Faery Wicca

Book One

Faery Wicca: Conveyer of the Great Mystery

For those new to the ways of Faery Faith, *Faery Wicca, Book One* will be both an educational workbook and a magical tome. Replete with practical instruction and exercises, historical documentation, poetry, meditations, and invaluable references, *Faery Wicca, Book One* imparts timeless wisdom along with the guidance necessary for apprenticeship.

But as the first publication on the oral Irish tradition, *Faery Wicca, Book One* will be of value to any follower of the Old Ways. The material on celebration and ritual, recipes, symbols, tools and faery contact will serve as a life-long reference and enrich the most venerable practitioners.

The publication of *Faery Wicca, Book One* reflects the resurrected pulse of the Nature People—our desire to return to a life of simplicity and spiritual balance. To this end, *Faery Wicca, Book One* will enlighten all who give it life by living its ways.

The Great Mystery will fulfill those who seek it.

Kisma Stepanich's book, *Faery Wicca*, excellently relates Celtic mythology to ritual working and practical magic. It is well researched and meticulously detailed. In our view it meets a long-existing need, and is essential reading for anyone practicing Celtic Wicca, whether starting on the path or already involved, and whether a solo worker or a member of a coven.

—Janet and Stewart Farrar

About the Author

Kisma K. Stepanich was born July 4, 1958, in Southern California. She has been actively involved in the Goddess community since the early 1980s. She founded Women Spirit Rising of Costa Mesa, and currently directs Moon Lodge Network, a woman's organization that provides ongoing New Moon ceremonies, monthly Goddess mythology circles, seasonal celebrations, and women's spirituality workshops. Of Irish and Romanian Gypsy descent, Kisma proudly claims her European heritage. A leading expert in the field of Faery Wicca, Kisma is a traditionally initiated Ollamh of the Faery tradition and holds Elder credentials with the Covenant of the Goddess (COG).

To Write the Author

If you would like to contact the author or would like more information about this book, please write to her in care of Llewellyn Worldwide. We cannot guarantee every letter will be answered, but all will be forwarded. Please write to:

Kisma Stepanich
c/o Llewellyn Worldwide
P.O, Box 64383, Dept. K694-7
St. Paul, MN 55164-0383, U.S.A

Please enclose a self-addressed, stamped envelope for reply or $1.00 to cover costs.
If outside the U.S.A., enclose international postal reply coupon.

Free Catalog from Llewellyn Worldwide

The Ancient Oral Faery Tradition of Ireland

Faery Wicca

Book One

Theory & Magick:
A Book of Shadows & Light

Kisma K. Stepanich

1996
Llewellyn Publications
St. Paul, Minnesota, 55164-0383, U.S.A.

FIRST EDITION.
Fourth Printing, 1996

Cover art and chapter illustrations by Renée Christine Yates
Editing, layout and design by Laura Gudbaur

Cataloging-in-Publication Data
Stepanich, Kisma K.
    Faery wicca / written by Kisma K. Stepanich
       p.   cm—
    Includes bibliographical references.
    Content: bk 1. Theory & magic, a book of shadows & lights
    ISBN 1-56718-694-7 (v. 1)
    1. Witchcraft--Ireland. 2. Gods, Celtic. 3. Ritual. 4. Magic. 5. Mythology, Celtic. I. Title.
BF1581.S74 1994   94-27464
299' .162—dc20   CIP

Llewellyn Publications
A Division of Llewellyn Worldwide, Ltd.
P.O. Box 64383, St. Paul, Minnesota, 55164-0383, U.S.A.

The Ancient Oral Faery Tradition of Ireland

About the Series

From ancient times comes the mention of the Oral Faery Tradition: A tradition mixed with magick and surrealism; a tradition that enchants the listener, drawing you into the mystery teachings hinted at in its mythos. The Oral Faery Tradition's teachings and its dimensions are not about little creatures flitting about with wings on their backs, as is so popularly misconstrued by individuals who are not a part of this authentic tradition. It is a tradition and world centered in the primal earth and the power contained therein, the stars inside the earth, the circles of existence. It is a tradition rich with the Ancient Gods, the ancestors, and the continuum. The Oral Faery Tradition has survived, and is alive today within these pages. Because the tradition of Faery Wicca is recognized as the backbone of many other types of Celtic Wicca, and because the tradition spans generations and therefore is replete with rich and varied practices, the complete study of this ancient oral tradition warrants coverage in two books: Thus, the Faery Wicca Series.

Faery Wicca, Book One is the first book to provide the mystery teachings of the ancient Oral Faery Tradition. The knowledge and practical expertise provided in its pages will benefit anyone who has a serious interest in the history of Witchcraft, the Faery and the Occult. While Book One provides a thorough overview of this intricate lifestyle, including instruction in initiation, Book Two deepens the focus on Shamanic practices of the tradition, including energy work, the Body Temple, healing techniques, developing Second-Sight, meditation techniques, journeys into the Otherworld, herbcraft, spellcasting, and a closing statement on the shamanic technique known as "remembering."

Anyone interested in Irish history and mythology, Paganism, Witchcraft, women's or men's studies, Celtic Wicca, Shamanism and the Occult will find this series an immensely rewarding and informative read.

Other Books by Kisma K. Stepanich

Faery Wicca, Book Two: The Shamanic Practices of the Cunning Arts, 1995

Sister Moon Lodge: The Power and Mystery of Menstruation, 1992

The Gaia Tradition: Celebrating the Earth in Her Seasons, 1991

An Act of Woman Power
   (Whitford Press, a division of Schiffer Publishing, Ltd., 1989)

Dedication

This book was written for the cunning women and men who lived in harmony with Mother Earth and worshiped the gods and goddesses, whose lives were violently taken from them by the oppressors of the Old Religion.

This book is dedicated to Goddess Ainé.

Acknowledgements

To unknown apprentices everywhere: thank you for believing in, and valuing the old ways, and keeping the Old Religion alive. I would like to thank my high priest and priestess, and the banshees and leprechauns who joined me in our dance together in the Cauldron of Cerridwen (in the good 'ole days). To all my apprentices—those I have thus far initiated of Luna Sea Coven, Rose Moon Tribe and Ancient Amber Coven, and those currently in apprenticeship in the Circle of Leanhuan Sidhe —blessings and deep peace to you all. Keep the Faith alive!

A special thank-you to Renée Christine Yates for her beautiful illustrations, and Danielle Michaelis and Sandi Sauer for their help with many of the figures found in this volume: blessings sweethearts! A fond remembrance to you, Debbie Sheehy, my Irish Spirit-Sister, your enthusiasm and help with my Irish is valued: thank you.

Thanks, Mom and Dad, for caring so much about the progress of this project, and Jack, my husband, thanks for your support and understanding. And a big thanks to Nancy Mostad for nursing me through the revisions and to my editor, Laura Gudbaur, whose keen interest in my material made the final process such a breeze. Bless you.

One will never be able to fully recover the ancient ways, for they are long gone, and what remains today is too fragmented to make complete sense—try though we may. The truth of any tradition is in the living of it! To all who feel the connection.

Gum Till Do Cheum, As Gach Cearn,
Fo Rionnag-iuil an Dachaidh!

(May your steps return from all corners of the globe,
under the guidance of the star, that points to home!)

Table of Contents

Section Two: Magickal Enchantments

Appendices

Guided Visualizations, Exercises and Rituals

Introduction

How to Use This Book

J began this project in 1990. The time had come for a comprehensive study on the oral tradition of Ireland to be printed, shedding light on the background of those beings known in this common day as fairies, and revealing their true nature, or origin, which would enlighten the minds of the Seekers of the Path.

Much has been written about the literary fairy, but relatively little has been written about the Faery, the Ancient Ones, the Irish gods and goddesses, who, like many of the Old Ones from ancient religions and spiritual belief systems, suffered demotion, resulting in a new classification of imaginary and mythological beings.

Today, Faery Wicca is a practiced branch of the Old Religion, or Witchcraft as has commonly been coined. Unlike other branches of Wicca, the Faery Tradition has remained a very elusive religion. Yes, it is a religion, Earth-centered, in which Dana (God), the Great Mother of all the gods, is the primary deity. It is a very simple Folk-Faith, not overly adorned with paraphernalia.

Faery Wicca is a way of living. There are, however, many skills expected of those who involve themselves with this tradition, and Initiation can only be acquired under the guidance of an Ollamh (Elder Priestess or Elder Priest). I feel very fortunate to be an Ollamh of the Faery Tradition, and find much joy and sovereignty in the passing-on of the tradition to those apprentices who truly desire to live it. Through the continuance of the Old Religion, the cunning women and men who were tortured, drowned, and burned at the stake also continue to live on— their sacrifice having ensured the unceasing worship of Goddess and God by the Nature People. We of Faery Wicca are the Nature People.

This first book of two, this Book of Shadows, is a beginning study in Faery Wicca. It is divided into two parts. Section One: Metaphysical Theory, provides lessons on the traditional history, the evolution of the Faery, the Celtic Irish Pantheon, esoteric beliefs, the practical mechanics of set-up and the understanding of how this aspect of the Old Religion survived and came to be the modern Faery Wicca.

Section Two: Magickal Enchantments, provides magickal application on the base materials presented in Section One, as well as guided visualizations, contacting and working with Faery allies, magickal tools, magickal symbols and alphabets, and ceremony and ritual.

To get the most from this volume, I highly encourage a complete reading of Section One, including contemplation and completion of all Journal Exercises, before working with the material in Section Two. Once the magickal work is acquiesced, each chapter is a continuation of the previous chapter; in other words, the magickal direction provided in the first chapter of Section Two is the foundation, and continues to be added to with each subsequent chapter.

The material knowledge of this volume is presented in such a way as to greater facilitate the neophyte in her or his understanding of the tradition, and is but a particle of the material knowledge one would acquire in a life-long involvement with the tradition.

Some of the material one will not find in this volume, that will be found in Faery Wicca, Book Two, is a study on the shamanic practices of Faery Wicca. Such material will cover working with the Three Worlds, the Four Cities, the healing arts, Irish herbology, spellcraft, divination, and minor rites of passages ceremonies and rituals; all of which are alluded to in this volume.

You will note I use two spellings of Faery/fairy. Faery is the formal spelling used when referring to the Tuatha De Danann, the Spirit Race of Light Beings who founded the Faery-Faith, while fairy is the common spelling used when referring to the literary creatures, the diminutive beings with gossamer wings who abound in children's fairytale books.

But for now, let us begin at the beginning, and before we do, I present to you the *pishogue*, modern incantation, which— upon beginning this project back in 1990— I first uttered to Brigid, asking her to flow through my veins, allowing me to convey the living knowledge of the Great Mystery found in the Irish Faery-Faith of Faery Wicca.

Breo-Saighit—Breed—Brihit —Saint Bridget
Fiery Arrow—Flame of Erin
You are known by many names~
Goddess of Poetry and Inspiration!
I call to You this day!

Come forth from your Cathedra Puellaris,
Come forth from Your Shrine in Kildare
and light the Flame of Inspiration
in me this day.

Give to me Your poetry.
Help me to see
that I contain the verse of wisdom;
that I have a story to tell.

I hold up the tool of the writer,
the first of its type,
the mighty wand of magickal poetry.
From the winged-one comes Your wand, Breede.

I praise the gentle beings
who rejoice in the air,
demonstrating the unencumbered passage
of the written word.
They sing and call to me:

"From the breath of Breed,
Her inspiration sails through the heavens,
lifted by the power of our wings.
To the earth Her verse is grounded,
through the quills we give way to you.
Onto the page the verse does manifest,
by you, daughter of Breo-Saighit!"

I call to You, Breed,
to bless my modern wands
of pen and pencil—and keyboard,
to carry forth in the tradition of the poet and writer
Your inspiration.

And though I no longer dip my quill
into the symbolic womb of
Your mighty dispensation
to draw forth from the well
the substance required to spread the word across the page

I grasp the magickal wand
of pen or pencil— or keyboard
in which is already contained the artery
of many-colored blood
As if drawing from my own veins
Your inspiration already
embedded in my heart.

Brigid, most excellent goddess,
sudden Flame of Inspiration,
may Your bright flame guide me into
everlasting communion through
usage of the written word!

Brigid, most knowledgeable One,
Flames of Wisdom,
May Your soul shine bright,
give me permission to keep
Our religion alive!

Poet's Invocation to Brigid
Kisma K. Stepanich

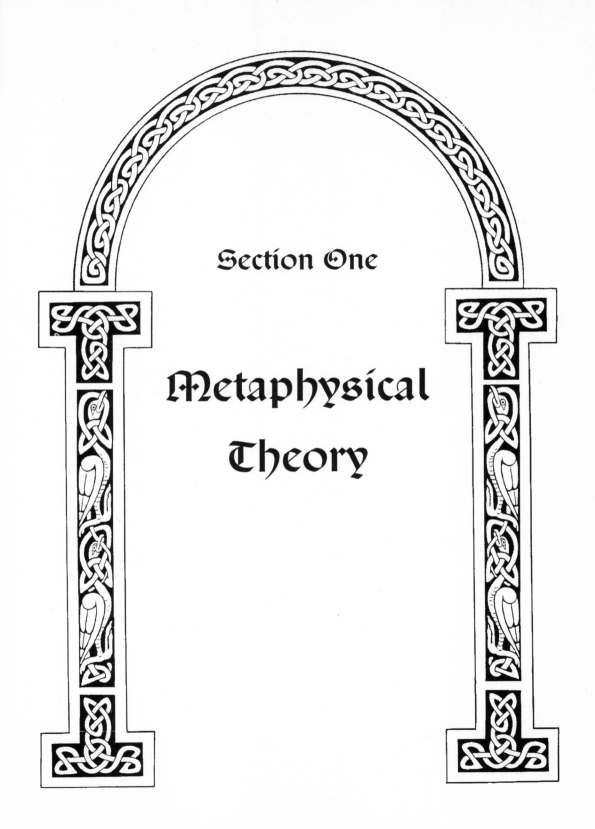

Section One

Metaphysical Theory

 *he wind blows strong*
off the sea
rain falls
Freedom.
Awaken to the mysteries
the call of Life
Onward—onward
Power.
Choice of devotion
old versus new
The roots.

—Kisma K. Stepanich

Lesson One

The Traditional
History

Unless one knows their tradition's origin, and has their roots firmly planted in this origin, one cannot successfully deepen their spirit.

Whether one is of Irish ancestry or not, it is most likely there is a familiarity with the myths or tales based on an ancient race of beings known as the Faery. Most modern children grow up being read such tales before bedtime; tales in which miniature creatures with gossamer wings flit about, often creating havoc in their wake. And, if like me, more often then not, children still anxiously await the part in the story where the mischievous beings bestow some wonderful gift on their victims, thus demonstrating their magickal abilities.

For the most part, children reach adulthood with a remembrance of the Faery, and if such an adult enters into the ever-deepening, ever-continuing world of the occult mysteries, they retain some belief in these creatures.

What most of the fairy tales do not convey is that such tales are based on the mythology of ancient Ireland, in the days when it was known as Eire, and that the miniature creatures in these tales are remnants of a past race of people who dwelled in Ireland—the Tuatha De Danann.

It was from this ancient race that the first religious tradition in Ireland developed. It was a Pagan tradition which came to be known as the oral Faery tradition; it was also an esoteric-Christian tradition, which flourished before the Roman Catholic Church began its crusade.

There is not one Irish alive today who will deny knowing of the ancient Faery-Faith, whether they have personally had a brush with the Sidhe (shee) or not.

From this Faery-Faith comes the modern Faery Wicca, which is a breathing, living tradition very much practiced; it is the shamanic tradition of a country, containing within it a wealth of Occult wisdom that ever deepens one's connection to Spirit.

In this first lesson, I provide a review of the traditional history of the Faery-Faith. This information is the roots, or the origin, of Faery Wicca, as based on the oral tradition of Ireland. This is the foundation from which the tradition's Initiates draw their magick.

Often, students eagerly want the recipes, secrets, and rituals of a tradition to perform magick, bypassing those aspects of apprenticeship which truly create a solid foundation. Most of us are guilty of trying to pull the wool over the mass population's eyes when it comes to systems of ancient and traditional magick. What may not be realized is that often harm, in the way of empty magickal results, frustration, chaotic energy, and spiritual deprivation is, more often than not, the outcome of such short-cuts.

If you are a serious student of esoterica, truly striving to deepen Spirit, then it is important to pay attention, observe, and learn before putting into practice the magick. And, so, let us now begin by looking at the origin of Faery Wicca.

The Four Irish Cycles

Medieval manuscripts provide us with four cycles of traditional Irish history. The four cycles are referred to as: the Mythological Cycle, the Ulster Cycle, the Fenian Cycle and the Historical Cycle.

These four cycles provide a vital account of the waves of invasions which swept through the Irish country, as well as the development of the Celtic Pantheon, and the cultural influences that formed the basis of the Faery-Faith belief system. The purpose of knowing such information is to understand the ancient foundation of Faery Wicca. In understanding the foundation of any tradition, one becomes not only educated, but also responsive toward the traditional practices. Below is a brief description of each of the four cycles.*

The Mythological Cycle is primarily based on the Tuatha De Danann (the tribe of Dana), from which the Faery Lineage is derived. Within this cycle an account of five waves of invaders are given, presenting three certain colonizations of Ireland, all of which were wrested through battle, and providing us with quaint glimpses of the ancient Irish ethics of war.

The traditions of this cycle are synchronized with the main events in ancient world history; the fifth wave of invaders, the Milesians, are fixed at about 1000 BCE (before common era)—the time of Solomon.

Many of the legends are based on the Tuatha De Danann, from which come the Ancient Ones, or gods (meaning both male and female) of the Celtic Pantheon,

---

* See Appendix-A: Ancient Manuscripts and Books, from which the material on these four cycles originated.

abounding in tales of enchantments and transformations, and victory gained by superior knowledge and wizardry.

Intelligence and magick are this cycle's distinctive features. As we work with the magickal enchantments of the tradition later in the text, we will see the connection between this cycle and the practices surrounding such magick.

The Ulster Cycle begins at the time of Christ, or the common era (C.E.). A reigning king, noted in ancient song and story, King Conchobar (Conor MacNessa) of Ulster, a powerful Ulster ruler who had become monarch of Ireland, residing at Emain Macha (Emania), founded the Rudrician line of Ulster kings. His memory is preserved in the tale of *The Sons of Usnach*, and in the greater tale of *The Tain Bo Cualigne (The Cattle-raid of Coolney)*.

Emain Macha was the headquarters of the famed Knights of the Royal Branch (also referred to as the Knights of the Red Branch). Most of the tales are of the rivalry between the two northern provinces of Ulster and Connacht.

In this cycle we have the appearance of the Amazonian Queen Medb (Maeve), daughter of Eocaid, the Ard-Righ (High King) of Ireland, who was the instigator of the great Connaught-Ulster war, and who became an immortal warrior-goddess. Another legend from this cycle revolves around Deirdre and the Sons of Usnach, which shows that King Conchobar, for all his kingliness, was sometimes no better than a king is supposed to be. The sorrows of Deirdre, as told in the story of *The Sons of Usnach*, is one of the Three Sorrows of Irish story-telling.

The most notable character of this cycle was the foster-son of King Conchobar, Cu Chulainn. He was the greatest, the most belauded, and the most dazzling of all the heroes, of whose life and wondrous deeds hundreds of stories still exist. His legends abound with Amazonian war-goddesses who teach him the skills of battle: Emer, the most beautiful woman in Ireland who becomes his wife, the Morrigan, the great Irish war-goddess, and Fand, Faery Queen and wife of the Irish sea-god, Manannan mac Lir.

The central group of characters in the tales that belong to this cycle are not wizards, like the tales found in the Mythological Cycle, but of warriors and war-goddesses who glory in their prowess and their unyielding endurance. Will-power, rather than intelligence, is the primary focus, as is fearless action in the face of terrifying odds that are celebrated.

The world of heroism thus begins. As we begin to work with the Five-Fifths of the Great Circle, found in the Magickal Enchantments Section, we will come to understand that the warrior attitude required in Faery Wicca comes from this cycle.

The Fenian Cycle is full of legends based on Finn mac Cumaill and his roving fiana (warbands). This cycle is also often described as the Ossianic Cycle because of the poems which belong to it that are attributed to Finn's son, Oisin or Ossian.

Finn and his fiana served Cormac mac Airt, who was unquestionably considered greatest by the poets of all the ancient kings of Ireland. Cormac reigned in the third century, and when he resigned the High-Kingship he ended one of the most fruitful as well as illustrious reigns that ever blessed Ireland. "He was the greatest king that Ireland ever knew," says one of the old historians. "In power and eloquence, in the vigour and splendor of his reign, he had not his like before or since. In his reign no one needed to bolt the door, no one needed to guard the flock, nor was any one in all Ireland distressed for want of food or clothing. For of all Ireland this wise and just king made a beautiful land of promise."[1]

Three great literary works are, by various ancient authorities, ascribed to him in his retirement—*Teagasc an Riogh (Instructions of a King)*, *The Book of Acaill (a book of the principles of Criminal Law)*, and *The Psaltair of Tara*, which is no longer in existence, and is known only by the frequent references to it of ancient chronologists, genealogists, seanachies, and poets; such references prove that it was a rich mine of very ancient historic and genealogical information, and that it was regarded as the greatest and most reliable authority of the very early days. "It proves to a certainty that in the third century of the Christian Era, there was a considerable amount of literary culture in Ireland,"[2] contrary to the Roman Catholic Church belief that the Irish were unscholared.

Cormac died in the year 267 C.E. more than a century-and-a-half before the coming of St. Patrick and the formal entrance of the Protestants.

The tales of the Ossianic, or Fenian Cycle, are similar to those found in the Ulster Cycle. Most focus on heroic fighters, but two groups of stories differ in their characteristics. The first characteristic is that the fiana are "foot" soldiers who walk rather than ride in chariots like the Ulster heroes, and the second characteristic is the camaraderie which they display, the intense pleasure found in a life shared with members of one's own special group, which is a marked contrast to the harsh individualism and clamorous rivalry that characterizes so many of the Ulster stories.

The fiana were soldiers in time of war, and a national police in time of peace. They prevented robberies, exacted fines and tributes, put down public enemies and every kind of evil that might afflict the country, and as this ancient poem declares:

> *We were heart companions,*
> *We were companions in the woods*
> *We were fellows of the same bed,*
> *Where we used to sleep the balmy sleep.*
> *After mortal battles abroad,*
> *In countries many and far distant,*
> *Together we used to practise, and go*
> *Through each forest, learning with Scathach*.*
> —The Tain Bo Cuailgne
> 4th Century

There is evidence from about the eleventh century that the Fenian tales were a part of popular traditions. Fianship was an honorable institution, recognized in the laws and considered essential to the welfare of the community.

The Fenian Cycle also differs in form and temper as it comes into prominence in the period of the poetry of the troubadour, and parallels the Arthurian legends of

---

1 Seumas MacManus, *The Story of the Irish Race, A Popular History of Ireland*, The Devin-Adair Company, 1921.

2 Ibid

* An Amazonian warrior-goddess from Alba (Scotland).

Britain. This cycle's greatest story, *The Pursuit of Diarmaid and Grainne* tells of romance, while many other tales give expression to a delight in the sights and sounds familiar to those who live an outdoor life in the waste and the wild and the woods, as we've seen above in the ancient poem.

For those seeking to enter this noble body, many and hard were the tests:

- No candidate was possible who had not mastered the twelve books of poetry.
- In a trench, the depth of the knee, the candidate, with a shield and hazel staff only, must protect himself from nine warriors, casting javelins at him from nine ridges away.
- Given the start of a single tree, in a thick wood, he has to escape unwounded from fleet pursuers.
- So skillful must he be in wood-running, and so agile, that in the flight no single braid of his hair is loosed by a hanging branch.
- His step must be so light that underfoot he breaks no withered branch.
- In his course he must bound over branches the height of his forehead, and stoop under others the height of his knee, without delaying, or leaving a trembling branch behind.
- Without pausing in his flight he must pick from his foot the thorn that it has taken up.
- In facing the greatest odds the weapon must not shake in his hand.

When a candidate had passed the tests, and was approved as fit for this heroic band, there were four *geasas*, or restrictions, (vows of chivalry) laid upon him, as the final condition of his admission:

- He shall marry his wife without portion, choosing her for her manners and her virtues.
- He shall be gentle with all women.
- He shall never reserve to himself anything which another person stands in need of.
- He shall stand and fight to all odds, as far as nine to one.*

Hard though they seemed, such accomplishment guaranteed an ensuing life of beauteous adventure and recompensation an hundred-fold, as described in this ancient song:

I feasted in the hall of Fionn,
And at each banquet there I saw
A thousand rich cups on his board,
Whose rims were bound with purest gold.

---

* *The Tain Bo Cuailgne*, 4th Century

9

And twelve great buildings once stood there,
The dwellings of those mighty hosts,
Ruled by Tadg's daughter's warlike son,
At Alma of the noble Fian.

And constantly there burned twelve fires,
Within each princely house of these,
And round each flaming hearth there sat
A hundred warriors of the Fian.

—17th Century song

The Agallam na Seanorach (the Colloquy of the Ancients) is by far the finest collection of Fenian tales; it is an account of the fiana's great doings, given to St. Patrick by Oisin and Caoilte, more than 150 years after their time.

Unlike the Mythological Cycle, which features intelligence and knowledge, or the Ulster Cycle, focusing on will-power, the distinctive quality of the Fenian Cycle is that of human warmth of feeling. It is this element—human warmth of feeling— that is connected to all Faery ceremony and ritual.

The Historical Cycle is a miscellaneous group of stories centered on various high-kings of Ireland and on a number of provincial or lesser kings. The tales in this cycle are ascribed dates ranging from the third century to the eighth century.

The renowned kings who figure prominently in these cycles are: Conaire Mor to Conn of the Hundred Battles, Niall of the Nine Hostages, and the Domnall, son of Aed.

Niall of the Nine hostages was the greatest king that Ireland knew between the time of Cormac MacArt and the coming of Patrick. His reign was epochal. He not only ruled Ireland greatly and strongly, but carried the name and the fame, and the power and the fear, of Ireland into all neighboring nations. He was founder of the longest, most important, and most powerful Irish dynasty. Almost without interruption, his descendants were Ard-Righs of Ireland for 600 years.

> *Under him the spirit of pagan Ireland upleaped in its last great*
> *red flame of military glory, a flame that, in another generation,*
> *was to be superseded by a great white flame, far less fierce but*
> *far more powerful, and one which was to shed its light far, far*
> *beyond the bounds of neighboring nations, to the uttermost*
> *bounds of Europe. That is the great flame that Patrick was to*
> *kindle, and which was to expand and grow, ever mounting*
> *higher and spreading farther, year by year, for three hundred*
> *years.*[3]

This cycle is also known as the Cycles of the Kings, and its tales are less magical than the Mythological Cycle, less heroic than the Ulster Cycle, and less romantic than the Fenian Cycle. The extensive group of tales found in this cycle are not only about kings, but about kingship, the founding of dynasties, dynastic succession, and the

---

3 Seumas MacManus, Ibid

fortunes of the royal houses of Ireland and her provinces.

The tales focus on the nature of kingship as being a marriage between the king and the realm; the country is a woman, spouse of the king, and before her marriage she is described as a hag. Once united with the king, her countenance becomes that of a goddess.

The Fives Waves of Invasions

In Faery Wicca the primary myths focused upon are drawn heavily from the Mythological Cycle, primarily those of the Tuatha De Danann. The Mythological Cycle is also the genesis of the Celtic Irish gods and goddesses.

The Faery-Faith was birthed during the golden age of the Tuatha De Danann, and from their magickal abilities comes the foundation for all ritual and ceremony within the modern tradition, as we shall observe in a later lesson.

Most importantly, within the Mythological Cycle are found the legends of five waves of invasions known as: Partholan, Neimheadh, Fir Bolg, Tuatha De Danann, and Milesian. The importance of containing this information is the connection to the source of the Faery-Faith, as well as the foundation of all Irish genealogies. This information, in essence, provides the origin of the tradition.

There are conflicting stories regarding many aspects of the five waves of invasions. The Mythological Cycle was simply retained orally, and not completely written down until about 1100 C.E. Furthermore, the tales were not recorded by those of the Faery-Faith, but rather by the Monastic chroniclers in medieval times of the newly established Catholic Church in Ireland.

However, some chroniclers, though they were churchmen, were not monastics. For that reason, many of the events may have been altered in accordance with the clergies' religious doctrines. It is continually noted by scholars, however, that the clergy who did indeed record the tales wrote them in such a manner as to suggest their belief in the characters of Tuatha De Danann as being ancient gods, and thus ascribing them as a true mystical race that came from the stars. Below is a brief historical account of the five waves of invaders taken from several ancient manuscripts. (See Appendix A: Ancient Manuscripts and Books.)

Partholan was the name of the first group of invader's respective leader. He fled his country after having killed his mother and father, and his descendants settled in an area between what is now called Tallaght and Howth, near Dublin. They remained in Ireland only some thirty-odd years before all eventually perished in a plague.

Neimheadh is the name of the leader of the second group of invaders, who came from Scythia. His people were terribly harassed by fleets of pirates called Fomorians, or sea-robbers, out of Africa, who descended upon the north coast, and endeavored to subdue the new settlers.

Neimheahd died in Ireland, but his people, after suffering great tribulations, ultimately abandoned the country. They dispersed in three groups, two of which were the ancestors of the people to next occupy Ireland.

Fir Bolg (Fir means men) was the third wave to come, 217 years after the Neimheahdians fled. This third group of invaders were escaped slaves from Greece who settled into Ireland, creating an agricultural community. The Fir Bolgs are the beginning of the country's recorded history. They were a pastoral people, creating raths and earthen-mounds in which they buried their dead without cremation. They had laws and social institutions, and established a monarchical government at the far-famed Hill of Tara.

They had three leaders who partitioned the kingdom into five provinces, and became known as three tribes: Fir Domhnann, Fir Gaileon, and Fir Bolg. They lived in Ireland for thirty-six years before the fourth wave of invaders, the Tuatha De Danann, arrived.

The Fir Bolgs were defeated by the De Danann in the First Battle of Mag Tuired. They fled to the islands of Islay, Arran, Man, and Rathlin. They returned as a subordinate people to Ireland about the beginning of the Christian era. However, there are tales which indicate the First Battle of Mag Tuired was fought between the two peoples and ended in a compact of peace, goodwill, and friendship.

Tuatha De Danann are the chief characters of the Mythological Cycle, and are considered the fourth wave of invaders. They are known as a people of magic wonders, learned in all the arts, and supreme masters of wizardry. Before coming to Ireland they are believed to have sojourned in the northern islands of the world, where they acquired their incomparable esoteric knowledge, and from where they brought with them four talismans: the Great Fal—the person under whom this stone shrieked was king of Ireland; the Spear of Lugh—no victory could be won against it, nor against him who had it in his hand; the Sword of Nuada—no one escaped from it when it was drawn from its scabbard; and the Cauldron of the Dagda, from which no company would go away unsatisfied. (More study will be given to these talismans in a later chapter found under the Magickal Enchantments Section.)

All the other groups reached Ireland by ship, but the De Danann where said to have come in dark clouds through the air and alighted on a mountain of Conmaicne Rein, and "for three days they cast a darkness over the face of the sun." They were described as being the most handsome and delightful company, the fairest of form, the most distinguished in their equipment and apparel, and their skill in music and playing, the most gifted in mind and temperament that ever came to Ireland, as well as the company that was bravest and inspired the most horror, fear, and dread. They were the "peoples of the world in their proficiency in every art."

In the *Book of the Dun Cow* (written about 1100 C.E.), it is said that the learned did not know from where Tuatha De Danann had come, but that "it seems likely to them that they came from heaven on account of their intelligence and for the excellence of their knowledge," and it was noted that they were worshiped as gods.

The Goddess Dana was the Great Mother of the Celtic gods and hence all people, and several of her people were individually described as gods. Dagda, the good god, also called Aed, fire; Eochaid Ollathair, the all-father; Ruad Rofessa, the Lord of Great Knowledge, also described as the god of druidism or draidecht (magic); Brigid, the daughter of the Dagda, who is a poetess, a healer, and a goddess of smith-work; Dian Cecht, the sage of leechcraft, as well as the god of health; Neit, the god of battle; Manannan mac Lir, a renowned trader who dwelt in the Isle of Man, who was called the god of the sea; Badb, the goddess of war; Nuada, the king of Tuatha De Danann when they came to Ireland; and, Lugh, the son of a De Danann and a Formorian, who battled and won against the Fomorians in favor of the De Danann. (Lesson Three will focus on the Ancient Ones.)

The First Battle of Mag Tuired was fought between the De Danann and Fir Bolg for occupation of Ireland. It was in this battle that Nuada lost his arm and was no longer suitable for king. The kingship was given to his adopted son, Bres, or Eochaid the Handsome, son of Elatha, who was the son of Delbaeth, king of the Fomore, and his mother, Eriu, daughter of Delbaeth, a De Danann.

The Second Battle of Mag Tuired is the subject of one of the greatest stories of the Mythological Cycle, for the adversaries of the De Danann in this battle were the Fomorians, the only beings comparable in mystery and magick to the De Danann themselves. However, before coming to Ireland, the De Danann made an alliance with the Fomore, and Ethniu, daughter of the Fomorian king, was given in marriage to Cian, son of Dian Cecht, a De Danann. From this marriage, Lugh was born.

The Fomorians had made themselves known in the time of Partholan in a "magic battle," and to Neimheadh, who defeated and slew two kings of the Fomorians, and later again defeated the Fomorians in three battles. However, after his death, his progeny suffered oppression at the hands of these same enemies under Morc and Conand. When the Fomorians arrived in Ireland during the De Danann occupation, they were led by Cichol Gricenchos son of Goll (One-eye) and Garb (Rough). They arrived on the shores of Ireland in four ships, each containing a company comprised of fifty men and thrice fifty women.

The Tuatha De Danann prepared seven years for battle, and in the end won when Lugh cut off the head of Balor, the king of the Fomorians. The Fomorians were never allowed to settle in Ireland.

The Dagda, who reigned just before the coming of the Milesian, was the greatest of the De Danann. He was styled Lord of Knowledge and Sun of all the Sciences. The Dagda was a great and beneficent ruler for eighty years.

The Milesian are the Celts, and wheresoever they came, had, before the dawn of history, subjugated the German people and established themselves in Central Europe. At about 1000 B.C.E, a great Celtic wave, breaking westward over the Rhine, penetrated into England, Scotland, and Ireland. Subsequently, a wave swept over the Pyrenees into the Spanish Peninsula.

> *They came from a land beyond the sea,*
> *And now o'er the western main*
> *Set sail in their good ships, gallantly,*
> *From the sunny lands of Spain.*
> *"Oh, where's the isle we've seen in dreams,*
> *Our destin'd home or grave?"*
> *Thus sang they, as by the morning beams,*
> *They swept the Atlantic wave.*

And lo, where afar o'er ocean shines
A sparkle of radiant green,
As though in that deep lay emerald mines
Whose light through the wave was seen,
'Tis Inisfail — 'tis Inisfail!
Rings o'er the echoing sea;
While, bending to heaven, the warriors hail
That home of the brave and free.

Then turned they unto the Eastern wave
Where now their Day-God's eye
A look of such sunny omen gave
As lighted up sea and sky.
No frown was seen through sky or sea,
Nor tear o'er leaf or sod,
When first on their Isle of Destiny
Our great forefathers trod.
                    —The Coming of the Milesians
                        by Thomas Moore, 1879

They were the fifth wave of invaders (often referred to as the Sons of Mil) to wash into Ireland, and who put an end to the supreme reign of the De Danann.

Their leader was Miled, or Milesius, whose wife was a Pharaoh's daughter named Scota. Miled's uncle, Ith, was first sent into Ireland, to bring them report upon it, but the De Danann, suspecting the purpose of his mission, killed Ith.

Miled, having died in Spain, his eight sons, with their mother, Scota, their families and followers, at length set out on their venturous voyage to their Isle of Destiny.

In a dreadful storm that the wizard De Danann raised up against them, when they attempted to land in Ireland, five of the sons of Mil, with great numbers of their followers, were lost. Their fleet was dispersed and it seemed for a time as if none of them would ever enjoy the Isle of Destiny.

Eventually they made land. Eber, with the survivors of his following, landed at Inver Sceni, in Bantry Bay. Afterwards, they defeated a De Danann host under Queen Eire, but lost their own Queen Scota in the battle.

Eremon, with his people, landed at Inver Colpa, the mouth of the Boyne, and when Eremon and Eber joined their forces in Meath, went against the De Danann in battle at Taillte. The three kings and the three queens of the De Danann were slain, many others also killed, and the remainder dispersed.

In the ancient *Book of Leinster*, Taillte was reported as left to Amergin, the Milesian poet and judge, to divide Eire between the two races, and that he shrewdly did so with technical justice, giving all above ground to his own people, and all underground to the De Danann.

However, the De Danann great immortal, Manannan mac Lir, at Brugh of the Boyne, assembled their host, and through council it was agreed that they should distribute themselves in their Spirit land. It was then that Tuatha De Danann went into hills and sidbrugaib (faery regions), so that sida (faeries) under ground were subject to them, and were rarely seen again, and where they have, ever since, enjoyed never-ending bliss.

The descendants of the Milesian generally have an *O* or a *Mac* before their surname.

When we dwell upon the nature of the above material, connecting it as the stuff folk-tales and "fairy" tales are made of, we realize that there is no use chasing the Faery with the techniques and disciplines of science and scholarship, if we lack a sense of wonder and humility of Spirit in these matters. "Fairy" tales certainly throw light on the origins and beliefs of our long past ancestors, but far more important they communicate a mood and an atmosphere concerned with intuition. The Faery-Faith, in essence, opens the door to religious awareness.

The Faery-Faith is inseparably connected with that same area of human consciousness that has to do with religious experience, with metaphysical insight. It is concerned with a greater reality beyond the everyday world of human frailty and limitations.

Journal Exercises

1. How can the historical background empower and give more meaning to a modern tradition?

2. What is your imagined image of the Faery?

Suggested Reading

The Fairies in Tradition and Literature, Katharine Briggs
The Story of the Irish Race, Seumas Mac Manus
Celtic Myth and Legend, Charles Squire
The Tain, translated by Thomas Kinsells

here the wave of moonlight glosses
The dim grey sands with light,
Far off by furthest Rosses
We foot it all the night,
Weaving olden dances,
Mingling hands and mingling glances
Till the moon has taken flight;
To and fro we leap
And chase the frothy bubbles,
While the world is full of troubles
And is anxious in its sleep.
Come away, O human child!
To the waters and the wild
With a faery, hand in hand,
For the world's more full of weeping
than you can understand.

— *The Stolen Child*
W. B. Yeats, 1889

RENEE '91©

Lesson Two

The Faery Lineage

Spirit is about forever. Magick is about 'change'. Like everything else we do in life, we must also take our mystical training one day at a time.

The primary folk of the Faery Wiccan tradition are the Tuatha De Danann, more commonly known as the Faery. Today, there are many ideas about the Faery.* Within their kingdom we find remnants of a magickal race of beings not of this world, as well as diminutive fairies, flower fairies with tiny wings, garden fairies, and elemental fairies, to mention only a few, each with their own virtues and traditions. Much of the lore creates the image that the Faery is based on fantasy.

Scholarly research brought forth many theories in regards to this tradition: i.e. the Naturalistic, Pygmy, Druid, Mythological, and Psychological, indicating that almost "all the essential elements upon which the advocates of the Naturalistic Theory, of the Pygmy Theory, of the Druid Theory, of the Mythological Theory, as well as ... (the) Psychological Theory"[4] was adequate evidence that the Faery-Faith was a living tradition, and that it's chief characters, the Faery, were, on some level, in existence.

Theirs became a study of human nature itself, proving that "all the world over, men interpret visions pragmatically and sociologically, or hold beliefs in accord with their own personal experiences; and are forever unconsciously immersed in a sea of psychological influences which sometimes may be explainable through the methods of sociological inquiry, sometimes may be supernormal in origin and nature, and hence to be explained most adequately, if at all, through psychical research."[5] Therefore, the most difficult problem of all was for human nature to interpret and understand its own ultimate essence and psychological instincts.

In modern psychology there is now a well-established interpretation of the Faery, as based on the Psychological Theory, which is that the Faery are inherent, either passively or actively, within the psyche, that they have no independent entity as actual living beings other than in human consciousness.

---

4 W.Y. Evans-Wentz, *The Fairy-Faith in Celtic Countries*, Oxford University Press, 1911.

5 Ibid.

* I use the spelling *Faery* when referring to the Tuatha De Danann, and *fairy* for the fantasy creatures that today are imagined as little people with wings.

In this school of thought, there are many psychological themes: the Faery are sexual images; they are archetypes, such as those of the classical gods and goddesses; they are embodiments and projected images of our fear of the unknown; they are the remnants of an old nature religion. The usage of archetypes is perhaps the leading avenue of practice in the Psychological Theory. The fact that consciousness consists of many images endlessly relating to one another around a central core is by no means a modern discovery; it has long been taught in esoteric traditions.

As R. J. Stewart denotes in his book *Advanced Magical Arts,* Element Books, 1988: "The higher order patterns, archetypes, or matrices, are traditionally taught as constants, or as undergoing changes of shape over such vast periods of outer time ... as to be imperceptible to individual human consciousness. In the human world, and in the innerworlds which form a major part of all magickal experience and practical work, the great matrices or universal archetypes ... are used as ritual patterns." He further explains that these matrices or archetypes appear as cosmologies, glyphs, maps, and portent symbols, enduring throughout magickal training from the exercises of the beginner to the adepts' advanced use of energies for specific chosen ends.

Not surprisingly, in orthodox religion, the Faery beings are regarded as evil, the host of the Devil, fallen angels, or, at best, frivolous and distracting influences.

However, the traditional understanding is that they are independent beings, of both a non-organic, immaterial state, which is close to humanity, as well as a mirror to humanity. They are a kingdom that will adapt themselves to whatever they find in our imaginations, be it positive mental images or negative mental images, as Shakespeare's Puck (*A Midsummer Night's Dream*) so eloquently articulates:

> *If we shadows have offended,*
> *Think but this, and all is mended,*
> *That you have but slumber'd here,*
> *While these visions did appear.*
> *And this weak and idle theme,*
> *No more yielding but a dream,*
> *Gentles, do not reprehend:*
> *If you pardon, we will mend:*
> *And, as I am an honest Puck,*
> *If we have unearned luck*
> *Now to 'scape the serpent's tongue,*
> *We will make amends ere long;*
> *Else the Puck a liar call:*
> *So, good night unto you all....*

The Faery-Faith is an ancestral tradition, connected to the powers of the Underworld, as we shall discuss in a later lesson, and which will be a subject of study in Book Two. The oral accounts continually report the "presence of deceased ancestors and humans who are physically translated to the [F]aery realm, either by [F]aery beings through acts of intent or by accident at sacred sites and other power locations in the land."[6] R.J. Stewart, in his many works on the

---

6 R. J. Stewart, *Advanced Magickal Arts*, Element Books, 1988

Underworld, gives us example after example of just such an occurrence.

Ancestral traditions, such as the Faery-Faith, contain the mysterious knowledge of communing with Faery beings through an avenue often referred to as Second-Sight.

Even the priests—Christian, Protestant, and Catholic—of Ireland were attuned to the power of the Faery-Faith and sought to keep their congregations away from Faery contact because of their knowledge of the true power found within the tradition. The Faery-Faith was acknowledged as a real, not fantasy, tradition, and it is no surprise that it was considered an early religion of Pagan Ireland.

Ancestral traditions are also closely connected to the land, and the land's environmental conditions, which explains why the nature of the Faery beings vary from land to land.

Let us now examine the Faery beings' chameleon-like nature, changing shape and size, light and insubstantial, made of cloud and vital substance, through their lineage, which sheds light on the changes they have undergone over several centuries.

From Tuatha De Danann we are given the source of the Faery-Faith and the gods of the Celts. The Faery, or Tuatha De Danann, are quite different from the modern day or commonly accepted fairy of the literary world. Through my own research I have created a Faery Lineage (see Figure 1).

The lineage, of course, begins with the most highly noted superior race of the Fay, the Tuatha De Danann. From them we have the first two branches: the Fenian Heroes and the Daoine Sidhe.

As I have already expressed in Lesson One, the Fenian Heroes were the noble warriors of Ireland. However, what was not told then was that the Tuatha De Danann were also of the fiana.

The Daoine Sidhe were the aspect of Tuatha De Danann that later became classified in tales as the Heroic Faery, the knights and ladies of the medieval romances, in whom we see a hint of the Fenian Hero, as well as the next branching, that of the Medieval Fairy.

The Medieval Fairy is woven with tales of magick and sorcery, wizards and witches, Morgan Le Fay and Avalon. This class of fairy drifts away from Tuatha De Danann and Ireland, becoming combined with a new breed of fairy springing out of the Arthurian Legends. It is with this fairy that the Tuatha De Danann become a reminiscent whisper on the breath. No longer of god-like quality, the fairy begin to grow smaller in size and are sometimes evil. It is also with this fairy that we see a shift take place, one which takes us away from the origin of the true Faery—the Tuatha De Danann—moving us into the world of mischievous spirits and the realm of phantasm.

Although during the Medieval Fairy period, the Heroic Faery come fleetingly back to life, the two merge and the Diminutive Fairy springs to life, becoming the traditional image for all fairies.

With the Diminutive Fairy, a list of euphemistic names* is birthed. The fairy become connected to the dead. By the sixteenth century, the literary fairy is introduced. They pinch and demand privacy. This literary fairy is introduced by John Lyly in his drama *Endimion*.

The Elizabethan Age brings another strain of fairy tradition into prominence. Rather than having romantic and fierce warrior attitudes, the fairy is mischievous

---

* See Appendix-B: Euphemistic Names for the Faery.

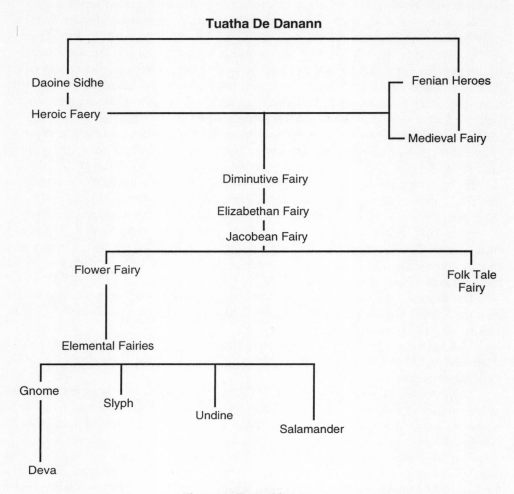

Figure 1: Faery Lineage

and bothersome. Nymphs become the new source of focus, and two new fairies are invented: the hobgoblin and Shakespeare's Flower Fairy in his *A Midsummer Night's Dream*.

The seventeenth century births the Jacobean Fairies, who are always adorned with gossamer wings and are so small that they are no bigger than microbes. With the Puritan influence, the fairies are firmly regarded as devils, and by the arrival of the eighteenth century they have been turned into flowery fertility spirits.

The first books are written expressly for the edification of children, and the stories in these books are about fairy godmothers who are relentless moralists. This trend persists into the nineteenth century where they become the Folk-Tale Fairy. The Golden Age of Faery completely comes to an end. Gone is the muck and muscle of the ancient gods, and in are the airy, tenuous creatures made of froth and whimsy. However, a sense of the old Fay is revived at the turn-of-the-century when the occultists bring forth the Elemental Fairy. Through these we catch a glimpse of the primal power and energy of the realm in which exist the Tuatha De Danann.

The Elemental Fairy are comprised of four classifications: Earth, Air, Water and Fire, the last of which is considered separate from the other three, and the first from which we draw the modern garden or wood fairy. From the garden or wood fairy we move into the Devas, who are known to be the soul of the plant kingdom.

Through my own efforts at understanding the different levels of the lineage, I have come to experience the Tuatha De Danann as a primal earth energy that can manifest in different forms when called upon. The Elementals are spiritual helpers from the kingdom of nature, who will assist us magickally. The Devas are the givers of plant medicine when befriended, assisting with healing magick.

When interested in working with the Faery kingdom, one will naturally touch upon the kingdom of the Elementals and the Devas; all are part of nature and Mother Earth. The Elementals and Devas are drawn to beautiful surroundings, such as gardens, parks and forests, wild-life areas in general; they are not interested in buildings and concrete. However, the energy of Tuatha De Danann can be worked with anywhere, for theirs is an ancient god-force of both a feminine and masculine nature. Let us now look at each branch of the lineage.

Tuatha De Danann (thanann)—The people of the Goddess Dana, or the people of the god whose mother was Dana. The Celts call them the Sidhe, Spirit-race, or the Feadh-Ree, a modification of the word Peri*.

In the traditional history of Ireland, this was the race who inhabited Erin after conquering the Fir Bolgs, and who were in their turn dispossessed by the Milesian and forced to take refuge under the grassy hills or in "lands beneath the waters."

Their country was the Tir na nOg (tyeer-nahn-ohgg), the Land of Perpetual Youth, where they lived a life of joy and beauty, never knowing disease or death, which was not to come on them. They were great masters of magick; a race who were said to have come from the stars to teach Earth's children about love and harmonious living. They became a Faery people, and many—both male and female—were great warriors who served under the Ard Righ, or High King, whose palace was in Tara. Many became known as the Fenian Heroes.

The Faery race, in the course of time, dwindled down into the Daoine Sidhe, although sometimes one can catch glimpses of them in their old form as a Heroic Faery.

Whether imaginary or a race of immortal beings, the Tuatha De Danann enriched the lives of the Celts, who wrote many a verse in praise of their magickal and Otherworldly attributes. The most beautiful praises are the poems that were sung, every word audible and expressive, flowing and changing with the flowing and changing of the magickal Faery energies.

I believe that it was during the changing tide of spiritual and religious beliefs that the Tuatha De Danann began to drift farther and farther away from our realm of existence. When a spiritual force is no longer being fed the energy of belief from the beings of this physical manifestation, then there is no longer a use for such a force.

Yet, as this Spirit-race receded from the material world, only to touch upon it in times of human need, it may well be that in a short time Fable, who changes mortalities to immortalities in her cauldron, changed the Sidhe into simply legendary beings—perfect symbols of the sorrow of beauty and of the magnificence and penury of humankind's dreams.

---

*See Appendix-C: The Etymology of the Word Fairy.

The Tuatha De Danann branches for the first time: to the right go the warriors, to the left, the romantic and peaceful people.

Fenian Heroes—The noble warriors of the Tuatha De Danann, who joined allegiance with the fiana (feen-a), the great fighting force of Ireland, and who were at their greatest when Finn mac Cumaill was their last and greatest leader.

Finn was the son of Cumhal (coo-al) mac Baiscne, the head of the fiana killed by the sons of Morna who were contending against him for the headship. Finn's mother was Muirne, granddaughter of Nuada Of The Silver Hand and Ethlinn, the mother of Lugh Of The Long Hand (both of the De Danann), and so he was of a godlike and Sidhe race. Finn was sent away to the care of a cunning woman, and was trained strenuously and in secret. He was trained in poetry and he acquired two magick skills. While he was in training to the poet Finegas he accidentally tasted the "salmon of knowledge and gained his magick tooth," and he drank a mouthful of water of the Well of the Moon which gave him the power of prophecy. It was for this reason, and the intermingled Sidhe blood in his veins, that the great warriors of the De Danann marched with him.

This was an active life for the De Danann, full of delights and dangers, and it went on until old age overtook Finn, and his fiana went down under dissensions, jealousies, and deaths. Of the De Danann, it was known that age and disease could not kill them, but they could be killed by violence; therefore, some of their hosts were lost to battle.

> *The remnant of our people*
> *Sweeping westward, wild and woeful,*
> *Like the cloud-rach of a tempest,*
> *Like the withered leaves of autumn.*
> *—The Tain Bo Cuailgne*
> 4th Century

The survivors of the Fenian Heroes, after the dissolution of the fiana, drifted, ever searching for another High King for whom to wield the sword and issue forth the battle cry. Perhaps Arthur, High King of Britain, received their homage. However, the Fenian Hero became intertwined with the Heroic Fairy of medieval times under the tutelage of the Daoine Sidhe, the left half of the lineages' first branching.

Daoine Sidhe (deena shee)—The Faery-folk of Ireland; dwindled gods of the early inhabitants of Ireland. They are supposedly Fallen Angels, too good for Hell. They were usually of human size, but it is not uncommon for them to be more than human stature and at times small in size.

Their inhabitations were generally underground or underwater, in the green raths or under the loughs (lakes) or in the sea. Of the Daoine Sidhe, two distinct classifications were extensively noted: the Heroic Faery and the Medieval Fairy; both greatly intercoursed with humans.

All was this lond fulfilled of faerie;
The elf-grene with hir jolie companie
Danced full oft in many a grene' mede.
—Chaucer

Heroic Faery—The knights and ladies of the medieval romances, and those that occur in the Celtic legends were of human or more than human size and of "shining beauty." They spent their time in aristocratic pursuits of hunting, fighting, riding in procession, as well as dancing and music which were beloved by all the Sidhe. A glimpse of the Fenian Hero is seen in the Heroic Faery, although of a more relaxed and gluttonous stance than of battle-worn.

By the year 1113 C.E., the sixth century warrior Arthur became a Heroic Faery; a king of fairy, one of the sleeping warriors whose return was confidently expected. The Matter of Britain and the Arthurian legends clearly become the new wave of fairy people.

He (Arthur) is a king y-crowned in Faerie,
With sceptre and pall, and with his regalty
Shalle' resort, as lord and sovereigne,
Out of Faerie, and reigne' in Bretaine,
And repair again the ould' Rounde' Table.
—*Fall of Princes*, bk.viii.c.24
Lydgate

Medieval Fairy—Out of Arthurian times the Medieval Fairy was born, moving away from Ireland and into England, and with them tales woven with magick and sorcery, wizards and witches, Morgan Le Fay and Avalon. The size of the fairy became variable, and there were both tiny and rustic fairy as well as hideous and monstrous ones. Often, they were depicted as beautiful fair maidens with long, flowing red hair and white skin, such as those portrayed in the paintings by J. Waterhouse.

Whether it were the train of beauty's queen,
Or Nymphs or Faeries, or enchanted show,
With which his eyes mote have delueded been.
—*The Shepherd's Calendar*
Spenser

The Monastic chroniclers in medieval times acted as hospices, and first-hand accounts of battles, crusades, and courtly politics were gathered by the monks of the new religion who were in charge of the chronicles.

Strange happenings and supernatural occurrences were eagerly recorded, and it is from these that we gain some of the early fairy anecdotes. Some chroniclers, however, though they were churchmen, were not monastics. The recordings of the Daoine Sidhe give indication of them enjoying the pleasures and occupations of medieval chivalry. It is, however, out of these chronicles that the typical and commonly used fairy attributes of modern times were born.

The fairy of the medieval romances are among the Heroic Faery in type, of human size and often amorous of mortals, expert in enchantment and glamour, generally beautiful, but occasionally hideous. Many of them were but half-forgotten gods and goddesses, euhemerized into mortals with magickal powers. The goddesses are more frequent than the gods, perhaps due to the patriarchal religion that forbade the mention or influence of the matriarchal belief system and its worship of the great Mother Goddess. It was, however, literary fashion which chose out this type of fairy, possibly because of the romances derived from Celtic hero tales founded on the Celtic Pantheon. Scattered references in the medieval chronicles show that very different types of Faery/fairy were available to the medieval poets if they chose to use them.

Diminutive Fairy—The Diminutive Fairies took part in life and became the traditional, and very first, little fairy. With its birth, a list of euphemistic names (Appendix B) became inevitable. These invisible and alert little things were always mentioned with a honeyed tongue. According to *An Encyclopedia of Fairies, Hobgoblins, Brownies and Bogies and Other Supernatural Creatures,* by Katherine Briggs, the wily, knowing not where they might be lurking, were careful to call them the Good Neighbours, the honest folk, the little folk, the Gentry, the hill folk, the forgetful people, the people of peace, etc., to prevent the "dint of their ill attempts and to bless all they fear harme of." Even the creatures, themselves, were known to give this warning to humans:

> *Gin ye ca' me imp or elf,*
> *I rede ye look weel to yourself;*
> *Gin ye ca' me fairy,*
> *I'll work ye muckle tarrie;*
> *Gin guid neibour ye ca' me,*
> *Then guid neibour I will be;*
> *But gin ye ca' me seelie wicht,*
> *I'll be your freend baith day and nicht.*
>   — *An Encyclopedia of Fairies,*
>   *Hobgoblins, Brownies, Bogies and*
>   *Other Supernatural Creatures*
>   Katherine Briggs

The fairy became connected with the dead; the soul was often thought of as a tiny creature which comes out of a sleeping man and wanders about—its adventures are the sleeper's dreams. By this means or others, the tradition continued, and came up into literature in the sixteenth century.

These literary fairies were introduced into drama by John Lyly in *Endimion.* They were brought in for a short time, to do justice on the villain by the pinching now traditional to the fairies. They punish not only the wrong done to Endimion, but the infringement of fairy privacy. In the tale, Corsites has been trying to move the sleeping Endimion when the fairies enter, and pinch him so that he falls asleep. They dance, sing and kiss Endimion:

Pinch him, pinch him, blacke and blue,
Sawcie mortalls must not view
What the Queene of Stars be doing,
Nor pry into our Fairy wooing.

Elizabethan Fairy—The romance and fierce warrior attitude of the Daoine Sidhe was gone. The fairy became mischievous and at times bothersome. And so, the poets and dramatists of the Elizabethan Age brought a different strand of fairy tradition into prominence. The yeoman class of the sixteenth century brought a spread of literacy and new class of writers. From the country, drawn up to town, such as Shakespeare, these new writers came forth bringing with them their own country traditions.

The fairy ladies of the medieval times, who were more humanized and sophisticated as time went on, became out of date. Nymphs became a new source of focus, as did the classical mythology. Two main types of fairies were introduced: the hobgoblins, with which we may rate the Brownie; and the small flower-loving fairies such as Shakespeare introduces in his *A Midsummer Night's Dream,* and which became all the fashion for the Jacobean Fairy. It is these small fairies that gain the addition of gossamer wings, a standard symbol of the modern fairy. These fairy writings came in toward the end of the century.

Out steps some Faery with quick motion,
And tells him wonders of some flowerie vale—
Awakes, straight rubs his eyes,
and prints his tale.
—*A Midsummer Night's Dream,* B.III. Sat. 6
William Shakespeare

It was the Elizabethan Fairy writers that perhaps gave us our first sense of social fairy life. Even the most flaccid and degenerate of the literary fairies had some point in common with the Faery in folk tradition, but, as a rule, the poets and story-tellers picked out one aspect from the varied and intricate world of Faery tradition, and the aspect chosen differed not only from poet to poet, but also from one period to another.

Jacobean Fairy—The Jacobean Fairy continued to extend the fashions in fairy lore set in Elizabethan literature, with an added emphasis on the minuteness of the small fairies, so that at one time people found it difficult to think of fairies at all without thinking of smallness. The hobgoblin type was exactly the same in both periods, except now the extreme Puritans regarded all fairies as devils.

A few verses of the following traditional poem show the quality of the Jacobean Fairy and its truth to tradition:

From Oberon, in fairyland,
The king of ghosts and shadows there,
Mad Robin, I at his command,
Am sent to view the night-sports here;
What revel-rout

Is kept about
In every corner where I go,
I will o'ersee,
And merry be,
And make good sport, with ho, ho, ho!

More swift than lightning can I fly
About this airy welkin soon,
And, in a minute's space, descry
Each thing that's done below the moon:
There's not a hag,
Nor ghost shall wag,
Nor cry, ware Goblin! where I go;
But Robin I
Their feats will spy,
And fear them home, with ho, ho, ho!

If any wanderes I meet,
That from their night-sport do trudge home,
With counterfeiting voice I greet,
And cause them on with me to roam;
Through woods, through lakes,
Through bogs, through brakes,
O'er brush and brier, with them I go,
I call upon
Them to come on,
*And wend me laughing, ho, ho, ho!**

These denizens affect the seasons; they have power over the unborn offspring of mortals; they can bless and ban. Though they are small, they can assume human size, and they have the power of rapid motion. The whole pleasure in them is in their littleness. It is a court intrigue through a minifying-glass, with a hint of surrealism about them which reminds us that the fairies are fertility-spirits, and toward the end of the seventeenth century, we reach the nadir of the fairies' power, who are now no bigger than microbes.

Flower Fairy—These are the gentle spirits of earth. Earth, lake, and hill are peopled by these fantastic, beautiful, willful, capricious child-spirits. These fairies passionately love beauty and luxury and hold in contempt all the mean virtues of thrift and economy. Above all things they hate the tight fistedhand that gathers the last grain, drains the last drop in the milk-pail, and plucks the trees bare of fruit, leaving nothing for the spirits who wander by in the moonlight.

They like food and wine to be left for them at night, yet they are very temperate and never become intoxicated. This fairy lives in the superstitious mouths of the peasantry:

---

*Hazlitt, *Fairy Tales, Legends and Romances Illustrating Shakespeare* (13 verses in total).

> *But people should not sit up too late; for the fairies like to gather round the smouldering embers after the family are in bed, and drain the wine-cup, and drink the milk which a good house-wife always leaves for them, in case the fairies should come in and want their supper. A vessel of pure water should also be left for them to bathe in, if they like. And in all things the fairies are fond of being made much of, and flattered and attended to; and the fairy blessing will come back in return to the giver for whatever act of kindness done to the spirits of the hill and the cave and the well and the lake and the sea.*[7]

Folk-Tale Fairy—The eighteenth century is the first period in which books are written expressly for the edification of children. Fairy Godmothers, already at one remove from the Folk-Tale Fairy, become relentless moralists, driving their protégés along the path to virtue. The trend persists into the nineteenth century, and it is not until a quarter of it has passed that the research of the folklorists begin to have some effect on children's literature. The Romantic Revival, however, had begun before this to affect the writings of the poets.

The Golden Age of Faery has ended, and all that is left are folk fairies turned into airy, tenuous, pretty creatures without meat or muscles, made up of froth and whimsy, as W. B. Yeats so classically mourns in the following passage from his book, *The Celtic Twilight:*

> *I seemed to hear a voice of lamentation out of the Golden Age. It told me that we are imperfect, incomplete, and no more like a beautiful woven web, but like a bundle of cords knotted together and flung into a corner. It said that the world was once all perfect and kindly, and that still the kindly and perfect world existed, but buried like a mass of roses under many spadefuls of earth. The faery and the more innocent of the spirits dwelt within it, and lamented over our fallen world in the lamentation of the wind-tossed reeds, in the song of the birds, in the moan of the waves, and in the sweet cry of the fiddle. It said that with us the beautiful are not clever and the clever are not beautiful, and that the best of our moments are marred by a little vulgarity, or by a pin-prick out of sad recollection, and that the fiddle must ever lament about it all. It said that if only they who live in the Golden Age could die we might be happy, for the sad voices would be still; but alas! alas! they must sing and we must weep until Eternity swings open its gates.*

Elemental Fairy—In the positive doctrines of mediaeval alchemists and mystics (e.g. Paracelsus and the Rosicrucians, as well as their modern followers), the ancient meta-

---

7 Katherine Briggs, *An Encyclopedia of Fairies, Hobgoblins, Brownies, Bogies, and other Supernatural Creatures,* Pantheon Books, 1976.

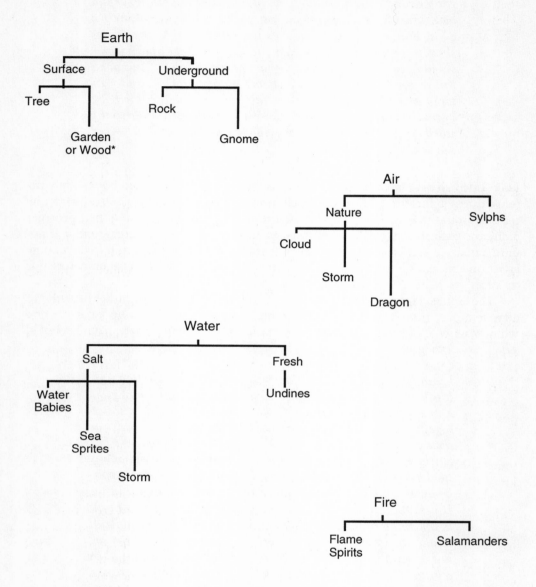

Figure 2: Map of the Elemental Group Classifications (and their subdivisions)

*This is the common Fairy of modern times, and is tied to the Devas.

physical ideas of Egypt, Greece, and Rome found a new expression; the folklore of the peasantry and the subject of fairies is turned into a study of beings of nature. They are quite scientific in their methods of study, and divide all invisible beings in four distinct classes:

> ⊱ Angels: who in character and function are parallel to the gods of the ancients, and equal to the Tuatha De Danann of the Irish, are the highest.

> ⊱ Devils or Demons: who correspond to the fallen angels of Christianity.

> ⊱ Elementals, sub-human Nature-Spirits: who are generally regarded as having pygmy stature, like the Greek daemons.

> ⊱ Souls: who are the shades or ghosts of the dead.

It is the third class, which includes spirits of pygmy-like form, that is most important in this present discussion.

The Elemental Fairy has four classifications (Earth, Air, Water, Fire), as each group inhabits one of the four chief elements of nature (Figure 2). Today, the subgroups found within each Elemental Fairy classification have been forgotten, retaining only the knowledge of that creature which in modern magick has become known as the elemental. The elemental inhabiting the earth is called the gnome; the air is the sylph; the water is the undine.

The fourth kind, those inhabiting the fire, are called salamanders, and seldom appear in the world of fairy: they are considered supreme in the elementary hierarchies.

All these Elemental Fairies, who procreate after the manner of humankind, have bodies of an elastic half-material essence, which is sufficiently ethereal not to be visible to the physical sight, and probably comparable to matter in the form of invisible gases. The visible world is merely thought of as their skin. In dreams, it is believed we go amongst them and play with them, and combat with them. They are explained as perhaps being human souls in the crucible.

These new forms of fairies are thought to be in different stages of evolution, and that all are concerned with the processes of nature. Their elemental life is also in close touch with human beings. The realm in which the Elemental Fairies exist are no longer referred to as Faeryland, but rather, the Middle Kingdom.

One might ask, where exactly is that country, and what is it in the middle of? This is the theory presented in answer. The world of the gods is of creative power, and ours is the world of created objects. The Middle Kingdom is the land of life that lies between them, serving as the bridge for their interaction. It is believed to extend wherever vital processes are going on: upward into sunlight and the warmth-realm called the troposphere, sidewise with the spreading flow of water, downward into the dark depths of earth, where roots grow and veins of metal run; which is a theory in keeping with the Faery-Faith tradition.

Figure 3 is a diagram of The Three Worlds, or Three Environments. R.J. Stewart, in his book, *Earth Light*, tells us, "Ideally the two realms, Over- and Underworld, should balance one another; what is found in one has a reflection or polar partner or opposite in the other. This includes humans and other, non-humans, beings …"

Alchemists, using this same rule, took the energies of above, below, and sideways to demonstrate this concept, thus further elucidating the movement of energy within the Elemental Fairy realm.

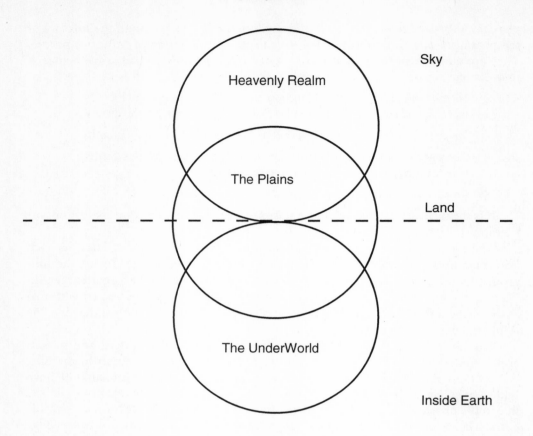

Figure 3: The Three Levels of Faeryland

There is one division within this Middle Kingdom which is quite clear, just as in the world of animals and plants, and that is between the fairies of the various elements. This division gives a natural and inevitable classification and one in which less departure from physical experience is involved. The groups merge into one another, just as in our solid world some fishes can fly a bit, some land creatures can swim, etc. It is nevertheless a clear-cut and real division.

However, there is among them all one type which most completely characterizes this new term of fairy, and this is the common woods or garden fairy who figures frequently in the minds of modern people. This fairy form is found everywhere, and varies as much from continent to continent as nationalities vary among humankind. Perhaps, it is in this form that the Tuatha De Danann have chosen to now communicate with us, mirroring back our need to reconnect with our environment, our earth.

Before we take a look at the individual group classifications of the Elemental Fairy, it is important to note that within each group, there exist some common attributes. All take notice of children and especially of quite small ones, as they have much affection for children, who are in the human order the nearest thing to them.

If they see a human being who truly feels attraction for a special plant or flower they take an interest in the admirer, as their vanity is flattered. Love for flowers and a conscious invitation to the Elemental Fairy to help is a way to come to know them, and perhaps even to see them. It is love of living things which is thought to be the great bridge between the two kingdoms.

The secret of their lives is rhythm. When they want to respond to another living species, they make their heart beat at the same pulse rate as the other life form. This synchronism makes them unified.

They are mainly concerned with the energy and life flowing around and within the form. They have no illusions, but rather have the power of seeing clearly and coming straight to the point. They are, however, very conscious of being part of a great cooperative scheme, and thus they have a feeling of certainty. Likewise, there is no sense of good or evil in their world, only a great love of beauty and perfection.

The four races of Elemental Fairy are by no means limited to one particular story in nature's three-tiered dwelling. It is quite the opposite: the liveliest exchange takes place up-and-down and sideways as the various groups go about their business, which, as mentioned earlier, is to serve life and its evolution. Let us observe how each Elemental Fairy functions in its own element.

Earth Fairy—has two subgroups: surface and underground. Each of these is again divided into two classes. On the surface, there are fairies with physical bodies, of which tree spirits are the finest example, and fairies without physical bodies, of which the common garden or woods fairy is the best illustration.

Underground (and of course to some extent upon it also) there are beings with physical bodies: those belonging to the great individual rocks, corresponding to the tree spirits. Associated with rocks there are fairies without physical bodies, generally called gnomes. These four vast categories are quite definite: trees, garden, or wood fairies of all kinds, rocks, and gnomes.

The earth fairies are almost universally tiny, about a foot or eighteen inches high, of a golden brown or dark green color. They have long ears and a general air of hopping about. A variant of this variety looks like a small teddy bear, generally light brown above and dark brown below the waist. They are cheerful, indeed gay, beings. They go on two legs with quick, jerky movements. They are also sociable and live in communities, and are exceedingly busy with immensely important affairs, or at least as it might seem to them. They inhabit the earth in forest areas, looking after the moss, and like to live among the roots of trees or in long grass. This variety seems to look after the life forces of aggregates of living things. They are attractive, amusing little things. They dart about impatiently when dealing with human beings. In fact, they are very like the leprechaun.

The tree fairy resides in each tree, and the form is much vaguer and practically invisible, for it really defines itself only when it projects itself outside. Most look alike: a tall, brownish form. Their job is to look after the tree and control its energies.

The wood fairies are beautiful little creatures that enjoy dancing and music. They like to dress-up and play among the flowers. Often they wear gossamer wings and gauzy tendril-like gowns (here we see a hint of the sixteenth century imagination still retained in this fairy's communion with modern women and men).

Dawn is a busy time for the garden fairy. As always at this time of the day, a special blessing is poured out upon the world. There is really an awakening of energy, and the fairies are kept busy receiving this and disseminating it.

The fairies think of the sun as a tremendous life-giving glove of light which is the source of all life, as they derive their nourishment principally from the sun's rays. They seem to draw the rays of the sun through their bodies; this is the nearest they come to eating.

Apart from deriving energy for the maintenance of their own bodies, they help to guide the energy from the sun for the plants' growth.

We may say, in truth, that the fairy life is the crown and perfection of a garden, helping to make it a place of rest and refreshment. The fairies are happy to work side-by-side with humans, to cooperate in making a spot of loveliness for mutual enjoyment, and if only more of us knew how eager this little Elemental is to help, gardens would be still more like fragments of heaven on earth than they are now to most.

Rock fairies are tremendously patient and contain vast wisdom, for they are grounded into the energy of Mother Earth. They represent a typical symbol of the greatness of soul. In essence, their appearance is a shining aura around the exterior of the rock.

Gnomes live close to, or actually under rocks. They are short, dumpy, and grey-brown in color. The limbs are of one color and the body another, which gives them the appearance of wearing a jerkin of leather. Usually the body is darker than the arms and legs. The feet are large, pointed and not very shapely, which gives them the effect of being shod in pointed shoes. The arms, in proportion to the body, are long and strong looking, with hands which are lumpy and not very well-defined. The space between the nose and eyes and mouth is wider than in human beings, and this gives the head a flattened, shovel-like appearance. The chin is exceedingly long and sharp, conveying the effect of a beard.

Gnomes are immensely clever Little People. They have what we might call a knowing eye, which understands at a glance everything it falls on. They send a message to us, constantly admonishing us to awaken. They are the knowers among Elementals. As such they possess a strong affinity to inner light. Of the Earth Fairies, gnomes are the least sociable, who are marked individualists, strongly ruled by antipathy.

Air Fairy—has two subgroups: the nature fairy and the Elemental itself, the sylph. The nature fairy is of three general types: cloud, storm, and dragon, and all are by nature part water and part air.

The cloud fairies live and have their being in masses in clouds; their size varies, but on the whole they are large, loosely knit, bulky forms, with slim, more or less human faces, with cloud-like hair thinly streaming behind them. Their whole texture is cloud-like. The cloud fairy is the sculptor of the imaginary world, and they get a sensation of achievement in floating about with their clouds and molding them. When clouds have vanished they retreat to mountain lakes, mist, and sea. They particularly love sunset and sunrise, because the sun shining through their clouds creates lovely effects, and they admire such sunrises and sunsets for the effects that are created in their world.

The most characteristic Air Fairy is the one that is associated with storms. The storm fairies are small, some four or five feet high, but shapely and beautiful. Their principal coloring is silver, with faint lights of pale blue and violet. They seldom come down to earth level and are seen mainly in great troops high up in the sky.

The third type, the dragon fairies, float idly across the sky, but very high above any cloud level and probably they are really moving rapidly. Storm fairies draw energy from them for some purposes of their own. They never descend to the lower atmosphere and are well above all storm levels. They are interesting because they are strange and so far removed from earthly life.

The sylphs are the most lovely to look at and to know. They have perfect human features and form, with beautiful childlike faces, except that they are far lovelier than the average human. Often they are surrounded by an opal-like shining glow. They are the easiest to communicate with. All of this kind of Air Fairy wear wings on their backs that are twice as large as their bodies and very frilly. The sylphs live in a world of tone, a realm of sounding glitter so vivid that even human ears and eyes catch glimpses of it.

Water Fairy—is divided into two subgroups consisting of salt water and fresh water. The salt water fairy consists of three groups: water babies, sea sprites, and storm fairies. The fresh water is the undine.

The first of the salt water fairies, the water babies, live on the surface of the ocean in sounds and bays near land. They are very jolly and have perfectly round faces, virtually no neck, an almost spherical body perhaps eighteen inches in diameter, almost no feet whatever, two vague flipper-like hands with fingers more or less well articulated, the whole affair a bright blue of soft texture, with great, merry eyes in a whitish face, almost no hair but with suggestions of baby fluff and faint knobs of ears. They roll and tumble against one another, and in the waves have the happiest of good times. They give their vital energy to us when we immerse ourselves in their salty playground.

The sea sprites are the golden jewels glittering just below the surface of the water; you can see them by looking out beyond the shore break. They are actually bigger than they seem, about five to six feet tall, and appear to look like humans, but with a fierce, gaunt beauty—more of a skeletal appearance than a fleshy one. They have elongated faces, sharp noses, slit mouths, and large blue eyes. A sea-windy hair of dark-blue floats around their heads. Their energy is one of happiness, and that of the Gypsy spirit—free and roaming.

The storm fairy dances with the open seas, rising up with the huge waves, but otherwise dwelling in the depths of the ocean. They are huge, fur-like creatures that are unpleasant because of their hugeness. They are one of the few hostile fairies.

The fresh water fairy is the elemental known as the undine—the beautiful and slender fairy of the ponds and lakes, who has been known to lure men to their death. Though they mean no harm, their love of singing and the enchantment they weave when singing naturally draws a wandering soul to the shore of the body of water in which they dwell.

This is the only elemental that perhaps has reminiscent qualities of the earlier Medieval Fairy. They are beautiful creatures, of a feminine nature, who are unclothed and are covered only by their masses of hanging curls. With sullen eyes and big lips, they appear to be mourning their inability to live on land.

Undines may be thought of as the great transformers; they are the chemists of the elemental world. It is undines who, in accordance with their inner life, and using fluids as their medium, cause substances to intermingle and undergo the process known as chemical change.

They, too, have a task assigned them. It is they who draw sap, the clear life-blood of vegetation, up the trunks of trees and stems of plants, to join forces with the light in foliage; they bring about change in the shape and composition of substances as they wield the fluid element to bind and loosen. They are also the dreamers.

Fire Fairy—is comprised of two types: flame spirits and the Elemental salamander.

The flame spirit is small, about three inches to two feet in height, rather like candle flames. They appear in little wood fires, called into being by the rhythm of the fire, which is the most powerful of vibrations, created by the sound of the fire; this is like a harmonic invocation, and ceases to exist when the fire goes out.

The salamander lives in volcanoes and is of an elongated, thin human shape, often dwindling away at the bottom. The largest ones are also present in forest fires; the bigger the fire, the bigger the fairy. These would be attracted to the fire from some distance, not called into existence, for there are actually places which are centers for these fire spirits, and when there is a fire they are called from there.

The Fire Fairies are indifferent to life, and though not exactly feared by the rest of nature, are held in awe. It is impossible to convey the vitality of this particular element in nature. It is both destructive and creative.

Fire is really mysterious to all of us in its many different aspects, but the fairies of this element are usually intelligent in our own sense of the word.

Were it not for the fact that warmth or fire, the province of fire spirits, is such a common phenomenon, witnessed every time we strike a light, we should hardly be able to contain our wonder at the properties of this element. These are among the first spirits we learn to see. But, it is in all groups that we are reminded that the Elementals are the living soul of nature; they do the work that makes the world go around—the living world.

> What a different view of the world dawns upon us when we open ourselves to the soul-life in Nature and begin to live it with her in our sense of movement! To do this deliberately, in willed awareness, is to experience a quickening that knows no end. It leads through door after door, over threshold after threshold, always in the company of the fairies, until, as we look back, the landscape we inhabited before begins to seem like the country of the dead and we ourselves wandering in it only half alive.
>
> We think of the seasons as periods of time, and of course they are that. But this is their least interesting aspect. They are also four distinct moods of Nature's soul, four different ways she relates to the interwoven worlds of earth and heaven. Furthermore, each season is, so to speak, a space in time, making four temporal kingdoms over which the four groups of the Elemental fairies rule.*

* Marjori Spock, *Fairy Worlds and Workers.*

Devas—Now we come to the final evolved form of the fairy, that of the "shining ones," who are known to be the soul of the plant kingdom. The spirit of the plant as it comes alive and takes new form allies itself with human beings and gives to them the secrets of the plant (i.e. medicinal properties, spiritual properties, nutritional properties, magickal properties, toxic properties, etc.).

These are the fairies without shape. They are simply a golden glowing, effervescent cloud of energy rising from the plant; a tingling energy that pin-pricks our skin when we enter their field. The Deva does not move from the plant, but remains closely attached. They are the life-side of Nature, an expression of the Divine energy—the Will—channeled in manifested Nature.

The Faery, the Elemental Fairy, the Devas, all the spirit beings of the world, cannot be captured, stuffed, and put on display in museums, like rare animals and birds of whose existence we have no doubt even if we have not seen them before viewing their carcasses. The beings of the Otherworld exist just as these animals and birds do, although we cannot see them.

I believe we all know that there is with us always an overshadowing consciousness of an invisible world, not in some distant realm of space, but here and now, blending itself with this world. This belief is what we call mysticism.

The noted author W. Y. Evans-Wentz said in his book *Fairy-Faith in Celtic Countries*: "And to the great majority of Europeans and Americans, mysticism is a most convenient noun, applicable to anything which may seem reasonable yet wholly untranslatable in terms of their own individual experience; and mysticism usually means something quite the reverse of scientific simply because we have, by usage, unwisely limited the meaning of the word *science* to a knowledge of things material and visible, whereas it really means a knowing or a knowledge of everything which exists."

Perhaps the study of the Occult truly is a science, therefore creating the term: Mystical Scientist. Perhaps....

I close this study with the poet and mystic, George W. Russell, who wrote *The Candle of Vision* under the name A.E.:

> *During all these centuries the Celt has kept in his heart some affinity with the mighty beings ruling in the Unseen, once so evident to the heroic races who preceded him. His legends and faery tales have connected his soul with the inner lives of air and water and earth, and they in turn have kept his heart sweet with hidden influence.*

Journal Exercises

1. Understanding the Faery Lineage gives great clarity when choosing to work with their energy; how has the above lesson altered your original beliefs surrounding the Faery?

2. Which branch of the Faery Lineage first fit your original view of them (it is okay if it was the literary fairy or the garden fairy; these are the two most common images); now which branch of the lineage has more validity to you?

3. How does this lesson enhance your overall sagacity of this tradition?

Suggested Reading

The Vanishing People, Katharine Briggs
The Fairy Mythology, Thomas Keightley
Irish Fairy and Folk Tales, W.B. Yeats

*L*ong, long ago beyond the misty space
Of twice a thousand years,
In Erin old there dwelt a mighty race,
Taller than Roman spears;
Like oaks and towers they had a giant
grace,
Were fleet as deers
With winds and waves they made their 'biding place,
These western shepherd seers.

Their ocean-god was Manannan Mac Lir,
Whose angry lips,
In their white foam, full often would inter
Whole fleets of ships;
Crom was their day-god, and their thunderer,
Made morning and eclipse;
Bride was their queen of song, and unto her
They prayed with fire-touched lips.

Oh, inspired giant! shall we e'er behold,
In our own time,
One fit to speak your spirit on the wold,
Or seize your rhyme?
One pupil of the past, as mighty souled
As in the prime,
Were the fond, fair, and beautiful and bold—
They, of your song sublime!

—*The Celts*
D'Arcy McGee
17th Century Irish Poet

Cu Chulainn
The hound of ULSTER

Lesson Three

The Ancient Ones

Save your majestic song, which hath their speed, And strength, and grace; In that sole song, they live and love and bleed— It bears them on thro' space. *

Since there was no written material from the Celts until the period of their arrival in their current homeland, the nature of their gods and goddesses is drawn primarily from Irish, Scottish, and Welsh tradition and literature. This does not mean that these beliefs were not held by the Celts of earlier periods, but suggests that up until the time they were recorded, they were preserved through tradition and oral recitation.

In this study, we focus on the Celtic Pantheon, richly abundant with goddesses mighty in magick, enchantment, and divination; and gods powerful in battle and wit.

In the traditional sense, the term *Ancient Ones* refers to both the goddesses and gods of Ireland, as does the term *the gods*; each list is extensive in names. Therefore, the terms god and goddess are used when referring to a specific deity of the Pantheon, such as Dagda or Brigid. We would then refer to Dagda as a god of ... and Brigid as a goddess of ... however, the most ancient name on record for the Celt's primary god is Dana.

The Primary God

In Faery Wicca, Dana is GOD, or the primary aspect of the gods. She is technically of a female energy, but contains the masculine; therefore, She is both a female god and a male god; the great Mother of all the gods and goddesses of the Celtic Pan-

---

* D'Arcy McGee, *The Celts.*

41

Faery Wicca

theon. Mother of the Gods, who is beyond them all, is one of the ancient definitions found referring to Dana.

Dana, or Danu (dawn-a, or dawn-uh)—The most ancient God on Celtic record. Evidence of this most ancient Celtic God is found in the Irish *Lebor Gabala* (Book of Invasions), dated at about 1000 C.E.. Dana is the Mother of the Tuatha De Danann, who later dwindled to the Daoine Sidhe, the Sidhe-folk of Ireland. She was praised as the Mother of the Gods, who is beyond all other gods of this world.

The name Dana means wisdom or teacher, as in the English word *don*, or giving, as in the root of the word *donate*. The following is part of her legend:

> In the twilight of the day whose light lingered longer than any other, there were prayers for abundance on La Baal Tinne's eve, the holiest of Dana's holy days. Worshippers carrying windblown torches of blazing bundled straw tied upon long branches made their way up the mountainsides, blessing the new cattle and the newly planted seed, explaining that they were commemorating the very day that the children of Mother Dana had first set foot upon the soil of Erin.[8]

Today, the Irish people, through their veneration for the good St. Bridget, render homage to the divine mother of the people who bear her name Dana—who are the ever-living invisible Faery-People of modern Ireland. For when the Sons of Mil, the ancestors of the Irish people, came to Ireland, they found the Tuatha De Danann in full possession of the country.

The Tuatha De Danann then retired before the invaders without, however, giving up their sacred island. Assuming invisibility, with the power of at any time reappearing in a human-like form before the children of the Sons of Mil, the People of the Goddess Dana became and are the Faery-Folk, the Sidhe of Irish mythology and romance.

Therefore, today Ireland contains two races—a visible race, which we call the Celts, and an invisible race, which we call Faery, or Sidhe. Between these two races there is constant intercourse even now, for Irish seers say that they can behold the majestic, beautiful Sidhe, and according to them, the Sidhe are a race quite distinct from our own, just as living and possibly more powerful.

The recorded mythology and literature of ancient Ireland have, very faithfully for the most part, preserved clear pictures of the Tuatha De Danann and their Goddess Dana so that, disregarding some Christian influence in the texts of certain manuscripts, much rationalization, and a good deal of poetical coloring and romantic imagination in the pictures, we can easily describe the People of Goddess Dana as they appeared in Pagan days, when they were more frequently seen by mortals.

Danu is recorded as being the Mother of the Dananns. Her name is usually associated with the Danube (Donau and Dunava in areas of eastern Europe). There is some speculation that in Proto-Celtic periods, the name Danu had been linked with the River Don in Russia. Don is the Welsh goddess who is equivalent to the Irish

---

8 *Lebor Gabala* (Book of Invasions) 2nd Century.

Dana, and it seems likely that she was an immigrant from Ireland, for the Children of Don correspond closely in character and functions to the Children of Dana. Don is also connected with the River Don in Scotland.

There is a possible link between the name Dana/Danu, the name Dione, as a goddess name in Greece, and the goddess name, Diana, as known by the Romans.

Celtic Goddess Pantheon

A major theme connected to the goddesses of the Celtic Pantheon is the association to a particular body of water—usually a river, but at times a spring, a lake, or the ocean.

The Divine Ancestress of the Celtic Boii tribe was known as Boann, and linked with the River Boyne in Ireland. Sequana, a goddess of France, became linked with the River Shannon of Ireland. And as I have already stated, there is some speculation that Dana might have been linked with the River Don in Russia, and that the Russian goddess, Don, was also linked to a river name in Celtic Scotland.

Linking their goddesses with various bodies of water in turn appears to have linked the Celtic reverence for the goddess as The Great Mare, for the white breakers of the ocean were described in Irish legend as the white mane of the Morrigan's head.

If we ponder how the sea and horse draw a parallel in the Celts' mind, we may see a connection in the double use of the word *mare*. It means sea in Latin and Russian, and is the root of the English word *marine*. At the same time it was used to designate a female horse. Both meanings of mare may have been derived from the same initial Indo-European source word, possibly the Sanskrit *mah* meaning mighty. This word may also be the foundation of the goddess names: Morrigan and Morgan—the roots *gan, gin*, and *gen* meaning birth, as in *genesis* and *begin*.

This interesting connection between the two words may suggest that the origin of the Pantheon was not in Ireland itself, but came from across the sea, and that the symbol of the first GOD—Dana—may very well have been that of a horse.

An aspect of the Irish goddesses worth noting is their wonderful and magickal ability to shape-change, not only as animals, but also alternating between an ugly Hag-state and that of a beautiful, alluring woman. The Morrigan becomes an eel, a wolf, a heifer, a raven, and several diverse images of mortal women. Macha and the Cailleach Bera take the form of horses, and the Badb takes the form of Royston crows, alternating between a Hag-state and that of a young woman.

In addition to these powers, there is the martial prowess of Celtic goddesses, who often acted as ambassadors in battles and rivalries between the Celtic tribes, sitting in on peace councils when disputes were discussed.

There is the less documented image of the goddess among the Celts as the figure of the Goddess of Victory, as well as the mother of some of the gods, such as Tailltiu, the step-mother of Lugh, and the goddesses of healing, poetry, and fate.

Rather than cover these various goddesses in this paragraph, let me present a listing of fifteen important Irish goddesses*, each in their own verse, in an attempt to honor the feminine regime of Erin.

Badb, or Badhbh (bav)—The primary Celtic war-goddess, who is of triple aspect, containing the goddesses Neman, Macha, and Morrigu in a single form, and who often takes the form of a Royston or hooded crow.

The narrative of the Battle of Moytura in *The Book of Leinster*, gives one of the most vivid descriptions of the activities of Badb and her attendant spirits:

> *There arose a wild, impetuous, precipitate, mad, inexorable, furious, dark, lacerating, merciless, combative, contentious badb, which was shrieking and fluttering over their heads. And there arose also the satyrs, and sprites, and maniacs of the valleys, and witches and goblins and owls, and destroying demons of the air, and firmament, and the demoniac phantom host shouted about him [Cu Chulainn], for the Tuatha De Danann were wont to impart their valour to him, in order that he might be more feared, more dreaded, more terrible, in every battle and battle-field, in every combat and conflict, into which he went; and they were inciting and sustaining valour and battle with them.* [9]

The Battles of Moytura seem in most ways to be nothing more than the traditional record of a long warfare to determine the future spiritual control of Ireland carried on between two diametrically opposed orders of invisible beings, the Tuatha De Danann, representing the gods of light and good, and the Fomorians, representing the gods of darkness and evil.

It is also written in the *Book of Leinster* that after the second of these battles "The Morrigu, daughter of Ernmas, proceeded to proclaim that battle and the mighty victory which had taken place, to the royal heights of Ireland and to its Faery host and its chief waters and its rivermouths."

Here we see the Tuatha De Danann with their war-goddesses fighting their own battles in which human beings play no part. For good had prevailed over evil, and it was settled that all Ireland should forever afterwards be a sacred country ruled over by the People of God Dana and the Sons of Mil jointly.

However, the course of victory was altered when "the Badb went up onto the summits of all the high mountains of Ireland, and proclaimed the victory." All the lesser gods who had not been in the battle came round and heard the news. And Badb sang a song which began:

> *Peace mounts to the heavens,*
> *The heavens descend to earth,*
> *Earth lies under the heavens,*
> *Everyone is strong....*

---

9 *Book of Leinster*, 10th Century.

* For a complete listing of the Ancient Ones, see Appendix-D: Irish Gods and Goddesses.

Then she added a prophecy in which she foretold the approaching end of the divine age, and the beginning of a new one in which summers would be flowerless and cows milkless and women shameless and men strengthless, in which there would be trees without fruit, and seas without fish, when old men would give false judgments, and legislators make unjust laws, when warriors would betray one another, and men would be thieves, and there would be no more virtue left in the world.

The Irish war-goddess, Badb, considered of old to be one of the Tuatha De Danann, has survived to our own day in the fairy-lore of the chief Celtic countries. In Ireland, the survival is best seen in the popular and still almost general belief among the peasantry that the Sidhe often exercise their magical powers under the form of Royston-crows; for this reason these birds are always greatly dreaded and avoided.

Badb, or Badhbh, originally signified "rage, fury, or violence," and ultimately implied a witch or cunning woman, Faery or goddess. There is also a definite relationship between the Badb and the Bean Si, as both wear the emblem of the crow, and both announce death.

Banbha (bawn-vwah)—One of the three queens of the Tuatha De Danann, and one of the three daughters of Dagda, who asked the Milesian to call Ireland after them. She is also the wife of Mac Cuill, Son of the Hazel, "whose god was the sea."

According to one myth, she was the first goddess who found Ireland before the Flood; according to another, she came over with Cesara. She told Amergin: "I am older than Noe; on a peak of a mountain was I in the Flood." Her name derives from banva, sow, or piglet.

Bean Si (ban-shee)—Which means Fairy Woman, or Woman of Peace. By one source, it is believed that this is a euphemism for any female spirit but usually representing the old toutal goddess, or goddess of the land and river of a particular region. However, more traditionally presented, the Bean Si is the messenger of death, or crone aspect of the Triple Goddess.

She is often depicted as having long streaming hair and a grey cloak over a green dress. Her eyes are fiery red with continual weeping, and when she is a messenger of death utters forth the "Ululu," the cry of death. Irish peasantry speak of this goddess as:

> *Sometimes the Bean Si assumes the form of some sweet singing virgin of the family who died young, and has been given the mission by the invisible powers to become the harbinger of coming doom to her mortal kindred. Or she may be seen at night as a shrouded woman crouched beneath the trees, lamenting with veiled face; or flying past in the moonlight, crying bitterly: and the cry of this spirit is mournful beyond all other sounds on Earth, and betokens certain death to some member of the family whenever it is heard in the silence of the night.[10]*

---

10 W. B. Yeats, *Irish Fairy and Folk Tales*, Walter Scott, 1893.

Song of the Banshee

By a Kerry Pishogue

Figure 4

The Bean Si could be as benevolent as the sacred women who used to sing the dying gently to sleep. When the Bean Si loves those she calls, the song (Figure 4) is a low, soft chant giving notice, indeed, of the proximity of death, but with a tenderness of tone that reassures the one destined to die and comforts the survivors—rather a welcome than a warning.

In the Highlands of Scotland she is also called the Bean-Niche, or the Little-Washer-By-The Ford, because she is seen by the side of a burn or river washing the blood-stained clothes of those about to die. She is small, and generally dressed in green, and has red webbed feet.

She portends evil, but if anyone sees her before she sees them and gets between her and the water, she will grant them three wishes. She will answer three questions, but she asks three questions again, which must be answered truly. Anyone bold enough to seize one of her hanging breasts and suck it may claim that they are her foster-child and she will be favorable toward them.

The Banshee (as is commonly spelled) is also considered a death spirit who wails only for members of the old families. When several keen together it foretells the death of someone very great or holy.

Breo-saighit (Bree-o-say-it)—The flame of Ireland, fiery arrow, was this goddess who latter became known as Brigid, the perfect example of the survival of an early goddess into Christian times. She is a goddess of fire and the hearth, a goddess of poetry worshiped by the poets, a goddess of healing, a goddess of the martial arts, a patron of warfare or briga, and a goddess of smith-work.

Brigid, or Brigit (breed, or bri-hit)—The Irish goddess Brigid seems to have been so much beloved that the Early Church could not bring itself to cut her off from the people, and she became St. Bridgit of Ireland.

She was a daughter of the Dagda, and was married to Bress, the son of the Fomorian king as an alliance. Brigid and Bress had a son, Ruadan, who was killed in battle, and his mother, Brigid, mourned for him, inventing the Irish keening. Her ancient song was:

Brigid, excellent woman, sudden flame,
may the bright fiery sun take us to the lasting kingdom.

One side of her face was ugly, but the other side was comely. Her powers are celebrated with the ritual of Imbolc on February 2 (one of the Four Great Festivals to be discussed in a later lesson), Bride's Day, when this chant is sung:

Today is the day of Bride;
the serpent shall come from the hole.

As a goddess of poetry, poets worshiped her, for her sway was very great and very noble. As a goddess of smith's work, it was she who first made the whistle for calling one to another through the night.

Brigid was born exactly at sunrise, and a great tower of flame reached from the top of her small head all the way into the heavens, thus signaling the birth of a holy babe, and her breath gave new life to the dead. It was this very same fire that was tended by the Daughters of the Flame, the nine who are Ingheau Anndagha, those who lived inside the fence of Brigid's shrine and could be looked upon by no man, to insure that the purity and sanctity of the fire would be protected.

Daring attempts were made to change the Tuatha De Danann from Pagan gods into Christian saints, but these were by no means so profitable as the policy pursued towards the more human-seeming heroes. However, as mentioned above, the one success was that of Brigid, the goddess of fire and the hearth. Today she is famous as Saint Bridget, or Bride. Most popular of all the Irish saints, she can still be easily recognized as the daughter of the Dagda. Her Christian attributes, almost all connected with fire, attest her Pagan origin.

Her sacred shrine in Kildare was active into the eighteenth-century. Originally, the undying flame was attended by nineteen virgins, but later was cared for by Catholic sisters.

Nineteen was her sacred number, representing the nineteen year cycle of the Celtic Great Year—the number of years it takes (18.61 years) for the new moon to coincide with the winter solstice. It was believed that on the twentieth day of each cycle, St. Bridget miraculously tended the fire herself.

The flame was extinguished once in the thirteenth century, but was relighted, and burned with undying glow until the suppression of the monasteries by Henry VIII. It was believed that this sacred fire might not be breathed on by the impure breath, just as the priestesses could not be looked upon by the impure.*

The lark is sacred to St. Bridget because its song woke her every morning before divinity, when she had service for the women who were her converts. The influence of St. Bridget remains a permanent power in Ireland even to this day, and she is much

---

* Sr. Mary Minchin, a Bridgedian at Kildare, will be relighting the sacred fire Feb. 2, 1996, and it will be kept burning.

47

feared by the enemy of souls and the ill-doer. She ordained bishops, and was head and chief of all the sacred virgins. She also held equal rank with the Archbishop; if he had an episcopal chair, so St. Bridget had a virginal chair (*Cathedra Puellaris*), and was preeminent above all the abbesses of Ireland, for sanctity and power.

Brigid was also a teacher of the martial arts, and a patron of warfare, or briga. Her soldiers were brigands, or as Christians called them, outlaws.

Brigid, the Gaelic Minerva, is also found in Britain as Brigantia, tutelary goddess of the Brigantes, a Northern tribe, and in Eastern France as Brigindo, to whom Iccavos, son of Oppianos, made a dedicatory offering, of which there is still record.

The name Biddy was commonly used when referring to St. Bridget. In Kerry, on the southwestern coast, when a girl impersonated the Saint (or a group carrying her effigy), and went begging from house to house, they sang:

Something for poor Biddy!
Her clothes are torn.
Her shoes are worn.
Something for poor Biddy!

When the group was comprised of only young men dressing in women's attire, they were called "Biddy boys." Giving money and food to the Biddy callers was thought to bring a good harvest. The rivers Brent and Braint may be named after her.

Cailleach Bera [koy-log vayra]—A very ancient Hag-aspect of the goddess who was known by many names throughout the Celtic countries. In the Irish Triads, the Cailleach is considered one of the three great ages:

(T)he age of the yew tree, the age of the eagle, the age of the Hag of Beare.

Although reference is made to her beauty, she was also described as having an eye in the middle of a blue-black face, red teeth, and matted hair. She controlled the seasons and the weather.

Cailleach Bera, or Beara, is almost identical with the Cailleach Bheur (cal yach vare) of the Highlands except that she is not so closely connected with the winter, nor with the wild beasts. She is a great mountain builder, and, like many other gigantic Hags, she carried loads of stone in her apron and dropped them when the spring broke to make dams, or mountains such as Loughcrew, where her stone seat is found.

The Cailleach Bheur of the Scottish Highlands, is a blue-faced Hag who personified winter, and is one of the clearest cases of the supernatural creature who was once a primitive goddess, possibly among the ancient Fomorians before the Celts. She has various facets of her character in which there is a striking resemblance to the primitive form of the Greek goddess Artemis. At first sight, she seems the personification of winter. She is called the daughter of Grainne, or the Winter Sun.

There were two suns in the old Celtic calendar, the Big Sun, which shines from La Baal Tinne, or Beltane (May Day) to Samhain (Hallowe'en), and the Little Sun, which shines from Samhain to Beltane eve.

The Cailleach was reborn each Samhain and went about smiting the earth to blight growth and calling down the snow. On Beltane eve she threw her staff under a holly tree or a gorse bush—both are her plants—and turned into a grey stone, therefore making lonely standing stones sacred to her.

In some tales, she does not turn to stone, but rather appears at the house where the fiana lay and begs for a place to warm herself at the fire. Gionn and Oisin refuse her, but Diarmaid pleaded that she might be allowed to warm herself at the fire, and when she crept into his bed he did not repulse her, only put a fold of the blanket between them. After a while he gave "a start of surprise," for she had changed into the most beautiful of woman that man ever saw. So, it would seem that the Cailleach represented a goddess of both winter and summer.

She is also the guardian spirit of a number of animals. The deer have the first claim to her. They are her cattle; she herds and milks them and often gives them protection against hunters. Swine, wild goats, wild cattle, and wolves were also her creatures. In another aspect, she is a fishing goddess, as well as the guardian of wells and streams. She also turns up in Manx-Gaelic as Caillagh ny Groamagh.

Dechtire—Queen of the swans, and mother of Cu Chulainn who was the reincarnation of Lugh. She was the daughter of Maga, the daughter of Angus, and was half-sister to King Conchobar.

Dechtire, on the point of being married to an Ulster chieftain named Sualtam, was sitting at the wedding feast when a may-fly flew into her cup of wine and was unwittingly swallowed by her. That same afternoon she fell into a deep sleep, and in her dream the sun-god Lugh appeared to her and told her that it was he whom she had swallowed, and bore within her.

He ordered her and her fifty attendant maidens to come with him at once, and he put upon them the shapes of birds, so that they were not seen to go. Nothing was heard of them again. But one day, months later, a flock of beautiful swans appeared at Emain Macha and Conchobar drew out his warriors in their chariots to hunt them.

They followed the birds until nightfall when they found themselves at the Brugh on the Boyne, where the great gods had their homes. As they looked everywhere for shelter, they suddenly saw a splendid palace.

A tall and handsome man, richly dressed, welcomed them and led them in. Within the hall were a beautiful and noble-faced woman and fifty maidens, and on the tables were the richest meats and wines, and everything fit for the needs of the warriors.

So they rested there the night, and during the night they heard the cry of a new-born child. The next morning the man told them who he was, and that the woman was Conchobar's half-sister Dechtire, and he ordered them to take the child and bring it up among the warriors of Ulster.

So they brought the child back, together with his mother and the maidens, and Dechtire married Sualtam.

Deirdre—The most beautiful woman in the world, who bore the curse that only sorrow would come of her beauty. Upon hearing the prophecy at her birth, the warriors of northern Ireland demanded her death. But the Ulster king, Conchobar, pitied her, and sent her into exile in the distant reaches of Ireland.

She lived happily in exile, and grew more beautiful each day. Then one day, she saw blood on the snowy ground with a raven nearby. She swore then to marry a young man whose hair was black, whose skin was white as snow, and whose lips were red as blood. She fell into a depression until her nurse Lavercam told her of a young man named, Naoise, who lived with his brothers nearby. Deirdre begged her nurse to arrange a secret meeting so she could see the man of her dreams, and when the meeting took placed, Deirdre placed a geasa on Naoise to free her from her woodland exile.

Deirdre's beauty gained the attention of the king, who laid plans to steal her from Naoise. So the lovers fled from Ireland across the ocean to Alba where they lived a rugged but happy life, until rumor reached them that Conchobar would welcome them back in Ireland. But the rumor had been deliberately planted; the king, angry at having his captive sprung from his grasp, wanted her back.

Deirdre knew that should they return to Ireland, tragedy would befall them, and begged Naoise not to return. Naoise, being a proud and loyal man to his king, over-ruled his lover and the party sailed back to Ireland. On the voyage home, Deirdre continued to have gloomy portents, although her lover and his brothers continued to ignore her warnings.

Her premonitions proved correct, and through treachery, Naoise and his brothers were murdered by the warriors of Conchobar. Deirdre was taken captive, and seeing that she had only one choice, threw herself from the king's speeding chariot in which she was being transported to the king, and smashed her head against a tree, splattering her blood and brains across the Irish soil.

Eire [eyr-ah]—This goddess, or queen of Tuatha De Danann, is one of the three daughters of Dagda, who gave the Melisian her protection when their Bard, Amergin, promised to call Erin (the ancient name of Ireland) "Ireland," which literally means the Land of Eire, in honor and homage to her.

Ich am of Irelande,
And of the holy lande
Of Irelande.
Good sire, pray ich thee,
Of sainte charite,
Come and daunce with me
In Irelande.
      —W. B. Yeats

Sometimes she appeared as a huge, beautiful woman, and sometimes as a long-beaked gray crow. She was considered a masterful magician, and lived on a hill in Ireland's center, which grew in size as the goddess aged.

Grainne (gran-ya)—The famed prehistoric mounds of Newgrange are thought to have been associated with this goddess. Newgrange lies along the coast between Dublin and Belfast, just a few miles west of Drogheda, and has been attributed to peoples as diverse as very early Celts to Phoenician colonists.

She was the wife of Finn mac Cumaill, the Fenian leader, whose nephew was Diarmaid. When Grainne saw Diarmaid she fell in love with him and put a geasa on him to run away with her. Because a warrior could never refuse a geasa placed upon him by a woman, he consented to do so and together the two lovers fled and stayed only one night in any place. They led a painful, dangerous existence. Grainne, the eternal mother of her lover-son, watched over him as he slept, singing a lullaby that contained all the love in the world, its joys and sorrows, and the triumphant strength that makes it inviolable by society. The name of her lullaby is known as *Duanaire Finn*.

Sleep for a little, a very small while,
And fear nothing.
Man to whom I have given my love,
Diarmaid, son of O'Duibhne.
Sleep here, deeply, deeply,
Son of O'Duibhne, noble Diarmaid,
I will watch over your rest,
Charming son of O'Duibhne...
My heart would break with grief
If I should ever lose sight of thee.
To part us would be to wrench
The child from his mother,
Exile the body from the soul,
Warrior of beautiful lake Garman...
The stag in the East does not sleep.
He does not cease to bellow
In the bushes of the black birds.
He does not want to sleep.
The hind without horns does not sleep.
She moans for her dappled child
And runs through the undergrowth.
Sleep for a little, a very small while,
And fear nothing,
Man to whom I have given my love....
                                   —Tain Bo Cuailgne

But Fionn pursued them all over Ireland for seven years, and finally caught them. He pretended to make peace with Diarmaid, but managed to bring about his death. Grainne died shortly after by throwing herself from a speeding chariot.

Grainne appears to be originally a sun-goddess (Grain, a feminine noun, meaning sun), and the conflict between Fionn and Diarmaid may reflect male resentment of the old matriarchal principle of the Young King replacing the Old King as mate of the goddess-queen. The love story between Diarmaid and Grainne can be compared to the love story of Guinevere and Lancelot, and Deirdre and Naoise.

Macha (ma-ka)—The name Macha literally means mighty. Though some myths associate her as one of the triple aspects of The Morrigan, in the Irish *Noinden Ulad*, Macha is represented as a separate deity. She is presented as the embodiment of the equine imagery of the goddess, suggesting a relationship to the Celtic Mare goddess known in Europe as Epona, and in Wales as Rhiannon.

Two sites in Ireland's county of Ulster still bear the name of Macha, one an ancient capital in Ulster known as Emain Macha, literally Twins of Macha, the other, Ard Macha, the present day city of Armagh.

She was the third wife of Crunnchu, of the Ulster Court, who boasted that Macha could run faster than any living horse, and, against her wishes, as she was full with child, he insisted she prove the truth of his claim to his men. Saddened in disbelief at Crunnchu's willingness to chance her life for his, Macha agreed to run the race.

She flew like the wind and calmly outran the steeds, crossing the finish line first. However, as she crossed the finish line, she gave birth to twins. The air was dense with quiet, and as she held each twin under an arm, her voice rang out into the silence, resounding the prophetic words that would never be forgotten, she cursed them for their pride and for the cold blood in their hearts and warned them that misery and suffering as painful as the labor of childbirth was to be her punishment of Ulster for nine generations. And with these words, she took her twins and left Ulster. Her death was certain doom on the men of Ulster.

She appeared in the Old Testament as Queen Maachah, whose spirit was worshiped as an idol in a grove until ousted by her son, King Asa (1 Kings 15:13).

As one of the triple forms taken by the ancient Irish war goddess Badb, the other two being Neman and Morrigu, all are in the shape of Royston or hooded crows. Macha is a Faery that "riots and revels among the slain." She is the personification of battle, and hovers over the fighters, inspiring them with the madness of battle. When the fight is over, the fighters revelled among the bodies of the slain; the heads cut off as barbaric trophies were called Macha's acorn crop.

Macha was considered one of Nuada's warlike wives and was supposedly killed by Balor, the king of the Fomorians, during one of the fights between the Tuatha De Danann and the Fomorians.

Maeve, or Medb (may-v)—In the Irish epic saga *Tain Bo Cuailgne*, Maeve's appearance is as a mighty warrior queen, and general of the army of the Irish county/state of Connacht. She led the Cattle Raid of Cuailgne in which the Brown Bull and the White Bull were captured, and whose passionate enmity had all but destroyed Ireland.

She was famous for her great display and her war chariots. The story of her raid and of the combats between her is retold by James Stephens in his book, *In The Land of Youth*, and also in Eleanor Hull's book, *The Cuchullin Saga*.

In the *Fled Bricrenn* of the Lebor na L'Uidre, she is portrayed as a judge of protocol and status among the Celtic people. As Queen of the Faery, Medb's tomb was said to be a cairn overlooking Sligo Bay, in an area that was once part of Connacht. In Elizabethan times, Medb becomes the model upon which Sheakspeare's Mab, Queen of the Fairies, is based.

The Morrigan, or Morrigu (more-ree-gun, or mohr-reeg-uh)—Her name literally means Great Queen. She was a major figure in the Irish epic *Tain Bo Cuailgne*. The narrative of the epic makes it clear that the Morrigan's loyalties are with the Tuatha De Danann and the Celtic tribes that had settled in the area of the large nation/state of Connacht.

In the *Tain*, she is acknowledged as having a threefold nature: "She is the three phases of the silver moon, waxing, full, and waning." In her aspect as a warrior goddess, The Morrigan is extremely active, and even aggressive. She is a vengeful crone, chortling in delight at spilled blood upon a battlefield, drowning enemy princes beneath her white waves, battling against the Fomorians to protect those of the tribe of Dana.

As one of the three war goddesses in the form of crows, Morrigu is the greatest. Neman confounds the armies of the enemy, so that allies wage mistaken war against each other, Macha revels in discriminate slaughter, but it was Morrigu who infused supernatural strength and courage into Lugh, so that he won the war for the Tuatha De Danann, the forces of goodness and light, and conquered the dark Fomorians, just as the Olympic gods conquered the Titans.

She flew across Celtic battlefields as the Royston crow, making herself visible only to those whose life would soon be over. Yet, to some she appeared as a young woman dressed in brightly colored cloths embroidered with threads of glistening gold. Changing shape and form was but play to the mighty Goddess, and poetry and prophesy Her natural tongue.

Her battle-cry was as loud as that of 10,000 men. Wherever there was war, either among gods or men, she, the Great Queen, was present, either in her own shape or in her favourite disguise, that of the hooded crow. An old poem shows her inciting a warrior:

> Over his head is shrieking
> A lean hag, quickly hopping
> Over the points of the weapons and shields;
> She is the gray-haired Morrigu.
> —Tain Bo Cuailgne

Whether the Tuatha De Danann came from earth or heaven, they landed in a dense cloud upon the coast of Ireland on the mystic first of May, without having been opposed, or even noticed by the Fir Bolgs. That those might still be ignorant of their coming, the Morrigu, helped by Neman and Macha, made use of the magic they had learned in Findias, Gorias, Murias, and Falias, the four cities of Faeryland (to be discussed in another lesson).

They spread "druidically-formed showers and fog-sustaining shower-clouds" over the country, and caused the air to pour down fire and blood upon the Fir Bolgs, so that they were obliged to shelter themselves for three days and three nights.

It was the Morrigu who, a week before the Day of Samhain, discovered that the Fomors had landed upon Erin and sent a messenger to tell the Dagda, the Battle of Moytura to follow.

In the *Tain Bo Cuailgne*, the war between Maeve and Cu Chulainn, the Faery watch the half-divine, half-mortal hero, amazed at his achievements. His exploits kindle love in the fierce heart of the Morrigu. Cu Chulainn is awakened from sleep by a terrible shout from the north. He goes in the direction from which the sound came, and meets with a woman in a chariot drawn by a red horse. She has red eyebrows, a red dress, and a long, red cloak, and she carries a great, gray spear.

He asks her who she is, and she tells him that she is a king's daughter, and that she has fallen in love with him through hearing of his exploits. Cu Chulainn says that he has other things to think of than love.

53

She replies that she has been giving him her help in his battles, and will still do so. Cu Chulainn answers that he does not need any woman's help. "Then," says she, "if you will not have my love and help, you shall have my hatred and enmity. When you are fighting with a warrior as good as yourself, I will come against you in various shapes and hinder you, so that he shall have the advantage."

Cu Chulainn draws his sword, but all he sees is a hooded crow sitting on a branch. He knows from this that the red woman in the chariot was the Great Queen of the gods.

The Morrigu comes against him three times: as a heifer, an eel, and then as a wolf. Each time Cu Chulainn, though hindered, succeeds. The Morrigu came back to Cu Chulainn disguised as an old woman to have her wounds healed by him, for no one could cure them but he who made them. She became his friend after this, and helped him.

Neman, or Neamhan—The ancient Irish war-goddess Badb took a triple form, Neman, Macha, and Morrigu, all in the shape of Royston or hooded crows, a form taken in modern Irish fairy-lore by the Bean Si.

Each manifestation has a different function. Neman is Venomous, the confounder of armies. It is she who causes bands of the same army to fight , mistaking each other for the enemy.

Tailltiu (tawl-tyeh)—She was the foster-mother to the god Lugh, and the goddess of August. Her name is cognate with the Latin *tellus*, from the same Proto-Indo-European root. She lived on the magickal hill of Tara, from which she directed the clearing of an immense forest, the wood of Cuan. It took a month to create the Plain of Oenach Taillten, where she then built her palace; Telltown is in County Meath.

Her festival, celebrated annually in her honor, lasted the whole of August. The Tailltean Games (the Irish Olympics) were created in an attempt to restore Irish culture when the medieval Taillte's festivities eventually died out.

Celtic God Pantheon

The heroes of the Tuatha De Danann make-up a warrior aristocracy of Irish gods, the major emphasis of what might be Solar gods. This thought is attached to Newgrange, the great megalithic mound which overlooks the River Boyne, believed to have been built by a thriving agricultural community which lived there around 3000 B.C.E.

Newgrange is often described as a passage grave. The whole structure covers an acre of ground, is estimated to contain about 200,000 tons of stone, and was made without metal tools or the use of mortar.

Over the entrance is a stone-framed slit which is called the Roof Box; on the morning of the winter solstice, the rising sun throws a pencil of light the whole length of the passage and chamber, to illuminate the central of the three recesses for approximately seventeen minutes. This same effect is seen, though less strongly, from three mornings before the solstice to three mornings after. This structure lends strong consideration to the credence that the Irish gods may have been annually worshiped.

Solar gods are often referred to as war gods. War gods are ambiguous; sometimes they represent the hope of victory, sometimes pure destructiveness. To the Celt they represented both, to be invoked or propitiated accordingly.

However, Irish gods are also connected to the trees, specifically the oak, symbolizing strength and longevity; its acorn is expressively phallic; its roots are said to extend as far below ground as its branches do into the air, thus showing that such a god had dominion over heaven, earth, and the Underworld.

The oak was central to Celtic religious symbology. It was the tree of the Dagda, the supreme Irish father god. The wood of the ritual midsummer fire was always oak, as was the Yule log.

The Celtic god as a fertility god is rare, which brings us to the Celtic Horned God, to which no certain origin of name can be placed. That he existed cannot be doubted. He is portrayed in many Celtic artifacts, such as on the medieval market cross in the center of Kells, County Meath, and on a stone in the churchyard on Tara Hill.

He is usually portrayed with horns and accompanied by animals. He either wears, or has looped on his horns, the torc (circular necklet) of Celtic nobility (although the Horned God of Animals, Nautre and fecundity was primarily a god of the ordinary people).

Unlike the Irish goddesses, many of the gods do not shapeshift, but retain possession of powerful weapons and magickal tools. Lugh has a bloodthirsty spear that never misses its mark; the Dagda has a cauldron of abundance; and Lir has a cloak of invisibility.

Most of the gods are connected to a wife in their myth. This careful detail to polarity defines the Celtic view that man required woman to exist, recognizing his need for procreation and thus emphasizing that the masculine and feminine principles were not mutually exclusive; each contained the seed of the other; each required the expression of the polarity, otherwise they could not relate to each other. Below I provide a listing of nine important Irish gods.*

Cu Chulainn (Coo-coolyn)—The Hound of Culannis the epitome of the superhuman war-hero of the Faery tradition. Cu (hound) is a common title for a great war-hero. Typically, he is destined to have a short, brilliant life covered with glory. He is unsurpassed in battle, young, valorous, of superhuman strength, and beautiful. He is closely associated with the gods, and he himself is of supernatural origin.

The oldest literature pertaining to Cu Chulainn is the part of the Ulster Cycle known as *The Tain Bo Cuailgne*. His introduction into the narrative probably dates from the seventh century.

Cu Chulainn's birth and youth are steeped in the supernatural. His mother was Deichtine, but his father was variously the Divine Lugh, Deichtine's brother Conchobar (birth due to incest was sometimes a mark of divinity), or the mortal Sualtaimh. He had many foster-fathers, including Ferghus and Conall Cernach.

At the time of his birth, two foals were born; they became his chariot horses, the

---

*For a complete listing of the Ancient Ones, see Appendix-D: Irish Gods and Goddesses.

Grey of Macha and the Black of Saingliu. Until he was seven years old, Cu Chulainn's name was Setanta. He arrived at the court of King Conchobar of Ulster, at Emhain Macha, having fought off 150 of Conchobar's boy-warrior troops on the way. He killed the fierce hound of Culann the Smith, and pledged to act as a guard for the smith in the dog's place; this is how he acquired his name, Cu Chulainn.

Cu Chulainn's war prowess is prodigious; he is larger than life, and *The Tain* is full of his incredible feats of battle. He was trained by a female warrior/prophetess Scathach in Alba. He was one of the heroes who quarrel over the champion's joint of pork at the Feast of Bricriu. He killed the monster Cu Roi and his own son Conla. The latter tragic deed was done because he was bound to his king, and Conchobar foretold that Conla was a threat.

His magickal weapons are Gae Bulga, a barbed spear given to him by Scathach, from whose wound no one can recover; and a visor, a gift from the sea-god Manannan.

One of his characteristics in battle is his habit of going berserk or into "arp spasm." On these occasions, he becomes a monster: his body revolves within its skin; his hair stands out from his head; one eye sinks into his head, the other bulges out into his cheek; his muscles swell to enormous size, and a hero-light rises from his head.

Cu Chulainn himself is linked with sacred numbers: he has tri-colored hair; seven pupils in each eye; seven fingers and toes on each extremity. He has three faults: those of being too young, too brave, and too handsome.

Emer, Cu Chulainn's wife, imposes superhuman tasks on him before she will consent to marry him. Upon performing the tasks, he has various encounters with the divine world: his Otherworld father, Lugh, appears to heal and comfort him after combat; he encounters the Morrigan as a beautiful woman, and when he spurns her, narrowly defeats her when she attacks him in the forms of an eel, a wolf and a heifer. The Faery king Labhraidh, invites him there, offering him the love of the Fay, Fand, in return for Cu Chulainn's killing of Labhraidh's rivals.

His death is devised by Medb: she uses the Children of Cailatin, whom she has trained, to lure the hero to his death, and she pits against him the entire force of Ireland. He dies fighting alone at Magh Muirtheimme. Many portents surround his end: there is a geasa on him not to eat dog flesh; he breaks the taboo, and this weakens him. When the Grey of Macha is saddled-up for him to go to battle, the horse cries tears of blood; and when Cu Chulainn mounts his chariot, his weapons all fall at his feet. Finally, he encounters the Bean Si, who washes his armor, thus presaging his imminent death. The hero is killed with a spear forged by Vulcan. His death is signalled by the presence of the Badb, the Battle Crow, alighting on his shoulder. A famous statue in the Gernal Post Office in Dublin portrays his death.

Dagda (da-dah)—The good god of ancient Ireland was known by many names. He was also called Aed (fire), Eochaid (All-Father), and Ruad Rofessa (Lord of Great Knowledge). Many sources attribute Dagda as being the god of druidism or draidecht (magick) of the Tuatha De Danann. The old Irish tract called *The Choice of Names* indicates that he was a god of the earth.

He had a cauldron called The Undry, in which everyone found food in proportion to his merits, and from which none went away unsatisfied. His favorite food was porridge. He had a living harp, and as he played upon it the seasons came in their order: spring, summer, autumn, and winter., He also had a huge club, of which one end killed the living and the other revived the dead.

The Dagda is a paradoxical character: endowed with great wisdom, he is portrayed as gross and uncouth. In an ancient tale, he is described as wearing a brown, low-necked tunic which only reached down to his hips, and over this a hooded cape which barely covered his shoulders. He wore horse-hide boots (the hairy side outward), and carried, or rather, drew after him on a wheel, an eight-pronged war club so huge that eight men would have been needed to carry it. The wheel, as he towed the whole weapon along, made a track like a territorial boundary. His hair was gray.

In his fertility role, the Dagda mates with Boann, the spirit of the River Boyne, exemplifying the union of tribal god and mother-goddess. He also mates with the destructive war-goddess, the Morrigan, which ensures security for his people. The goddess Brigid was his daughter.

When the Sons of Mil invaded Ireland, according to the Mythological Cycle, the divine race of the Tuatha De Danann were driven underground to establish Otherworld kingdoms beneath the hills. The Dagda assigned each member of the De Danann one of these mounds, or sidh. Nuada was lord of the sidh of Almu; Midhir of the sidh of Bri Leith, and so on. The Dagda's sidh possesses three trees which perpetually bear fruit, a pig which is always alive, and an inexhaustible supply of drink.

Diarmaid, or Diarmuid ua Duibhne—He appears in the Fenian Cycle. He is a lieutenant of the aging hero Finn, leader of the war-band, the fiana, and hero of the archetypal love story of *Diarmaid and Grainne*. Grainne, daughter of the King of Ireland, was betrothed to Finn Mac Cumaill but at a feast in her father's house fell in love with Diarmaid O'Duibne and persuaded him to run away with her.

At first, he refuses her because of his bond of loyalty to his leader, but Grainne binds him with a geasa to take her away from the court of Tara. Finn pursued them for seven years (or, in other versions, a year and a day), but they are aided by Diarmaid's foster-father, Oengus, the god of love. The couple reach the Forest of Duvnos which contains a magic tree of immortality, guarded by a giant, Sharvan the Surly.

In the seven year period, the two lovers live together happily, producing five children. Finally, Finn, still thirsting for revenge, organized a boar hunt, in which Diarmaid is invited to take part. However, the boar is the magic boar of Boann Ghulban in County Sligo; this creature had once been Diarmaid's foster-brother, and it was prophesied that Diarmaid would meet his death through him. Finn knows the prophecy and deliberately exposes Diarmaid to danger.

In one version of the story, the boar kills Diarmaid; in another, the boar is killed, but the hero is fatally wounded by one of its poisonous spines. The pursuit is commemorated by many dolmens in Ireland being known as Diarmaid and Grainne's Bed. The dead Diarmaid was taken to Brugh na Boinne (Newgrange) by the love god Oengus, who breathed aerial life into him.

The elopement of Diarmaid and Grainne is first mentioned in the tenth century *Book of Leinster*. The stories of the Fenian Cycle were developed during the twelfth century; and the tradition concerning Diarmaid's death dates from between the twelfth and fifteenth century.

Diarmaid is of divine origin: he is closely linked with Oengus, and he is sometimes known as Diarmaid Donn (dark) or Diarmaid, son of Donn. Donn is the god of the dead. Diarmaid is irresistibly attractive and is described as Master and Charmer of Women.

Lamhfada, or Lugh (loo)—The name of this Irish sun-god means long-handed, or far-shooter. He was also called Ioldanach, or the Master of All Arts, named so by the Tuatha De Danann when he became their king. Although Lugh's father was Cian, son of Etan of the Tuatha, his mother was Ethniu, daughter of Balor the Fomorian. It was Lugh, who, seeking the favor of the Tuatha De Danann, killed his grandfather Balor the Fomore in The Second Battle of Mag Tuired, and thus became king of Tuatha.

The word *lugos* means raven, and there is a tenuous link between Lugh and ravens; before The Second Battle of Magh Tuired, Lugh is warned by ravens of the coming of the Fomorians.

Towns such as as Luguvalium (Carlisle) and Lugdunum (Lyon) are linked by scholars to Lugh, and at Lugdunum, coins depict images of ravens.

In the Irish tradition, Lugh is portrayed as a shining god of light, but also as a warrior, sorcerer and master of crafts. He appears at Tara, the royal court of Nuada, king of the De Danann, presenting himself as the master of all crafts and skills. This had led to a link between Lugh and the Gaulish Mercury, whom Caesar refers to as inventor of all the arts. Lugh appears at Nuada's court to encourage him to stand up to the Fomorians. Nuada surrenders the kingship to him, and Lugh then orchestrates the military campaign.

He engages the three craftsman-gods, Gobihniu, Luchta and Creidhne to forge magic weapons. He himself has a magick spear, but it's with a slingshot that he kills his grandfather.

To help the De Danann against the Fomorians, Lugh brings with him such magic objects as Wave-sweeper, the boat of Manannan, the sea-god, and Answerer, a sword which will cut through anything. Lugh himself is a magician; he chants spells to encourage the army of the De Danann.

He was celebrated at Lugnasadh (Lammas) on August 1 (one of the Four Great Festivals to be discussed in a later lesson) as a reminder of the De Danann victory over the Fomorian. Unlike the Dagda, Lugh was handsome and polished, and owned a spear that was extremely powerful; if he were to say *ibar* as he threw the spear, it would not miss its mark. It would come back to his hand if he said *athibar*. When not in use, he kept the tip of the spear immersed in the Dagda's cauldron, to prevent the village where it was stored from going up in flames. After the De Danann are driven underground by the Sons of Mil, the Dagda assigns to Lugh the sidh of Rodruban.

In the Ulster Cycle, Lugh is associated with Cu Chulainn. He is a kind of Otherworld father to the young hero, and when Cu Chulainn is wounded and exhausted by his battles against Connacht, Lugh appears to soothe his hurts and heals him by causing him to sleep for three days.

Manannan mac Lir (manan-awn mac lir)—Manannan was the son of the Irish sea-god, Lir. In early texts, Manannan is not specifically listed as a member of the De Danann, but in later documents he is included.

He was the special patron of sailors, who invoked him as God of Headlands, and of merchants, who claimed him as the first of their guild. He protected Ireland, enclosing the island with his own element to guard it. His favorite haunts were the Isle of Man, to which he gave his name, and the Isle of Arran, in the Firth of Clyde, where he had a palace called Emhain of the Apple-Trees.

Apart from being a sea-god, Manannan is also a master of skills, wisdom, trickery, illusion, and magick. The divine warrior Lugh, in helping Nuada and the De Danann to vanquish the Fomorians, obtains magickal gifts from Manannan: a boat which obeys the thoughts of its sailor and requires neither oar nor sail; a horse that can travel with equal ease on land or sea; and a dreadful sword named Fragarach, the Answerer, which can penetrate any armor. Cu Chulainn has a visor as a present from Manannan. The sea-god possesses magick pigs which are killed and eaten on one day, and are alive and ready for the same fate on the next. Many other tales of magick surround the character of this god.

He had many famous weapons of his own: two spears called Yellow Shaft and Red Javelin; a sword called The Retaliator, which never failed to slay, as well as two others known as the Great Fury and the Little Fury. His boat was called Wave-sweeper, which propelled and guided itself wherever its owner wished, and he also had a horse called Splendid Mane, which was swifter than the spring wind, and travelled equally fast on land or over the waves of the sea.

Lir wore a magick coat of mail and breast-plate through which no weapon could pass, and on his helmet there shone two magick jewels as bright as the sun. He endowed the gods with the mantle which made them invisible at will, and he fed them from his pigs, which renewed themselves as soon as they had been eaten.

The Feast of Age was his famous banquet at which those who ate never grew old. It is his figure that outshines all the other gods. Up to the latest days of Irish heroic literature, reference is made to his luminous figure.

His wife was the Faery, Fand. From lack of Manannan's attention, she fell in love with Cu Chulainn, but, in the end, was persuaded by Manannan to return with him to Tir Taingiri. Upon her consent, Manannan wove a web of forgetting around both Fand and Cu Chulainn, and upon waking neither remembered the other.

Mider, or Midhir—King of the Gaelic Underworld, son of the Dagda and Boann, goddess of the River Boyne. His wife was the oustandingly beautiful Etain Echraidhe, personification of reincarnation. He had a magick cauldron which his daughter, Blathnat, helped Cu Chulainn to steal.

In the Mythological Cycle, Midhir is the lord of the sidh of Bri Leith. The *Book of Invasions* tells of the invasion of Ireland by the Milesian, who drove the divine De Danann underground to become lords of the Otherworld beneath the hills.

The most important story of Midhir concerns his wooing of Etain. He incurs the wrath of his wife Fuamnach by bringing home his new bride, and she uses magick to transform her young rival into a butterfly, buffeted about the world for many years.

Midhir makes desperate attempts to find Etain, and finally tracks her down, reborn more than 1,000 years after her initial birth, as a beautiful young woman. But the new Etain is married to Eochaidh, king of Ireland, and she is at first reluctant to return to Midhir, since she has forgotten him.

By means of trickery, he manages to kiss Etain; she remembers and loves him, and the pair finally escape from the royal court at Tara in the form of two swans. They are pursued by the king, but Midhir magickally configures fifty women, all identical to Etain. By mistake, Eochaidh chooses not the real Etain, but their daughter, and thus commits the horror of incest.

Another story about Midhir also concerns his association with birds. *The Book of Leinster* has a tale in which Midhir possesses three hostile cranes who discourage travelers from stopping at his dwelling, and who rob warriors of their courage.

Nuada—Was the supreme god of battles. He was also given the name Argetlam (He of the Silver Hand) when he lost his hand in The First Battle of Mag Tuired, between the De Danann and the Fir Bolgs. Upon losing his arm, he had to relinquish the kingship, because he no longer met the criterion of physical perfection which was a rule of sovereignty. The new king, Bres (meaning beautiful), reigned as surrogate for Nuada until the divine smith/leech, Dian Cecht, made Nuada an artificial arm of silver and thus made it possible for him to resume his power.

During the wars with the Fomorians, Nuada is daunted by the terrible power of the Fomorian leader, Balor of the Baleful Eye, and he again gives up his kingship to the hero Lugh. Lugh takes over the organization of the war and overcomes Balor himself.

He was possessed of an invincible sword, one of the four chief treasures of Tuatha De Danann, over whom he was twice king. Nuada is one of the original kings, or gods, in direct lineage to the ancient Mother Goddess Dana.

Although Nuada, the supreme war-god, vanished early out of the Pantheon after being killed by the Fomorians in The Second Battle of Mag Tuired, he lived on through his greatest proteges: the five great war-goddesses of the Celts, Fea, the Hateful, Nemon, the Venomous, Badb, the Fury, Macha, a personification of Battle, and over all of them, the Morrigu, or Great Queen. After the Milesian invasion, Nuada was given the sidh called Almu, which was later wrested from him by Finn.

Nuada has various counterparts. In British archaeology, he may be identified with Nodens, the god of Lydney on the River Severn. Both names mean cloud-maker. In Welsh mythology, Nuada may be identical with Nudd or Lludd, who was probably a sun-god. The loss of his arm gives Nuada a resemblance to the Germanic Tyr whose right arm was bitten off by a wolf.

Oengus, or Anegus (ang-us) **of the Birds**—The son of the Dagda. In the early literature, he is presented as one who is himself in love, and he also helps other lovers in adversity. He was also called Mac ind Oc, or In Mac Oc, which means The Young Son, or The Young God. He received this name from his mother, Boand, who decreed upon his birth: "Young is the son who was begotten at break of day and born betwixt it and evening." Dagda had concealed Boann's pregnancy by causing the sun to stand still for nine months, so that Oengus was conceived and born on the same day.

In the *Tain*, Oengus is represented as a Gaelic Eros, a god of love and beauty , described as "slender and as swift as a wind. His hair swung about his face like golden blossoms. His eyes were mild and dancing and his lips smiled with quiet sweetness. About his head there flew perpetually a ring of singing birds, and when he spoke his voice came sweetly from a center of sweetness."

As was his way, one could not know him, unless he made himself known. He called himself Infinite Joy and Love. Like his father, he had a harp, which was gold rather than oak like the Dagda's, and when he played it, his music was so sweet that anyone who heard it would follow.

Three main stories surround him. In two, he is presented as a helper of lovers. In the story of Midhir and Etain, Oengus woos Etain on Midhir's behalf. Later, Oengus is able partially to remove the butterfly spell cast on Etain by Midhir's jealous wife Fuamnach. She is thus restored to human form from dusk to dawn and is cherished in Oengus' palace on the River Boyne. In the story of Diarmaid and Grainne, Oengus intervenes to help Grainne and Diarmaid against Finn, who desires Grainne. Oengus is Diarmaid's foster father, and on one occasion he takes on Dairmaid's form to lure away Finn's companions who are hunting him. Oengus also spirits Grainne away to safety on two occasions where her discovery is threatened by Finn.

In the tale, *The Dream of Oenghus*, it is the god of love himself who is smitten by passion. He dreams of a young woman whom he does not recognize, and falls desperately in love with her. He learns that the girl's name is Caer Ibormeith (Yew Berry), and he finds her with her companions on a lake. He also learns that Caer is a shape-changer, and every other year she transmogrifies from human form to that of a swan. King Ailill of Connacht intercedes with Caer's father, Ethal Anbual of Sidh Uamain, on behalf of Oengus, but to no avail. The only way to win Caer is to take her when she is in swan form.

The shape-change occurs on the Feast of Samhain, on the first of November, and it is now that Oengus approaches Caer and flies off with her, having transformed himself also into swan form. The two fly three times round the lake, sending everyone to sleep for three days and nights by their magick song, then fly off to Brugh na Boinne, Oengus' palace. Newgrange is his burial place.

Oengus is the archetypal young man, or divine youth. As such, he may be identified with the British Maponus and the Welsh Mabon.

Oghma Grianaineach (of the Sunlike Countenance)—Irish god of wisdom, learning and writing. As one of the Tuatha De Danann and son of the Dagda, he was said to have invented the Ogham script. This script appeared about the fourth century in *The Book of Ballymote*, but almost certainly continues an older system of magickal symbols. The ogham is a system of writing which consisted of horizontal or slanting strokes and notches cut on stone or wood and branching out on either side of a vertical line or corner.

Oghma was shrewd and quick thinking in warfare; he was also a champion in battle. Not only is he described as a strong man, but he is likened to the classical demi-god hero Hercules. He is also connected to the Greek Ogmios, an old man, bald and burnt by the sun. Like Ogmios, Oghma is described as holding a club and lion-skin, drawing crowds of prisoners along with golden chains connected by their ears to the tip of his tongue.

The Ancient Ones that we invoke depend chiefly upon our own individual tuning, which, more often then not, is determined by a tradition's historical, cultural, and environmental factors. For there to be an effective resonation with or to the cosmic source, depends upon our choice. Based on this, such choices need to be individual, not prescribed from outside of self, unless directly contacted by the Ancient One.

Janet and Stewart Farrar broach this in their book *The Witches' God*: "Magical or religious practice is a communion with the reality which lies behind such god-forms, which are tuning-signals to aspects of that reality." Thus, understanding the nature of our chosen Ancient One, defining precisely the aspect, can help to prepare you for a more perfect tuning.

The Ancient Ones do exist; they ensoul the archetypes. The aim of communicating, or making contact with an archetype in the traditional esoteric way, is not to become the archetype, not even to identify with the archetype in a personal way. Such an overlapping of one reality with the next, such a superimposition, contains the danger of possible delusion.

"True meditation is always accompanied by a disturbing echo of undeniable deep personal insight; it often indicates areas of weakness that require inner attention and development of rebalance. In this role alone, work such as mediation of advanced forms of consciousness or god- and goddess-forms is of immense value to us, though its resulting personal insight is only one of many side-effects and not a major aim."[11]

The true aim is to surrender ourselves to the mystery of communion with the Ancient Ones, to allow the tuning to take place; thus allowing our own special creative flow to be unleashed into the earth's plane, into our lives, to enliven us and help us achieve a more perfect sense of balance.

---

11 Janet and Stewart Farrar, *A Witches' Bible, Volume I: The Sabbats,* Robert Hale, Ltd., 1984.

Journal Exercises

1. What does the term *God* mean to you? Can this term resonate a feminine polarity, or must it always be assigned a masculine identity?

2. When you think in terms of choosing a personal deity with which to commune, how can choosing one from your tradition bring about a more perfect tuning?

Suggested Reading

The Witches' Goddess, Janet and Stewart Farrar
The Witches' God, Janet and Stewart Farrar
Dictionary of Celtic Myth and Legend, Miranda J. Green
Women of the Celts, Jean Markale
The Book of Goddesses and Heroines, Patricia Monagham

he fairies went from the world, dear,
Because men's hearts grew cold;
And only the eyes of children see
What is hidden from the old;
And only the magic of love, dear,
Can ever turn the key
That unlocks the gates of Fairyland
To set the Sidhe folk free.

— *The Little Good Folk*
Kathleen Foyle

And for the hardness of men's hearts
The wee folk went from us.
— Old Irish Legend

~ THE MORRIGAN ~

Lesson Four

The Celtic Division of the Year

As it was, As it is, As is shall be Evermore, O Thou Tri-
une of grace! With the ebb, with the flow, O Thou Triune
of grace! With the ebb, with the flow.*

Faery Wicca focuses on the balance of polarities. To everything there is a negative and a positive side. This fundamental duality can be expressed through the
day and the night being the times of light and darkness.

The day—light—belongs to the physical world—the world made manifest. The
night—dark—belongs to the Otherworld and those realms that cannot be seen in the
stark light of day. To the Celt, it is believed that a person born during the night can
see ghosts and phantoms which are made invisible to those born during the day, and
unless the day-born are of the Faery-blood, second-sight will elude them.

The two most important times of the twenty-four hour cycle are the times of
dawn and twilight. Dawn, or first light, is thought of as dispelling the darkness, and
so is considered the "banisher of spirits to their abodes." Dawn is the Rose Door
through which the mind moves into the Lunar Sphere, or conscious-waking state.

The Lunar Sphere encompasses the body, or manifest elements—the mind, the
emotions—and includes transcendent consciousness (Figure 5). When we begin to
fully work in this sphere, we begin to access our inner power, thus initiating change,
or self-transformation.

Faery magician R. J. Stewart explains that "One of the basic premises of magic
at all stages of development is that if consciousness and energy may be aroused,
transformed, or exchanged upon one of the higher metaphysical levels or spirals, then
the effects upon the lower or outer world are far greater."[12]

Through our working the Lunar Sphere we are given flashes of illumination and
enlightenment, igniting our inner fire, our inner power, which resides in the Lunar

---

* An ancient Irish blessing; Triune means "Trinity."
12 R. J. Stewart, *Advanced Magickal Arts,* Element Books, 1984.

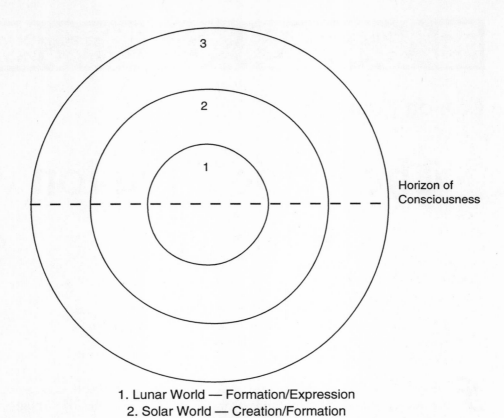

1. Lunar World — Formation/Expression
2. Solar World — Creation/Formation
3. Stellar World — Origination/Creation

Figure 5: The Three Worlds

Sphere, causing our energy to turn through a spiral or octave, becoming the Solar Sphere: a permanent state of enlightenment beyond personality, but the personality is included within it through the thoughts, emotions, and foundational energies.

The other most important time of day is twilight, or two-lights. Twilight moves nearer the other realm, and so is considered the "invoker of spirits from their abodes." Twilight is the Purple Door through which the mind moves into the Solar Sphere, or subconscious-dreaming state.

The Solar Sphere is traditionally said to admit the initiate to the Convocation of Light, meaning a state of consciousness, though it is frequently represented in visual terms as a place or inner dimension, with landscape, features, people, and other attributes. It is in this state that a universal mind can be touched.

The importance of working in this sphere relates to the higher, or "more drastic, initiations in magic: they involve transformations which are deep and permanent, and may not be easily rescinded or regressed."[13]

The last transformation shown in Figure 5 involves crossing the Abyss (in connection with the Tree of Life, which we will not work with in this volume), and

---

13 Ibid.

merging consciousness with the supernal Stellar Sphere, which is the crown of wisdom and understanding, the universal being, Outgoing and Ingoing principles (Spirit, Father, Mother), a further step which leads into the Void, known in Kabbalah as the Ain Soph.

The division of day and night, light and dark, is also applied to the year. The year is divided in two: the winter and summer (Figure 6). Winter is the season of night, dark, and cold; while summer, maintaining the alternation of opposites, is the season of day, light, and warmth.

Interestingly, the first half of the year is that of winter, for, as was common in ancient times, day followed night. The beginning of the next day was always the eve before the actual sunrise.

So it is with the Celtic year. The beginning of the new cycle, or wheel of the year, is celebrated on the eve of winter at Samhain (SOW-an), November 1 being the calends* of winter. The second half of the year is summer, which begins on the eve of La Baal Tinne, May 1, being the calends of summer.

As with any shamanic tradition, the seasonal wheel of the year is vitally important, and like any other tradition, the Celtic Division of the Year is composed of four seasons:

- ⭐ Geimhreadh(GEV-rah)Winter
- ⭐ Earrach(Are-uckh)Spring
- ⭐ Samhradh(Sour-ah)Summer
- ⭐ Fomhar(FOE-war)Autumn

The four seasons each have a place in the Division of the Year. Geimhreadh and Earrach belong on the first half, which is the dark side of the year, known as the Time of the Little Sun. Samhradh and Fomhar belong on the second half, which is the light side of the year, known as the Time of the Big Sun.

The Time of the Little Sun
The season of Geimhreadh (GEV-rah)—Winter
Begins at Samhain (SOW-an)—October 31
Contains the months:

- ⭐ Samhna(SOW-nah)—November
- ⭐ Nollag (NULL-ug)—December
- ⭐ Eanair (ANN-irr)—January
- ⭐ Feabhra(FYOW-rah)—February
- ⭐ Marta (MAWR-tah)—March
- ⭐ Aibrean (Ah-brawn)—April

The first half of the year begins on the evening of October 31. This half of the year is considered the time of the Little Sun, referring to the moon. The moon is the

---

* This Gaelic word means calender; thus, the calends of winter means the calender of winter.

natural light that shines brightest in the dark of night. During the winter season, day-light diminishes quite drastically, night becomes more prevalent, and so more of our waking time is spent during the dark hours of night. Thus, the moonlight can become a primary source of inspiration. In Faery Wicca, moon rituals are always important during the Little Sun.

Winter is the realm of the spirits and Faery. This is the negative polarity of the year when night is most powerful. The doorway into night, twilight, is handled with extreme caution. To offset the foreboding of the evening-tide, sunrise is greatly uti-lized during the time of the Little Sun in maintaining the great balance.

To the Celts, winter was filled with the uncanniness of the night, when humankind seemed powerless in the hands of Fate, prevailing until the dawn of another summer. Because of this, most people hurried to the sanctity of their homes when twilight neared. To be out-and-about during the night, especially in the time of the Little Sun, was strictly warned against, for it was the time when one would surely be approached by a spirit or Faery of the Otherworld.

In Faery Wicca, during the Little Sun, twilight becomes the time at which we per-form, or begin, our magickal enchantments. Twilight, as the "invoker of the spirits from their abode," provides the necessary energy that will aid us in our journeys to the Otherworld, as well as in dreamwork, meditation, or contemplation, contacting allies, and all acts of visioning.

The dawn is then used to birth the information received during journeys, dreams, meditations, and ally contacts into our conscious mind, as well as the time for the empowerment of, or enactment of, our visioning.

Winter, the time of night or darkness, consists of six months: November through April; two seasons: winter itself, and spring; and two of the Four Great Festivals: The Feast of Sam-fuim (Samhain), October 31; the eve of winter, and Imbolc, February 1; the eve of Oimlec, the old festival of spring, which divides the first half of the year from winter into spring. Two smaller events take place within this season: Yule, or the winter solstice, signifying the middle of the winter season; and the vernal or spring equinox, signifying the middle of the spring season.

The Time of the Big Sun
The season of Samhradh (SOUR-ah)—Summer
Begins at La Baal Tinne (Law BAL-tene)—April 30
Contains the months:

- Marta (MAWR-tah)—May
- Meitheamh (MEH-hev)—June
- Luil (YOO-ill)—July
- Lunasa (LOO-nassa)—August
- Mean Fomhair(MAN fore)—September
- Deireadh Fomhair(JERR-ah fore)—October

This is the second half of the year beginning on April 30, the eve of May Day. This half of the year is considered the time of the Big Sun. The earth, on her ecliptic,

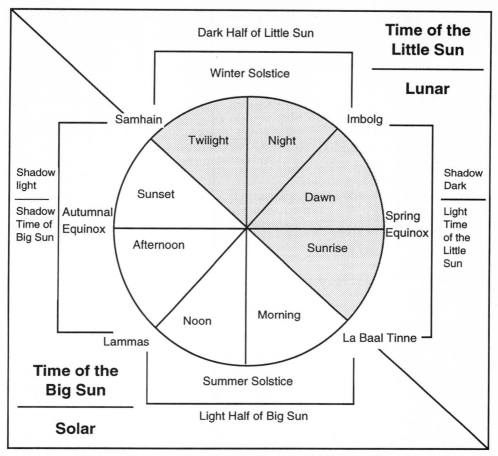

Figure 6: Celtic Wheel of the Year—Northern Hemisphere

is closest to the sun during the majority of this time of year, and, therefore, the warmth of the sun is more prominent, as is the length of daylight hours. In Faery Wicca, sun rituals become more important during the Big Sun.

Summer is the positive time, when those things that are shadowed by the dark seem not to exist because of the abundant light hours. The world is no longer swamped by the world beyond.

The Celts believed that during this time one's luck in the ensuing year seemed to be in balance, and, unlike the set Fate of winter, one is not brought face-to-face with their unalterable destiny. Now are the joys of summer, hard work, and hard play. Movement is outside of the home, unlike the confinement that the bad weather of winter oftentimes brings.

To offset the overzealous energies of the sun, however, the twilight is given special attention with its coolness and settling beauty. The Purple Door is welcomed with a sigh of refreshment when the hard work and hard play of the day can be turned into the mellow sweetness of a cool summer's night.

Traditionally, we work our magickal enchantments at the time of dawn during the Big Sun to receive the full strength of the energy made naturally available to us.

Most of the magick during this time is focused on activities, planting of seeds (metaphorically speaking), harvesting, celebrating the bounty of our efforts, and giving thanks.

At twilight, our practices turn toward sharing the great wisdom learned through private lessons, releasing our hold on desires and needs, focusing on the growth that is taking place. When we journey to the Otherworld, we do so playfully, to receive guidance on current projects.

Summer, the time of light, consists of six months: May through September; two seasons, summer, itself, and autumn; and two of the Four Great Festivals, La Baal Tinne (Beltane), April 30, the eve of May Day, beginning the summer half of the year; and Lughnasadh (LOO-nasa), July 31; the eve of August, dividing the second half of the year from summer into autumn. Two smaller festivals also take place in the summer: the summer solstice, signifying the middle of the summer season, and the autumnal equinox, signifying the middle of the autumn season.

The Four Great Festivals

In Faery Wicca, we have four major Sabbats, or High Holy Days with which we celebrate the tradition, that are called The Four Great Festivals. As in any tradition, the Holy Days usually hold a specific importance based on the mythology of the tradition. On these days, such myths are re-enacted to re-establish the origins of the tradition in the minds and hearts of the participants.

Myth enactment transforms each participant, drawing them into the characters and events of the myth, thus evoking a remembrance, or a tie-in to the past. Myth enactment transmutes the energy of the tradition, placing it into the realm of a living tradition.

When we remember the origin of the tradition through ritual, we gain a deeper sense of belonging; such ceremonies create a psychological lineage; although for some, such a lineage may be genealogical.

Shamanically, each of the Four Great Festivals are connected to an energy shift and a season. By attuning oneself to such an energy shifting, one becomes open to the greater cosmic energies available to us from the source, for we encourage our minds, our egos, to surrender and journey into a place between the worlds. Such a journey diminishes all sense of space and time, bringing into a harmonious balance the meeting point of past, present, and future.

As previously discussed, the first half of the year, known as the Little Sun, contains the seasons of winter and spring, and the two Great Festivals the Feast of Samfuim (Samhain) and Imbolc.

Accordingly, the second half of the year, known as the Big Sun, contains the seasons of summer and autumn, and the other two Great Festivals, La Baal Tinne (Beltane) and Lughnasadh.

Although today the winter and summer solstices and the vernal and autumnal equinoxes are included in most Wiccan circles*, these four minor holidays were traditionally considered seasonal markers, thus taking on a personal nature and celebrated privately. In keeping with the tradition of Faery Wicca, they will not be discussed here.

Below, we shall look at each of the four seasons and their Great Festivals†. We will begin with the first half of the year, the time of the Little Sun, the season of winter and the Celtic New Year.

Geimhreadh and the Feast of Sam-fuim (Samhain)—The time when the Big Sun dies, the powers of darkness exercise great influence over all things. The light of the darkness is known as the Little Sun, the moon. The Feast of Sam-fuim (summer's end) takes place October 31, the actual eve of the winter season. The feast is performed under the moonlight and never during daylight.

Traditionally, it was a pastoral festival, which marked the time at which livestock were rounded up and brought in from the fields; some were chosen for slaughter, others kept for breeding purposes. The Feast of the Dead was celebrated at the end of one pastoral year and the commencement of the next. The great assemblies of the five Irish provinces at Tara took place at this time, the festival being marked by horse races, fairs, markets, pastoral assembly rites, and political discussions, along with ritual mourning, too, at the death of summer.

The Celts believed that on this night all entrances into the Otherworld opened—even the great entrance in Ireland, located a little north of the town of Sligo, on the southern side of Ben Bulben, some hundreds of feet above the plain on the white square in the limestone, where no mortal has ever touched with their hand, where there is no more inaccessible place upon the earth, and "few more encircled by awe to the deep considering of how to gain entrance."

This is the true door to Faeryland. It was believed that in the middle of night it would swing open. In *Celtic Twilight,* W.B. Yeats writes about the door to Faeryland: "All night the gay troops sweep to and fro across the land, invisible to most, visible to but a few, and it is to the trained eye and ear that the fields become covered by red-hatted riders, and dancing red-gowned figures, and the air full of shrill voices—a sound like whistling."

Through this door of white stone, and the other doors of that land, where "geabheadh tu an sonas aer pighin,"# have gone kings, queens, and all the hosts of Faery, and who come out into the wide green valley of Drumcliff and Rosses lying at the foot of Ben Bulben.

Rosses is a little sea-dividing, sandy plain, covered with short grass, like a green tablecloth, and lying in the foam midway between the round carin-headed Knocknarea and Ben Bulben. At the northern corner of Rosses is a little promontory of sand and rocks and grass, a mournful, haunted place, where the traditional Feast of Sam-fuim was once celebrated.

---

* For general material on celebrating the solstices and equinoxes, refer to my book: *The Gaia Tradition*, Llewellyn Publications. The Irish ritual celebration will be covered in *Faery Wicca, Book Two.*

† Ritual outlines for each of the Great Festivals can be found under the Magickal Enchantments Section, in the chapter: Ceremony and Ritual.

You can buy joy for a penny.

To the Celts this time of year was considered a time of great danger and vulnerability, for it stood at the boundary between two halves of the Celtic year. It was considered as outside, or suspended from time, when the normal laws of the world were temporarily in abeyance.

With the barriers between the real world and the supernatural dissolved, and with the Otherworld spirits and Faery moving freely from the sidhe to the land of the living, mortals could also penetrate the Underworld.

In Faery Wicca, we refer to this time as Samhain (SOW-an), All Hallow's Eve. In the traditional sense, it marks a time of immense spiritual energy, when the gods of the Otherworld have to be accorded special rituals to appease them, and when strange happenings are apt to occur.

Because the death of the year is acknowledged, so are all ancestors of the Spirit realm. Paying honor to one's dead becomes a joyous event rather than a sorrowful one, for out of death comes rebirth and a journey into another Circle of Existence (discussed in Lesson Five), where the dead are stronger than the living, and where every principal existence is derived from the dead.

In ceremony, it is traditional for the cunning women, (the witch women) or the Banshees (priestesses), to dance the Dance of the Dead, or the Dance of the Ancestors. This dance is also performed to enact the myth of remembering the bloodthirsty deity, Cromm Cruaich (The Bowed One of the Mound), the Fomorian God of darkness, to whom the clans of Ireland were once forced to sacrifice their children until Tuatha De Danann came, putting an end to such sacrificing.

The cunning men (the witch men), or Leprechauns (priests), tell the following traditional poem, which they chant in memory of those who died:

> *There came*
> *Tigermas, the prince of Tara yonder,*
> *On Hallowe'en with many hosts,*
> *A cause of grief to them was the deed.*
>
> *Dead were the men*
> *Of Banba's host, without happy strength,*
> *Around Tigermas, the destructive man in the North,*
> *From the worship of Cromm Cruaich—'t was no luck for them.*
>
> *For I have learnt,*
> *Except one-fourt of the keen Gaels*
> *Not a man alive lasting the snare!*
> *Escaped without death in his mouth.*
> —The Tain Bo Cuailgne

Divination by fire, by earth, and by water is practiced. The most usual spell worked on Samhain is to wash a garment in a running brook, then hang it on a thorn bush and wait to see the apparition of an ancestor who will come to turn it.

Another spell is the Building of the House. Twelve couples are taken, each being made of two holly twigs tied together with a hempen thread; these are all named and stuck round in a circle in the clay. A live coal is then placed in the center, and whichever couple's holly-twig house catches fire first will assuredly be married.

Aside from the folly of such spell-casting, the Dance of the Dead is of most importance. The sacred fires are lit and in a Ronde or Ridee (circle dance), the participants gather and solemnly revolve around themselves, three times from east to west, and then begin moving as a whole widdershin (a moonwise or counter-clockwise movement).

All faces are covered with masks depicting demons, spirits, creatures of the night. The dance is performed in honor of those who have been, but who have passed into another Circle of Existence.

In the center of the dancing circle, on an earthen mound, is spread the Feast of Sam-fuim: the fruits of summer's end and the grains of the harvest. After the feasting, bowls of warm water are put out, and all gathered wash their hands and faces with the water.

Those who are chosen to enact the custom of throwing out the water, pick up a container and move to the outside of the circle and face the dark of night. In a loud voice they cry out:

Hugga, Hugga, salach! (Away, Away, here is water!)

warning the spirits of the dead last buried, who may still be wandering about, not to get their clothes wet.

On this night, it is traditional to leave food out for the ancestors, spirits, and Faery who might be wandering about. If the food disappears by morning, it is a sign that the beings of the Otherworld have taken it (for no one would dare to touch or eat of the food so left!), thus insuring a blessing of prosperity and protection upon the giver.

The new church, in an attempt to abolish the peasantry from honoring the Great Festival, adopted the Feast of the Dead, changing its anniversary to the first day of November. The feast was transformed into the Fete in Commemoration of the Dead by the Roman Catholic clergy.

Today, the Roman Church acknowledges the first and second of November as Holy days devoted to those who have passed out of this life. The first day, the Fete of All the Saints or La Toussaint, (established by St. Odilon, Abbot of Cluny, in 998 C.E.)originated thus:

> *The Roman Pantheon—Pantheon meaning the residence of all the gods—was dedicated to Jupiter the Avenger, and when Christianity triumphed the pagan images were overthrown, and there was thereupon originally established, in place of the cult of all the gods, the Fete of all the Saints, and became one of their holy days.*

And though the Fete in Commemoration of the Dead , established the church's Holy day to fall on the first of November, it is in direct accord with the Faery Wiccan Samhain.

Earrach and Imbolc—The beginning of spring is traditionally called Oimelc, or the First Milk of the Lamb, afterwards called Bride's Day, and later St. Bridget's Day.

Traditionally, the celebration focuses on the return of Breo-saighit (Fiery Arrow) of the sun. A procession of torches were carried from the participants' homes to the ceremonial Rath or mound.

The Irish would dance around the Rath, spiraling up it until at last all reached the top to find a bonfire waiting to be ignited. They would converge on the pit and throw their torches onto the brambles, and as the flames reached into the night, they would chant:

> Bride is welcome,
> Bride is come,
> Bride is welcome,
> Bride is come!

This form of sympathetic magick was performed to acknowledge the approach of the sun's warmth back to the earth. As the sacred fire grew in strength and brightness, the celebrants would know the season was changing and all life would soon be warmed and rebirthed by the warmth of the Breo-saighit. A feast of milk and bread followed, and many a tale was told as all gathered around the sacred fire for warmth.

Imbolc was traditionally celebrated on the evening of February 1, but was later changed to February 2, when in the ninth century the Pope abolished the festival and substituted for it the Feast of the Purification of the Blessed Virgin, when candles were lit in her honor, hence, the modern name of Candlemas.

Samhradh and La Baal Tinne (Beltane)—The time of the Big Sun arrives, and the second half of the year begins. This is perhaps the most memorable and auspicious of the Four Great Festivals, for it is the Holy day marking the arrival of Tuatha De Danann on the shores of ancient Erin.

This Great Festival is called La Baal Tinne (The Bright Fire), and is also known as La-Beltaine, Beltain, Beltaine, Beltene, or simply as May Day. It is also known in Ireland as Cetshamain, and is one of the few specifically Irish festivals. The fact that it was linked with stock-rearing may mean that it was not an appropriate ritual activity for the whole of the Celtic world, although traces of this festival are found in many traditions as a fertility festival.

Traditionally, the festival was associated with the start of open pasturing, with the beginning of summer, and the welcoming of the sun's heat to promote the growth of livestock and crops. Again, bonfires were kindled in sympathetic magick to encourage the sun's warmth to penetrate the earth. The ancient festival site was the His of Uisneach, County Westmeath.

The Celts believed that at this time in the Otherworld the sacred fire of Tamhair-na-Righ (Tara of the Kings) was lit every three years, and then with great ceremony. To light the fire, the sun's rays were concentrated by means of a brazen lens on some pieces of dried wood (which was the manner in which all sacred fires in Sidhe were kindled).

They also believed that the Faery were at their jolliest and in the best of humors upon May eve, and the music of their pipes and harps were said to be heard all through the night, while their companies danced upon the Raths.

Traditionally, in Faery Wicca, the ceremonial fire was obtained from the friction of wood, or the striking of stones. This was only done at the invocation of the spirits of fire, who were thought to dwell in these objects. It was from the sacred fire that all participants then lighted brands and took them home to light the domestic fires.

Bonfires always played a role in the ceremonies, but the most dangerous role was when the men who drew lots and whoever received the burnt piece, was obliged to leap three times over the flames when they were at their highest. The women jumped over the flames when they were low. These fire ceremonies were a practice which interposed a magick protection between the Celts and the powers of evil.

Cattle—whose horns were decorated with garlands of vervain and rowan in honor of the May Queen (the maiden aspect of the triple goddess)—were driven on a path made between two fires, while continually being sprinkled with the Sgaith-an-Tobar (water from The Purity of the Well), or the first water drawn from the sacred well after midnight on May Eve. (Whomever succeeded in being first at the well had to cast into it a tuft of grass called Cuisheag grass, to show that the Sgaith-an-Tobar had been abstracted.) The cow whose skin was singed when passing between the fires became the sacrificial animal for the feast. Milk, butter, and corn made up the balance of the feast.

If on the first day of May, a sacred heifer, snow white, should appear among the cattle, the Celts believed the highest good luck would come, and this verse was recited to insure the blessing:

> *There is a cow on the mountain,*
> *A fair white cow;*
> *She goes East and she goes west,*
> *And my senses have gone for love of her:*
> *She goes with the sun and is not burned,*
> *And the moon turns her face with love to her,*
> *My fair white cow of the mountain.*[14]

Round the May-bush that was hung with garlands the Baila* (waltz) was danced. In this dance the women wore garlands and the men carried wands of green boughs. At the end of the dance, a woman would toss her garland to the man of her choice. If he succeeded in catching the garland on his bough, much intercourse was believed to transpire between the two; but if he missed and the garland fell to the ground, heartache was sure to come around. Another mystic dance performed at the festival was the snake dance. The gyrations of the dancers were always westward in the track of the sun.

Pipes and harpers, dressed in green with gold sashes, played the most spirited dance tunes, and through the dance tunes the magick was often woven by a story teller. A story, such as this one, was often to be heard:

---

14 Lade Wilde, *Ancient Legends, Mystic Charms and Superstitions of Ireland,* Lemma Publishing Corporation, 1887.

*See Lesson Twelve: Ceremony and Ritual: The Irish Jig and Other Faery Dances.

Once, about a hundred years ago during the festival a cele-brated tune, called Moraleana, was taught to a piper of another race as he traversed the hills and came upon our festi-val; and he played it perfectly, note by note, as he heard it from the Faery pipes; on which a geasa was given him in exchange for the melody that he would be allowed to play the tune three times in his life before all the people, but never a fourth, or a doom would fall on him.

However, one day he had a great contest for supremacy with another piper, and at last, to make sure of victory, he played the wonderful Faery melody; when all the people applauded and declared he had won the prize by reason of its beauty, and that no music could equal his, the crowd crowned him with the garland, but he had played the melody four times, and at that moment he turned deadly pale, the pipes dropped from his hand, and he fell lifeless to the ground.

Nothing escapes the Sidhe race, we know all things, and our vengeance is swift and sure. Let this tale serve as a reminder that our powers are greatest at La Baal Tinne![15]

Herbs gathered on May Eve were traditionally considered to have a mystical and strong virtue for curing disease, and powerful potions were then made by the skillful; such potions, which no sickness could resist, were made chiefly of the yarrow—known as the herb of seven needs.

Divination was also practiced by means of the yarrow. The girls would dance around it singing:

Yarrow, yarrow, yarrow,
I bid thee good morrow,
And tell me before to-morrow
Who my true love shall be.
— Ancient folk saying

The herb would then be placed under the head at night, and in dreams the true lover of the girl was believed to appear.

Love spells are traditionally the central theme of all magick performed at La Baal Tinne. A remembrance of very powerful herbal remedies and love potions are even now frequently in use. In ancient times, they were generally prepared by an old woman, but must be administered by the person who wishes to inspire the tender passion while repeating:

---

15 Lady Wilde Ibid.

You for me,
and I for thee
and for none else;
Your face to mine,
and your head turned away
from all others.
— Ancient folk saying

This was to be repeated three times secretly over a drink made with hemlock, mint, and a few other things, and given to the one beloved. At the same time, it was considered wise to remember that to give a love potion was a very awful act, as the result could be fatal, or at least full of danger. Here is an example of a story that would be attached to the above type of warning:

> *A fine, handsome young man, of the best character and con-*
> *duct, suddenly became wild and reckless, drunken and disor-*
> *derly, from the effect, it was believed, of a love potion*
> *administered to him by a young girl who was passionately in*
> *love with him.*
>
> *When she saw the change produced in him by her act, she*
> *became moody and nervous, as if a constant terror were over*
> *her, and no one ever saw her smile again. Finally, she became*
> *half deranged, and after a few years of a strange, solitary life,*
> *she died of melancholy and despair.*

This was said to be "The Love-potion Curse." However, a safe love-potion is no more than gathering yarrow in the light of the full moon, following La Baal Tinne, and repeating this charm:

Moon, Moon, tell unto me
When my true love I shall see?
What fine clothes am I to wear?
How many children shall I bear?
For if my love comes not to me,
Dark and dismal my life shall be.
— Ancient folk saying

Then, the girl would be instructed to cut three pieces of clay from the sod with a black-hafted knife, carry them home, tie them up in the left stocking with the right garter, place the parcel under her pillow, and dream a true dream of the man she is to marry, and of all her future fate.

Another mode of divination for this future fate in life was by snails. The young girls would go out early before sunrise to trace the path of the snails in the clay, for always a letter was marked, and it was the initial of the true lover's name. A black snail was very unlucky to meet first in the morning, for its trail would read death, but a white snail brought good fortune. Other animal omens were: a white lamb on the right hand was good; but the cuckoo was an ominous of evil.

A white lamb on my right side,
So will good come to me;
But not the little false cuckoo
On the first day of the year.

Prophecies are also made from the way the wind blew on May morning.

Where did you leave the wind last night?
If in the north,
then the country is lost to the Clan Gael
and our enemies shall surely triumph.
If in the south,
then victory will surely come our way.

The following were the geasas (taboos) of La Baal Tinne:

➵ The marsh marigold is of great use in divination, and is called the shrub of Beltaine. Garlands are made of it for the cattle and the door-posts to keep off the evil power.

➵ Milk is poured on the threshold, though none be given away; nor fire, nor salt—these three things being sacred. Again I repeat, neither fire, nor water, nor milk, nor salt should be given away for love or money, and if a wayfarer is given a cup of milk, they must drink it in the house, and salt must be mixed with it. Salt and water as a drink is at all times a potent charm against evil, if properly prepared by a Fay and the magick words said over it.

➵ It is not safe to go on the water the first Monday in May.

➵ If the fire goes out on May morning it is considered very unlucky and it cannot be rekindled except by a lighted sod brought from a cunning woman or cunning man's house. And the ashes of this blessed turf are afterwards sprinkled on the floor and the threshold of the house.

➵ Do not marry in the month of May for it is a sacred month and all rejoicing should be for the Faery, and they alone.

When the Druids formed their priesthood in Ireland, they put forth the belief that unless the life of man was repaid for the life of man, the will of the immortal gods could not be appeased, and thus developed the private human sacrifices that have shadowed the Celts as if a part of the Faery-Faith, which they were not.

The Druids continued the re-lighting of the sacred Faery fires, but added the sickening custom of constructing huge wicker-work images, which they filled with living men and women. And setting it on fire, they burned alive those unfortunate victims.

St. Patrick determined to break down the power of the Druids; and, therefore, in defiance of their laws, Patrick had a great fire lit on May Eve, when he celebrated the paschal mysteries, and, henceforth, Easter or the Feast of the Resurrection eventually took the place of the Festival of La Baal Tinne.

Fomhar and Lughnasadh—Autumn begins. August 1 is the time of Lughnasadh, which was later altered to Lugh-mass or Lammas.

Lugh, or Lamfhada (Of the Long Arm) put an end to the long war between the Fomorians and the Tuatha De Danann when he killed Balor, the Fomorian god-king. We celebrate him on Lughnasadh, for this is the day he chose to begin his sojourn into the Circles of Existence, and like the death of the Big Sun, Lugh's sunlight left the race of the De Danann.

The sun-god himself is said to have instituted the Elembiuios festival, and it was once of hardly less importance than Beltaine or Samhain. It is noteworthy, too, that the first of August was a great day at Lyons—formerly called Lugudunum, the dun (town) of Lugus.

We honor Lugh with games of skill, for Lugh was a stealthy warrior. He possessed a magick spear which thirsted for blood and flashed fire or roared aloud in battle; and he was the first to use the horse in warfare.

When he approached from the west at The Second Battle of Mag Tuired, in which he slew the one-eyed Balor, the dead king's grandfather cried out, "I wonder that the sun has risen in the west today rather than in the east." His druids answered, "Would that it were no more than the sun! It was the glowing face of Lugh the Long-handed"—which nobody could gaze upon without being dazzled.[*]

The Lugh-mass is observed with mourning and a feast, the mourning procession being always led by a young man carrying a hooped wreath. A feast of corn is enjoyed, for Lugh is celebrated as the Corn-king.

After the feast the Tailltean Games begin with chariot races and sword-play. Trial marriages for a year and a day can be performed on this day, and should after 365 days the couple choose to dissolve their marriage, they return to the place where they had been celebrated, and standing back-to-back in the center of a Black Rath, walk apart; one to the north, the other to the south.[†]

Lammas Towers are built and dancers circle around a female doll who represents not only the Harvest Mother, but also the Great Mother, who ensures the continuation of life through the rebirthing of the corn, as well as the future incarnations of the De Danann.

Today, there are many holidays dotting our calendars. As Pagans, the celebration of our holidays are not acknowledged in today's society.

At one time I felt as if I were forced to schedule time off from work, losing pay, to celebrate my spiritual belief. This left me feeling frustrated. On top of that, I felt confused about celebrating the holidays of other religions.

As the great wheel of the year turned many times over since I began living the life of Faery Wicca, my world not only transformed so that the celebration of the Four Great Festivals has become a normal and accepted event each year in my life, but I've also come to realize that—yes, I can celebrate the religious holidays of all belief systems.

I believe, when we take the time to honor the holy days of other belief systems we gain the ability to transcend religious barriers, and in doing so, begin creating a universal language in which everyone, from every nationality, of every religion can understand.

---

[*] Seumas MacManus: *The Story of the Irish Race.* 1921

[†] More on the Trial Marriage Ritual will be included in my upcoming book, *Faery Wicca, Book Two.*

My husband, Jack Reidling, a biological scientist, once said: "the best world will be that which has no country borders; a world where all people belong everywhere and can go wherever their hearts lead them." This same theory, I believe, applies to the religions of the world.

Journal Exercises

1. When we view the year as a polarity, how can this create a greater balance in our lives?

2. Ritual myth enactment has two sides; what might the pros of such myth enactment be; what might the cons be?

Suggested Reading

The Power of Myth, Joseph Campbell
Celtic Heritage, Alwyn and Brinley Rees
Advanced Magical Arts, R. J. Stewart
The Fairy-Faith in Celtic Countries, W. Y. Evans-Wentz

elightful is the land beyond all dreams,
Fairer than aught thine eyes have ever seen.
There all the year the fruit is on the tree,
And all the year the bloom is on the flower.

There with wild honey drip the forest tress;
The stores of wine and mead shall never fail,
Nor pain nor sickness knows the dweller there,
Death and decay come near him never more.

The feast shall cloy not, nor the chase shall tire,
Nor music cease for ever through the hall;
The gold and jewels of the Land of Youth
Outshine all splendours ever dreamed by man.

Thou shalt have horses of the fairy breed,
Thou shalt have hounds that can outrun the wind;
A hundred chiefs shall follow thee in war,
A hundred maidens sing thee to thy sleep.

A crown of sovranty thy brow shall wear,
And by thy side a magic blade shall hang,
And thou shalt be lord of all the Land of Youth,
And lord of Niav of the Head of Gold.

— *The Fenian Cycle*
(Niav of the Golden Hair
describing Tir na nOg to Oisin.)
The Tain

Lesson 5

The Land of Faery

If an apprentice is unwilling to undergo a complete training, both mundane and magickal, as well as physically, mentally, emotionally, and spiritually, then they will never receive the gift of the gods!

The Land of Faery is the dimension where the Faery dwell, which is comprised of the Otherworlds, plains, or realms of existence (Figure 3, Lesson 2). Time within Faeryland is different from ours. The commonly reported theme has been that a short period of time in the realm of Faery may be centuries in our world.

Early fairy specialists had a vivid sense of the relativity of time, founded, perhaps, on experiences of dream or trance, when a dream that covers several years may be experienced between rolling out of bed and landing on the floor. Occasionally, the dimension is in this direction.

Another suggestion behind all the stories is that Faeryland is a world of the dead, and that those who entered it had long been dead, and carried back with them an illusory body which crumbled into dust when they returned to our realm or dimension.

In the last approximately 300 years our world and the realm of Faery have grown apart. It may be that this period of time is a brief period of time in their realm—perhaps days or a few months. "But as there is no moon or sun in the Faery realm, there is no rotational clock of nights, days or lunar and solar cycles."[16] Their world is illuminated by the light within the earth, a direct light, that of Spirit living within matter.

Everything in the Faery realm is intensified, amplified, sometimes painfully or ecstatically real. It is not a fantasy land, not a child's imagination, but the primal land within, both within our consciousness and within the planet. We do not just imagine this realm, for it has a true nature and firm identity of its own, existing even if one never thinks of it. It is so real that once visited, one returns truly changed.

There are complex power traditions associated with the Faery realm. By exploring it, one begins to make contact with only one aspect of an obscure and potent

---

16 R. J. Stewart, *Earth Light, the Ancient Path to Transformation; Rediscovering the Wisdom of Celtic and Faery Lore,* Elements Books Ltd, 1992.

perennial wisdom tradition. R. J. Stewart tells us that "At the very foundations of religion, mysticism and magic is an almost forgotten concept of power and light, not revealed in the sky or far away in divine dimensions, but utterly close, below and within the Earth"[17]—alias: the Underworld.

In Faery Wicca, the journey into the Underworld becomes inevitable, for the true Faery teachings are part of this Underworld lore, powerful traditions in which humanity, the land, and the planet interact with one another, often through the agency of non-material or non-organic beings: the Faery.

As mentioned in an earlier lesson, the Faery reflect or mirror back our ideas or attitudes, assuming the shape and image of what our minds hold, be it positive mental images or negative mental images.

Likewise, the Faery realm mirrors back; this may be the very reason why, throughout the centuries, the thought of Faeryland has held such a seduction for people, for it has retained the image of a place of peace, beauty, luxury, and pleasures. Even after the Roman Catholic Church denounced it as hell, Faeryland remained alive, even if now in the convoluted form of a fantasy land.

In Faery Wicca, the most basic way to make contact with the Otherworld is through the skill development of visualization, using our imagination to begin the journey for us. Because of this, the most valuable tool is not a material one, but an inner tool—the mind. Through developing the ability to let go of Ego, the mind can then sojourn.

As the primordial landscapes within begin to materialize, access to Faeryland almost certainly follows. Entering Faeryland is not difficult, it takes only belief, belief that Otherworlds do co-exist, and that it is possible to become a co-walker between the worlds.

The term *co-walker* was coined by the seventeenth century fairy scholar, Reverend Robert Kirk. Only 300 years ago it was commonplace for people to see Faery beings of different types, to converse with them, to pass physically in and out of the Underworld or Faery realms. And though the worlds have moved farther apart than ever before in the history of human kind, there still remains a thread connecting them.

We find the thread first in our minds. It is a thread that is held by the Weaver Goddess of the Heavenly Realm. Once we willingly grab hold of the thread, she tosses the ball of yarn to which the thread is attached, allowing the ball to drop down into the Underworld, down into the primal land, down into the realm of the Faery and the ancestors, down into the level of transmutation.

As already described above, Faeryland is comprised of many Otherworlds, plains, or realms. Each world, plain, or realm is located on one of the following three levels: the Heavenly Realm; the Plains or earth; and the Underworld. Each level serves a function and is very similar to the shaman's traditional concept of the upper world, the middle world and the lower world. All worlds overlap and deal with different aspects of spiritual evolution.

---

17 Ibid.

The Heavenly Realm—It is from this realm that the origin of the universe as we know it was birthed. From the great cosmic mother's womb came forth life.

In Wiccan, Pagan, and Goddess circles, a common creation myth explains how the Great Cosmic Mother became lonely after creating most of the universe, and decided to give birth to a sun. This sun lit-up the universe and favored his sister the earth, and so made his way over to her and from that day until this, has remained relatively close to earth at all times.

As the sun grew into manhood, he acquired the potent magick of initiating life through the releasing of his energy, and so impregnated his sister, and thus life on earth began.

In almost every creation myth, Spirit has moved down into the physical; God sent his own son down to earth; the angels fell down to earth, etc. This theory suggests that the movement of Spirit is downward.

One of the earth's natural laws is the law of gravity: what goes up, must come down; as we grow older, the body begins to sag; as plants die, their foliage droops; as the season changes at autumn, trees drop their leaves. At death, we are either buried, submerged, or our ashes are released down into the earth.

Therefore, in Faery Wicca, the Heavenly Realm teaches us about Spirit-light and decension, as well as astral travel, connecting with the light source, universal energy, the concept of Father-Sky, and super-consciousness. A common chant sung to the Heavenly Realm is:

I am opening up in sweet surrender
to the luminous love-light of the one above ....

This love-light is the moonlight, sunlight, starlight—all light that falls down onto our plain from the Heavenly Realm.

It is within this realm that the Over-lords reside—the Archangels, the Christian god, the galactic brotherhood, and the beings from neighboring universes. If one were to physically travel into this realm, such travel would require a machine (such as an airplane, helicopter or spaceship), with life-sustaining equipment for travel into higher altitudes.

The Heavenly Realm generally denotes the great unknown because of its vastness, darkness and deepness of space. All the known laws of earth, for the most part, do not apply. Yet, it does communicate with us. The adage: As Above, So Below* is demonstrated every second of every day.

The heavenly bodies align, conjunct, sextile, square, trine, oppose, quincunx, parallel, semi-sextile, semi-square, septile, quintile, sesqui-square, and biquintile, in hundreds of aspects, mirroring to us in such a way the roles they are playing, whether flowing and harmonious, or challenging and inharmonious, to such a degree, that the complexity of interpreting the messages becomes either impossible or a life-time career of study.

The study of the Heavenly Realm is a two-fold science. One side is known as astrology, and the other side is known as astronomy. In this form of science we truly see the sharing of the rational and the irrational.

---

* A Hermetic maxim ascribed to the mythological Egyptian founder of science, Hermes Trusmegistus.

Yet, once made aware of the messages being sent to us from the Heavenly Realm, integrating such knowledge into consciousness, and striving to cooperate with the energies of the heavenly bodies, one finds that living life on the earth can easily mirror these realities.

There are many plains found within the Heavenly Realm in the Faery Wiccan tradition. The most common ones are:

- Magh Ildathach—The Many Colored Plain
- Magh Mel—The Plain of Honey
- Magh Mor—The Great Plain
- Magh Findargat—The Plain of White Silver
- Magh Argatnel—The Plain of Silver Cloud
- Magh Rein—The Plain of the Sea
- Magh Mon—The Plain of Sports
- Magh Aircthech—The Bountiful Plain
- Magh Ciuin—The Gentle Plain
- Magh Imchuin—The Very Gentle Plain
- Cluiche Magh—The Sporting Plain
- Sen Magh—The Old Plain

Traditionally, these are the plains from where the Tuatha De Danann, dwelled before descending to earth. Sen Magh was the plain from where Dana gave birth to the Ancient Ones.

As in any other realm in which the gods are known to have originally dwelled, entrance by a mortal has never been proven triumphant, for it is a realm closed to our Circle of Existence and spiritual level of evolution. I believe that it is a realm in which all life once existed, but like every system in the universe, evolution or devolution seems to be the normal flow of energy. Thus, we see the flow of Spirit energy down into the second level, or realm, of existence.

The Plains—This is the level that embraces the earth. It is in this realm that the Tuatha De Danann dwelled at one time alongside humans. In fact, it is not uncommon to find myths from around the world telling us of the gods coming to earth and living with mortals. One tradition tells us that because their gods chose the daughters of men to mate with, the first tribes of earth were born.

It is this level and the next, the Underworld, which is of great interest in Faery Wicca. The Plains teaches physical activation, elemental compatibility, cycles, ego development, mind/body connection, functioning in physicality, the concept of Mother-Earth and wakeful consciousness.

The earthly realm of Faeryland was once known as Erin or Ireland, and her heart center, Cathair Crofthind, was the stronghold—the psychical center—of the Faery power, and was known by many names. Each of the five waves of invaders called the heart center by different names:

The Heavenly Realm

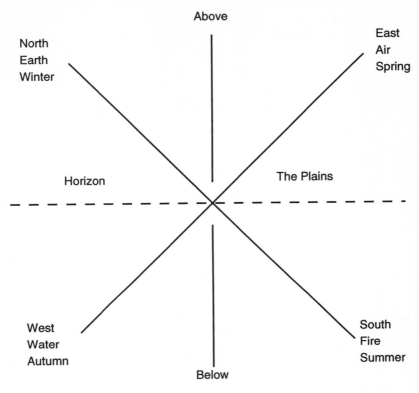

Above

North
Earth
Winter

East
Air
Spring

Horizon

The Plains

West
Water
Autumn

South
Fire
Summer

Below

The Underworld

Figure 7: The Directions

- Fordruim—Partholan
- Druim Leith—Neimheadh
- Druim Cain—Fir Bolg
- Cathair Crofthind—Tuatha De Danann
- Temair—Milesian
- Tara— the modern name

It is no wonder that the land of the Irish goddess, Erin, was so important, for Faery Wicca is deeply attuned to the land. It is considered an environmental tradition (Figure 7). Becoming oriented to the Directions and the Elements realigns energies that need to be patterned before entry into the realm of Faery can be achieved. When one begins to work with the Directions and the Elements they begin to align with the idea of the land as being sacred. These esoteric teachings revolve around reducing our separation from, and antagonism toward, the planet through cathartic meditative or visualizing experiences, as shall be given under the Magickal Enchantments Section. In doing so, we make contact with our inner power.

Inner power allows us to begin undergoing personal transformation within our minds, emotions, and hearts. This involves bringing the outer- and inner-realities together. We begin to see ourselves as an extension of the land, other life-forms and humans, as well as the land, other life-forms and humans as extensions of self.

The compilation of opening self to the cosmic energies falling down from the Heavenly Realm into this Plain, and surrendering to the downward flow of Spirit, can help to gently ease one toward the Underworld, the realm where the Faery now dwell.

Many insights into our natural world and its subtle energies are conferred through interaction with this realm.

The Underworld—R. J. Stewart warns that "The proper place for the encounters of the [F]aery realm is, initially, in the attuned imagination, and for beneficial transformative purposes with no ulterior or selfish motives. Whatever motives we may have are reflected back to us in the [F]aery realm, hence the traditional requirement that we be pure of heart, steadfast of will, and honest. Deceit breeches deceit, and greed acquires only [F]aery gold, which turns to leaves in daylight. What we should seek, perhaps, are the leaves of the trees in the [F]aery realm, which turn to regenerative gold in our upper world, the gold of a restored healthy environment."

As an environmental tradition, Faery Wicca has methods of restoring the land to health through working with the image of the primal land within the polluted land, as ours has become. This is done through re-attuning our land to the Faery land.

When we begin to work with the Underworld, we shift images in our mind (Figure 8). We begin to think of earth as the Overworld in the attempt to generate a polarity. The ideal image would be of the Over- and Underworlds balancing one another, creating a mirror image of each other, so that what is contained within one has a reflection or polar partner in the other. This theory does not only apply to the land itself, but also to humans and other beings of a non-human nature.

The Underworld teaches the release of Ego, the rich darkness of creation, descension into the soul, connecting to death without fear, Initiation, hearth-source and delving into the subconscious. At its deepest levels, the Underworld leads us to a realization of universal consciousness within—not merely within our minds, but within the planet. The stars are within the earth!

There are also a number of Underworld realms in the Faery tradition. They are:

- Tech Duinn—House of Donn
- Tir na nOg—Land of Youth
- Tir na mBan—Land of Women
- Tir nAill—Land of the Otherplace
- Tir na mBeo—Land of the Living
- Tir fo Thuinn—Land under the Wave
- Tir Tairngiri—Land of Promise and Ever Young
- Emhain Abhlach—Apple Orchard in the Land of Promise

Like the other two levels, the Underworld also exists according to its own laws that are opposite to our own. Unlike our law of cause and effect (popularly misconstrued as the law of karma), the Underworld has no such cause and effect law. Per-

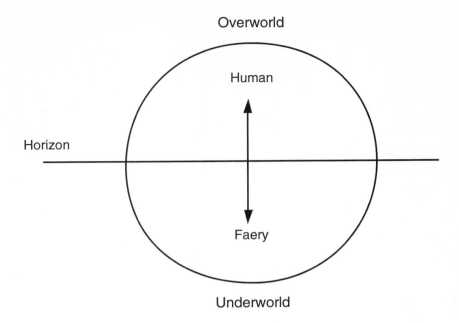

Overworld

Human

Horizon

Faery

Underworld

Figure 8: The Primal Land

haps this is because of the difference in the time cycle. Theirs seems to be a realm that resonates beyond such cycles of energy as we know it.

We are bound to the cycles of the moon, sun, and stars (although less powerfully then the former two). Since the Faery realm does not contain, nor is lit by, the sun or moon, but by an inherent light within the land itself, they are not governed by our time cycle, as discussed at the opening of this chapter.

In Faery Wicca we are taught that the Faery realm, or the Underworld, also draws light from the stars within the earth, which are images of the patterns seen in our own sky. Yet, the absence of sun and moon in their realm depicts the absence of certain human characteristics in the Faery. Just as we use the method of healing our land by imaging the primal land within the earth, exchanging energies, realigning and regenerating through the Over- and Underworld balancing one another, so we can exchange certain energies which the other may lack. This imaging of unification has the proficiency to generate a fusion of perfect being through regeneration.

In Faery Wicca there are found Three Stabilities of Knowledge, which pertain to this regeneration:

- To have traversed every state of life.
- To remember every state and its incidents.
- To be able to traverse every state, as one would wish, for the sake of experience and judgment.

These three tenets make-up the foundation of the Celtic Circles of Existence. This is a very ancient wisdom found in Faery Wicca to which no origin can be placed. The first publication of this wisdom appeared in 1862, *Barddas of Iolo Morganwg**, by D. J. Roderic (Llandovery), Longman & Co. (Figure 9).

Celtic Circles of Existence—There are three states, or Circles of Existence, in which living beings are subjected. Each of these three states or circles, provides a function of evolution. They are:

- ⚒ Circle of Ceugant (Infinity), where there is neither animate nor inanimate save Dana, and Dana only can traverse it.
- ⚒ Circle of Abred (Re-birth), where the dead are stronger than the living, and where every principal existence is derived from the dead, and humankind has traversed it.
- ⚒ Circle of Gwynvyd (White-life, i.e. the Circle of Perfection), where the living are stronger than the dead, and where every principal existence is derived from the living and life, that is, from Dana, and humankind shall traverse it; nor will humankind attain to perfect knowledge, until they shall have fully traversed the Circle of Gwynvyd, for no absolute knowledge can be obtained but by the experience of the senses, from having borne and suffered every condition and incident.†

In the Celt's mind, it was believed that Dana, or GOD, caused that every living and animate being should pass through every form and species of existence endured with life, so that in the end every living and animate being might have perfect knowledge, life, and Gwynvyd; and all this formed the perfect love of GOD, which in virtue of the individual's divine nature, Dana could not but exhibit toward woman and man and every living being.

According to the late Ross Nichols, the Chosen Chief of the Order of Bards, Ovates and Druids, "All living beings below the Circle of Gwynvyd (Perfection) have fallen into Abred (Rebirth), and are now on their return to Gwynvyd (Perfection). The migration of most of them will be long, owing to the frequent times they have fallen, from having attached themselves to evil and ungodliness; and the reason why they fell was, that they desired to traverse the Circle of Ceugant (Infinity), which Dana alone could endure and traverse." In other words, Spirit fell because of pride. The following is an ancient teaching on this matter.

> *The disciple asked, "Did all who reached the Circle of Gwynvyd after the primary progression of necessity from Annwn, fall in Abred from pride?*

---

* Much controversy raged over the *Barddas*, however, it was instrumental in reviving the Druidic forms and ceremonies in Wales and England. Because no earlier written sources of the *Barddas* could be found, the material was considered fraud. I present it here, because it has a part in the philosophy of Faery Wicca since the Celtic Church first formed

† *Barddas of Iolo Morganwg*, by D. J. Roderic (Llandovery), Longman & Co. 1862.

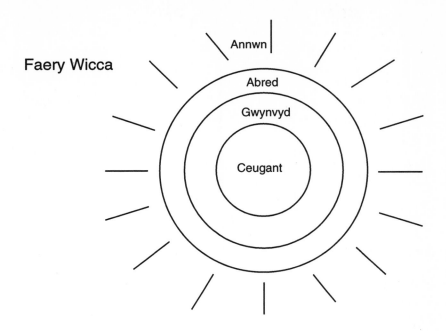

Faery Wicca

Annwn

Abred

Gwynvyd

Ceugant

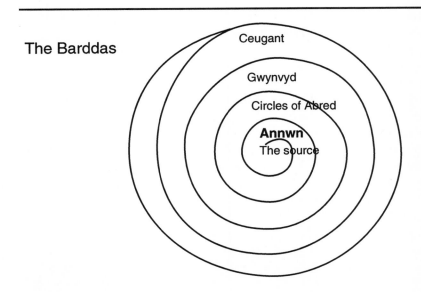

The Barddas

Ceugant

Gwynvyd

Circles of Abred

Annwn
The source

Figure 9 : The Circles of Existence

"No," answered the Master, "some sought after wisdom, and hence saw what pride would do, and they resolved to conduct themselves according to what was taught them by GOD, and thereby became divinities, or holy angels, and they acquired learning from what they beheld in others, and it was thus that they saw the nature of Ceugant and eternity, and that GOD alone could endure and traverse it."

"Does not the danger of falling in Abred, from the Circle of Gwynvyd, exist still as it did formerly?" asked the Disciple.

"No," answered the Master. "Because all pride and every other sin, will be overcome before one can a second time reach the Circle of Gwynvyd, and then by recollecting and knowing the former evil, every one will necessarily abhor what caused him to fall before, and the necessity of hatred and love will last and continue for ever in the Circle of Gwynvyd, where the three stabilities, namely, hatred, love and knowledge, will never end."

The Disciple asked: "Will those, who shall return to the Circle of Gwynvyd after the fall in Abred, be of the same kind as those who fell not?"

Answered the Master: "Yes, and of the same privilege, because the love of Dana cannot be less toward one than toward another, nor toward one form of existence than another, since She is GOD and Mother to them all, and they will all be equal and co-privileged in the Circle of Gwynvyd, that is, they will be divinities and holy angels for ever."

Disciple: "Will every form and species of living existence continue for ever as they are now? If so, tell me why?"

Master: "Yes, in virtue of liberty and choice, and the blessed will go from one to another as they please, in order to repose from the fatigue and tediousness of Ceugant, which GOD only can endure, and in order to experience every knowledge and every Gwynvyd that are capable of species and form; and each one of them will hate evil of necessary obligation, and know it thoroughly, and consequently of necessity renounce it, since he will perfectly know its nature and mischievousness — Dana being a held, and Dana being Great, supporting and preserving them for ever."

According to the three principals, qualities of woman and man shall be her and his migration in Abred, from indolence and mental blindness she and he shall fall to Annwn; from dissolute wantonness she and he shall traverse the Circle of Abred, according to her and his necessity; and from her and his love for goodness she and he shall deepen to the Circle of Gwynvyd. Therefore, all living exists within Gwynvyd, and vacillate between this circle and Abred when we die and prepare for a rebirth.

When we are in sacred space, having cast the Great Circle, we move between the worlds. It is possible that we stand at a threshold which is of a triple nature, a threshold that allows us to catch a glimpse of Ceugant, the realm of Dana, as well as Abred, the realm of the ancestors.

Ancestral Worship—The traditional realm of the ancestors is connected to the Underworld. The Underworld is that realm which is technically inside the earth. Spirit deepens, spirit moves downward, or ultimately strives to move down into the center which is Ceugant.

Ancestral worship is greatly misunderstood in today's society. When thinking in terms of communing with an ancestor, thoughts of talking to the dead are usually generated. The Faery ancestral worship is not of this mediumistic intercourse, nor of the New Age variant, channeling. Rather, it is a striving to connect with the Spirit of the land, the light inside the earth.

Ancient wisdoms are connected to the earth; the earth teaches us how to live. As R. J. Stewart, in his work with the Underworld tradition, so eloquently states, ancestral worship "affirms that universal wisdom and regeneration are not found exclusively in heavenly or ethereal dimensions, but also in the heart of the sacred land, the planet, within Mother Earth."[18]

When we move into the Underworld, we may enter into a collective, or individual, awareness of Ancestral memories and beings. Why is that? Because the earth contains all knowledge, all wisdom, all life experiences—of every aspect of creation —that have taken place on and within her.

In Wiccan, Pagan, and Goddess circles we recite this truth each time we say Starhawk's modern version of the *Charge of the Star Goddess*:

From Me, all things proceed
and unto Me, all things return ...
I have been with you from the beginning
and I am that which is attained
at the end of desire.[19]

When we strive to connect with the ancestors, it is not done in the attempt to resurrect them, to bring back the dead. Faery Wicca is not necromancy*, nor strives to be.

The Faery ancestors can only help us remember ancient wisdom that may be gone from the earth plane at this time, buried deep in the subconscious matters of our minds, and in the realm of the Underworld, as well as provide us with direction in polarizing the Over- and Under-Worlds, thus achieving balance of the primal land. Contact with such beings can also provide us with information that will help us individually in our efforts to understand the evolutionary process, preparing us to delve deeper into Spirit.

Ancient deities are also found within the Underworld. The knowledge which they transmute to us is called High Faery Lore. This is the body of tradition that talks

18 R. J. Stewart, *Earth Light, the Ancient Path to Transformation; Rediscovering the Wisdom of Celtic and Faery Lore,* Elements Books Ltd, 1992.
19 Starhawk, *Spiral Dance*, Harper Row, 1986.
* See Lesson Seven: Modern Faery Wicca, The Witch-Trials of Ireland.

of the gods and goddesses of the land, the tradition of kingship and ceremony, the Great Goddess, and the memories of the megalithic Bronze Age culture.

However, many Celtic deities are not found in the Underworld, for they belong on the surface of land, in the seas, rivers, sky, stars.

Let us return to the theory of the Circles of Existence. In Faery Wicca, all worlds, all realms, all dimensions intersect, and this intersection is possible to reach if one is willing to develop the necessary skills. When we think of life as being spiraling vortexes of energy, unwinding and winding, then the possibility that one can move in either direction begins to resonate with truth.

The theory is that life birthed from Annwn, the outermost circle from GOD, not abyss but outer darkness (as shown in Figure 9), and spirals downward through Abred into Gwynvyd. We vacillate between Gwynvyd and Abred between lifetimes, moving upward and downward, or spiraling up and down, until we have achieved and experienced all forms of life, thus accomplishing a state of perfection.

When this state of perfection is achieved, we spiral downward, deepening into the most potent energy vortex, that of Ceugant—the center or the Divine. One cannot help but wonder whether or not Ceugant is a blackhole. When ones moves into it, do they move into the threshold of another universe, another cycle of existence, containing within it its own circles? And if Ceugant is a blackhole, then, as scientific theory implies, does one reach the other side elongated like a spaghetti noodle?

Yes, this thought provokes humor, because such questioning does not contain an answer. At our current level of experience we have not yet traversed Ceugant, and, therefore, all we can do is surmise.

For the time being, let us resume our understanding of our current realm of existence, and the up- and downward spiraling that takes place between Gwynvyd and Abred, and the idea of re-birth or regeneration. This theme of regeneration or resurrection after death is known in Faery Wicca as the Doctrine of Rebirth.

The Celtic Doctrine of Rebirth—The idea of rebirth, or reincarnation (literally meaning refleshing), is an ancient view of cyclic rebirth after each death—the original meaning of being born again. The archaeology of Pagan religion in Ireland represents a strong belief in rebirth. Many tombs contain elaborate grave gods; the iconography implies that regeneration is a function of the gods. Wine motifs associated with many deities represent the symbolic blood of rebirth, resurrection. Mother-goddesses are venerated as deities of life, death, and rebirth, and associated with the seasonal symbolism: the death of winter is followed by the rebirth of spring. Deciduous trees die and are reborn, as is the corn seed buried in the dark tomb of earth. Stags, too, with their autumnal shedding and spring re-growth of antlers, possess a seasonal, cyclical symbolism.

The Doctrine of Rebirth teaches that our souls do not die, but pass from one body to another in the physical once we have chosen to incarnate in the physical. The esoteric secret of rebirth is: "if you know what you sing, death is the center of a long life!"

Death, as many Initiates have proclaimed in their mystical writings, is but going to the Otherworld from this world, and birth a coming back again; Buddha announced it as his mission to teach humankind the way to be delivered out of this Circle of Existence.

This knowledge became very available among the great nations of antiquity—the Egyptians, Indians, Greeks, and Celts. It was taught in the Mysteries and Priest-Schools, and formed the corner-stone of the most important philosophical systems like those of Buddha, Pythagoras, Plato, the Neo-Platonists, and the Druids.

The Alexandrian Jews, also, were familiar with the doctrine, as implied in the Wisdom of Solomon (viii.19, 20), and in the writings of Philo. Interestingly, it was one of the teachings in the Schools of Alexandria, that directly shaped the thoughts of some of the early Church Fathers; for example, Tertullian of Carthage, who lived from circa 160 C.E.–240 C.E., and his contemporary, Origen of Alexandria.

The Christians in the first centuries held, or were greatly influenced by, the Celtic Doctrine of Rebirth. It was the theologians who created the Greek canons of the Fifth Council, further expounding the Doctrine of Rebirth as a teaching of Jesus Christ, but also as a universal law governing the lives of all humankind:

> *The Saviour answered and said unto his disciples: 'Preach ye unto the whole world, saying unto men, 'Strive together that ye may receive the mysteries of light in this time of stress and enter into the kingdom of light. Put not off from day to day, and from cycle to cycle, in the belief that ye will succeed in obtaining the mysteries when ye return to the world in another circle. **

In addition to the many Gnostic-Christian sects, the Manichaeans, who comprised more than seventy sects connected with the primitive Church, also promulgated the rebirth doctrine. However, along with the condemnation of the Gnostics and Manichaeans as heretical, the Doctrine of Rebirth was likewise condemned by various ecclesiastical bodies and councils. This was the declaration by the Council of Constantinople in 553 C.E.:

> *Whosoever shall support the mythical doctrine of the pre-existence of the Soul, and the consequent wonderful opinion of its return, let him be anathema.*

After centuries of controversy, the ancient doctrine ceased to be regarded by the Catholic Church. However, the Celtic Doctrine of Rebirth was retained in myth, and was transformed into a symbol: the cauldron of regeneration, eventually leading to rebirth. Within the tales of the four Cycles is found the persistent reference to this magickal cauldron, which brought the dead warriors back to life, though often they cannot speak. In the Otherworld, each bruidhen (hostel) has its own inexhaustible cauldron of plenty.

The cauldron also took on the symbolism of being the belly of the Great Cosmic Mother, from whom all life is birthed, and to whom all souls return before their transmigration to another life.

---

* *Pistas Sophia, Book II.*

As we've discussed above, the concept of rebirth is closely associated to the Otherworld, which is perceived as being essentially similar to life on earth, or a polarity reflection. From the Doctrine of Rebirth we have the creation of the Transmigration of Souls.

The Transmigration of Souls—Although Caesar remarked that the Gaulic Druids created the concept of the Transmigration of Souls ("The Druids attach particular importance to the belief that the soul does not perish, but passes after death from one body to another..." Lucan [Pharsalia I, 446ff]), we've already seen that the concept existed long before their cult was formed.

Death was acknowledged as merely an interruption in a long life, as a bridge between one life and another, or one realm and another. The human soul was believed to remain in control of their bodies in another world after death. It was perceived that the souls of humankind were immortal and that after a definite number of years, people lived another life, when their souls inhabited another body.

To the Celts, the holding place was in the Otherworld, wherein the cauldron of regeneration and rebirth is contained. The concept of reincarnation was not only the general belief of Pagan Europe, but was also found in the beliefs of the Eskimos, Greeks, Hindus, and the Orient. Even Jewish tradition retained traces of reincarnation.

In the *First Book of Adam and Eve*, Adam offered God a sacrifice of his own blood, saying, "Be favorable to me every time I die, and bring me to life.*"

Pythagoras believed in the Transmigration of Souls from one body to another: "The spirit wanders, comes now here, now there, and occupies whatever frame it pleases. From beasts it passes into human bodies, and from our bodies into beasts, but never perishes."[†]

The Transmigration of Souls parallels the Celtic Doctrine of Rebirth so closely that additional attention to the theory of regeneration and rebirth here would only be redundant.

In our Western culture, the thought of karma or reincarnation is often looked-down-upon. I believe the denial of reincarnation and its product of not harming other life-forms, as well as viewing oneself as apart of all life, as enforced through Christianity, has been the result of the present-day crisis of human kind's dominance over nature.

By destroying Pagan animism, Christianity attempted to remove the soul from nature, resulting in an exploitation of nature in a mood of indifference to the feelings of natural objects and other life-forms, and the sanction to exploit the environment by science and technology, thus creating an ecological imbalance of air and water pollution, overpopulation, and other ecological threats, which has directly threatened the spiritual evolution of the planet as a whole.

Whether one directly believes in regeneration or rebirth, the wisdom not to be forgotten, as taught through the Celtic Doctrine of Rebirth, as well as the Druidic Transmigration of Souls, is the attitude of oneness, which is one of the primary focuses found in Faery Wicca.

---

* de Lys, *The Giant Book of Superstitions.*
† Joseph Campbell, *The Masks of God: Primitive Mythology.*

Every aspect of life cooperates with the other in an exquisite system. To offset one aspect of this system, no matter how insignificant that aspect may seem, disrupts the entire system. Such a disruption generates an energy disharmony.

As an environmental tradition, Faery Wicca encourages the participants to look upon all aspects of the system as vitally important and relevant to their own life. Seeking the ultimate connection of being an extension of the system, and seeing the system as an extension of self, bridges the gap that current religions have unfortunately created.

The blame is not to be put entirely on current religions, however, for man and woman are the creators of such religions. Therefore, religions simply reflect the mass consciousness of a people at a given time in history.

We can amend the damaging effects of such causes that at one time seemed righteous; it takes concerted effort, though. And, of course, the change begins with the idea. Giving voice to the idea and sharing it with others generates an energy spiral into this and other realms of existence, allowing it to become manifest.

This concept is the truth behind magick, and is the basis for understanding cause and effect. The time has come for us to birth the new world vision that we dreamers have been dreaming: Oneness.

Journal Exercises

1. What is your belief surrounding regeneration, rebirth, or reincarnation?

2. As a dreamer, what new world vision have you been dreaming; how can you give birth to this vision?

Suggested Reading

The Book of Druidry, Ross Nichols
An Act of Woman Power, Kisma K. Stepanich
Earth Light, R. J. Stewart

here is a secret pool, dew-fed and still,
Ringed by the blossomed gorse
and heather hill,
Whose waters,
changing not with drought or cold,
Know sailing pomp of cloud and mirrored gold;
Shy creatures of the glen stoop there to drink
And sleeping lilies freight the shallow brink.

Never fish swims, dark roach or speckled trout,
Darting from burnished stones swift in and out;
Sunken deep down, yet strangely green and near,
The swinging elfland city may appear,
With tranced turret reared and lights to stream
As now the sunset colours glance and gleam.

Red mosses bind the edge, and dim blue flowers
So small that they might gem Titania's bowers;
The heron drowses; and the dragon-fly
Makes minute music there, sustained and high;
And when the moon-dappled shadows stretch and bar
The tangled reeds net each a silver star.

— *The Magic Lake*
Kathleen Foyle

Lesson 6

Sacred Space

Vanished the angelic trees and being all! The wood darkens: the wind has ceased to fan the glade to flame. Oh, it was magical! Can I recall? [*]

To ask one involved with Wicca, magick, Paganism, or Goddess worship what Sacred Space might be, the most common answer received is: it is the space designated as sacred within the boundary of the cast circle. But Sacred Space is more than this. There are typically three types of Sacred Space:

→ Permanent Sacred Space
→ Temporary Sacred Space
→ Personal Sacred Space

Permanent Sacred Space is usually formed on, or near, energy vortexes which are concentrated points of psychic or soul energy, as Frank Joseph explains, "put there by cosmic and natural forces of earth and sky, or through states of altered human awareness still resonating at the site." [†]

Most of the Permanent Sacred Space sites of today have been with us from ancient times, i.e. the Serpent Mount (Locust Grove, Ohio), the Heian shrine (Kyoto, Japan), the Mani shrine (Dju Gompa, Bhutan), the Seven Springs (Biskey, Gloucestershire, England), the White Horse and Dragon Hill (Uffington, Oxfordshire, England), Needle Rock (Le Puy, France), Burrowbridge Hill (Somerset, England), Glastonbury Tor with St. Michael's Church (Somerset, England), Corroboree Rock (central Australia), Temple of Apollo (Delphi, Greece), Sacred grotto (Kilnacanogh, County Wicklow, Ireland), The Avebury Complex and Stonehenge (England), and those of Ireland: Newgrange, Bruagh na Boinne, Cashel Aenghus, Duma of the Mound of Bones, Tailtin, and Tara—to name only a few of the sacred sites found throughout the world.

---

[*] A.E. *Natural Magic*, "Voices of the Stones."

[†] Frank Joseph (ed), *Sacred Sites: A Guidebook to Sacred Centers & Mysterious Places in the United States*, Llewellyn Publications, 1992.

Plato in his Laws refers to Hesiod's myth of the age of Cronus when "all that life requires was provided unasked and in abundance," the reason being that the women and men of that time were ruled not by other women and men, but by spirits, these corresponding to the eternal element in human nature.

The men and women of the age of Cronus were wanderers, living under the direct guidance and protection of the Earth Spirit, following the migratory paths of their ancestors, vitally concerned with the cycles of animal and plant life, the progress of the seasons, the movements of the heavenly bodies.

The earth was held sacred. Before civilization set in, the earth was the one universal deity, not the material earth, but the Spirit by virtue of which, according to the ancient philosophers, is a living creature: a female, because she receives the power of the sun, is animated thereby and made fertile. Her great body is like that of humankind. It is corruptible and subject to change, but her Spirit is unchanging, and, therefore, the essential nature of this planetary being is spiritual.

Porphyry states that the "physical earth is merely a symbol of the earth as she really is." The orthodox view that survived into the middle ages from prehistoric times is expressed by the alchemist Basilius Valentinus: "The things, minerals included, draw their strength from the earth spirit. This spirit is life, it is nourished by the stars, and it gives nourishment to all the living things it shelters in its womb. Through the spirit received from on high, the earth hatches the minerals in her womb as the mother her unborn child."

Before literature, we can only begin to understand the deep spiritual beliefs of ancient civilizations through the creation of the sacred spaces; for such sites can be considered the record of sacred history. The philosophy that seems to go with the lifestyle of the wandering tribes is that of Herclitus: "All is in flow." Every river is as sacred as the Ganges, according to the Indian saying.

Yet, we must not view our ancient ancestors who honored the sacred land as ignorant, for it is evident that these civilizations of historical antiquity derived the better part of their scientific knowledge from the traditions of a more developed, unified, and widely disseminated system belonging to a previous age unknown to history. The evidence of Stonehenge and other megalithic sites shows the existence 4,000 years ago of advanced scientific knowledge combined with a natural, unobtrusive technology, suggesting that the present world civilization is not the first, merely the most materially developed and materialistically directed.

The land of Ireland has always been held sacred as the Emerald Isle, untouched by even the hands of the Roman Catholic Church. Strangers may have conquered the land, imposing their own gods and cults on the natives, but the sacred places and the dates of the Faery-Faith festivals remained the same as before. The attributes of the new deities may have been accommodated to the old, and the invaders became in time subjected to the traditions of the country, but the sacred land remained sacred. It was even the policy of the early Christians to follow antique precedent in this respect, with the result that almost every old church occupies a site with sacred associations far earlier than the present building, while the feast day of the saint to whom the church is dedicated has in many cases been inherited from the Irish god or goddess.

At these sites of Permanent Sacred Space, one may still attune themselves to the greater Spirit, that of the sacred land, and ultimately that of the Underworld, wherein the Spirit of the land, the ancestors, and the Faery dwell.

The Great Circle

Temporary sacred space is that space designated as sacred within the boundary of the cast circle. Casting a circle is part of almost every earth tradition*. It is practiced in Wiccan, Pagan, Magickal, and Goddess circles. The casting of a circle, whether in a formal way or by acknowledging the earth boundary of our planet, is performed to create a sense of sacredness, designating the space which is being occupied as being removed or in-between the worlds: between the Plains and the Otherworlds, between everyday living and the invisible realms of which we do not generally partake.

By casting the circle we remove ourselves, mentally, physically, and spiritually from linear existence, placing our consciousness into the Great Circle which represents the natural cycles of living: birth, growth, decay, death, and rebirth.

Although there are many ways to formally cast a circle, depending upon the tradition, the most important aspect of the function is the act of creating Sacred Space; to become part of the sacredness.

In Faery Wicca, it is traditional to cast the Great Circle on open land. In ancient times the thought of constructing a permanent enclosed structure seemed anti-sacred. Structures separate worshippers from the natural world, enforcing an anthropocentric attitude, while segregating the participants from other humans who do not come to take part in the worship held within such a structure.

The symbol of the circle boundary is to show that what is in the boundary is within the center of the universe, and what is without is part of the infinite which contains many things of both a positive and negative characteristic.

Traditionally, the Great Circle is cast on the earth, demonstrating an embrasure of all life-forms, while representing the equality of all life-forms. The people who gather within the sacred space of the Great Circle may be at different levels of spiritual evolution, as well as different degrees in their traditional training, but once the circle is cast all who stand within are considered to be on the same level in the eyes of the Ancient Ones.

In Faery Wicca we call the Great Circle the Faery Ring. When cast, it is approximately eighteen feet across. Eighteen is a double-sided nine. Nine figures prominently in Celtic tradition as explained under the Magickal Enchantments Section in the Magickal Faery Tools chapter. Most importantly, nine symbolizes the whole—in other words: the circle.

The Faery Ring is divided into five parts: the four quarters—North, East, South, West—and the Center of the circle is the fifth. Interestingly, when a circle divided in five parts is drawn on a piece of paper, the four quarters resemble the lattice archway of a portcullis, and the center is the design of the lozenge; (Figure 10) two of the Celtic sacred symbols.

---

* Directions on casting a circle will be covered under Section Two.

It is not by chance that these sacred symbols are found within the Great Circle, because the circle itself is a great symbol. As many creation myths indicate, the Universe begins with roundness—the Great Circle, the cosmic egg, the bubble, the spiral, the moon, the zero, the wheel of time, the infinite womb—such are the symbols that try to express a human sense of the "whole"-ness of things.

Unlike the cross, which symbolizes up/down, left/right, lending way for the linear thinking of one side being in a better position, and creating the power-over-mind-set which has been known to destroy equality and a sense of wholeness, the

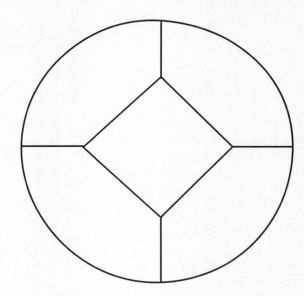

Figure 10: The Five-Fifths of the Great Circle

Great Circle expresses the essential unity of all peoples, creatures, and nature on this earth. The Great Circle is without status clues, promoting "O"neness.

However, within this oneness of circle, there are different aspects of experience to be learned as demonstrated by the division of it into fifths. When the Faery Ring is cast and you stand within the center of the circle, you are within the great womb of the universe, awaiting rebirth into a new level of consciousness. When standing in the center, you can turn to each of the four quarters. There, a threshold into that quarter realm rises before you, a reminder that on the other side lies only "one" aspect of the Great Mystery.

The Five-Fifths of the Great Circle—The expression "Five-fifths of Ireland" is familiar to all who speak the Gaelic, or Irish, tongue. Originally, the five-fifths was Ireland herself, and the antiquity of this five-fold conception cannot be doubted if you know Irish history. For the island was divided into five-fifths, or five provinces, when the Fir Bolg invaded.

Four of the five provinces geographically related to one of the four directions, the fifth fifth being that of the central heart of the land. There is, however, a disagreement in the tradition as to the true identity of the fifth fifth.

In early literature, the Fir Bolg division consisted of Connacht, Ulster, Leinster, and the two Munsters—East Munster and West Munster. (Figure 11). The five provinces met at the Stone of Divisions on the Hill of Uisnech (in Meath), which was believed to be the mid-point, or center of Ireland.

However, present day Ireland provides an alternative tradition claiming that the fifth province was Meath (Mide), the Middle (Figure 12). Even though Meath is today considered the center. In the Faery-Faith, it is almost commonly acknowledged that Tara, located in Brega, is the true heart of Ireland.

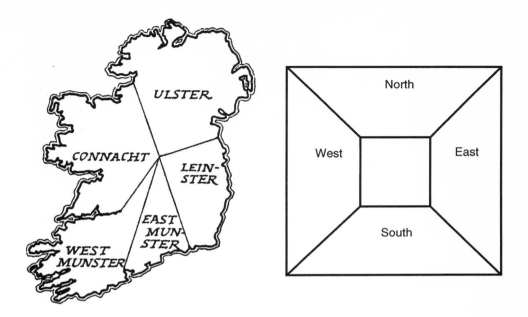

Figure 11: The Five Provinces

As will be described below, in Faery Wicca we use the five-fifths of Ireland to study the division of the Great Circle in an attempt to better understand the different functions found within each of the fifths.

Ulster—This fifth represents the North quarter and is ascribed the primary function of Cath (battle). Other functions of this fifth are: contentions, hardihood, rough places, strife, haughtiness, unprofitableness, pride, captures, assaults, hardness, wars and conflicts.

In this province/quarter, you learn to unleash your warrior spirit. The warrior spirit is that part of the personality which encourages the novice to walk the path of apprenticeship toward initiation.

In the process of creating sacred space by casting the Great Circle, the North is the gateway through which the warrior enters the circle. The North is also the first province/quarter acknowledged within the circle.

The warrior spirit, which represents inner strength, is called into the realm of the living to enable a person to continue forward on his or her personal journey.

Leinster—This fifth represents the East quarter and is ascribed the primary function of Blath (prosperity). Other functions of this fifth are: supplies, bee-hives, contests, feats of arms, householders, nobles, wonders, good customs, good manners, splendor, abundance, dignity, strength, wealth, house-holding, many arts, accouterments, many treasures, satin, serge, silks, cloths, green spotted cloth, and hospitality.

This province/quarter teaches partnership with nature as in farming and gardening.

The first battle the warrior spirit is brought face-to-face with is the attitude of anthro-procentrism. The natural world is revealed in the East through the light of Spirit. The warrior begins to see the partnership that exists between other life-forms and the earth.

The warrior begins to understand the hostile environment humankind has created which has resulted in an imbalanced eco-system: polluted resources, extinction of animal species, the unhealthy state of Mother Earth through the continual raping of her minerals and forests, and the threat of nuclear annihilation.

Through this new understanding of nature, the warrior spirit begins to honor and defend the planet and all relations, rather then continue to battle for man's foolish ego desire for world-domination.

Munster—This fifth represents the South quarter and is ascribed the primary function of Seis (music). The other functions of this fifth are: esa (waterfalls), oenaigi (fairs), nobles, weavers, knowledge, subtlety, musicianship, melody, minstrelry, wisdom, honor, music, learning, teaching, fiansa (warriorship), fidchell playing (a game similar to chess), vehemence, fierceness, poetical art, advocacy, modesty, code, retinue, and fertility.

In this province/quarter the power of the feminine is represented; the inner power/medicine is received through the connection with the feminine energy of goddess.

Munster also plays a peculiar role in the wider cosmology of the Faery Tradition. The House of Donn and the world of the dead lie off the coast of West Munster. This is also the province of the aborigines of Ireland, who were believed to have been the progeny of Cessair, and who utterly perished in a great flood just as the first invaders, led by Parthalon, utterly perished in a great plague.

Munster is pre-eminently the province of female supernatural personages. The Sid of Munster is known as the Land of the White Women. In this province the primary landmarks commemorated to the ancient goddesses are found: the Paps of Anann, near Killarney in Munster; Ebliu, sister of Lugh, is associated with a district in Munster; Knock Aine, a Munster hill named after the goddess Aine; the Beare peninsula of West Munster, which is the haunt of the ancient Crone goddess, Cailleach.

Munster is the primeval world, the place of origin. On its west coast are the landing places of Cessair, known as Dun na mBarc in Coirco Duibne; the Sliab Mis, again in Corco Duibne, where the goddess Banba met the Sons of Mil; Tul Tuinde where Fintan, or Banba, survived the Flood; Valentia Island off the west coast of Munster where the wizard Mug Ruith dwelled for nineteen reigns, it is in Munster that the Sen Erainn (the Old Erainn), believed to be the aboriginal inhabitants, presence is recorded.

To say the least, Munster is the province of the Fay: the cunning women (witch women, or midwives; the healers) of Erin who were banned and outcast as new waves of invaders poured into Ireland through the North province, and who acknowledged the province as a realm of music and low-class entertainers.

However, in both early literature and folk-tales, sweet music is revealed to be one of the essential attributes of the Otherworld, into which men are lured by the enchantment cast over them by beautiful women who dwell therein.

When the warrior spirit moves into the awareness of the South province, the understanding of balance is revealed. Not only has the warrior begun the balance on

Figure 12 : Present Ireland

a planetary (physical) level, but now on an energy (inner) level. The idea of the only supreme energy being that of a masculine nature is negated, and the realization that the balance on all levels can only be achieved by bringing into partnership the masculine with the feminine supreme energies, introduces the warrior to her or his power, the power of the heart and the law of the feminine: Love.

Connacht—This fifth represents the West quarter, and is ascribed the primary function of Fis (learning). The other functions of this fifth are: foundations, teaching, alliance, judgement, chronicles, counsels, stories, histories, science, comeliness, eloquence, beauty, blushing (modesty), bounty, abundance, and wealth.

This is the province/quarter in which Eldership is achieved. Through the death of the old self, the warrior undergoes descension into the inner (Solar) realm. As the hermit, she or he walks into the realm of the Great Mystery on a vision quest to receive the health and help required to walk his or her power in balanced beauty and strength.

After three years of hard work, the warrior reborn is initiated into a new cycle of spiritual evolution. The new Elder begins to understand that in their occult (inner mysteries), Connacht and the powers beyond it are supreme; that here, the last is first.

Meath— This fifth represents the Center, and is ascribed the primary function of: King- and Queen-ship. The other functions of this fifth are: stewards, dignity, primacy, sta-

111

bility, establishments, supports, destructions, warriorship, charioteership, soldiery, principality, high-kingship, Ollamhship, mead, bounty, ale, renown, fame and prosperity.

This is the province of the Ancient Ones; the power of oneness and heart. To rest in this province requires the Elder to have three essential attributes: justice; victory; the power to give fruitfulness to the earth and health to humankind.

All three attributes are derived from the ability to perpetually dwell within Truth, as stated in this ancient proverb:

By ... truth great peoples are ruled.
By ... truth great mortality is warded off from [humankind].
By ... truth great battles are driven off into the enemies' country.
By ... truth every right prevails and every vessel is full...
By ... truth fair weather comes in each fitting season, winter fine and frosty, spring dry and windy, summer warm with showers of rain, autumn with heavy dews and fruitful. For it is ... falsehood that brings perverse weather upon wicked peoples, and dries up the fruit of the earth*.

Idealistically, the above attributes teach about the nature of jealousy, fear and niggardliness, for jealousy would be a fatal weakness in a judge, as would fear in a warrior, and greed in a farmer.

Attaining Eldership and moving into the center brings one to their throne of king- or queen-ship. As mentioned earlier, there is a tradition in Irish mythology where the king was fundamentally bound-up with the fortunes and prosperity of the land. The Celts believed that if the king's character was good, Ireland would flourish.

In the Faery tradition, Tara was the sacred site of kingship from very early. Here, the pre-Christian Feast of Tara legitimized the new king, and it was here that the ritual marriage took place between the king and the land.

The concept of sacral kingship was intimately associated with sacred places and, in particular, sacred trees, which were present at the site of the king's inauguration as symbols of wisdom, sovereignty, and, perhaps also, representative of the land itself.

The kingship was of a feminine nature; the kings of Ireland were men who showed favor to, or were accepted by, the lady who personified the realm, thus the ritual of the king-marriage was to the land, or goddess of the land.

An example of this is the marriage of Eriu, the eponymous goddess of Ireland, who sealed her union with her royal spouse by handing him a golden goblet full of red liquor. The queen-goddess Medb cohabited with nine kings of Ireland; she would not allow any king in Tara who did not mate with her.

Many of these goddesses underwent transformation once the union had taken place. This may take the form of a change from old hag to young girl or from wild and mad female to sane and beautiful woman. A third form of transformation concerns the girl of royal birth brought up among peasants who is restored by union with the king to her rightful status. However, the favored kings were brought into the center of Ireland. Therefore, they were brought into the heart of Dana.

As each of the four quarters of the Great Circle provides a lesson in one aspect of the Occult, so the Center of the Great Circle contains within it the greater Mystery of the tradition.

---

* Dillon, *Modern Philogy*, XI, 81, "The Hindu Act of Truth in Celtic Tradition."

To dwell in the Center of the Great Circle, one must be in the quintessent state of marriage to both the masculine and feminine principles of life: a partnership of both god and goddess.

Standing in the Center means standing in the Otherworld, the "navel" of the cosmos. In the cosmologies, the Center is often an axis which extends from the Underworld to the Heavenly Realm, uniting the universe vertically as well as horizontally. In the Center is found the heart, or a fire-altar. This fire-altar represents the sacrificial fire, the navel of the earth as well as the fire of the universe.

Having looked at the Great Circle, we now turn our attention to the most important fixture used in the Great Circle, which is the Altar.

The Face of the Altar

The true altar is the earth, and the face of the earth altar would be the physical world. Ceremony was quite often held outside in some remote area in an attempt to commune with the holiness of nature, thereby allowing a greater connection to the Ancient Ones.

The Ancient Ones, or Tuatha De Danann, were known to have pulled away from the physical realm and melted into the other realms paralleling this dimension. The doorways into their realm, or Faeryland was found only in the wildest places. Today, the altar can also act as the doorway to Faeryland.

The modern altar has taken on new meaning. Every religion works with some type of altar upon which rests its sacred tools. Altars have become a focal point for meditation, the items adorning the altar representative of Spirit. These items are placed on the altar in an attempt to invoke into our lives the quality they represent or symbolize.

Although the traditional Faery altar was a center flame or hearth-fire, today, in the modern practice of Faery Wicca, a different form of altar has been created and put to use which is similar to most Wiccan, Pagan, and Goddess circle altars. Most commonly, it is a free-standing table with a flat surface made out of wood, but can also be a felled tree-trunk, dresser-top, book shelf, as well as a designated place on the ground.

The Face of the Altar refers to the altar surface upon which is placed various items. The altar face is designed to look at us, conveying the expression produced by the various influences of the items adorning it. Simply put, the Face of the Altar is a mirror upon which we gaze to see the qualities of Spirit we wish to embody.

In Faery Wicca, we have three primary altar faces with which we work: the Five-Fifths, the Mirror, and the Polarity. Each altar face represents a different set of valuable concepts, as further explained below.

The Five-Fifths Altar: This altar face is based on the five provinces of Ireland: Ulster, Leinster, Munster, Connacht, and Meath, the province correspondences as discussed above, as well as the elements of Earth, Air, Fire, Water and Soul, and the corresponding Elemental-Fairy, Gnomes, Sylphs, Salamanders, Undines and Devas.

This altar face is used when working solely with Tuatha De Danann energy, for it is based on their mythology. Thus, it is a Faery altar. However, it is more an altar of the Ancient Ones than of the Elemental Fairy, as might be thought by the usage of such beings.

It is traditional to place the altar either in the Center of the Great Circle, or in the North Province. In the Center, it represents the Fire of Spirit, while placed in the North Province it represents the Journey of the Warrior. To design the face of the Five-Fifths Altar, the following guide-line can be used (Figure 13):

> *North Province:* The formal gateway/doorway through which the warrior enters the Great Circle.
>
> *Item/Symbol Correspondences:* Ulster, warrior spirit, earth, gnome, winter, midnight, regeneration, colors of green and white (green for the color of the earth during the time of The Big Sun; white for the color of the earth during the time of The Little Sun).
>
> *East Province:* Although the North is the quarter of the earth element, it is in the East where the warrior begins to learn her or his connection to the earthly realm, thus entering a formation of partnership with other life-forms of this planet. In this direction the attitude of the warrior spirit is initiated.
>
> *Item/Symbol Correspondences:* Leinster, attitude, air, sylph, dawn, spring, birth, colors of yellow and green (yellow for the mental stimulation required for enlightenment; green for the new growth of earthly partnerships.)
>
> *South Province:* This is the province of emotion, feelings, and passion. This is the quarter in which the warrior spirit begins to understand the balance of life-energies which must include the feminine aspect of nature. This is the realm of goddess and inner power.
>
> *Item/Symbol Correspondences:* Munster, fire, salamanders, mid-day or noon, summer, experience and growth, color of red (red for the blood which contains the passion of Spirit).
>
> *West Province:* In this province the warrior spirit learns to integrate the partnership of knowledge and wisdom, moving into a phase of ego-death which births Eldership. This is the realm of the inner mystery, the womb of life from which all life began and to where all life returns in order to begin again.
>
> *Item/Symbol Correspondences:* Connacht, water, undines, twilight (two-lights) or evening, autumn, decline and death, colors of blue, gray and black (blue for the cooling energies of decline; gray for the time of death; black for the journey into the unknown).

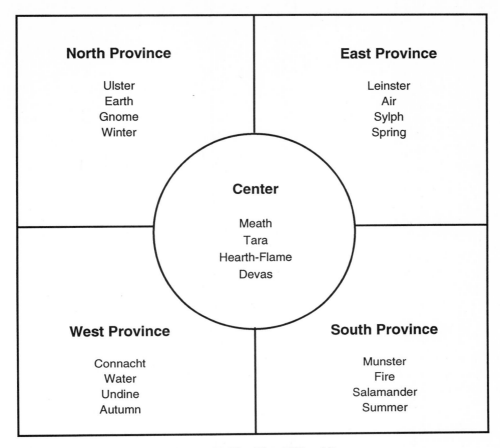

Figure 13: The Five-Fifths Altar

Center: The province of the heart, oneness and balance rests in the Center. The three attributes: justice, victory, and fruitfulness are the keys to perpetually dwell in Tara. The hearth flame, or Fire of Spirit, burns in the Center. The warrior spirit has journeyed successfully through all the provinces, and now, if she or he can pass through the doorway of the unknown without fear, she or he is enabled to find the path of Truth. Upon treading the path of Truth, the warrior spirit, turned into an Elder Spirit, arrives at the heart-center, the fifth province, and is rewarded by being allowed to sit in the throne of the Ancient Ones, and obtain true Spirit-Power.

Item/Symbol Correspondences: Meath, Tara, Faery, the unknown, fire, heart, Devas, Spirit.

The Five-Fifths Altar face is, in essence, a mandala, representing the warrior immram (voyage of apprenticeship). This altar face is used when deeper insight in spiritual evolution for the benefit of all relations is required. Meditating upon the altar of the Ancient Ones opens you to communion with their wisdom. Through such an act of meditation, direction is often provided; their help providing the querist with the powerful medicine of health.

Mirror Altar: The face of the Mirror Altar is laid-out with a horizontal division (Figure 14), representing the term: As Above, So Below. Within each part of the horizontal division, a second division takes place turning the two halves into fourths.

In the center of the altar face, at the borderline between the upper and lower horizontal division, a fifth division is created, bringing the face of the altar into the traditional five-fifths. The first focus of the altar face is in splitting it in half, creating an above and a below.

> *Above:* The Above half of the horizontal division is the realm of the Ancient Ones or Deity, the Heavenly Realm and all its plains (see Figure 3 in Lesson 2). The Above half is next divided into two halves: the top-half represents the Heavenly realm; the second-half represents the place where the Heavenly Realm and the Plains meet.

> *The Top-half of Above:* In this half, which is the Heavenly Realm, place images or symbols of Deity of both a female and male nature. There is no need to worry about which side of the Heavenly Realm you place such images or symbols. Remember, this top-half of the Above represents the Heavenly Realm, not polarities, as we will work with in the Polarity Altar discussed next. Before each image or symbol place a single white candle in an appropriate holder; the flame is lit in honor of the Deity before which the candle is placed. When we work with Deities, it is important for us to understand the full nature or aspect the Deity represents. As discussed in an earlier lesson, such information allows us to attune to the cosmic source more intimately. To the sides of the image or symbol of the Deity place votive offerings: small bundles containing food and other objects the Deity is known to favor. If images of the Deity are not available, the white candle and votive offerings are sufficient representations.

> *The Second-half of Above:* This is the level where the Heavenly Realm meets the Plains. This is the surface of the earth, the realm in which humans dwell. This is the realm that we also look upon as being the Overworld (see Figure 8 in Lesson 5) to the Underworld. Place natural items that are deemed the physical-earthly representation, or incarnation, of the Deity placed in the Heavenly Realm, such as a rose to represent the law of the goddess, a stag horn to represent the fertility of the god, a cauldron for Dagda, a dove for Brigid, etc. However, this is an important point: place the natural object opposite the Deity. For example, if you have an image of Brigid placed on the left-side of the Heavenly Realm, place her dove on the right-side in the Plains. Remember, this altar face mirrors to us. What this means is that where something is in the realm above or below another realm, then that something is mirrored back, reflect-

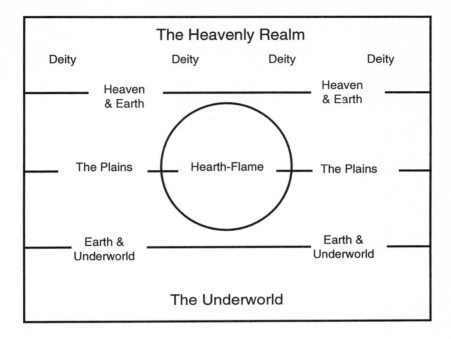

Figure 14: Mirror Altar Face

ing the opposite. What is above, is now below, or what is below is now above. What is left, becomes right, and vice-versa.

Below: The Below-half of the Mirror Altar is the realm of ego death, apprenticeship, the Elemental Fairy, the Ancestors, earth-light, Faery and the Underworld with its various plains. Like the Above-half, the Below-half is also divided in the following way: the lower-half, representing the place where the Plains and Underworld meet; the fourth-half, representing the Underworld and the stars inside the earth.

The First-half of Below: This is the level of the warrior on her or his journey of apprenticeship. It is the place where the Over- and Under-worlds come together (see Figure 8, Lesson 5). In Wiccan, Pagan, and Goddess circles, this is the place we refer to as being in-between the worlds when the Great Circle is cast. This is also the place of the Elemental Fairy, Ancestors, Faery, and other earth-spirits. Contact made with any of these is represented in this realm, and items or symbols that represent such beings are placed here. Also, items or symbols that represent change, release, ego death, and apprentice-ship are included in this realm. These are the items that represent inner consciousness. For example, the Hermit and Death tarot cards work well in this realm, because the former card represents the war-rior's willingness to journey into the unknown, while the latter card represents the warrior's desire to release and transmute energy into a higher vibration. Magickal tools, such as the Silver Branch*, the four Talismans and the cup, are placed in this level, for each represents a different aspect of apprenticeship and the journey into the Underworld. Personal affirmations written out on paper, to transform areas of imbalance, or unhealthiness, can also be placed in the lower-half.

The Second-half of Below: This is the Underworld and the stars inside the earth. This is also the place where the Underworld Deities and Ancient Ones dwell. Items that represent conscious and subconscious awareness, death and rebirth, transformation and regeneration are placed here. Sprouting seedlings, butterflies, and smiles are a few symbols that represent conscious transformation. However, it is better not to place images or symbols of the Underworld Deities and Ancient Ones on the altar; for they are moving deeper and deeper into and through matter, on into another realm of existence. I believe that to continually invoke or strive to represent them will create the doorway and opportunity for actual physical death. Communing with the Underworld Deities and Ancient Ones provides us with valuable tools to help our self-transformation, but unless we are ready to move completely into their realm and leave this physical realm completely behind, they are better left alone. Remember "Spirit deepens," and to follow the Underworld Deity means to continue to move down and away from the realms above.

Center: This is the place of the Fire of Spirit. The hearth-fire candle is placed here and kept burning without interruption (only if it is safe to do so), representing the flame of life or the sacred fire of creation. Also, symbols of the heart can be placed here, for the heart is the center of our personal universe. This lay-out is used when the warrior is working with her and his Spiritual Benefactor[†] for spirit deepening.

The Polarity Altar—On this altar face the division is split down the middle, creating a left and a right side. (Figure 15) This division focuses on polarity—balance. The entire left side represents the negative polarity of life: the feminine nature, goddess, receptive energy, the moon. The entire right side represents the positive polarity of life: the masculine nature, god, transmitting energy, the sun.

A second division occurs within both the left and right sides, creating four smaller parts, with the addition of the fifth being the Center, in the middle on the borderline where the left- and right-sides join. Again, we see the demonstration of the five-fifths.

Left-side: The entire left side represents the Negative Polarity, the feminine nature, and Goddess. This aspect of life contains the negative quality of destruction, regeneration, fertility, and the receptive quality of conception.

---

* See the Magickal Enchantments Section, Magickal Faery Tools lesson.

† Under the Magickal Enchantments Section, in the Working With the Ancients Chapter, direction is provided for contacting personal Spiritual Benefactor.

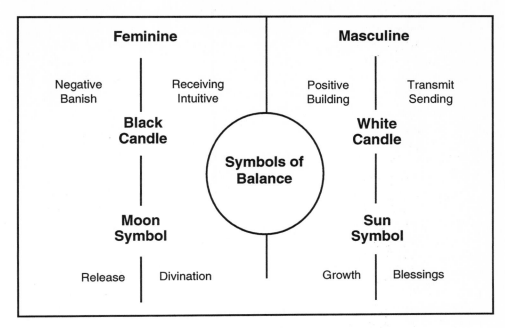

Figure 15: Polarity Altar

In the very middle of the left side, a symbol of the moon and a black candle are placed to represent the lunar realm from which the subconsciousness is birthed into consciousness.

Outer-left: This is the field of the true negative polarity. Into this area are placed those items which represent things that we are releasing from our lives; the banishment of illness, emotional instability, weakness. Since this panel is the farthest area left from our heart-center, we can look upon these things as being on their way out of our lives, in much the same way as the left cards in a tarot spread are read.

Inner-left: This is the field of receptivity. The items that are placed here act as symbols of intuition, fertility, regeneration. Receiver crystals, seeds, and divining tools, such as tarot cards, pendulums, and runes are a few of the items that would be placed here. When someone is working spellcraft which focuses on creativity, whether to conceive a child or to conceive inspiration for an artistic endeavor such as writing, painting, sculpting, etc., those items from the spell would be worked with here.

Right-side: The entire right side represents the positive polarity, the masculine nature, and God. This aspect of life contains the positive quality of construction, growth, activity, and the transmitting quality of animation. In the very middle of the right side a symbol of the sun and a white candle are placed to represent the solar realm in which consciousness is given life and light. Like the left side, the right side also contains two divisions: an inner-right, representing the positive energy; and an outer-right, representing transmitting energy.

Inner-right: This is the field of positive energy used to put into action, to build, expand, and generate growth in all areas of life. In essence, this field represents animation. This field can focus on those areas in life that deal with health, balance and strength. Usually, the items placed in this panel represent the positive results we are envisioning from the negative areas we are releasing, or banishing, from our lives. Therefore, what is being worked with and represented in the outer left panel, the inner right panel shows the opposite, or "positive" outcome desired. For example, if in the outer-left panel we were banishing laziness from our lives (a picture of self sitting in front of the television wasting time), we would place a positive symbol in the inner right panel showing activity (a picture of self walking, running, or standing-up, with a smile). Thus, we see how both sides work in polarity and partnership. What is being released or banished from our life in the outer-left panel, the opposite and positive transformation is being highlighted on the inner-right panel: one is on its way out; the other on its way in.

Outer-right: This field represents transmitting energy. With this energy we send blessings, healings, prayers, best wishes, and spell charms out to the Spirit Realm. Usually, the items placed here correspond with the messages, or inspiration, received from the items focused on in the inner-left panel. Therefore, we would place written requests/blessings/prayers/best wishes, etc. in this panel. If we performed spellcraft for healing, the ashes or other charms from the spellcraft would be placed here in order to manifest them. Likewise, the answers, messages, and inspiration being received from the divination tools are placed on the inner-left side, which have been worked with and put into effect by sending them out on the outer-right side: what is conceived on the inner level is being birthed on the physical level. For example, if during divination the Tyr rune was pulled (meaning: justice, discrimination, victory, faith, strength, spiritual discipline, the spiritual warrior) and placed on the inner-right panel for meditation, a message of inspiration would eventually come through. Let us say that the message received was: It is important to be fair. Perhaps being fair is best symbolized by the balanced scales attached to the Libra sign, or the Justice tarot card; then this symbol would be placed in the outer-right panel with a written affirmation stating: I am fair.

Center: Like the Center of the other two altar faces, the Center of the Polarity Altar also represents the Fire of Spirit, and so, a hearth-flame would also be placed here and kept burning (if not a hazard). The items placed in the center of this altar face would focus on representing the balance of polarities, the partnership between the feminine and masculine natures, Goddess and God, receiving and transmitting energies, and the dance between the moon and sun. The Chinese symbol of Yin and Yang is an ideal symbol to place in this Center.

This altar face is exclusively worked with when the warrior is striving to obtain a personal balance between their lunar and solar nature, or when spellcraft is performed.

There is a fourth altar face that can be used. However, it is an altar face that requires complete understanding and knowledge of its energies, for it is a composite of two of the above altar faces.

In Faery Wicca as a warrior becomes more adept with her or his altar work, the Mirror Altar and the Polarity Altar grids can be combined (Figure 16). This new altar face, consisting of seventeen parts, provides the serious student with a new tool, that of specificity in all areas of study.

As shown in the figure, each compartment becomes an area of intensity. Deities are chosen whose energy or qualities assist the function for the column it heads.

For example, on the left-side of the altar face, the first column becomes a focus on banishing, releasing, and protection. The deity chosen would have the energy, or quality of destruction, such as the Cailleach, who is a crone aspect of goddess. Crone aspects have the ability to destroy that which is no longer of use.

The next square below deals with banishing areas of an unseen nature (remember we are dealing with the plane of Spirit, and here the Heavenly Realm meets the Plains), and so in our life, this is the area of negative attitudes and unhealthy emotions—basically the more destructive qualities of character. This is the square in which affirmations are written to banish those qualities from affecting us.

The third square down would focus on the negative or unhealthy areas effecting physicalness, i.e. an illness, a bad relationship, a material item. Again, we write an affirmation of releasing these physical items from physical space.

The bottom square deals with the Underworld, the realm of the dead, and so this is the realm from which we can invoke protection against negative influences that may come to us arbitrarily. A talisman representing protection could be made and placed in this quarter.

However, I caution against using this altar face unless you have worked with the other two altar faces individually for at least six months to a year.

My new apprentices are encouraged to work with the Mirror Altar for the first six months of their immram. The second six months, they work with the Polarity Altar. In the second year of their immram, the apprentice, now an Initiate, works with the Five-Fifths Altar.

Only when the Initiate has successfully worked through each of the five-fifths, holding the warrior spirit attitude in contemplation, do they combine the Mirror and Polarity Altar grids. A study is given to each of the squares in order to gain an in-depth understanding of the complexity of this altar face before putting it into use; this study usually takes six months.

However, whichever altar face you work with, it is important to keep the altar face simple. In doing so, a better focus can be achieved on those areas of life that truly need transforming and healing.

Just as altars are mobile, so is Temporary and Personal Sacred Space. They can go with us anywhere. As already discussed, Temporary Sacred Space is used to define the casting of the Great Circle for ceremony, magickal spellcraft, and healing rituals. Personal Sacred Space is within us, and can be entered at anytime, any place, without the usage of the casting of the Great Circle when shielding, or protection is required, as well as when meditation and shamanic journeys are endeavored.

Personal Sacred Space is the body Temple, the physical shell in which our spirit and soul is housed. In Faery Wicca, the use of Personal Sacred Space is vitally important, especially when we journey into the Otherworlds. In the chapter on Ceremony And Ritual, under the Magickal Enchantments Section, a guided visualization will be provided to connect with Personal Sacred Space.

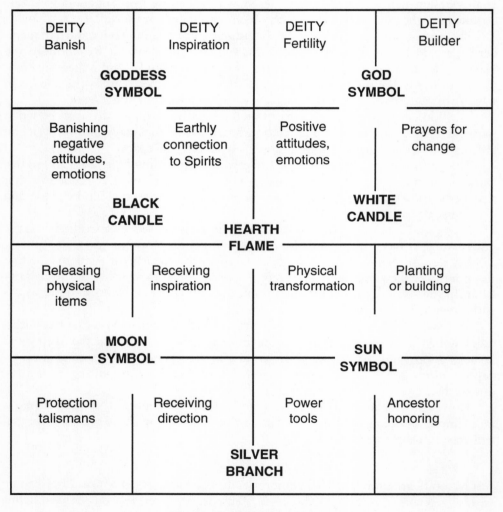

Figure 16: Combined Altars

Journal Exercises

1. Take time to contemplate the meaning of the Great Circle, what it represents to you, how it can contain sacred space, and journal your thoughts.

2. If your body is the Temple of your personal sacred space, how would you want to take care of such a Temple? List the ways in which you are harming your Temple. List the ways in which you can balance your Temple.

Suggested Reading

Sacred Sites, Frank Joseph (ed)
The Earth Spirit, John Michell
Sister Moon Lodge, Kisma K. Stepanich

n the cool of the evening they used to gather
'Neath stars in the meadow circled near an old oak tree
At the times appointed by the seasons of the Earth
And the phases of the Moon
In the center often stood a woman, equal with the others
And respected for her worth
One of the many we call the Witches,
the Healers and the Teachers of the wisdom of the Earth

The people grew through the knowledge she gave them
Herbs to heal their bodies
Spells to make their Spirits whole
Hear them chanting healing incantations
Calling forth the Wise Ones
Celebrating in dance and song
Isis, Astarte, Diana, Hecate, Demeter, Kali, Inanna*

Now the Earth is a Witch and the men still burn her
Stripping her down with mining and the poisons
of their wars
But to us the Earth is a healer, a teacher, our mother
The weaver of the web of life that keeps us all alive
She gives us the vision to see through the chaos
She gives us the courage, it is our WILL to survive.
Isis, Astarte, Diana, Hecate, Demeter, Kali, Inanna.

— excerpt from *The Burning Times*
Charlie Murphy
*Goddess Chant
Deena Metzger

Lesson 7

Modern Faery Wicca

No Faery shall wile them, No seed of Faery Host shall life them. No Sea-sword shall pierce them, Between sole and throat, Between eye and hair. No flood shall drown them, No brine shall drown them, No water shall drown them, Now and forever, Come forth! *

T he dealings with what we know as Wicca or Witchcraft were really very few in Ireland compared to the scourge that flashed through England, or the Continent. One of the reasons for this is because the practices of pishogue (spellcraft) in the Faery-Faith was far removed from those found in the spellcraft of other countries.

The Irish had their own superstitious beliefs and did believe in the cunning woman and cunning man, or witches; however, they did not involve themselves with sorcery, nor believe in the Devil and his cult known as Satanism[†].

In England and Scotland during the mediaeval and later periods of their history, Witchcraft became an offense against the laws of the Catholic Church, God, and man. However, in Celtic Ireland, dealings with the unseen were not originally regarded with such abhorrence, and had the auspices of custom and antiquity.

The Witch Trials of Ireland

Ireland has always remained aloof from the surrounding countries, lying far away on the verge of ocean, remote from those influences which so profoundly affected

---

* Oral traditional saying of the Protection of the Faery onto those who keep the Faery-Faith alive.

† Satanism is, however, a by-product of the Roman Catholic Church, and was never found in any ancient earth tradition. There, it is safe to say that Satanists are the rebels of the Roman Catholic Church.

popular thought in other countries. The scourge that hit Ireland and Scotland was a result of the Protestants and the Roman Catholic Church. The cunning women and men were stigmatized as heretics and associates of the church's evil god, Satan, who held no role in the Faery-Faith of Ireland and so, therefore, was never accepted into the tradition.

However, the Protestants who dwelled in Ireland soon acted similarly to the Roman Catholic Church because of the Holy Writ which contained the grim command:

Thou shalt not suffer a witch to live.

In England from the sixteenth century, an enormous literary output relative to Witchcraft took place, the majority of the works being in support of the belief. While in Ireland, on the other hand, with the exception of only one pamphlet of 1699, which may or may not have been locally printed, there is not the slightest trace of any Witchcraft literature being published in the country until the opening years of the nineteenth century.

In 1324, the first case of Witchcraft was reported in Ireland; Dame Alice Kyteler, known as the Sorceress of Kilkenny, was the subject. She had been married four times, first to William Outlawe of Kilkenny, a banker; secondly, to Adam le Blund of Callan; thirdly, to Richard de Valle—all of whom she was supposed to have got rid of by poison—and the fourth, to Sir John le Poer, of whom it was said she "deprived of his natural senses by philters and incantations."*

Her covey (coven) confederates were arrested and sent to prison. Their names: Robert of Bristol, a clerk, John Galrussyn, Ellen Galrussyn, Syssok Galrussyn, William Payn de Boly, Petronilla of Meath, her daughter, Basilia, Alice, the wife of Henry Faber, Annota Lange, and Eva de Brownestown. Of the confederates, Petronilla was condemned to death after she was flogged six times, and under the repeated application of this form of torture made the required confession of magical practices. She admitted the denial of her faith and the sacrificing to Robert, son of Art, and as well that she had caused certain women of her acquaintance to appear as if they had goats horns.

Petronilla's execution sentence was to be burnt alive in Kilkenny on November 3, 1324, which fell on a Sunday. This was the first instance of the punishment of death by fire being inflicted in Ireland for heresy. Although Petronilla is the only solitary name mentioned, the following was recorded in *"Narratives of Witchcraft and Sorcery" in Transaction of the Ossory Archaeologoical Society, vol. i:*

> With regard to the other heretics and sorcerers who belonged to the pestilential society of Robin, son of Art, the order of law being preserved, some of them were publicly burnt to death; others, confessing their crimes in the presence of all the people, in an upper garment, are marked back and front with a cross after they had abjured their heresy, as is the custom; others were solemnly whipped through the town and the marketplace; others were banished from the city and diocese; others who evaded the jurisdiction of the Church were excommuni-

*Seymour, St. John. *Irish Witchcraft and Demonology*, Causeway Books, New York, 1973

*cated; while others again fled in fear and were never heard of
after. And thus, by the authority of Holy Mother Church, and
by the special grace of God, that most foul brood was scattered and destroyed.*

In 1327, Adam Dubh, of the Leinster tribe of O'Toole, was burnt alive on Col-
lege Green for denying the doctrines of the Incarnation and the Holy Trinity, as well
as for rejecting the authority of the Holy.

Again, in 1353, two men were tried at Bunratty in County Clare for holding
heretical opinions, and were sentenced to be burnt. Thus, we find in Ireland a ripple
of the wave that swept over Europe at this period.

For another 100 years nothing is recorded, while the second half of the sixteenth
century furnishes us with two cases, and a suggestion of several others.

The following entry in the table of the *Red Council Book of Ireland*, in the year
1544, briefly mentions the possibility of another witch trial, without the addition of
further mention: "A letter to Charles Fitzarthur for sending a witch to the Lord
Deputie to be examined."

The next notice of Witchcraft in Ireland occurs in the year 1578, when a witch-
trial took place at Kilkenny, though again, unfortunately, no details have been preserved. In November of the same year, sessions were held there by the Lord Justice
Drury and Sir Henry Fitton, who in their letter to the Privy Council on the twentieth
of the same month, "inform that Body that upon arriving at the town:

> [T]he jail being full we caused sessions immediately to be held.
> Thirty-six persons were executed, amongst whom were some
> good ones, a blackamoor and two witches by natural law, for
> that we find no law to try them by in this realm.

The blackamoor was a black man, who then was uncommon in Ireland. He may
have been a confederate of the two witches, as it was mentioned he was a negromancy.
The modern word *necromancy* was originally spelled, by old writers, as nigromancy,
meaning that divination was practiced through the medium of negroes instead of
dead persons as we are lead to believe*.

The natural law mentioned above was to soon change. Two statutes against
Witchcraft had already been passed in England, one in 1541, which was repealed six
years later, and a second in 1562. In 1586 the Irish Parliament passed its first
Statute—the principal points of it may be gathered from the following extract:

> *Where at this present there is no ordinarie ne condigne pun-
> ishment provided against the practices of the wicked offences
> of conjurations, and of invocations of evill spirites, and of sor-
> ceries, enchauntments, charms, and witchcrafts, whereby
> mainie fantasticall and devilish persons have devised and prac-
> ticed invocations and conjurations of evill and wicked spirites,
> and have used and practiced witchcrafts, enchauntments,*

---

* In an old vocabulary of 1475, "Nigromantia" is defined: *divinatio facta per nigros.*

charms, and sorceries, to the destruction of the persons and goods of their neighbours, and other subjects of this realm, and for other lewde and evill intents and purposes, contrary to the laws of Almighty God, to the peril of their owne soules, and to the great infamie and disquietnesse of this realm. For reformation thereof, be it enacted by the Queen's Majestie, with the assent of the lords spirituall and temporall and the commons in this present Parliament assembled.

1. That if any person or persons after the end of three months next, and immediately after the end of the last session of this present parliament, shall use, practise, or exercise any witchcraft, enchauntment, charme, or sorcery, whereby any person shall happen to be killed or destroied, that then as well any such offender or offenders in invocations and conjurations, as is aforesaid, their aydors or councelors being of the said offences lawfully convicted and attainted, shall suffer paines of death as a felon or felons, and shall lose the privilege and benefit of clergie and sanctuarie; saving to the widow of such person her title of dower, and also the heires and successors of such a person all rights, titles, etc., as though no such attaynder had been made.

2. If any persons (after the above period) shall use, practise, or exercise any witchcraft, enchauntment, charme, or sorcery, whereby any person or persons shall happen to be wasted, consumed, or lamed, in his or their bodie or member, or whereby any goods or cattels of any such person shall be destroyed, wasted, or impaired, then every such offender shall for the first offense suffer imprisonment by the space of one yeare without bayle or maineprise, and once in every quarter of the said yeare, shall in some market towne, upon the market day, or at such time as any faire shall be kept there, stand openlie in the pillorie for the space of sixe houres, and shall there openly confesse his or theire errour and offense, and for the second offense shall suffer death as a felon, saving, etc. [as in clause 1].

3. Provided always, that if the offender in any of the cases aforesaid, for which the paines of death shall ensue, shall happen to be a peer of this realm: then his triall therein to be had by his peers, as is used in cases of felony and treason, and not otherwise.

4. And further, to the intent that all manner of practice, use, or exercise of witchcraft, enchauntment, charme, or sorcery, should be from henceforth utterly avoide, abolished, and taken away; be it enacted by the authority of this present Parliament that if any person or person... shall take upon them by witchcraft, etc., to tell or declare in what place any treasure of gold

or silver shall or might be found or had in the earth or other secret places, or where goods or things lost or stollen should be found or become, or shall use or practice any sorcery, etc., to the intent to provoke any person to unlawful love [for the first offense to be punished as in clause 2], but if convicted a second time shall forfeit unto the Queen's Majesty all his goods and chattels, and suffer imprisonment during life.

Considering what was taking place in England and Scotland, this Statute was exceedingly mild. It made no provision whatsoever for the use of torture to extract evidence, nor did it offer any particular encouragement to the witch hunter, while the manner of inflicting the death penalty was precisely that for felony, viz. hanging, drawing and quartering for men, and burning (preceded by strangulation) for women, all of which was sufficiently appalling, but far more merciful than burning alive at the stake.

Ireland was a blessed country, indeed, to have escaped the notice of the most horrendous witch hunter, King James I of England and VI of Scotland, 1566-1625; otherwise, the country would have unfortunately contributed its share to the list of victims in that monarch's reign. Also, in Ireland the various methods of applying the question extraordinary to victims preceding their trials in the attempt to extract from them their confessions was mostly void of repetition of torture, but the infamous Inquisitor, James Sprenger, imagined a subtle distinction by which each fresh application was a continuation and not a repetition of the first; it is recorded that one sorceress in Germany suffered this continuation no less than fifty-six times.

The hellish approach taken by inquisitors toward the accused can only be described as the appalling work of demons, rather than supposed men of God; highlighting the more charitable work of that of the cunning women and men who helped heal the sick and assist the birthing of life.

Although how the accused witches of Ireland were put to death before the subsequent passing of the Act of 1586 is not recorded, one can only assume the method of execution would have been that for felony. On the Continent the stake was in continual request.

In 1514, three hundred persons were burnt alive for this crime at Como. Between 1615 and 1635, more than six thousand sorcerers were burnt in the diocese of Strasburg, while, according to Bartholomew de Spina, in Lombardy a thousand sorcerers a year were put to death "for the space of twenty-five years."*

The total number of persons executed in various ways for this crime has, according to the *Encyclopaedia Britannica,* been variously estimated at from one hundred thousand to several million.

During this scourge that flared across the country, in the persecution of those who practiced magickal arts, no rank or class in society was spared; the noble equally with the peasant was liable to torture and death. This was especially true of the earlier stages of the movement when sorcery rather than witchcraft was the crime committed. The difference between the two was distinct: sorcery was more of an aristocratic pursuit, while anybody might become a victim of the witch epidemic.

---

* Francais, *L'Eglise Et La Sorcellerie.*

Noblemen, scholars, monks, nuns, titled ladies, bishops, clergy, common folk, none were immune from accusation and condemnation.

Another Act of the Parliament of Ireland passed in 1634 and designed to facilitate the administration of justice, makes mention of Witchcraft, and it is there held to be one of the recognized methods by which one human could take the life of another.

> *Forasmuch as the most necessary office and duty of law is to preserve and save the life of man, and condignly to punish such persons that unlawfully or wilfully murder, slay, or destroy men ... and where it often happeneth that a man is feloniously strucken in one county, and dieth in another county, in which case it hath not been found by the laws of this realm that any sufficient indictment thereof can be taken in any of the said two counties... For redress and punishment of such offences ... be it enacted ... that where any person shall be traiterously or feloniously stricken, poysoned, or bewitched in one county (and die in another, or out of the kingdom, etc.), that an indictment thereof found by jurors in the county where the death shall happen, shall be as good and effectual in the law as if, etc. etc.*

Between the years of 1606 and 1656, miscellaneous accounts of Witchcraft in Ireland are reported. A clergyman was tried in 1606 for the practice of "unhallowed arts." However, he was sent to England for the trials, and his ultimate fate is unknown. In 1609, a strange story of magickal spells being counteracted by the application of a holy relic was recorded in the County of Tipperary, and in 1613, a John Stewart was apprehended as the accomplice of a Scottish witch named Margaret Barclay. A Rev. Robert Blair, M.A., was excommunicated in November, 1634 because of his "impression of spirits," and in a letter dated 13 August 1640, the Lord of Castleconnell's Castle four miles from Limerick was reported as being a sorcerer. In all the above, however, no death sentences are reported.

The most famous Witchcraft Trial of Ireland is reported in 1661. The woman accused was Florence Newton at Youghal. She was committed to Youghal prison by the Mayor of the town 24 March 1661, for bewitching a girl named Mary Longdon. The Mayor had contemplated using the water experiment* on Florence, but did not actually go through with such a horrendous form of torture. Two other women were suspected during the above trial, a Goody Halfpenny and Goody Dod, but neither were punished.

Florence Newton, however, was tortured in several ways. According to *Witchcraft Further Displayed*, written by Francis Bragge in 1712, the accuser's "water" (urine) was boiled and then "dropped on the witch," awls were put into both of the "witch's hands" to see if she would bleed, and there is mention of her having the

---

* For those unfamiliar with this form of torture, the water experiment was based on taking the right thumb of the suspected witch and tying it to her left great toe, and vice versa. She is then thrown into the water: if she sinks (and drowns, by any chance) her innocence is conclusively established; if on the other hand, she floats, her witchcraft is proven, "for water, as being the element of baptism, refuses to receive such a sinner in its bosom."

"test of the tile," but unfortunately no description of this method of torture is to be found.

Although no records provide formal entry of sentencing, it was recorded that the Attorney-General went down to Youghal to prosecute, and there can be little doubt that Florence Newton was probably found guilty, and if so would have been sentenced to death in pursuance of the Elizabethan Statute, Section 1.

There are only a few other mentions of Witches in seventeenth century Ireland following the Florence Newton trials. A Margaret Matthews was the wife of an accused man described by Bragge as "a man of considerable talents and legal knowledge, but of a violent overbearing temper and a litigous disposition." He was sent to prison for being a sorcerer. His wife, Maragret, was taken into custody and refused to claim guilt, and although not sentenced, died about a month latter (November 1, 1685) of the "injuries she had received at their violent hands."

A case of supposed witchcraft occurred in Cork in 1685-6, the account of which is contained in a letter from Christopher Crofts to Sir John Perceval (the third Baronet, and father of the first Earl of Egmont). The "bewitched" was the man's son, Jack. The accused was an old woman, the mother of Nell Welsh, who was reputed a bad woman. The woman was committed to Bridewell, and no further record given of a sentencing.

The next reporting of a Witch trial was recorded in a 1699 pamphlet, *The Bewitching Of A Child In Ireland*. According to the pamphlet, in 1698 a beautiful girl of nine was bewitched, and the accused woman was apprehended, condemned, strangled, and burnt.

Finally, the last instance of Witches being tried and convicted in Ireland as offenders against the laws of the realm, took place on the Island Magee, near Carrigfergus, in the County of Antrim, and Province of Ulster in 1710-11.

The case began as a haunting of Mrs. Anne Haltridge, widow of the Rev. John Haltridge, began experiencing in her room by a black-haired youth. The haunting continued for two years until her death on February 22, 1711. The case had been fully reported and involved one Presbyterian minister, Robert Sinclair, and two of his Elders, John Man and Reynold Leaths, who spent "many a day with the distressed family in prayer."

After the death of Mrs. Haltridge, a girl of eighteen years of age, Miss Mary Dunbar, who had come to stay with Mrs. Haltridge, junior, to keep her company after her mother-in-law's death, received the same haunting the elder Mrs. Haltridge had. She went into a fit, and upon recovering, cried out that a knife had been run through her thigh by three women she was able to describe.

About midnight she was seized by a second fit. She received a vision of seven or eight women who conversed together, and in their conversation called each other by their names. When she came out of her fit she gave their names as Janet Liston, Elizabeth Cellor, Kate M'Calmont, Janet Carson, Janet Mean, Latimer, and one whom was termed Mrs. Ann. She also gave a description of each.

The women from the district who matched the descriptions were sent for. Between March 3 and 24, depositions were sworn to by several people, and the Mayor of Carrigfergus issued a warrant for the arrest of all suspected persons. Seven women were arrested; their names: Janet Mean, of Braid Island; Jane Latimer, of Irish quarter, Carrigfergus; Margaret Mitchell, of Kilroot; Catherine M'Calmont of

Island Magee; Janet Liston, alias Sellar, of Island Magee; Elizabeth Sellar, of Island Magee; and, Janet Carson, of Island Magee.

The accused were brought up for trial at Carrigfergus before Judges Upton and Macartney on 31 March 1711. They all denied the charge of Witchcraft, and the one woman who was the "ugliest and who was the greatest suspected," called god to witness that she was wronged. The jury found all guilty, and in accordance with the Statute, the prisoners were sentenced to a year's imprisonment, and to stand in the pillory four times during that period. Thus ended the last recorded trial for Witchcraft in Ireland.

Significantly, all Witch trials stopped in all countries within a decade of each other. The last in England was 1712, and in Scotland in 1722. But even as late as the summer of 1911 the word *witch* was heard in an Irish law-court, when an unhappy poor woman was tried for killing another, an old-age pensioner, in a fit of insanity (*Irish Times* for 14th June; *Independent* for 1st July).

In fact, the insidious accusations of Witchcraft against women, and some men, continued to dot the court records. In modern times, the shame of such an hysterical period of our civilization is truly mentioned with a honeyed tongue.

However, a very important note in regards to the horror of the legal systems and unlawfulness of the ancient shamanic religion of the European cunning women and men must be acknowledged: although the Statutes against Witchcraft in England and Scotland were repealed, it is said that that passed by the Irish Parliament was not similarly treated, and is consequently and theoretically still in force.

Therefore, Witchcraft is still officially recognized in Ireland, today, as an offense against the law.

Irish Witchcraft Comes to America

Unfortunately, the horrible witch persecutions of Salem, Massachusetts, in the United States of America, may very well have been attributed to an Irish-American witch in 1688. The story is of interest as showing that at this time there were some Irish-speaking people in Boston, Massachusetts. Shortly after the date of its colonization, the State of Massachusetts became remarkable for its cases of Witchcraft; several persons were tried, and some were hanged for this crime.

The case in point was reported by Cotton Mather. He first gave an account of it in his *Memorable Providences Relating To Witchcraft*, published at Boston in 1689, the year after its occurrence, and subsequently reproduced it in his better-known *Magnalia Christi*, published at London in 1702. Here is the story as recorded in Memorable Providences:

> *Four children of John Goodwin in Boston which had enjoyed*
> *a Religious Education, and answere'd it with a towardly Inge-*
> *nuity; Children indeed of an exemplary Temper and Carriage,*

and an Example to all about them for Piety, Honesty, and Industry. These were in the year 1688 arrested by a stupendous Witchcraft.

The Eldest of the children, a Daughter of about Thirteen years old, saw fit to examine their Laundress, the Daughter of a Scandalous Irish Woman in the Neighbourhood, whose name was Glover (whose miserable husband before he died had sometimes complained of her, that she was undoubtedly a witch, and that wherever his head was laid, she would quickly arrive unto the punishments due to such a one), about some Linnen that was missing, and the Woman bestowing very bad language on the Child, in the Daughter's Defence, the Child was immediately taken with odd Fits, that carried in them something Diabolical.

It was not long before one of her Sisters, with two of her Brothers, were horribly taken with the like Fits, which the most Experienc'd Physicians (particularly our worthy and prudent friend Dr. Thomas Oakes) pronounced Extraordinary and preternatural; and one thing the more confirmed them in this Opinion was, that all the Children were tormented still just the same part of their Bodies, at the same time, though their Pains flew like swift lightning from one part to another, and they were kept so far asunder that they neither saw nor heard each other's Complaints.

At nine or ten a-clock at Night they still had a Release from their miseries, and slept all Night pretty comfortably. But when the Day came they were most miserably handled. Sometimes they were Deaf, sometimes Dumb, and sometimes Blind, and often all this at once. Their tongues would be drawn down their throats, and then pull'd out upon their Chins, to a prodigious Length. Their Mouths were forc'd open to such a Wideness, that their Jaws were out of Joint; and anon clap together again, with a Force like a Spring-lock: and the like would happen to their Shoulder-blades, their Elbows and Hand-wrists, and several of their Joints ... Their Necks would be broken, so that their Neck-bone would seem dissolv'd unto them that felt after it, and yet on the sudden it would become again so stiff, that there was no stirring of their Heads; yea, their Heads would be twisted almost round. And if the main Force of their Friends at any time obstructed a dangerous Motion which they seemed upon, they would roar exceedingly.

But the Magistrates being awakened by the Noise of these Grievous and Horrid Occurrences, examin'd the Person who was under the suspicion of having employ'd these Troublesome Daemons, and she gave a Wretched Account of herself that she was committed unto the Gaoler's Custody.

(Goodwin had no proof that could have done her any hurt; but the hag had not the power to deny her interest in the enchantment of the children; and when she was asked, Whether she believed there was a God? her answer was too blasphemous and horrible for any pen of mine to mention. Upon the commitment of this extraordinary woman all the children had some present ease, until one related to her, accidentally meeting one or two of them, entertain'd them with her blessing, that is railing, upon which three of them fell ill again.)

It was not long before this Woman was brought upon her Trial; but then (thro' the efficacy of a charm, I suppose, used upon her by one or some of her crue) the Court could have no Answers from her but in the Irish, which was her Native Language, although she understood English very well, and had accustom'd her whole Family to none but English in her former Conversation.

(It was long before she could with any direct answers plead unto her Indictment, and when she did plead) it was with owning and bragging rather than denial of her Guilt.)

And the Interpreters, by whom the Communication between the Bench and the Barr was managed, were made sensible that a Spell had been laid by another witch on this, to prevent her telling Tales, by confining her to a language which 'twas hoped nobody would understand. The Woman's House being searched, several Images, or Poppets, or Babies, made of Raggs and stuffed with Goat's Hair, were found; when these were produced the vile Woman confess'd, that her way to torment the Objects of her Malice was by wetting of her Finger with her Spittle, and stroaking of these little Images.

The abus'd Children were then produced in Court, and the Woman still kept stooping and shrinking, as one that was almost prest to death with a mighty Weight upon her. But one of the Images being brought to her, she odly and swiftly started up, and snatch'd it into her Hand. But she had no sooner snatch'd it than one of the Children fell into sad Fits before the whole Assembly.

The Judges had their just Apprehensions at this, and carefully causing a repetition of the Experiment, they still found the same Event of it, tho' the Children saw not when the Hand of the witch was laid upon the Images.

They ask'd her, Whether she had any to stand by her? She reply'd, She had; and looking very fixtly into the air, she added, No, he's gone! and then acknowledged she had One, who was her Prince, with whom she mention'd I know not what Communion. For which cause the Night after she was heard expostulating with a Devil for his thus deserting her, telling him, that because she had served her so basely and falsely she had confessed all.

However to make all clear the Court appointed five or six Physicians to examine her very strictly, whether she were no way craz'd in her Intellectuals.

Divers Hours did they spend with her, and in all that while no Discourse came from her but what was agreeable; particularly when they ask'd her what she thought would become of her Soul, she reply'd, You ask me a very solemn Question, and I cannot tell what to say to it.

She profest herself a Roman Catholick, and could recite her Paternoster in Latin very readily, but there was one Clause or two always too hard for her, whereof she said, She could not repeat it, if she might have all the world. In the Upshot the Doctors returned her Compos Mentis, and Sentence of Death was past upon her.

Divers Days past between her being arraign'd and condemn'd; and in this time one Hughes testify'd, that her Neighbour (called Howen), who was cruelly bewitch'd unto Death about six years before, laid her Death to the charge of this Woman (she had seen Glover sometimes come down her chimney), and bid her, the said Hughes, to remember this; for within six years there would be occasion to mention it.

(This Hughes now preparing her testimony, immediately one of her children, a fine boy well grown towards youth) was presently taken ill in the same woful manner that Goodwin's were; and particularly the Boy in the Night cry'd out, that a Black Person with a Blue Cap in the Room tortur'd him, and that they try'd with their Hand in the Bed for to pull out his Bowels.

The Mother of the Boy went unto Glover on the day following, and asked her, Why she tortured her poor Lad at such a rate? Glover answered, Because of the Wrong she had receiv'd from her; and boasted That she had come at him as a Black Person with a Blue Cap, and with her Hand in the Bed would have pulled his Bowels out, but could not.

Hughes denied that she had wronged her; and Glover then desiring to see the Boy, wished him well; upon which he had no more of his Indisposition.

After the Condemnation of the Woman, I did my self give divers Visits to her, wherein she told me, that she did use to be at Meetings, where her Prince with Four more were present. She told me who the Four were, and plainly said, That her Prince was the Devil. (She entertained me with nothing but Irish, which language I had not learning enough to understand without an interpreter.)

When I told her that, and how her Prince had deserted her, she reply'd (I think in English, and with passion too), If it be so, I am sorry for that. And when she declined answering some things that I ask'd her, she told me, She could give me a full answer, but her Spirits would not give her leave: nor could she consent, she said, without this leave that I should pray for her. (However against her will I pray'd with her, which if it were a fault it was in excess of pity. When I had done she thanked me with many good words, but I was no sooner out of her sight than she took a stone, a long and slender stone, and with her finger and spittle fell to tormenting it; though whom or what she meant I had the mercy never to understand.) At her Execution she said the afflicted Children should not be relieved by her Death, for others besides she had a hand in their Affliction.

Mrs. Glover was hanged. Three years after the Boston incident a similar outbreak occurred amongst the children in the house of the Rev. Samuel Parris at Salem, a small village about nineteen miles northeast of Boston.

Numerous persons were brought to trial, and in only sixteen months, twenty-five were hanged, approximately 150 were put in prison, and more than 200 accused of Witchcraft.

In April 1693, the Government finally put a stop to the trials and the remaining accused were released from prison. Although Mr. Parris is acknowledged as being the "Beginner and Procurer of the sorest Afflictions," Mrs. Glover may be considered the first cause, for had the case of the Goodwin's children not occurred at Boston, it is probable that the Salem trials would never have occurred.

The historical accounts above are the sad stories of how the shamanic practices of Northern European women were abolished. It is no wonder that today American women with European heritages feel very lost and fragmented. As modern women living in Western Civilization, we recognize our missing roots; this applies also to American men with European heritages.

There are no teachers who can hand-pick those from the crowds who have the natural cunning abilities, take the chosen under their aegis to nurture and train in the Craft, in the Ways of the Wicca (Wise).

Today, all mention of our indigenous roots are tainted with rumors of evil and Devil-worship, just as any ancient tradition of a non-Christian nature has been labeled.

Author and Scottish Initiate Raymond Buckland reminds us that "With the coming of Christianity there was not the immediate mass-conversion that is often suggested. Christianity was a man-made religion. It had not evolved gradually and naturally over thousands of years, as we have seen that the Old Religion did. Whole countries were classed as Christian when in actuality it was only the rulers who had adopted the new religion, and often only superficially at that. Throughout Europe generally, the Old Religion, in its many and varied forms, was still prominent for the first thousand years of Christianity."[20] And, in all reality, still is through our modern practice of Wicca.

---

20 Raymond Buckland, *Buckland's Complete Book of Witchcraft*, Llewellyn Publications, 1986.

As important as it is for women and men of color to reach back to their roots and ground in them, so it is just as important for the white woman and man to unshamefully reach back into theirs.

All of us, all women and men of any color, have been stripped clean from our true origin. Today, we are coming back full circle, to breath awake the inner fire of our cell memories and awaken into our powerful pasts.

Taking hold of this hidden past, we birth it into our modern living, finding a new avenue of expression. We are being creative with our expressions, for we have no standard system of basic laws or codes by which to follow, except one: The Wiccan Rede:

An it harme none,
do what ye will,
for the goodwill of all.

With only a collection of fragmented pieces of the basic laws and codes of our lost traditions, we have had to create new traditions based on what we know of the old ones.

We can truly attribute the resurgence of Witchcraft to the literary efforts of Dr. Margaret Alice Murray in 1921, when she produced *The Witch Cult In Western Europe*, and ten years later, *The God of the Witches* (1931).

This brings us to the modern grandfather of Witchcraft: Dr. Gerald Brousseau Gardner. In 1954, Gardner's book *Witchcraft Today* was published, and in it he confirmed that the Old Religion was, indeed, very much alive. And through his efforts, the oral tradition that had existed for perhaps twenty to thirty thousand years, was written down and made available to any who sought after the Ways of the Wicca.

From Murray to Gardner to Aleister Crowley, Doreen Valiente and Janet and Stewart Farrar, modern Witchcraft was birthed, and to America it came by way of the Scottish Initiate, Raymond Buckland, who had been initiated by Gardner's High Priestess. Soon to follow were Sybil Leek, Gavin and Yvonne Frost and other individuals.

Today, there is a wide selection of traditions to choose from: Gardnerian, Celtic, Saxon, Alexandrian, Irish Faery-Faith, Scottish, Sicilian, etc. It is not surprising that there are so many forms of the Craft in which to practice the Old Religion, for just as there are many different types of people, each person has a different heart-beat; although similar, we must find the rhythm that resonates with our heart. When we find it, we breath deep into our bellies, gather our traditions and proudly display them to the world.

Different Branches of Wicca

Wicca is a religion based on love and pleasure, tuned to the cycles of nature and the rhythms of the universe. It is a religion of polarity (goddess and god) and balance. Within our rituals are found music, dance, song, and laughter—lots of laughter, for Wicca is a life-oriented religion.

The following list of branches, although similar, represent slight differences in the tradition. Regardless of which branch of Wicca one is drawn to, it is important to know that there exists today a set of Principles of Wiccan Belief (Appendix E), which I would encourage anyone to read and understand no matter which branch of Wicca one practices.

Before we look at the branches, which I have listed alphabetically, a word about the usage of the term *Wicca* in place of the term *Witchcraft* might be needed. Technically, they both mean the same thing, but because of the negative connotations the word *witch* has created in the mind-set of the mass population, witches have found that reclaiming the word has been quite a challenging fete. The next step in claiming the term *witch* is the words origin, which—consensus agrees—is Wicca.

The term *Wicca* truly has a softer vibration surrounding it, and when used, rather than provoking fear to the uninformed, usually generates curiosity. However, whether one chooses to call it Witchcraft, Wicca, Old Religion, or simply the Craft, it is one and the same.

Alexandrian Wicca—English; founder: Alex Sanders. Rituals, although basically Gardnerian, are modified with many Judeo-Christian and Ceremonial Magick elements. Covens work skyclad (naked). The eight Sabbats are observed. Goddess and God observed.

Celtic Wicca—This is a difficult branch to define, because the term *Celtic* basically covers about eight countries, and often combines the mythological traditions found in those countries. However, for the most part, Celtic Wicca in America is centered around the English and Welsh traditions, combining two systems of magick: druidism, and the more modern aspect of Witchcraft as introduced by Gerald B. Gardner.

However, Doreen Valiente has also had great influence in Celtic Wicca in terms of her published material on natural-magick (which is based on the cycles of earth, moon and sun).

The primary mythological lore used is that of the Matter of Britain and the High King, Arthur, who became the fairy people in the sixth century, and their offspring the Medieval fairy, who became variable in size and both tiny and rustic as well as hideous and monstrous.

Often, Ceremonial Magic is blended into Celtic Wicca. Ceremonial Magic is a form of high magick that was developed by Occultists in the late 1800s and early 1900s. Eliphas Levi, S. L. MacGregor Mathers, Dr. W. Wynn Westcott, Dion Fortune, A. E. Waite, Aleister Crowley, Paul Foster Case, and Israel Regardie are among the names connected with the many groups founded within this branch, and who founded such groups as the Hermetic Order of the Golden Dawn, Qabalists, Freemasons, Theosophists and Rosicrucians, Enochian; all generally referred to as the Western Mystery Tradition. Ritual is very formal, the magical system blends Pagan esoteric teachings with the Judeo-Christian Qabalah-Archangel systems. There is a degree of hierarchy found within their priesthoods. They work within Temples, using excessive magickal paraphernalia.

Circle Wicca—American; founders: Selena Fox and Jim Alan, 1974. Circle Sanctuary is a 200-acre Nature preserve in Wisconsin. Circle differs from many traditional Wicca in that it is more aligned with Shamanism and the American Indian Ways than it is with European Wicca.

Dianic Wicca—Although this is an older tradition of Italy, in America it has become synonymous with lesbian separatists' groups. In its original sense, it was a tradition that included both female and male practitioners, and worked with the Triple Moon Goddess and the Horned God. Rituals took place outdoors, usually in oak groves.

Faery Wicca—Irish; founders: Tuatha De Danann. Although there is no exact date of origin, it is one of the lasting folk-traditions found in Wicca, and because of this has been one aspect of Wicca that has—up until current times—been taught orally. Because of this, self-initiation is discouraged.

Janet and Stewart Farrar, located in Ireland, are modern practitioners of this form of Celtic Wicca, as am I, located in America, and R. J. Stewart, located in England. This book is based on the metaphysical theory and magickal enchantments practiced in the tradition of Faery Wicca.*

Druidism is often linked to Faery Wicca. However, it is an entirely different system; originally a priesthood, that while based on the Faery-Faith, merged with the Esoteric Christian Church. Druidic practices can be successfully traced back to 1717 and John Tolan, who was then the Chief of the Order of Bards, Ovates, and Druids. The succession of the Chiefs, which bring us to current times are: William Stukeley, Edward Finch Hatton, William Blake, MacGregory-Reid, Philip Ross Nichols, and Philip Carr-Gomn.

Frost's Wicca—Welsh; founders: Gavin and Yvonne Frost, early 1970s. Known as The Church and School of Wicca, apprentices are gained through a twelve-lesson correspondence, and because of this, apprentices undergo a self-initiation. Although originally there was no mention of work with the goddess, they have modified their tradition to include Her.

---

* If interested in learning more about, or becoming part of this tradition, send a query, with a self-addressed-stamped-envelope (this guarantees a response) to: Kisma K. Stepanich, c/o *Llewellyn New Worlds*, P.O. Box 64383-K694-7, St. Paul, MN 55164-0383, U.S.A.; if international, please include the correct return postage required.

Gaia Wicca: American; founder: Kisma K. Stepanich, 1985. This earth Wicca is a unique weaving of Native American Traditions and European Wiccan Traditions into a Holism, which I call the Gaia Tradition. Apprenticeships are based on the traditional year and a day, with a degree system of advancement, and it does not allow for self-initiation. Covens are predominantly female at this time, but open to men. Both Goddess and God energies are put into use, with the aim toward balance. The eight sabbats are celebrated, and magickal workings are at the monthly esbats.

Gardnerian Wicca—England; founder: Gerald B. Gardner, 1950s. This is considered the first modern denomination of the Craft*. The Gardnarian tradition places emphasis on the Goddess over the God. It has a degree system of advancement and does not allow for self-initiation. Covens work skyclad, and aim to have equal numbers of male and female initiates.

Seax-Wicca—American; founder: Raymond Buckland, 1973. This tradition has a Saxon basis, but is considered, by the founder, to be a new denomination of the Craft. Main features of the tradition are the fact that it has open rituals, it has a democratic organization that precludes ego trips and power plays by coven leaders, encourages both group and solitary practice, supports self-initiation, skyclad optional.

Coven or Solitary

After viewing the different branches of Wicca, let us turn to the consideration whether one should work with a Coven or as a Solitary. As was traditional, working with a Coven or Covey was the only manner in which the Mysteries of the Craft were taught. The concept of working Solitary came about when it was too dangerous for Covens to meet.

Fortunately, thanks to a handful of strong women and men who chose to continue the Craft even during the burning years—albeit solitary—the Craft remained alive and is with us today.

There is only so much experience one can gain working Solitary. However, working in a Coven provides a great range of experience, from energy exchange, group journeys, powerful psychic exchanges, positive magickal results, to group celebrations. With the Coven, one receives sharing, validation, confirmation, information, support, rejuvenation, pleasure—the list is endless.

As an elder priestess of Faery Wicca, I know that there are certain teachings I will only pass on through my Coveners. There are certain aspects of the Mysteries I

---

* For a detailed examination of the birth of Gardnerian Witchcraft, see Janet and Stewart Farrar's books: *Eight Sabbats for Witches* and *The Witches' Way*.

simply can never write about, because the experience of the Mystery is the teaching/lesson. To try and convey such information through the written word defeats the purpose.

Covens are not to be found everywhere, and finding one can be hard. However, there is an old saying in Wicca: When the student is ready, the teacher will find them. This saying speaks truth. For when a student is ready, they will take the steps necessary to make contact with other people of a like-mind. This attempt to make contact, and join with kindred spirits, brings the student and teacher together, which ultimately leads to the Coven.

When people ask me: "How do I find a coven?" I tell them to start visiting local Metaphysical, Occult, or New Age bookstores in their neighborhoods; take classes offered through these centers, because two-to-one, if classes are being offered on: Wicca, Spells, Goddess, Psychic Development, Ritual, and Ceremony, etc., the teacher is most likely a priestess or priest of Wicca. At the very least, attending such classes will hook the querist up with others who are either looking for a Coven or already belong to a Coven.

I would like to end this lesson and first Section on a personal note. As a modern woman with a European heritage, I have learned through Wicca to stand up and say, in a proud and strong voice: "I am Kisma, I am an Irish Witch and Romanian Gypsy."

I have been able to claim my birthright without fear of the ugly taboos other religions may have placed upon the esoteric traditions of my heritage. I no longer hear those derogatory slangs tossed so freely by the historians and clergies who have created such a negative reputation against my heritage. Rather, I hear: Kisma is a Fay, a cunning woman, Dark Queen of the Wheel of Life.

I feel the powerful vibration of Ireland rise up through my bones, and my Gypsy fire flame to life inside my womb! This is the gift of the gods that I have been given. This great and powerful gift of reclaiming proudly and passionately my divine healing rights, my traditional background, and yes, my woman's mysteries.

My Initiate soul found true freedom through her apprenticeship, for I delved into the unknown, I leapt back into the flames of my burning sisters and brothers, to understand! To understand why they were considered a threat! To find the answers to such questions as: Why was their healing power loathed? Why were they murdered so nefariously?

Yes, the rage, the sorrow—the weeping sorrow for my soul who was alive somewhere then, who was tortured and raped and ravaged and burned—has flashed through every particle of my being until I emptied out everything … emptied it all out, released it, re-grounded, took a deep, full belly breath, looked at my face in the mirror, saw the cunning woman, saw the Gypsy, claimed, proudly, my heritage, my roots, set the intent of my woman spirituality, smiled, and said: "So Be It!"

Journal Exercises

1. How does the remembrance of the Witch trials affect you?

2. When you hear the term *Witchcraft* or *Witch* what images come to mind? When you hear the term *Wicca* what images come to mind?

3. What is your ideal image of Wicca? After journaling, reread the different branches and see if one of them fits it.

Suggested Reading

Buckland's Complete Book of Witchcraft, Raymond Buckland
Irish Witchcraft and Demonology, Seymour
Ireland and the Anglo-Norman Church, Stokes
Wars of Turlough, Westropp
Transactions of the Ossory Archaeological Society, vol. i, "Narratives of Witchcraft and Sorcery."

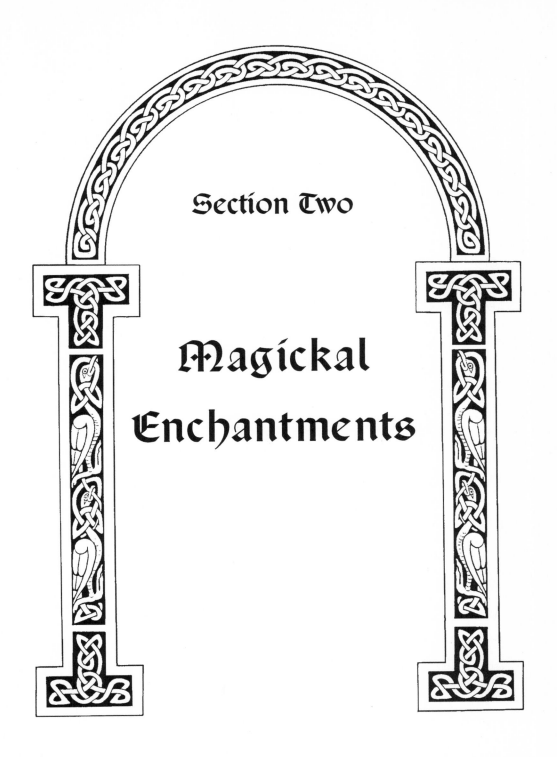

Section Two

Magickal Enchantments

arewell! Farewell! Farewell!
Far hence we lost ones go:
Hearken our knell,
Hearken our woe!

Farewell! Farewell! Farewell!
With breaking hearts we flee:
For none can tell
Our wild home on the sea.

For ages on the Moyle
In loneliness and pain,
Our feet shall tread no soil,
Wild wave, wild wind, wild rain.

For ages in the west,
Fierce storms and fiercer cold
Shall be alone our rest,
While ye grow old.

Let not our memories pass,
O ye who stay behind —
Who are as the grass
And we the wind

Farewell! Farewell! Farewell!
Far hence we lost ones go:
Hearken our knell,
Hearken our woe!

— *The Tale of the Four White Swans*
Fiona Macleod, *The Laughter of Peterkin,* 1897

Lesson Eight

Working with the Ancients

We will keep faith until the sky falls upon us and crushes us, until the earth opens and swallows us, until the seas arise and overwhelm us. *

One of the first areas of interest within magickal workings is usually with the Pantheon of the tradition, which is why the first three lessons of this book focused on the traditional history of Ireland, the Faery Lineage, and the Ancient Ones. As an elder priestess of Faery Wicca, I know that if an apprentice is unwilling to undergo a complete training, both mundane and magickal, as well as physically, mentally, and spiritually, then they will never receive the gift of the gods, which is often in the form of direct communion with the Ancient Ones, as well as the other beings that exist within the Otherworlds.

In this chapter, I will provide several exercises and journeys to make contact with the Elemental Fairy, the Ancient Ones, and their host of beings. I present the exercises and journeys in a specific order, encouraging the readership to follow this order for best results. This does not mean that later chapters cannot be worked with prior to undergoing the exercises laid out in this one—for each chapter is an exclusive whole—however, what this does mean is that before deciding to perform, or undergo, any of the exercises and journeys found within a given chapter, I highly encourage you to first read the entire chapter in order to understand the process of the journey, and the reasons why I provide each in a given order.

Before we begin any of the exercises, or I take you on a journey, it is important to first focus on the Book of Shadows. Although this item could be considered a tool, it is not a magickal tool, it is a practical tool, for it becomes the magickal journal of the adept.

---

* Celtic oath of the elements.

Book of Shadows

Traditionally, the magickal journal was known as the Black Book. Today, the magickal journal is often referred to as a Book of Shadows. Both are the diary of an adept or apprentice, containing within the results of experiments tried and true, chants and prayers that touch the Spirit of Faery, mystical teachings handed down mouth-to-ear, magickal words of power, visionary guidelines, ceremonial outlines, recipes for herbcraft, as well as the dreams and desires of the scribe.

Keeping a Book of Shadows is very important when undergoing an apprenticeship or performing the exercises and journeys found in this book. As already defined, this journal becomes the recipe book for spiritual evolution.

When one takes the time to record the messages received during meditation, or experiences from a shamanic journey, the results of an energy exercise or ritual, a practical tool is developed. Each entry becomes a continual focus for meditation. On the pages of the Book of Shadows the messages and guidance from Deities are usually recorded—albeit, sometimes hidden.

This book, *Faery Wicca*, for example, was made possible through the journal entries I kept in my Black Book, not only during my varying degrees of apprenticeships, but even today as an adept and elder priestess of Faery Wicca. Therefore, this book could be considered a Book of Shadows, for in it I provide information, words of wisdom, guidelines, exercises, journeys and rituals, to help others begin their spiritual immram (voyage of apprenticeship) into the Land of Faery, just as I do with my apprentices whom I physically work with in my Coven's outer court circle.

A Book of Shadows can be anything: a three-ringed notebook, an artist's hardbound sketchbook, a diary, the blank books readily available at most bookstores and stationary supply shops.

The key to keeping a Book of Shadows is to record personal transformation; the motto to always have in mind when one delves into the spiritual kingdom of life is that "change is the magick." When one cannot make the necessary changes in their life, then they possess no magick. Life is about change. Through the Book of Shadows one can learn about change—the flowing richness of wealth that comes through change—and then one will become the magick that is naturally held within.

Faery Allies

Working with allies is a common denominator found in most indigenous traditions. Faery Wicca is no exception, being the indigenous tradition of Europe. Whether one calls them an ally, companion, or ancestor, the spirit beings of the other realm are there to help us if we but take the time to seek them.

In Lesson Two: The Faery Lineage, we discussed the Elemental Fairy* (elementals, sub-human Nature-Spirits who are generally regarded as having pygmy stature, like the Greek daemons), and its four classifications:

- ⚔ Earth-Gnome
- ⚔ Air-Sylph
- ⚔ Fire-Salamander
- ⚔ Water-Undine

In Faery Wicca, allies are found within these four groups. In truth the Celts can be considered the Clan of the Elements, for they believed there were no greater forces than those of air, fire, water and earth, the elements that shape the physical world.

Many prayers of protection were based on the elements, as described below in this ancient Charm for Fear By Night:

Who is there on land?
Who is there on wave?
Who is there on billow?
Who is there by door-post?
Who is along with us?
The gods of the elements' guarding?

The elements were also sworn by, or used in oaths, as demonstrated in this ancient Celtic oath of *The Three*:

The Three Who are over me,
The Three Who are below me,
The Three Who are above me here,
The Three Who are above me yonder;
The Three Who are in the earth,
The Three Who are in the air,
The Three Who are in the heaven,
The Three Who are in the great pouring sea.

Working with the elemental kingdom becomes very invigorating.[†] They are the spiritual helpers from the kingdom of nature who will assist us magickally. To connect with them, the following guidelines are provided for each Elemental Fairy classification. Once contact has been made, putting such beings to work for us is as easy as saying: So Mote It Be!

---

* For best results reread this lesson.

† In my first book, *An Act of Woman Power*, Whitford Press, I share an experience I had with the Elemental Fairy kingdom that was truly transforming.

Earth Fairy—Surface: Tree, Wood or Garden; Underground: Rock, Gnome

I knew you when the earth was cold,
I knew you when the earth was hot,
I knew you when my hands in soil sought
the light within the earth.

The Earth Fairy is found during the dawn—their busy time—out in a garden, wood, or meadow. To truly connect with this ally, one must be willing to get their hands soiled without repulsion to dirt.

By planting a crystal in the soil at dawn (before a tree if a Tree ally is desired; in a flower bed, herb plot, or vegetable garden for a Wood or Garden ally; next to a rock for the Rock ally; in the middle of a clearing or deep in the forest for a Gnome), settling yourself before the crystal, and chanting the above call will encourage the ally to present itself.*

Using a bodhram (traditional Celtic drum similar to the Native American Indian medicine drum) to call the Earth Fairy ally is also helpful. After performing the above guidelines, beat a steady rhythm on the bodhram, allowing the vibration of the rhythm to connect with your heartbeat and ground it into the heart of the earth. Often the Gnome will respond to this method.

Once an Earth Fairy ally has been found, theirs is the energy of grounding, shifting awareness to the physical, to the here-and-now. Putting them to work magickally is asking this ally to see the physical for you and communicate it to you in the act of awakening your awareness.†

When you have made contact with an ally, don't forget to ask what type of Earth Fairy it is (Surface or Underground, etc.); what name it would like to be called; how it would like you to make contact with it again; times for best contact; days for best contact, etc. It is important to inform the ally that the crystal you have planted in the earth is a gift to their realm.

By giving first, you will receive generously back. Never journey into the spiritual realm, never seek an ally, companion, ancestor, Ancient One, Deity, without giving the first gift.

This concept of giving first and then receiving will help teach you the ancient law: "What you give of yourself freely, without attachment to what you will receive in return, will be returned to you ten-fold."

Air Fairy—Nature: Cloud, Storm, Air-Dragon; Elemental: Sylph

The power of the eagle
The power of the storm
And the hand of valor
Which a blade well becomes~
Come now breath of Dana.

---

* Be prepared to visit the spot several times before an ally presents itself, as they are cautious of our kind.

† For more information on working with elementals, refer to my book, *The Gaia Tradition*, Llewellyn Publications.

The Air Fairy is found easiest during the sunset, or on a foggy or misty day. To connect with such an ally means allowing time for cloud watching. The Air Fairy is the sculptor of the imaginary world and will reveal itself through a cloud formation, in a thunder cloud, or a glittering glimpse from the corner of the eye.

To call this kind of ally, one must go outside where there is open space, turn three times in a deosil (clockwise; sunwise) circle, each time throwing a handful of glitter into the air. On the completion of the third round, lay down, looking up into the air and chant the above call.

The use of a whistle or flute will help call the sylph. Sylphs love music, they love vibration. After performing the above guidelines, use the whistle or flute to continue to attune your energy with the realm of the Air Fairy.

Once an Air Fairy ally has been found, theirs is the energy of inspiration. They will help free the mind by drawing you into their imaginary realm, floating you into unfettered territory so mind disengages Ego, and inner-child dances freely. You will know you have made contact with an Air Fairy when you have returned from your daydream refreshed and inspired!

Don't forget to ask the Air Fairy ally to identify itself, providing instructions on how to further commune with it. Like the Earth Fairy ally, it is important to present their realm with a gift; in this case the glitter doesn't work as a gift. I would encourage tossing a decorated feather into the air and letting it fall where it may, leaving it behind when you depart.

Water Fairy—Salt Water: Water Babies, Sea Sprites, Water-Storm; Fresh Water: Undine.

> *Guile! Guile! of the dark waves.*
> *Guile! Guile! of the Dirge.*
> *Guilog! Guilog! voice of the swans.*
> *On their bodies,*
> *by the warrior Michael.*
> *On their protection,*
> *By Brigid, daughter of Dugall the brown.*
> *In ocean and narrow,*
> *Deep in the trough of the whirlpool*
> *May the Three follow them*
> *And in the suckling cauldron of Cerridwen!*

The Water Fairy allies are the great transformers. They can help to bind or loosen any magickal working; for they are the chemists of the Elemental Fairy.

The Water Fairy are found during the mid-point of the day, when the full sunlight sparkles upon the ocean water or glistens off the lake, pond or stream. The Water Fairy can lure us away from reality, drawing us into the depths of their enchantments. Once there, they teach us to dream. Through dreaming, we begin to perceive new visions of self. With a new vision of self we can begin the transformation required to become the new image.

To contact a Water Fairy, go to a body of water. If you go to the ocean, a lake or a pond, wade waist-deep into the water; if you go to a river or stream, sit in the

153

water. Blow bubbles from a bubble-soap mixture, splash the water across the surface, and set-sail a handcrafted boat decorated with flowers, shells and moonstones. Sing the above call to their realm, then lie back and release yourself into the ebb and flow of the water.

You can also submerge your feet, ankle-deep, in the water and play a harp, dulcimer or psaltery, letting go of your control over the music and freeing self-consciousness by using your voice.

The Water Fairy ally will make their presence known by either physically brushing against your skin, or by tugging firmly at your body through the ebbing tide of the water. Fear of water will hinder contact with this ally. Fear of water can also be connected to fear of emotions. If you hold such fear you can actually transform the fear by using the Water Fairy ally. Rather than working with the ocean, a lake, pond or stream as given above, work with a bowl of water, a sink or bathtub. Once you feel more confident, then venture to the wild body of water; the cauldron of our emotions.

If you relax into their realm, this ally will instruct you how to flow in a situation; guide you to the blockage preventing a flow; still you where calm and peace is needed; become rough when there is stagnation and action is required; drown you by washing over your head or splashing into your mouth when you need to wake-up and swim. Once you have an ally, don't forget to ask for identification and direction as to future contact. Be sure to inform it that the handcrafted boat is a gift to their realm.

Fire Fairy—Flame Spirit, Salamander

> *Burn it with fire.*
> *Golden, bejeweled.*
> *Clasped by magick,*
> *About her slim hips,*
> *Loose the girdle.*
> *Burn it with fire.*
> *Burn it with fire!*

The Fire Fairy ally has an intelligence of its own, and, as already discussed in Lesson Two: The Faery Lineage, is really not considered part of the Elemental Fairy. Rather, Fire is acknowledged as the Power of Faery, as the Flame of Spirit, as the Hearth-Fire. This is not to say that one cannot ally fire; for we can, but to do so, we must be willing to get burned. I tell you true, this ally will reach out and lick you, which, unfortunately, usually burns the skin or singes the hair at the very least.

Therefore, when seeking a Fire Fairy ally, I highly encourage you to proceed with great caution, remembering fire is both a symbol of creation and destruction. On our plane the destructive energy of fire precedes the creation energy of fire. Due to this fact, in order to contact this ally a certain degree of willingness to let it destroy you must exist, and it is germane to begin seeking this ally through the Flame Spirit: the candle flame*.

---

* To some degree we will work with the Salamander in Book Two's Faery Divination chapter when we study the art of Scrying, otherwise, I do not encourage seeking the Salamander ally. To do so would involve working with a very large fire out in the wild—such as a bonfire. Unless one is skillfully trained as a fire-fighter, please let the Salamander ally, and its realm, exist untouched.

To contact a Flame Spirit ally light a candle and focus on the flame, chant the call and commit to the flame something burnable which you value. Have a container ready to lay the burning item in, and as you witness the destructive energy of this ally, seek the flames for the birth of the Flame Spirit ally. Obviously, there is a very short period of time in which this ally will present itself. When it does so, a distinct image of a face will appear in the flame. Once this happens, focus back on the candle flame and re-image the face into the flame of the candle.

Ask the ally to identify itself and give guidance for further contact. Don't forget to inform it of your gift which you gave to their realm, which it ate in order to come more alive.

Working with the Flame Spirit ally will help focus you into a state of no-mind, aiding you with the development of meditation skills. Meditation involves removing all mental chatter, holding a thought in contemplation, thus opening to meditation, in which the ally realm can communicate more efficiently with your consciousness.

Once you have made contact with your allies and have received identification and guidance from them, you can then begin putting them to work whether it be through spellcraft, or simply in gaining clarity on personal direction.

Know that allies do not possess you, nor can they, for they are helpers. In the manner in which I am guiding you to work with this kingdom, I am not having you evoke them into our realm, nor try to control them by becoming their master. You are simply asking them to be your helper when needed, in exchange for a gift you render their realm each and every time you work with it.

This next section contains several journeys that will help identify you with one of the Four Cycles as presented in Lesson One: The Traditional History. The Four Cycles are:

- The Mythological Cycle
- The Ulster Cycle
- The Fenian Cycle
- The Historical Cycle

Before working with the following material, you may want to re-read the material in Lesson One to refresh your memory with the historical background of Faery Wicca.

The Arousal of the Flame

Before you begin further research and study on the above cycles, I would like to take you on a short journey which will arouse your inner flame.

The inner flame is located in what is called the power center of the body: alias the navel area, located between the sacral and solar plexus chakras. This power center is the point of gravity within the body; the place where the energy of the Heavenly Realm meets the energy of the Underworld. Therefore, this power center actually represents The Plains.

By arousing the inner flame, we begin to awaken a deep sense of consciousness, one that will connect us with the universal mind helping us to remember the experiences we undergo during each journey and the ancient wisdoms conveyed through each journey.

This first journey will help pinpoint which of the four cycles will best serve you at this time, pointing you in a direction for further research and study. This journey will attune you to the lessons of a particular cycle, providing you with insight as to which tales will most likely resonate with the current lessons you are undergoing.

I do not include The Historical Cycle in this journey, as The Historical Cycle is the cycle wherein Ireland became Christianized: the old gods were turned into Saints, and the pre-Celtic/pre-Christian Faery-Faith was pushed rapidly underground*.

This journey, which I call The Journey of Perception, will require the quiet and undisturbed space of thirty minutes. I offer the following format as a guideline to use prior to beginning each journey provided in this book. This format will help prepare your space, as well as ground and center your energy.

Preparation Format
Please prepare your space by:

- ⚹ Burning a favorite incense to help awaken your deep-seated ecology.
- ⚹ Lighting a white candle to lead you through the tunnel of perception.
- ⚹ Playing gentle music on your stereo (such as Enya, Kim Robertson, or Anne Williams) to connect you with the vibrational side of life, which will help your trancing abilities.
- ⚹ Arrange a sitting place before a mirror hung at eye-level.

Ground and Center Format
Before we begin each journey, or ceremony, it is important for us to first ground and center our energy. By doing so, we move away from linear thinking, releasing our hold on the day-to-day activities which have a tendency to dominate our mental faculties.

Grounding and centering brings us completely into the NOW, allowing our conscious awareness to focus on what we present to it by staying focussed, rather than being distracted by floating thoughts[†].

When your space has been altered by the influences of the Preparation Format and, thus, turned into a sense of Sacred Space, sit down before the mirror and relax.

Let your eyes rest on your image in the mirror. Blink very gently a few times and relax them so that the lids shut half-way, and now, stop trying to see, thus attaining soft-sight.

Next, focus on your soft-breath by following its natural flow in ... and out, in ... and out, in ... and out (three times).

Take a full belly breath in through your nose, filling your belly first then your lungs, and now initiate the out-breath with your diaphragm by releasing your breath through your mouth. Do this once for mind, a second time for body, and a third time for Spirit.

---

* However, for those interested in the tradition of druidism, the Historical Cycle could be worth your investigation.

† For additional grounding and centering techniques, see my book *An Act of Woman Power*.

Let your breathing resume its normal rhythm. By performing the above breathing exercise you ground and center your energy into your spine.

The Journey of Perception*

The way of life is a cycle. A huge wheel that slowly turns—forever. We understand this concept when we chant:

Spinning, Spinning,
round and round,
the wheel of life
does slowly spin.

The wheel of life is based on the cycle of Grandmother Moon, who teaches us about change; it's based on the cycle of Grandfather Sun, who teaches us about the seasons; it's based on the cycle of life, which teaches us about acceptance.

Your breath is also a wheel, a cycle. Follow the cycle of your breath. As you inhale, your awareness falls deeper inside your consciousness, and as you exhale, your consciousness raises into your awareness. Falling and rising. Falling and rising. Falling and rising.

The wheel of your breath is also a cycle: a cycle of perception. Just as perception is also a wheel, a cycle. You are now going to begin following the cycle of your perception as it takes you through your inner functions of thinking, willing, and feeling. Thinking, willing, and feeling. Thinking, willing, and feeling.

Allow yourself to rest on one of these three functions. Slow down and allow your perception to rest on either thinking, willing, or feeling. You are now resting in only one function. Confirm to yourself which function. [pause]

This function is an area of perception. Hold this area of perception in your consciousness, and allow yourself to open to any messages that may need to come through with regards to this area of your life. Relax and open.

[Meditation time permitted/approximately 5 minutes.]

Focus back on your area of perception. Take a full belly breath and exhale, committing any messages received to your conscious awareness. [pause]

With your next full belly breath, raise your awareness back to your eyes, blinking them open.

[pause]

Taking a third full belly breath, lower your focus back to your image in the mirror. Let your breathing resume its normal rhythm and focus on your image in the mirror, gradually opening your eye-lids back to a normal attention.

Your Journey of Perception has now ended.

---

* Pre-record the journey, including the chant rune, and play it back as you do the journey, or have someone in your group act as the mediator, or guide, and read it outloud.

Once you have undergone the above journey, be sure to record the experience in your Book of Shadows, noting the area of perception (thinking, willing, or feeling) you rested in, and any messages received during the meditation. You will continue to work with this information, building upon it. Now find your are of perception below:

- **Thinking:** If you rested in the area of thinking, begin your study of the traditional history with tales from The Mythological Cycle. This cycle features intelligence and knowledge. The information gained from this cycle will be your foundation for this current cycle, or phase, of your life. Key words: thinking, intelligence, knowledge.

- **Willing:** If you are resting in the area of willing begin your study of the traditional history with The Ulster Cycle. This cycle features will-power and heroism. The information gained from this cycle will be your foundation for this current cycle, or phase, of your life. Key words: willing, will power, heroism.

- **Feeling:** If you are resting in the area of feeling, begin your study of the traditional history with the tales from The Fenian Cycle. This cycle features human warmth and cherished memories. The information gained from this cycle will be your foundation for this cycle, or phase, of your life. Key words: feeling, human warmth, cherished memories.

As you begin to work with Faery Wicca, remember your area of perception. Remember your key words. Under-go research pertaining to the Cycle connected to your area of perception. Read the tales from the Cycle, not only to familiarize yourself with the tradition's evolution, but to grasp the meaning of the lesson your Spirit is striving to learn today.

Often I have students ask, "How long will I be working with this area of perception?" Cycles, especially those connected to spiritual growth, are traditionally four years long. To many apprentices, remaining in one area of perception for four years seems too long a time, and because of their impatience, most students will quickly move on to another area of perception, or another tradition.

If an apprentice, however, applies patience to their training, then during the course of a four year cycle they will come to know many things about their spirit and how they function in life.

When we are drawn to an ancient tradition, we truly learn from the old tales, because in some aspect the life myth we are creating through our own living parallels the lessons revealed in the tales. Therefore, perceive, with wakeful consciousness, what that lesson may be.

As we study our Cycle and its historical aspect, it is important to keep in mind the research may take several months. In fact, it could take an entire year. Relax in this knowledge.

If you are in a rush to know everything at the beginning, then you will never be able to endure the trials and errors of spiritual evolution. Let us always remember:

Spirit is about forever. Magick is about change. Like everything else we do in life, we must also take our mystical training one day at a time.

With this in mind, we are going to focus our attention on the next journey, which will help deepen personal power.

What do I mean by power? When I use this word, I do not suggest developing power that will enable one to exercise control-over, domination, or authority, in a forceful or restraining way against other individuals.

When I use the word *power*, I am referring to inner energy; the source of means of supplying the energy which is Motive Power; the power that is a latent spiritual ability to act or act upon which generates the energy that helps one to expend that energy to transform their weakness and fears into strength.

The word *power*, stems from the Latin, *poti* or *potis*; which means powerful, able (having the power), from where the words potent, possess (have power over), and possible are derived. In the original sense of the word, power means: being able to do something.

Other traditions, such as Native American Indian traditions, refer to this power as medicine. The Lakota word for medicine is *Wakan*; which means holy, or sacred. In general the power, or sacredness of a being, is connected to an object, person, or idea which one defines as sacred or powerful. Thus, such an object, person, or idea becomes a prototype.

Once we define our individual prototypes, we consciously, as well as unconsciously, try to become the mirror of such a prototype, thereby connecting the concept of power in proportion to the ability of the prototype, or acting to reflect most directly the principle, or principles, which are found in the prototype.

Personal power, or personal medicine, is that which, if grounded into, will enable us to receive inspiration or, as referred to in Faery Wicca, the gift of the gods.

Within your power now is seeded the area of your perception, which you clarified during The Journey of Perception. This seed-power (of thinking, willing, or feeling) can now be aroused and turned into energy; an energy that will feed your spirit and help you learn the lessons drawn from the Cycle you currently walk.

I am going to take you on another journey called: The Seed Power Journey. This journey is the act of arousing the flame of will. Once will is aroused, once your personal power is aroused, it becomes so much easier to continue deepening spiritually, as well as begin defining where imbalance may exist.

This journey will require the quiet space of fifteen minutes, and before you begin, review the Preparation/Ground and Center format guidelines given above. Next review the keywords connected to your area of perception, and re-read any Book of Shadows entries you made after undergoing the first journey.

When you are ready to begin, enact the Preparation format. When your space is ready, sit before the mirror and relax, shifting into the Ground and Center format. Let your eyes rest on your image in the mirror. Blink very gently a few times and relax so that your eyelids shut half-way. Stop trying to see, moving into soft-sight.

Begin to follow the natural flow of your soft-breath in … and out, in … and out, in … and out. Take your first full belly breath of air in through your nose and release out through your mouth—this is the breath for mind. Take your second full belly breath, and release—this is the breath for body. Take your third full belly breath, and release—this is the breath for Spirit. Relax, and breath normally.

The Seed Power Journey*

Deep within is a dormant power, and within this dormant power is the seed of our deepest sense of self. This seed is the seat of power, the influence behind all energy that rises through the body.

> I invoke thee, power,
> deep, deep seed within me,
> fertile, fertile, power
> flowing, flowing, energy through me.

This seed-power rides on the current of breath. Follow this current of power. As you inhale, gather this deep current of power, and as you exhale, spread this deep current of power through your body. Gathering and spreading. Gathering and spreading. Gathering and spreading.

A current of seed-power is flowing through you now. Feel the energy of this current of seed-power feed your Spirit. Feel the arousal of inner flame, bursting into life.

[pause]

Into this current of energy, into this flame, awaken your area of perception: thinking, willing, or feeling. Reaffirm your area, and after you have confirmed it, offer it as fuel to your seed-power.

[pause]

As your seed-power receives this offering it becomes nourished, and from the seed-power a tender green shoot begins to emerge. The shoot grows and stretches. This new growth is your personal power.

From the shoot comes new branches. On the branches sprout buds. From the buds come the fruit of your area of perception keywords. Connect each of your keywords to a bud. Now, you are going to meditate on each bud, each keyword, one at a time, to receive a message that will help activate personal power into your life. Relax and open.

[Meditation time permitted/approximately 5 minutes.]

Focus now on the entire plant; for this plant represents personal power. Take a full belly breath and exhale, committing to consciousness the messages connected to each keyword.

[pause]

With your next breath, gather-up your inner current of energy, your personal power, and as you exhale ground this energy into your seed-power, into your personal power.

[pause]

Take a third full belly breath, raise your awareness back to your eyes, and as you

---

* Again, either have someone act as a mediator and read this to your group, or pre-record it on tape and play it back as you take the journey.

exhale, blink your eyes open and lower your focus to your image in the mirror. Let your breathing resume its normal rhythm and focus on your image, gradually opening your eyelids back to a normal state of attention.

Your Seed Power has been activated.

Now that you have finished the journey, record the message received for each of the keywords in your Book of Shadows. Study each message and turn it into a positive affirmation to be used throughout the day when one of the keyword qualities is required. We will continue to build on this work.

Thus far, you have connected to the origin of the Faery Wiccan tradition through an area of perception and the study of the old tales connected to its Cycle, and you have been rooted into your seed-power, through which you received direction on how to use keywords to enact personal power. From these two connections inner magick is being brought forth.

This work has been in preparation to connect with one of the Faery, who will become a Spiritual Benefactor. The purpose of connecting with a Spiritual Benefactor is in finding that quality of Spirit which resonates with your mundane living, that through such a connection can aide in developing and strengthening personal power.

Before I guide you toward this connection, the time has come to meet a Faery companion. This companion is known as a Fetch. They act as a companion who, in essence, will fetch the Spiritual Benefactor for you each time an audience is sought.

The Faery Companion

The Faery Companion is quite different than an Elemental Fairy ally, because we can never control the Faery Companion, nor put him to work for us. If the Faery Companion is indifferent to us, he will simply not fetch our Spiritual Benefactor, and we might have to endure a lesson from him on how to be polite. It is the companion who will teach us about Faery morality, should we lack any of the virtues so deemed as necessary by them for successful communion with their realm.

They have a strict code of morality that is enforced. Lack of generosity, rudeness, and selfishness are unpopular with them. Anyone who seeks contact with gloom in their heart will have a harder time, for the Fay truly love merriment; music, song, and dance are passages into the Land of Faery.

Once contact is made, the Faery will begin to visit our dwelling places uninvited, and they expect to find them neat, orderly, and beautiful. If you have a fireplace, the hearth must always be swept clean, with fresh water set out for their use; the old tales surrounding this is that the Fay will wash their babies with it.

Most importantly, the Faery Companion will scold us if we are unfair and hold deceit in our hearts, for even the Hosts (the negative polarity of the Faery) do not lie; they only evade.

It is important to remember that Faery do not have the same emotional sentiments as we humans; theirs is a world of balance. To infringe on their realm, or privacy, without prior announcement can result in being cut off from their realm and any further contact with them. Learning to beckon the Fetch and send him to announce your eagerness for an audience is the most profitable way of gaining deeper entrance into their realm. With this in mind, I will now take you on a journey to meet your Fetch. This journey will take approximately thirty minutes.

Perform the Preparation and Ground and Center format.

The Faery Fetch Journey[21]*
Very quietly you rest within, flowing with the breath. Sinking your awareness deeper and deeper into your power. Deeper and deeper into your power. Deeper and deeper into your power.

> *Earth the power*
> *beneath my feet,*
> *forming the road*
> *I am ready to greet.*

The earth is below your feet. You stand within a vague and shadowy landscape. Before you is a hill. Begin walking up the hill toward the peak.

Half-way up, three figures are sitting in the road, stopping your progress. They are quite naked, and each of them gazes on you with intent earnestness. You look at each one.

The first being is so beautiful that your eye fails upon him, flinching aside as from a great brightness. He is mighty in stature, and well proportioned, so exquisitely slender and graceful that no idea of gravity or bulk goes with his height. His face is kingly and youthful, and of a terrifying serenity.

The second being is of equal height, but broad to wonderment. So broad is he that his great height seems diminished. The tense arm on which he leans is knotted and ridged with muscle, and his hand grips deeply into the ground. His face seems as though it has been hammered from hard rock, a massive, blunt face, as rigid as his arm.

The third being can scarcely be described. He is neither short nor tall. He is muscled as heavily as the second being. From the way he is sitting, he looks like a colossal toad squatting with his arms about his knees and upon these his chin rests. He has no shape nor swiftness, and his head is flattened down and is scarcely wider than his neck. He has a protruding, dog-like mouth that twitches occasionally, and from his little eyes there glints a horrible intelligence.

The first being speaks. He asks: "For what purpose do you go abroad this day

---

21 The three Fetches are based on James Stephen's, *The Crock of Gold*, The Macmillan Company, New York, 1935.

* Again, either have someone act as a mediator and read this to your group, or pre-record it on tape and play it back as you take the journey.

and on this hill?" You tell him that you travel searching for your Faery Companion.

He ponders this answer. Then states: "We are the Three Absolutes, the Three Redeemers, the Three Alembics: the Most Beautiful Fay, the Strongest Fay and the Ugliest Fay. In the midst of every strife we go unhurt. We count the slain and the victors and pass on laughing, and to us in the eternal order come all the peoples of the world to be regenerated forever. Why have you called to us?"

You tell him a second time that you are seeking your Faery Companion. He responds: "There are no paths closed to us. Even the gods seek us, for they grow weary in their splendid desolation. You must now tell us why you have called to us?"

You tell him a third time that you are seeking your Faery Companion, adding that you seek a Faery Fetch of the Ancient Ones, a Faery Fetch who will be able to help you find your Spiritual Benefactor.

He responds: "Then you must choose now one of us to be your Fetch, and do not fear to choose, for our kingdoms are equal and our powers are equal." Look at each one of the beings before you. Choose one to be your Faery Fetch. [pause]

Point to your Faery Fetch and tell him you have chosen him, and open yourself to communing with him. Allow your Fetch to school you in the ways of Faery morality. Hear what he has to share, and know that he is gifting you with his wisdom, preparing you for deeper journeys. Relax and open.

[Meditation time permitted/approximately 15 minutes.]

The time has come to return to the outer world. See if you have something to offer your Faery Fetch as a gift, and then offer it to him.

[pause]

Take a full belly breath and focus on your Faery Fetch, as you exhale, allow his form to dissolve, but know that you will retain him in your consciousness. [pause]

With your next full belly breath you are going to raise your awareness back to your eyes.

[pause]

Taking a third full belly breath, blink open your eyes and focus on your image in the mirror. Gradually open your eyelids back to a normal attention. Let your breathing resume its normal rhythm.

You now have your Faery Fetch.

⁘

Journal in your Book of Shadows. The Faery Fetch you chose is very important to remember, for he is the being that you will send to fetch your Spiritual Benefactor whenever you need to communicate with her or him.

The same Faery Fetch will be worked with until he tells you that he is no longer available. This does occasionally happen, and when it does, it simply means that you need to choose one of the other two beings. To find out who your new fetch is, simply perform the journey over. However, don't be surprised if your original Faery Fetch stays with you for several years.

Each of the three Faery Fetches have a name. The first being is named Beauty. The second being is named Strength. The third being is named Ugliness. Find your Faery Fetch below:

⚹ **Beauty** is Thought (thinking). The home of Beauty is the head of humankind. When you work with Beauty you will know all delight. Beauty will help you live unharmed in the flame of the Spirit, and nothing that is gross will be able to bind your limbs, or hinder your Thought.

Beauty allows you to move as a queen or king amongst all raging passions without torment or despair. With Beauty, never shall you be driven or ashamed, but always you will choose your own paths and walk with Beauty in freedom and contentment.

The lesson Beauty teaches is: All things must act according to the order of their being, and so Thought can hold you against your will by binding you, and then you bind Thought against your will. Thus, the holder of any unwilling mate becomes the guardian and the slave of their captive.

⚹ **Strength** is Love (feeling). The home of Strength is the heart of humankind. When you work with Strength you will know safety and peace, for Strength's days have honor and his nights quietness. There is no evil thing that walks near Strength's lands, nor is any sound heard but the lowing of cattle, the songs of birds, and the laughter of happy children in Strength's domain.

Strength will give protection and happiness and peace, assuring that you will not fail or grow weary at any time on your journey.

The lesson strength teaches is: Strength is complete, it cannot be increased, and Love, when it exists, is also complete and it cannot be added to, for both are whole ingredients within themselves, and therefore when one is with Strength and Love they are with whole ingredients and the only way to change the two is to diminish them by adding the shadow of doubt.

⚹ **Ugliness** is Generation (willing). The home of Ugliness is in the loins of humankind. When you work with Ugliness you will be given the wild delights which have been long forgotten. All things which are crude and riotous, all that is gross and without limit is Ugliness.

With Ugliness, you shall not think and suffer any longer; but you shall feel so surely that the heat of the Sun will be happiness: the taste of food, the wind that blows upon you, the ripe ease of your body, these things will amaze you who have forgotten them.

When Ugliness puts his great arms about you, they shall make you furious and young again; you will leap on the hillside like a young goat and sing for joy as the birds sing.

Ugliness teaches: The torments of the mind may not be renounced for any easement of the body until the smoke that binds you is blown away, and the tormenting flame has fitted you for that immortal ecstasy which is the bosom of Dana.

Compare your Faery Fetch to your area of perception, noting if they are of the same function (of thinking, willing, feeling), and record your thoughts on this comparison in your Book of Shadows.

Spiritual Benefactor

Finally, we come to the Spiritual Benefactor. As was discussed in Lesson Three: The Ancient Ones, the Ancient Ones that we invoke depend chiefly upon our individual tuning. The Ancient Ones do exist, they are esoteric archetypes to which we can attune ourselves by surrendering to the mystery of communion with them. This allows our own special creative flow to enliven us, as well as help us achieve a more perfect sense of balance in our mundane and spiritual living.

The Ancient One who comes can help us learn more about our personalities by using their ancient tales to demonstrate what influence their energy will have in our lives—but, only should we chose to call upon them. I have chosen seven Irish goddesses and five Irish gods to consider as your Spiritual Benefactor.

The seven goddesses are: Aine, Airmed, Breo-saighit, Cailleach Bera, Cesara, Eire, and Tailltiu.

The five gods are: Dagda, Lamhfadha, Manannan mac Lir, Nuada and Oengus.

Before undergoing this journey you do not need to pre-choose one of the above goddesses or gods. It is okay to undergo the journey, allowing the goddess or god to choose you. However, should you decide to allow the Spiritual Benefactor to choose you, then it would be best to re-read the information previously given on each, as well as remember the list of names.

This journey will require the quiet and undisturbed space of forty-five minutes. When your space has been altered by the influences of the Preparation format, and you are in Sacred Space, sit before your mirror and relax. Perform the Ground and Center format.

As before, let your eyes rest on your image in the mirror. Blink a few times to relax your eyelids, and allow them to shut half-way. By now you will begin to feel the difference between relaxed eyes or soft-sight and attentive eyes or focused-sight.

When your eyes are attentive, you are reaching your awareness out through them, using vision to touch or grab-hold of images to bring back to your mind. When your eyes are relaxed, your vision is no longer reaching out, but allowing images to come into your pupils and be received by your third eye or field of intuition.

With soft-sight, focus on your soft-breath, following its natural rhythm in and out, for three breaths. By now you are probably equating soft breathing with the three full belly breaths that you will soon take for mind, body and Spirit.

When the three soft-breaths have been taken, take your three full belly breaths in through your nose and release out through your mouth, once for mind; twice for body; and thrice for Spirit. Let your breathing resume its normal rhythm.

The Spiritual Benefactor Journey*

Within you is forming an Energy Triad. In the bottom right corner of the Energy Triad is your area of perception and its Cycle of study—Thinking and The Mythological Cycle, Willing and The Ulster Cycle, or Feeling and The Fenian Cycle. See this corner of the Energy Triad, with your area of perception, form in your mind.

[pause]

In the bottom left corner is your Seed-Power which contains the buds of each keyword. One at a time the buds reveal themselves to you, bringing into your conscious awareness the message of each of keyword. Take a moment to reaffirm your affirmations.

[pause]

A strong foundation of this new Energy Triad has now been formed. Allow your breath to spread the strength of this foundation through your body. Spreading and paving a new road. Spreading and paving a new road. Spreading and paving a new road.

This road leads to a new horizon, the horizon which forms the top point of your Energy Triad.

Like the rising moon,
Be mine a good purpose
Towards each creature of creation.
May thy course be smooth to me,
Thou fair and Ancient One of the seasons,
Kindly be each deed that you reveal.

This inner Energy Triad was the hill upon which sat the three beings from whom came your Faery Fetch. See your companion materialize now before you, and journey up the hill to the place where he sits, which is half-way up the hill.

Take a few moments to greet your Faery Fetch. Acknowledge his presence, call him by name, give to him a gift you've brought and allow him to speak to you. Open and relax.

[Meditation time provided/approximately 5 minutes.]

Ask your companion if he will now go fetch your Spiritual Benefactor. If you have already chosen, tell him the name now. If you have not already chosen, ask him to go fetch the Spiritual Benefactor who chooses you. [pause]

Your Faery Fetch now departs in a twinkling of light. The road is now open and you continue walking toward the top of the hill.

As you reach the top, all is quiet and dark. You sit down and wait for your Faery Fetch to return. Suddenly, the energy around you begins to shift. An intense feeling of electricity moves around you. Tiny sparks of light flash, and a buzzing sound is in the air.

[pause]

---

* Again, either have someone act as a mediator and read this to your group, or pre-record it on tape and play it back as you take the journey

Your Faery Fetch reappears. Looking very intently on you, he says: "Behold, I bring your Spiritual Benefactor." As your Faery Fetch disappears, there before you, still in shadow, stands one of the Ancient Ones.

Now is the time to present your gift to the Spiritual Benefactor. Now is the time to invite your Spiritual Benefactor to step into the light and become the top point of your Energy Triad. Now is the time to allow your Spiritual Benefactor to speak and convey a message. Now is the time to also ask her/him for help in healing your Spirit. Do not forget to ask your Spiritual Benefactor to tell you, or confirm, her/his name. Relax and open.

[Meditation time permitted/approximately 15 minutes.]

The meeting of your Spiritual Benefactor has come to an end, and she/he is preparing to depart back into the Faery realm. Take a moment to thank her/him.

[pause]

As your Spiritual Benefactor fades back into the Faery realm, focus on your inner Energy Triad. See once more the bottom right and left corners, and now see the top peak of the Energy Triad as complete. See it shining with the energy of your Spiritual Benefactor. Take a full belly breath and solidify this form into your conscious awareness.

[pause]

With your next full belly breath you are going to raise your awareness back to your eyes, blinking them open.

[pause]

Taking a third full belly breath, lower your focus to your image in the mirror. Let your breathing resume its normal rhythm and gradually open your eye-lids to a normal attention.

You now have a Spiritual Benefactor.

Each Spiritual Benefactor has a quality that can help you integrate the current lesson you are undergoing. Find your Spiritual Benefactor listing below and review her/his qualities. After you have done this, don't forget to make an entry in your Book of Shadows.

The Goddesses
Aine has the quality of transformation. Whether that transformation be in regard to altered states of consciousness (such as traveling into the Dreamtime), or the ability to change things in the physical (such as your job or hair style), she emphasizes the use of intuition.

Her symbols are those of the element of air, the swan, and red mare. The air is connected to the east and spring, as well as the quality of clear thinking. The swan is the symbol of life energy. The Bird-Goddess is often the guardian of the family and clan, overseeing the continuity of life energy, the well-being and health of the family, and the increase of food supply. Swans are seen to glide between the worlds. The Faery also look upon the swan as bringing luck and wealth.

The mare is a symbol of strength and endurance, as well as regeneration and fertility. The Mare-Goddess represents personal power, both in physical and spiritual domains. In shamanic rites, the horse will often carry the rider into other dimensions.

If Aine is your Spiritual Benefactor then the time has come for you to open and allow altered states of awareness to come into your experience by developing your intuitive abilities. The time has come to surrender to the power of Spirit and accept the healing and transformation you require. During this time of transformation, do not forget where you have come from, for Wisdom comes by remembering pathways you have already walked.

Airmed has the quality of healing and earth-magick. Whether one works with the plants of their own garden, or store-bought and packaged herbs, the Devas of the plant kingdom are her allies.

Her symbols are earth, flower, herb, the circle, and the hummingbird. Through the touch of a plant she can create, or restore life. Earth is in the north and is connected to the qualities of strength and solidness. Herbs and flowers renew themselves every year as does the earth, as does the circle in its never ending cycle. Healing is also an act of renewal. The circle teaches the continuum of life.

The song of the hummingbird awakens the medicine flowers, and teaches you to perceive the presence of joy and beauty and love in your life.

If Airmed is your Spiritual Benefactor, then the time has come for you to bring forward your personal magickal qualities of working with earth-magick. To do so you must be willing to drop your judgmental attitude and relax. The time has come for you to be filled with joy and experience a renewal of the magick of living.

Breo-saighit has the qualities of inspiration and clarity. Her symbols are that of fire and the hearth. Fire is the element that cannot be controlled by humankind. It is also the vital heat of the body and the lightest of the elements, for it rises on the air. Fire is associated with life and the birth-giving aspects of nature. The human spirit is considered fire, and when we are birthed into this world, the fire of Spirit awakens within.

The hearth is a symbol for the womb. As in a hearth, the womb bakes the fetus into shape as the hearth does the dough into bread. Hearth and fire are symbols of transformation of the physical. Through her flame of inspiration, one may gain the clarity required to begin developing a new physical reality.

If Breo-saighit is your Spiritual Benefactor, then the time has come for you to let the child within shine. Through this innocence you will be reminded about trust, trusting your sparks of inspiration to lead you forward. The time has come for you to balance your personality and trust in your intuition to help transform your weakness into strengths.

Cailleach Bera has the qualities of builder, doer, and renewal. She also contains the qualities of gentleness and peace; they can be found as we understand the environment in which she dwells, usually that of lonely places, away from the villages and clans.

Her symbols are water, deer, cattle, swine, goats, and the wolf. She rules the water, the emotions, the intuition, and feelings, and illustrates the duality of water—stagnant and flowing—through her ability to dam-up a stream when she drops the rocks from her apron to build a mountain in much the same way one might resolve hurtful weeping to find inner strength, or to dismantle the dam to allow the water to flow in much the same way one might allow themselves to feel the emotion that is moving within them.

Deer are symbols of gentleness, the tender relationship that would exist between a mother and child. Cattle are connected with the more earthy aspect of this goddess in her fertility aspects, as well as in the nurturing ability to feed offspring and others with her milk.

Swine represent both life and death; the fertility aspect of the fast-growing, rounded body, as well as the dark aspect of nature that does not tolerate weakness or incompetence just as the sow will eat any of her young that are flawed. Pig was also considered the feast of the gods and was served at the ritual table.

The goat is the symbol of warmth, for the skin was valued for clothing. Finally, the wolf is the symbol of the pathfinder, the teacher.

If Cailleach Bera is your Spiritual Benefactor, then the time has come for you to find the gentleness of your Spirit. The time has come for you to nurture yourself by applying gentleness, warmth, and caring. Within you, this new Energy Triad you have just built, is your mountain. Frequent this mountain often, for in the aloneness of your power place you will find your true self. Look within for your teacher.

Cesara has also the quality of the pathfinder. She is the sojourner, who is not afraid to journey into unknown territory and face possible hostile forces. The ability to bridge gaps and unite people is her gift. Her symbol is the great above, the heavens. From out of nowhere she arrived, and into nowhere she disappeared.

If Cesara is your Spiritual Benefactor, then the time has come for you to face the obstacles that may be in front of you. Be willing to find new ways to overcome them. The time has come to renew estranged relationships with those people who, in some way, have left their mark on you and have become part of the obstacle. Receive the expansive quality of the sky and bring that feeling into your life.

Eire has the quality of truth. Exacting a fair promise and keeping it is tied into her magickal abilities. She is an energy that demands recognition, honor and homage, and in return she opens the doors and gives her protection. She is the land, or body, of Ireland, the below, supporting all those who walk upon her.

Her symbol is that of the crow. Although the crow is often associated with the war-goddesses, or death-goddesses, the crow as the symbol of Eire represents the power of regeneration, an omen of change. Through this symbol you are allowed to learn your personal integrity.

If Eire is your Spiritual Benefactor, then the time has come for you to pause and reflect on where your life may be out of balance. You are not alone, and the time has come to allow your personal will to emerge so that you may stand in your truth and speak boldly out in support of that truth.

Tailltiu has the quality of courage and endurance, skills and perfection. When called upon she will tell us the answers, or at least guide us in the right direction. She resides at the sacred heart of Ireland, Tara, and teaches us to center.

If Tailltiu is your Spiritual Benefactor, then the time has come for you to focus on your trade in life and develop those skills that will help secure your path. The time has come for you to move in the right direction and get to the center of what you do best.

The Gods

Dagda has the qualities of abundance and balance. He is the god of the earth, the Celtic Pan, representing the masculine aspect of fertility, family and home-life. He is a good provider, and a reliable and sturdy worker.

The Dagda is like the King of Pentacles in the Tarot, the Yod-Fire force of the Tetragrammation in the element of earth. This makes him a solid extension of the Father-Fire energy in the physical universe. Therefore, his energy is one that stimulates vegetation, growth, and material production. He can be thought of as the sperm which fertilizes the Mother's egg.

His symbol is the cauldron, the symbol of the womb. This womb cauldron is known for its abundance; any who eat from it are filled. The Dagda and his female cauldron represent balance between the male and female, and the willingness to be in partnership. Through this partnership the Spirit is reborn, or renewed and can begin celebrating the sense of family that has been united within.

If Dagda is your Spiritual Benefactor, then the time has come for you to renew your balance between your male and female energies. Take your responsibilities seriously, and when called upon to provide for yourself as well as others, do so with joy and celebration. Laughter and smiles are keys to opening the doors closed around you. The time has come to find the abundance in your life, finding creative ways to renew your surroundings.

Lamhfadha has the qualities of strength and protection. He is the sun-god, or Father Sky energy. He reigns over his domain, assuring that his warmth and light will shower down upon all his subjects. In his mightiness, he takes his charge seriously, and will fight to his own death in defense of those he loves, if need be.

Lugh can be compared to the King of Wands of the Tarot, representing the Fire of Fire aspect. This extremely dynamic Father Force is a volatile igniting spark; the first action. This energy can be fierce and unpredictable, but not durable. Like a volcano, its force great and uncontrollable, Lugh can be wild and warlike, a raw, unleashed energy when not worked with.

His symbol is a mighty spear that drips blood from its tip. Although it represents a weapon, which is used to defend, the spear is also phallic in nature and suggests not only strength, but also virility.

If Lamhfadha is your Spiritual Benefactor, then the time has come for you to be willing to stand up for yourself. Strengthen your environment by creating a sense of protection. Look at those areas in your life where you have allowed others to push you around.

By using Lugh's spear, you can pierce through the obstacles in your life and be triumphant. Will-power is very important, as is action, taking action for your life. No one else will make it happen for you, you must be willing to do it for yourself.

However, the lesson is also to use your energy wisely. Channel it to those areas of your life that require transformation. Do not burn yourself out.

Manannan mac Lir has the qualities of youth and long life. His realm is the vast ocean upon whose crest he walks as if the water were solid. In his palace, Emhain of the Apple-Trees, he serves the Feast of Age, at which those who eat never grow old. His helmet reflects the sun, while his body is surrounded by the moon. He is the greatest sea-god, and in his boat, Wave-sweeper, he will assure safe passage from one body of land to the next.

Like the King of Cups card of the Tarot, Lir represents the Water of Fire element. He symbolizes the subconscious realm of the human mind and the creative spark which ignites and gives birth to unconscious images. These are the qualities of sensitivity, attraction, and grace.

His symbols are water and a magick mantle that when worn produces invisibility. As the god of water he represents the emotional, intuitive element of a masculine gender. His feeling nature, and his ability to safely cross the water, demonstrates his levelheadedness.

The mantle of invisibility represents the quality of knowing when to make oneself noticed and when to remain quiet, and skirt around the edges. This emotionally balanced god teaches us the blending of wisdom and knowledge.

If Manannan mac Lir is your Spiritual Benefactor, then the time has come for you to become more aware of your emotional outbursts. The watery side of your personality is in need of grounding. By learning to wear Lir's mantle, you will be able to fit in when you feel out-of-place, and in doing so, learn from an experience that otherwise you would have avoided because of your own insecurities. The time has come to not continually draw attention to yourself, but to listen and learn.

Nuada has the qualities of competition and battle. He was the supreme war-god. He can be compared to the King of Swords in the Tarot, representing the Air of Fire. This quality symbolizes the violent, fiery power of movement as well as the vitalizing power which lies behind the Astral Realm of image and inspiration. He can be likened unto the first spark of intellectual inspiration, but in this element, it is a swift and agitated energy.

His symbol is an invincible sword that can aggressively slice through any obstacle placed before it. The sword is an instrument created specifically for killing humankind, unlike the spear, or bow-and-arrow, that were created for hunting food for survival. The sword is an attitude of attack.

If Nuada is your Spiritual Benefactor, then the time has come for you to begin working with your anger and hostilities. Are you quick to judge, find fault with, or attack others? Nuada will help you work with the brave skill of harnessing this great mental power and learn to reconcile opposing energies. When one is too quick to take action and attack any situation, then the more subtle details, or messages, will not be identified, or received, and thus applied in life.

Oengus has the quality of love and beauty. This is the Celtic Eros, the Greek Cupid. He teaches us to find the beauty in all areas of life. His symbol is that of a golden harp, upon which he plays, and all who hear follow. Music and song are his gifts; the vibration of Spirit and spreading that vibration to all life. Divine Imagination is what Oengus represents. Balancing the male common sense and the female happiness will result in an embrace in love of immense will.

Oengus' greatest gift is to gather women and men to the center, from the far without to the deep within, trembling from the body to the soul until the head of woman and the heart of man are filled with Divine Imagination.

If Oengus is your Spiritual Benefactor, then the time has come for you to look at the beauty of life and begin seeing the love that exists within it. Examining the shadow of your desires will bring you face to face with your fear. Oengus teaches you that what you fear is that your strength will be taken from you and then you can no longer be a tyrant.

The time has come to question whether you are embracing beauty, or considering it just to be a thing called virtue. What is it you call wisdom? Is it misdirected courage? The real virtue is courage, and the real courage is liberty, and the real liberty is wisdom, and wisdom is Beauty.

Traditionally, the same Spiritual Benefactor is worked with for one year; for that is only one full turning of the Great Wheel of the Year, and to fully understand the message of such an archetype, surrendering to their communion will not be completed until you have traveled through each season with them in their confidence.

In my circles, when the warrior or apprentice is ready to move into year two of their immram, then I encourage a new Spiritual Benefactor be fetched.

All of the information received from the four journeys you have undergone, provides you with the necessary ingredients in forming a very strong foundation for understanding the tradition of Faery Wicca.

This foundation is, in essence, the origin from which personal power and energy—for health and help in your life—is drawn. This foundation becomes the warrior's shield.

The Warrior's Shield

We are going to take this foundation and create a Celtic shield, which is akin to the Native American Tradition's medicine shield and the Eastern Tradition's mandala.

A mandala is a symbolic diagram, usually round or oval with radial symmetry, but sometimes square, triangular, diamond-shaped or polygonal. Oriental mandalas, especially in India, can become enormously complex. They are often viewed as mystical maps of the cosmos, or the realm of Deity, and are intended for contemplation as a religious exercise.

The mandala is the archetypal symbol of whole experience, a state in which all aspects of the self have been fully integrated and realized, and where the psychic center of the personality reigns, as Carl Jung has said.

In Sanskrit, mandala means magic circle. Practitioners of Eastern Religions meditate upon the mandala, which create specific states of awareness that foster spiritual growth.

Other mandalas may be simple personal expressions of feeling or awareness. The graphic material included in a mandala may be anything at all, from recognizable human, animal, or vegetable forms, to highly abstract designs. Spiritual insight is conveyed when one sits still and contemplates the mandala. For the whole soul, all knowledge is always present and needs only to be accessed.

In Faery Wicca our mandala is called the Warrior's Shield. The legendary giant Finn mac Cumhaill was said to have developed the most powerful Warrior's Shield by incorporating the ogham alphabet into cryptic runes, making the alphabet unintelligible, except to all but those who held the secret key, and combining them with spirals and lattice work.*

This method, known as Sluag ogham, increased the number of strokes threefold, making it into the ogham of the Multitudes, also becoming known as Finn's Tooth, Finn's Window, and Finn's Shield.

Finn's oghams are based on position within a circular or square framework, and, as such, can also be related to certain aspects of traditional cosmology, such as the directions and elements, time of day, or spiritual states of being.

His Warrior's Shields were so powerful, that to look upon the face of the shield, dazzled the viewer, often disorienting them, rendering them senseless.

Making a Warrior's Shield requires having undergone the above four journeys in order to form the inner Energy Triad, which is the foundation of the shield's design.

Creating a Celtic Shield

To create your Celtic Shield, take the information that forms your Energy Triad and turn it into a mandala for meditation when working with your Spiritual Benefactor.

Whether or not you are an artist has no bearing on the making of the shield; for all that is required is your imagination, intuition, and the information already recorded in your Book of Shadows.

Figure 17 shows the basic Energy Triad. To begin, in your Book of Shadows draw this triangle. At the bottom right corner write your Cycle and its area of perception: Mythological—Thinking; Ulster—Willing; Fenian:Feeling.

Next, in the left corner of the Energy Triad, list your area of perception keywords:

- Thinking: thinking, intelligence, knowledge.
- Willing: willing, will-power, heroism.
- Feeling: feeling, human warmth, cherished memories.

Next, on the top point of the Energy Triad, write the name of your Spiritual Benefactor: Goddesses: Aine, Airmed, Breo-saighit, Cailleach Bera, Cesara, Eire, Tailltiu; Gods: Dagda, Lamhfada, Manannan mac Lir, Nuada, Oengus.

Finally, in the center of the Energy Triad, write the name of your Faery Fetch: Beauty, Strength, Ugliness.

Study each point of the Energy Triad and connect a color and symbol to each. Then begin to create a design that represents each point; use your own creative talents or cut pictures out of magazines. Let the design of each point weave together, creating a mandala-like effect. Use your Book of Shadows to design several shield faces before you actually create the real one.

The width of the shield face needs to be approximately twelve inches and can be made of anything: a round ceramic platter, a round wooden plate, a circular piece of metal (copper is best), construction paper cut in a circle, canvas or leather stretched on a wooden embroidery hoop.

---

* Magickal symbols and the ogham magickal alphabet will be looked at in Section Two Lesson Nine: Magickal Faery Tools.

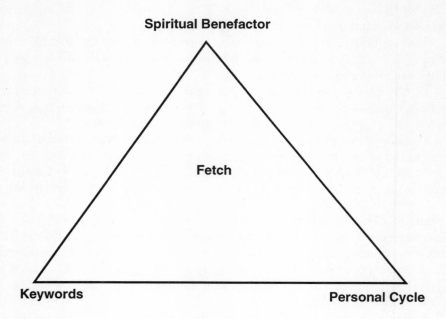

Figure 17: Energy Triad

Once you have the shield face, transfer the mandala design from your Book of Shadows onto the shield's surface. Use paint, needlepoint, markers—whatever you like. Glue on the pictures cut from magazines as well as other items chosen. Make the face of the shield as complex or as simple as you would like it to be. And above and beyond everything: Remember to take your time and be neat—this is a virtue esteemed by the Faery.

When your Celtic Shield is complete you will be hanging it on the wall before your altar for contemplation and meditation.

As you follow the roadmap of your Spirit through the creation of your shield, you will begin to grasp a better understanding of who you are. Use the shield, the roadmap of your spirit, to ground and center deeper into your personal power.

Know that with this act—of bringing forth your Warrior's Shield from within—your transformation is, indeed, beginning. Without even being aware of it, you have begun to perform magick, and as we are taught in Faery Wicca: Spirit is about forever. Magick is about Change. Let the magick that dwells within you become the foundation upon which you begin changing.

Element that is older
than the ancient earth!
O Element that was old
when Age was young!
O second of the Sacred Three
in whom the seed of Alldai
In whom the seed of the Unnameable
became the spawn of the world,
Whence the old gods,
and the fair Dedannans,
and the sons of men —
O Element of the Elements,
show me the fish of Manainn,
Show me the fish of Manainn
with the arrow in the tongue
O Element, in the name Manannan, son of Lir!

—The Dominion of Dreams
Under the Dark Star
Fiona Macleod, 1985

Lesson Nine

Magickal Faery Tools

*Take the mastery of your accomplishments in both hands
and become effective in your own realm of influence!* *

Like any other religious tradition, Faery Wicca has its standard magickal tools. Magickal tools are used for several reasons: to direct energy, to enhance personal power, and to focus attention. These three reasons are not inconclusive of tool usage, but are the primary ways in which such tools are utilized.

Magickal tools also aid in understanding the mechanics of ritual and ceremony, as well as developing psychical abilities. For these reasons, tools are a major part of the novice's spiritual development in apprenticeship. The basic tools are: the Faery wand, the cup, the athame, the pentacle, and the four talismans.

The Faery wand is the most important tool of the tradition. Above and beyond everything, it is acknowledged as the Branch of Peace, and is used in all councils and magickal workings. Traditionally, three Faery wands are eventually acquired, but only one is received during the novice's immram (voyage of apprenticeship).

The first Faery wand is called the Silver Branch of the sacred apple-tree, bearing blossoms, or fruit, which the queen of the Land of Promise and Ever-Young (Tir Tairngiri) gave to those mortals whom she wished as companions, as this ancient poem suggests:

> *A branch of the apple-tree*
> *from Emhain I bring,*
> *like those one knows;*
> *Twigs of white silver are on it,*
> *Crystal brows with blossoms.*
> —Anonymous, 10th Century

---

* Caitlin Matthews, *The Celtic Book of the Dead*, pg 94, St. Martin's Press, 1992.

Faery Wand

In myth, the Silver Branch often produced music so soothing that mortals who heard it forgot all troubles and even ceased to grieve for those whom the Banshee (death) took. The apple-branch is an ancient talisman, a key which unlocks the secret of the Land of Faery from which such talismans are brought; for the Silver Branch is the symbolic bond between the Otherworld and this world, offered as a tribute to the gods by all initiates who make the mystic immram in full consciousness. This Faery wand is considered a passport into Faeryland.

In Faery Wicca, the Silver Branch is the wand of healing and is received after the novice has journeyed into the Underworld through their own inner (Solar) realm of Spirit. The success of such a journey highlights where unhealthiness may exist. As an apprentice, bringing unhealthiness to consciousness allows transformation to take place.

When unhealthiness is identified, leaving it in a state of imbalance promotes decay of Spirit. As an apprentice, healing self is the number one priority and the first magickal working sustained.

Unless we are healed, unless we can heal ourselves first, then we cannot really expect the healing energy to successfully flow through us into another person. Therefore, when the Silver Branch is acquired, it is used on self.

The Silver Branch is, therefore, a tool of transformation. The simple act of waving the Silver Branch over the body and meditating with it in the hands activates an ability within consciousness to discern between truth and falsehood.

Creating a Silver Branch

Making your own Silver Branch requires finding a living apple tree. This is the traditional wood required for such a Faery wand.

Because this will be your first traditional Faery wand, and because it focuses on the beginning of your apprenticeship, or the beginning of your transformation from an unhealthy state to a healthy one, the ritual to obtain the branch will traditionally occur at dawn, following the evening of the new crescent moon.

Begin scouring your neighborhood and wildlife areas for apple trees. When you have found an apple tree, and if it is on somebody's property, ask permission from the owner if you can cut a branch approximately eighteen inches long and about a half-inch in thickness (try to find a branch that does not taper too thinly toward its tip). When permission has been granted, inform the owner that you will come back at a later time—which will be on the day of the next new crescent moon.

Between the time you find the apple tree and the morning you perform the ritual, visit the tree as often as possible. Sit before the tree, resting your back against its trunk, and pray to the Tree Fairy to send love and healing into the branch which you have chosen to cut. By communing with your chosen tree, the Elemental Fairy will feel respected and will give you the health and help you seek.

The following is a ceremony outline that can be used when performing your wand-cutting ritual. Take with you the following items:

- A special knife to cut the branch from the tree.
- An offering/gift to the Tree Fairy, which will be buried at the base of the tree's trunk.
- A black cloth (cotton, muslin, or wool is best) in which to wrap the branch.
- Pure spring water.

Faery Wand of Promise Cutting Ceremony

At dawn prepare yourself to visit the apple tree from which you will cut the Faery wand of promise. When you arrive at the tree, at the base of the tree trunk lay out the above listed items on the ground, then face the tree. Close your eyes and perform the Ground and Center format.

Espurge (sprinkle) the spring water on the ground around the base of the trunk in a deosil (clockwise) direction, creating a circle large enough in which to walk around the trunk. By performing this act you are designating a boundary of Sacred Space in which both you and the tree now stand.

Sit with your back against the trunk and pray to the Tree Fairy. Tell the Spirit why you have come, that you will be cutting away a branch from its boughs to use for healing yourself, and eventually for bringing health to your relations. Allow the Tree Fairy to speak to you by remaining quiet. Should the Spirit indicate that the time you have chosen is not right to perform such a ceremony, then honor this message by thanking the Tree Fairy and leaving.

When the message to continue has been received from the Tree Fairy, present the offering/gift you have brought. Explain the meaning behind the gift and then bury it in the ground at the base of the trunk.

Next, take the knife, stand before the branch soon to be cut away, and sing an honoring song, such as:

Many go into the soul,
with eyes shut tight
and mind asleep,
But Silver Branch upon this tree,
I call to you
come unto me.
Gently guide my soul to health,
with open eyes
and mind awake.
For health and help, I come to you.
For health and help, I cut you free.
For health and help, let healing begin this day.

Continue to sing this chant/song as you cut away the branch. When it comes away in your hand, hold it to your heart and envision it filled with the health and help of the loving Spirit of the Tree Fairy. Wrap the branch in the black cloth, and once again, thank the Tree Fairy for giving away part of itself to you.

You now have been gifted with a branch to transform into your Faery wand: the Silver Branch.

⁓�֍⁓

Now the work begins. Transforming the branch into the Silver Branch requires time, patience and commitment.

First Step: Strip the bark completely from the branch, using a sharp knife. When this is done, place the branch in a window that gets both sunlight and moonlight (an east or south window is best), and leave it there until the next dark moon, when the moon begins a new cycle.

In the meantime, begin preparing for the transformation of your wand by gathering together the following items that will be used to adorn it:

The Wand Crystal: In the tip of the wand will be placed a crystal. The crystal used ought to be a single terminated crystal (i.e. pointing in only one direction) so the energy flow is amplified.

You also want your crystal to be a male, or shooter, crystal. A shooter crystal radiates energy. When you hold it in the palm of your hand it will feel as if it is throbbing when you point the tip of the crystal toward the palm of your other hand. Move the crystal up and down; your palm will feel a tingling sensation, as if the crystal is shooting a stream of energy.

If a crystal pulls you into it, which means you feel a trance-like state or a desire to meditate, then the crystal is female, a receiver crystal. There are several different types of crystals to choose from, however, the best ones to use for the Faery wand are:

> Amethyst (purple) is an effective healing stone, as it acts as a sponge, absorbing the forces which are effecting the body either mentally or physically. By absorbing these forces, it is able to repel away those vibrations which the body does not need.

> Quartz (clear) mainly amplifies the energies of the one who is working with the stone. Thus, it amplifies the healing energy that is flowing from the user of the wand.

> Rose Quartz (pink) works on the emotional body and helps to balance the love emotions that often cause imbalance when misdirected. Rose quartz specifically focuses on the heart, throat, third-eye and crown chakras.

After you have chosen the crystal for your wand, it is important to clean it by smoking it over a censor (incense burner) in which sage, cedar, and sweetgrass are smoldering. Sage and cedar purify, while sweetgrass sweetens the vibration of the crystal. This method of crystal cleaning is very much like the Native American Indian traditional method of purification called smudging.

When you have smoked your crystal, bury it in the earth during the three days of the full moon (the last night of the waxing moon phase, the night of the full moon and the first night of the waning moon phase) to energize it with the influences of earth and moon, both of which affect our physical and subtle bodies.

When this is done, wrap the crystal in a black cloth and put it away until ready for use.

The Cloth Handle: A cloth handle will be put around the base of the wand where your hand grasps hold. Since this area is relatively small, you will need a piece of material approximately five inches square.

A natural fiber material, such as cotton, wool or raw silk, is the best to use because it is a pure material and has a higher vibration. As for the color and design of the fabric, keep in mind that this wand is the Silver Branch of healing. Therefore, you will want to select colors that promote healing, such as green, blue, and yellow, as well as a design that signifies wholeness and growth.

The Magickal Symbols: You will either carve or paint certain runes and magickal symbols on the shaft of the wand, such as your initials, astrological information, name of the wand, etc. If you are going to use paint, then the color of paint must be chosen, or blended. Again, you want the color to carry the vibration of healing.

If carving, I encourage the purchase of any basic wood-carving tool set that can be found at most hardware stores, or any arts-and-crafts store. Unless experienced at wood carving, using a knife is very tedious and prone to mistakes.

Choosing the magickal symbols and runes for the wand must be given deep consideration. The following chapter provides information on the traditional Celtic magickal symbols, the Gaelic alphabet, and the Irish oghams.

Writing your name in ogham, or your initials with the Gaelic alphabet, requires foreknowledge of what energy the symbol will carry. When designing your wand, remember the simpler the symbology, the better. Also, don't forget to use your Book of Shadows to illustrate different designs and layouts for possible use. Be creative and let your intuition guide you.

There are many aspects to be considered in the designing of your Faery wand. Because this is going to be used as a tool for healing and transformation, it is not something you want to simply throw together.

On the evening of the dark moon you will perform the following Faery Wand Ritual. This ritual will require the quiet and undisturbed space of one hour. Before beginning, use the Preparation Format to alter your space into a sense of sacredness. When you are ready to begin, place all materials needed before you. In addition, have the following items:

- A clean washcloth.
- A bowl of chamomile tea (pre-steeped).
- A censor and smoking mixture (as given above).
- Red paint and a small paint brush.
- An awl or sharp object to bore the hole for the crystal.
- A new black pouch to carry your Silver Branch.

Faery Wand Ritual

Hold the branch in your hands while you perform the Ground and Center format. Relax and close your eyes, focusing on the branch. In your mind, connect with the Tree Fairy. Get a sense of the Spirit's energy surrounding you and flowing through the branch.

When the healing energy of love is felt, open your eyes and hold the branch over the smoking mixture to cleanse it. As you smudge the branch, focus on healing love energy.

Soak the washcloth in the bowl of tea and wipe the branch three times with the cloth, each time re-wetting the cloth. This is the act of sealing the branch against outside influences that may be attracted to it once you begin to work with it. Again, run the branch through the smoke rising from the smudge.

On the tapered end, or end chosen to be the male end of the wand, use the awl or other sharp object to bore a hole big enough to slip the crystal in half-way. Do not make the hole too big as you do not want the crystal to fall out. Keep in mind you will not be using glue to keep the crystal in the hole, so you want it to be snug.

When the hole is just right, paint the inside of the hole with red paint, and while the paint is still wet, push the crystal down into the hole. Paint the opposite end of the branch, which is now the designated female end of the wand. By painting both ends red, you are performing an act of sympathetic magick. The red paint is symbolic of your blood. In this act, you are giving your blood to the wand in an act of bringing the Silver Branch to life. When this act is complete, the flat end of the branch is now the female, or receiver, end, and the end holding the crystal is now the male, or sender, end.

Hold the female end in your left hand and the male end in your right. Close your eyes and follow your breath into your navel center, the point of gravity wherein the Heavenly Realm and the Underworld meet. As you relax your mind, call to your Faery Fetch.

When your companion has arrived, send him to fetch your Spiritual Benefactor. Once your Spiritual Benefactor has arrived, share the living branch with her/him. Explain to her/him that you are transforming the branch into your Faery wand and would like her/him to bless it as your Silver Branch. Explain that you will use this magickal and sacred tool as an aide for healing yourself and eventually helping to heal others. Then allow your Spiritual Benefactor to speak to you.

[Meditation time provided/approximately 15 minutes]

Now is the time to either finish adorning the Silver Branch with the cloth handle on the female end and adding the symbols and runes already chosen, or wrap it in the new black pouch and put it away until you are ready to adorn it. Remember, that when you adorn your Silver Branch, each time you do so, focus on the intent of the healing love energy sealed within it. Complete the adornment of the Silver Branch by the next full moon, at which time you perform the Magickal Tool Consecration Ritual given at the end of this chapter.

You now have your first traditional magickal and sacred tool, your Silver Branch. Use it wisely.

Now that you have your Silver Branch, how might you use it? This is a common question. Your Silver Branch is a magickal tool. The more you care for it as if it is alive, and the more you work with it by using the following Faery Wand Exercises, the more you will develop a psychic connection with your Silver Branch.

All magickal tools become based on such a connection. If we do not have a psychic link with a tool, then it cannot really be considered magickal. All magickal tools become sacred when we care for them with respect. Treating a magickal tool as an inanimate object enforces the mental image that it is a useless object. By linking-up with a magickal tool as if it were a living energy and exposing it to both sunlight and moonlight on a regular basis reinforces our psychic link to the tool.

Faery Wand Exercises

Before we take a look at the following exercises, I would like to say a few things regarding the care of your wand. Like other items in which you have placed a value or worth, the wand should be viewed in this vein.

The wand likes being wrapped with softness and kept warm when not in use. So take the time to create a special black pouch for your wand of velvet or soft flannel. Keep a fresh sprig of lemon balm or lavender inside the pouch, as the essence of both these herbs resonate with Faery wands.

Also, Faery wands love twilight, as this is the time of entrance into their realm. Let your wand visit the outdoors during twilight at least once or twice a month, and especially at both the dark moon and full moon. This will keep your Silver Branch energized, or it will begin to withdraw from you. Remember, you have created the Silver Branch to use as a magickal tool. If you don't use it, you lose it!

The following exercises are given to help you become more familiar with the Faery wand as a working tool, thus creating a psychic bond with it. Most of the exercises are derived from the Grimoire of the Shadows of the Outer Court of Clach Nam Fitheach Dubh.

Thought and Meditation

What does your wand mean to you? When you hear the words wand, rod, club—these are a few of the terms applied to the Faery wand—what images come to mind? As the owner of a Faery wand it is important to have a clear understanding of the sensual responses created by each of the above words.

In the Tarot system of divination, one of the minor arcana suits is called Wands or Rods. If you lay the suit (ace to ten) out and study it, a message is given in relationship to the meaning or lesson of the suit of Wands or Rods. The suit of Wands is connected to the direction of south, and the element of fire. The suit teaches us to pay attention to the face we present to the world, as well as asks us to answer these questions:

- Who are you?
- What do you want to do out there, in the world?
- How do you want others to perceive you?
- Do you work better in partnerships or alone?
- Is status quo more important to you then ethical consideration of others?
- Do you repel or attract others to you?
- Do you create struggle?
- How do you use the scepter of your skill?

Playing cards, the modern offspring of Tarot cards, contain the Wands or Rods of the Tarot in the form of Clubs. Unlike the suit of Wands, the Clubs have a very different feel. Try laying out all the Club cards and see if you get the same message you did from the Tarot Wands. Try it and see.

This first exercise is to give thought and meditation toward understanding, very thoroughly, what the terms Wands, Rods, and Clubs really mean to you. In your Book of Shadows set up a worksheet page with columns like those shown in Figure 18.

Under each category, list all the types of Wands, Rods, and Clubs you can think of (listing material objects all the way through to spiritual meanings) as shown. Study each meaning and begin to understand what type of meaning you would like to attach to your Faery wand.

Attraction and Repulsion

This is a visualization exercise that will help you build a psychic connection with your wand. The psychic connection is established when you realize that your wand is an extension of you. As you develop this connection, using the wand as a diviner or pendulum takes on significant new meaning.

Find a blank section of wall (no pictures hanging on it, and no furniture against it). Stand approximately one foot from the wall and then position a soft chair about a foot directly behind you.

Subject or Symbol	Material Manifestation	Mind Manifestation (how you think it)	Soul Creation (how you feel it)	Principle Spirit/Origin
wand	pen	word	meaning	intention
	match	lighting	illumination	fire
	stick	support	help	aid
	bar	separate	forbid	prevent
rod	steel	strength	support	fire
	fishing pole	sport	food	survival
	lamp post	light	illumination	electricity
club	weapon	defense	strong	survival
	chair	support	help	aid

Figure 18: Wand Exercise 1

Hold the female end of your wand with your left hand, press the end firmly against your solar plexus chakra (about an inch above the belly button). Grip the middle of the wand, halfway between both ends, with your right hand, pointing your thumb and forefinger of each hand forward. The male end of the wand will point directly toward the wall.

Close your eyes and visualize the wand drawing you toward the wall. As you feel the forward pull, gently move with it until you feel the male end of your wand settle against the wall.

Remain at the wall, but now visualize the wand repelling you away from the wall. Allow the push to get stronger and stronger until you feel as if you are losing your balance and fall back into the chair. Repeat both operations several times. Perform this daily for a week.

An alternative form of using this exercise would be to perform the above with an imaginary (astral) wand sticking out of your solar plexus, allowing it to draw you forward or repel you backwards. You would continue to practice both methods until satisfied with the results.

When you use your wand this way you are developing a language with it, and in time the wand will actually begin to speak to you. As it attracts you toward an object, place, or person, it is giving you a positive, or yes, response. If it repels you away from an object, person, or place, your wand is telling you the situation is negative, or is giving you a no response.

The Blue-Energy
This exercise is designed to begin moving your own energy out from your body by using the wand as a channel. Because the wand is the primary tool of the tradition it is used to cast the Great Circle.

In a dimly lit room, clasp the female end of your wand in both hands. Hold it to your heart and ground and center using the breath exercise already taught in the second chapter. When you feel your energy quiet down and your awareness focused on the exercise you are about to perform, take a deep belly breath and relax.

Transfer the wand completely into your right hand. Allow your forefinger to lay on top of the wand, pointing toward the male end, and clasp your left hand on top of your right.

Point the wand out before you and exhale. As you exhale, visualize your energy flowing through your right hand into your wand. As your energy flows out of the tip of the wand, imagine it coming out in a thin blue stream. Very gently move the wand to the right in a circling motion. Concentrate.

Repeat the above a few more times. Practice until you truly begin to see the blue-energy shoot out of your wand. This may take a couple of months to achieve, but the first time you actually see the blue-energy will be a great reward.

Preparation for Spellcraft
We use our wands to imbue something with a positive energy, or send energy out to manifest a desire in our physical lives. We also use the wand to release and send away negativity. The following two methods will help develop the skill to imbue and send energy during spellcraft.

Imbuing: Find a small and very commonplace object, such as a glass, or book, or statuette. Place it somewhere in your room. With your wand in your right hand, draw a single circle deosil around it, then point the wand at the object and imbue (fill) it with some interesting quality, such as a musical tone to be heard in the mind, a faint mist about it almost invisible to the eye, or a feeling of happiness. Continue to imbue the object with your intent until you feel you have strongly built the energy around the object.

For the next few days, let your attention go immediately to the object every time you enter the room, in an act of rebuilding the intense quality. Remove the object and put it back where it is normally kept.

If the object continues to conjure your attention to it each time you enter the room where it is kept, then your work was successful. However, if you completely forget about the object, and one day remember this exercise, then your attempts were unsuccessful, and you need to continue practicing this exercise until your focus becomes stronger and the exercise becomes successful.

Sending: Find an odd, incongruous object and place it in your room. Draw a widdershin (counterclockwise) circle about it. Point the tip of your wand at it and send the command: "Go out! Go out!" at it. Try to feel an intense rejection.

Continue sending this rejection at the object until you have strongly built this energy around it. In the following couple of days ignore the object whenever you enter the room.

The exercise is accomplished when you can stay in the room and truly not notice the object. When you become aware that this is indeed the case, the exercise has ended and you can return the object to its normal place of keeping. However, if you were unsuccessful, repeat the exercise until your results are successful.

Astral Stairway
The next exercise will show you how to use your wand as an astral ladder when going on shamanic journeys.

Stand the wand upright with your right hand (possibly resting it on some object for extra height). Close your eyes and imagine it as the central post of a spiral stairway, and walk around it as if climbing stairs.

Climb thirty-five steps, imagining that you are ascending into the Heavenly Realm. With your eyes still closed, reverse your steps at the top and descend, widdershin, the thirty-five steps until you come back into your body. Repeat.

NOTE: You can also use this to descend into the Underworld to go on a deep inner journey, in which you would return to your conscious awareness by ascending, deosil, back up the stairway into your body.

Protection
This exercise will teach you to begin using your wand for protection work, as if the wand were actually going to prevent a bad fall through an open window, securely barring unwanted intruders from coming into your home through open windows and doors, or keeping you and your family safe from a wild, raging storm.

Hold the wand horizontally before you with the female end to the left and the male end to the right. Make sure your thumbs touch together in the middle of the wand.

Slowly approach an open door. Stand a foot before the door. Close your eyes and focus on the wand. Begin to build up a feeling of protection and send that feeling of protection into the wand.

When you feel you have successfully built up the protection energy in the wand, allow the wand to gently pull you forward toward the door. As you begin to move slowly forward, trust that the wand will stop you safely within the doorway, as you feel the protective check of the wand, and sense a secure feeling, say "Stop!"

Open your eyes and see if you are standing in the doorway. If you stopped before the doorway, you did not trust enough to allow the wand to protect you. If you walked through the doorway, you did not build-up enough protection energy in the wand.

Repeat until you begin to work with the wand in a balanced way, allowing the wand to use the protection energy by stopping you exactly in the doorway.

Passing

This exercise is similar to the preceding one. However, the focus is on feelings of peace and blessings.

Hold the wand in the doorway as in the previous exercise, then switch your right hand so that both thumbs point to the male end. Close your eyes and lift the male end of the wand up, holding the wand parallel to your body. Say: Proceed in peace!

With eyes closed, very slowly pass through the door. Repeat until you feel a sense of peace come over you as you pass through the door.

A variation on the above: repeat the same action, but rather than move forward, step back as if inviting a well-liked and very good friend into your home, saying: You are blessed and welcome. Repeat until you feel a sense of love come over you.

If you develop a communication with your wand through the above exercises, your wand will very clearly begin to speak to you. I've had my wand suddenly fly out of my hands and fall to the floor between me and another individual. The wand fell horizontally blocking the individual's energy from me. Thus, my wand immediately created a protection energy before me, while sending me the message to stop.

As stated earlier, wands become an extension of your Spirit, so the more you bond with it, the more the wand will work in cooperation with you. Be sure to record all exercise results in your Book of Shadows.

⁕⁕⁕

As I mentioned earlier in the chapter, there are traditionally three Faery wands acquired—the first being the Silver Branch of apprenticeship. The second and third wands are the Bronze Branch of the Initiate, and the Gold Branch of the Elder.

The Bronze Branch is often made of oak, willow, or birch. It is the wand which represents the mystery of life and death, as undergone during the ceremony of Initiation, and is used in herbcraft and spellwork.

The traditional design of the Bronze Branch is a wand ending with a little spike or crescent with gently tinkling bells attached to the sending, or masculine, end of the branch. The crescent represents the Initiate's secure connection with their Lunar/Solar nature, which is the relationship that is formed during apprenticeship.

Embedded in the receiving, or feminine, end of the branch is a smooth circular stone, usually representing the Initiate's personal power. The power stone acknowledges that the Initiate has, indeed, connected with their power, has awakened such power, and is consciously working in cooperation with it and Spirit.

The Gold Branch of the Ollamh (Elder Priestess or Elder Priest) is received by those Initiates who answer the calling of becoming a spiritual teacher. This branch takes years to receive. Because of the amount of work required to attain the adeptness of an Elder in Faery Wicca, few ever acquire the Gold Branch.

The Gold Branch is the Elder's representative of their level of adeptness and leadership in the spiritual community. The Gold Branch is the true Branch of Peace, for it is taken to all councils and used for working with the natural world.

The traditional wood used for this is the yew; the tree of death. The tip of the Gold Branch divides into three smaller branches, representing the Trinity or threefold nature of life: the mother, father, and holy child, with whom the Elder works in coalition for the health and help of all relations who walk the earth. The other details of the Gold Branch are known only to those of us who have undergone such a rite of passage, and is kept within the realms of that wisdom to be kept secret.

Because this volume deals only with the immram toward the first degree of Initiation, I will not go further into the Bronze and Gold Branches of the tradition, for each require another level of traditional wisdoms and esoteric teachings not set forth here, as well as each a specific ritual. Rather, I leave you to the acquirement of your first Faery wand, the many lessons that will be learned through the usage of such a magickal tool, and these words of the oral tradition:

> *Wand of magick healing light, send forth this love by full moon light to the apprentice near and far, and as the dawn breaks on yonder day, I pray you learn its wisdom by working it in a Sacred Way.*

Athame, Cup, and Pentacle

The athame, cup, and pentacle are considered the working tools of Faery Wicca. In other words, they are the tools that are used to cast the Great Circle, for the ritual offering of Cakes and Cream to the Ancient Ones and to perform spellcraft.

The Athame (ceremonial knife)—This is the tool of the east quarter, of mind, the power of air, and of a masculine nature. It is used to cut the boundary of the Great Circle before each ceremony and ritual.

Traditionally in Faery Wicca, athames were not used. Metal, specifically iron, was held as a protection against Faery, and, therefore, kept them at bay.* In modern Faery Wicca we have incorporated the use of the athame, seeking that the blade be made of silver, copper, bone, or gold, with either a wooden or bone handle.

---

* To understand the ancient Pagan's alarm against using iron tools in ceremony, I would highly encourage a reading of Riane Eisler's book, *The Chalice and the Blade.*

Unlike other Wiccan traditions, especially Gardnarian, Ceremonial Magic, or other orders of high magick, our athames are basic and can be any shape or size; the handle can be of any color.

Should the owner of an athame wish to etch magickal runes and other symbols on the blade or in the handle, so be it. There are no hard rules in Faery Wicca, other than that no part of the ceremonial knife be made of iron. Once an appropriate knife is chosen, it is then dully consecrated, using the ritual format at the end of this chapter.

The Cup— This is the tool of the west, the heart or emotions, water, and of the feminine energy. Its counter-magickal tool is the athame, which represents the masculine energy. When the two are joined—the blade of the athame lowered into the liquid held in the womb of the cup—male and female join, enacting hierogamos: the union of god and goddess toward which all people unconsciously aspire.

Aside from all other symbolism connected to the cup (i.e. the womb of the Great Mother, the container of the elixir of life [blood], cauldron of regeneration) the most basic symbolism the cup represents in Faery Wicca is Truth.

In Faery Wicca, we first begin working with the Faery wand, the magickal tool which puts us in touch with our own power, so that we are truly ready to begin working with our truth.

The symbolism of the Faery wand promoted balance, encompassing both male and female energy aspects, with an emphasis on self-healing and self-balance. The cup promotes truth through reembracing, for some, the feminine polarity of life, or the Great Mother Goddess from whose womb all life sprang.

Earth is also symbolic of the Great Mother, and the ocean of Her womb, for all physical life as we know it on our planet literally crawled from the depths of the ocean. It is not coincidental that the ocean is connected to the womb, which is connected to the cup. The cup is the tool of the west and the west is the element of water, and the element of water is of a female energy (Figure 19).

Through the heart, through truth, the polarities found within life can be grounded into the earth, by acknowledging that both earth and water are required for survival.

In ceremony, the cup is used to offer the traditional cream to the Ancient Ones, in remembrance that from them comes wisdom.

Copper, pewter, and silver are the materials used for the cup, which normally has a stem, making it more a goblet then an actual cup. As for inscribing the outside with magickal runes and symbols, that is left to the decision of the owner; it is an act neither encouraged nor discouraged. Once the appropriate cup is obtained it is then consecrated, using the ritual format provided at the end of this chapter.

The Pentacle— This is the tool of the north, of the body, of the earth, and is of a feminine and masculine nature. It is through the symbol of the pentacle (the five-pointed star within a circle) we see the balance of the other three elements coming together to form a whole.

In Faery Wicca, air, fire, and water are believed to have existed before the formulation of the fourth element earth. Therefore, when these three elements joined, the addition of the fourth was created. With the fourth comes the living Spirit, which

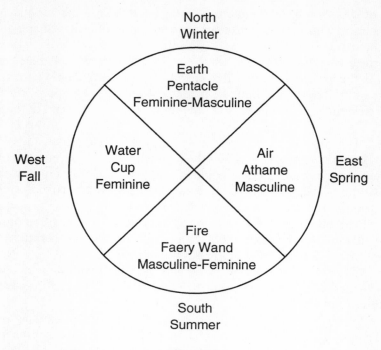

Figure 19

is symbolized by the fifth point on the pentacle. (Again, the five-fifths of the Great Circle enacted.)

Naturally, life constitutes both female and male energy, therefore, the earth exemplifies this by being of a feminine-masculine nature. Also, north is the Above, south is the Below. South is of a masculine-feminine nature, and north, as the Above, works as a mirror, reflecting the balance, although in a reversal of feminine-masculine.

In ceremony, the pentacle is used as a platter upon which are carried the cakes offered to the Ancient Ones. These cakes represent the substance of the earth. The pentacle is also used for meditation, gaining deeper insight into the macrocosm of the universe*.

Pentacle Platters are preferably made of wood. Obtaining a nine-to twelve-inch circular wood plate, the pentacle can thus be burned into the wood or painted on the surface.

Should the pentacle design be painted, the colors green and white would be used (refer to Lesson Six: Sacred Space; The Five-Fifths Altar Face). Once a suitable pentacle platter has been created, it is then properly consecrated, using the ritual format provided at the end of this chapter. Acquiring the four magickal tools—the Faery wand, cup, athame, and pentacle—provides a complete, basic working set of magickal tools.

---

* For more work with the pentacle in meditation, refer to my book, *An Act of Woman Power*. Whitford Press.

The Four Sacred Talismans

The final magickal tools to be worked with are the Four Sacred Talismans, which were considered the four great treasures of the Tuatha De Danann. Each of the four Sacred Talismans are connected to one of the Four Cities where the De Danann are said to have learned all their magickal abilities: Falias in the north, Gorias in the east, Finias in the south, and Murias in the west.

> *There are four cities that no mortal eye has seen but that the soul knows; these are Gorias, that is in the East, and Finias that is in the South; and Murias that is in the West; and Falias that is in the North. And the symbol of Falias is the stone of death, which is crowned with pale fire. And the symbol of Gorias is the dividing sword. And the symbol of Finias is a spear. And the symbol of Murias is a hollow that is filled with water and fading light.* *

As already discussed, orienting oneself to the land, the directions, and the elements is a powerful key to working within the Land of Faery. By using these, we attune ourselves to the holism of the primal land.

The Sword of Nuada—In the myths surrounding Nuada's sword, no one escaped from it when it was drawn from its scabbard. As a talisman, it is the key that opens the door leading into the sacred city of Gorias, and is a dagger or small sword of bronze or stone (not iron or steel).

In visualization, this talisman is connected to stone pillars, stone circles, that help to align us to the rising of the light, or dawn, in just such a way that the stone monument of Newgrange is aligned to the winter solstice sun.

Connecting with this talisman brings forth insight into the direction of east, the element of air, the season of spring, the mental body, illumination, clarity and inspiration. As the symbol of the dividing sword, it is used to cut through the veil, enhance Second-Sight and connect us to the breath of Spirit.

The Spear of Lugh—In the myths surrounding the spear, no victory could be won against it nor against him who had it in their hand, and, continually from the tip of the spear, blood dripped. When not in use the tip of the spear was submerged in the Dagda's cauldron. The use of the word *ibar* meant the spear would hit its mark. The use of the word *athibar* meant it would come back to the hand that threw it.

As a talisman, it is the key that unlocks the door to the sacred city of Finias, and is a straight branch that has been pulled in one swift motion or cut, without steel or

---

* Fione Macleod, *The Little Book of the Great Enchantment.*

iron, from a tree with white or silver bark. The bark is then incised with a spiraling pattern design.

In visualization, the spear is connected to trees, as if seeking their shade from the hot, noon-day sun. Two groups of trees are worked with in connection to the Spear. In one case, two trees that are standing side-by-side like pillars, one of green leaves and branches, the other of brilliant orange, white, and red flames that continually reverse the image of the other tree, are used. The other group are tall and slender trees, similar to poplar trees, but with silver-grey bark and white, pale-green, and silver leaves, with many white flowers. Such a connection to trees ties in the ancient alphabet and magickal symbols of the Celts, which are primarily those of trees, as will be discussed at a later time.

Working with this talisman generates insight into the direction of south, the season of summer, the element of fire, the will, passion, innocence, and trust. As a symbol of the staff, it is phallic in nature, and speaks to us of the fire of creation.

The Undry, The Cauldron of the Dagda—In the myths surrounding the cauldron of regeneration, no company would go away unsatisfied. As a talisman, it is the key which opens the door to the sacred city of Murias, and is a cauldron, or bowl, containing pure water.

In visualization, the cauldron is connected to a clear stream of flowing water that flows to a golden-red sea with dark green and blue waves. The stream flows through low hills, framing the sea with the setting sun at the horizon. Harp music is also connected to the cauldron, as are lakes and waterfalls, which ultimately move to the sea.

To connect with such a talisman brings forth insight into the direction of west, the element of water, the season of autumn, the emotional body, love, wisdom, decline, and release. As the symbol that is filled with bubbling water and fading light, we are eased into the realm of intuition, which can only flow when we relax our attentive focus on the physical realm and move into a state of relaxed attention, or as we have already discussed, soft-sight.

The Great Fal, The Stone of Destiny—The person under whom this stone shrieked was king of Ireland; thus, many aspired to become king and many stood upon it without acknowledgement. The Stone of Destiny was brought with the Tuatha De Danann from the land of Falias—a sacred and unknown realm located in the north. From this land they brought the Fal, which they placed on the heart center of Cathair Crofthind.

From the Fal forms of divination developed by using white stones (quartz crystals) found in Ireland. As a talisman it is the key that unlocks the door into the sacred city of Falias, and is either a quartz crystal rock or a stone with quartz crystal veins.

In visualization, the Fal is connected to a low thorn hedge, wild and uncut, as well as a cave in which we enter a maze eventually leading to a open cavern in the midnight land, or the Underworld.

To connect with such a talisman brings forth insight into the direction of the north, the element of earth, the season of winter, the physical body, the stars inside the earth, death and rebirth. As the stone of death crowned with a pale fire we are brought into kinship with the Ancestors and the wisdom of the great Earth Spirit.

In Faery Wicca, magickal tools are consecrated at the time of dark moon, when the moon begins her new cycle, thus birthing a new wave of energy. For astrologers, it would be wise to choose a dark moon when the energy is compatible with the aspects of your natal chart, but for those of us who are not so intensely tapped into the movement of the heavens, the next dark moon will always serve the purpose.

The following is a basic consecration ritual as practiced in Faery Wiccan circles. Simply make the necessary name/tool changes, and any other descriptive adjustments for each usage. The format I've presented here is with emphasis on the consecration of the Silver Branch.

This ritual will require the quiet and undisturbed space of thirty minutes. The following items will be needed:

- The magickal tool and its black pouch.
- The smoking mixture and censor.
- Consecration oil, such as heather or yarrow.

Undergo the Preparation Format, setting up all necessary items required for the ritual, along with the magickal tool being consecrated. When your space has been altered, perform the Ground and Center format.

Magickal Tool Consecration Ritual
Hold the Silver Branch [tool name] to your heart and pray. Pray to your concept of what God or Goddess or the Great Spirit may mean to you. Pray and charge the Silver Branch [tool name] into the sacred way of healing [or however the magickal tool or talisman will be used]. Speak your prayer four times, each time including this statement:

> *I consecrate this Silver Branch [tool name] of healing [function of tool or talisman] for the positive benefit of all my relations. Help me to know what is right. Help me to heal [use of tool or talisman].*

When you have finished speaking your prayer four times, quiet yourself. Smoke the Silver Branch [tool name], passing it through the incense smoke once for each side of the wand [three times in the case of the wand].

Cradle the Silver Branch [tool name] in your hands, relax and move into your inner realm. Call your Faery Fetch to you. Once he has appeared, send him to Fetch your Spiritual Benefactor. When the Spiritual Benefactor has appeared, inform her/him that you are ready to consecrate your magickal tool, but before doing so, need to receive a blessing from Faery. Relax and open to receive the blessing from the Spiritual Benefactor.

[Meditation time provided/approximately 15 minutes.]

With the blessing received, commit it to consciousness. Thank your Spiritual Benefactor. Come back to a normal attention, using the three breaths of awakening.

Now is the time to consecrate the Silver Branch [tool name], by marking it three times with the Consecration Oil, each time reciting the Blessing of Faery given you by the Spiritual Benefactor. When complete, say:

Wind comes from the spring star in the East
Fire from the summer star in the South
Water from the autumn star in the West
Wisdom, silence and death from the winter star in the North
By the powers of earth, moon and sun
By the powers of air, fire and water
The will of the great art be done.

Blow your breath three times over the Silver Branch [tool name]. Place it back in its black pouch. You have now charged this magickal tool. Use it wisely, remembering the ancient rune:

> *What good be tools without the inner light? What good*
> *be magick without wisdom-sight?*

*hey're glancing through
the glimmer of the quiet eve,
Away in milky wavings of neck
and ankle bare;
The heavy-sliding stream
in its sleepy song they leave,
And the crags in ghostly air:*

*And linking hand in hand, and singing as they go,
The maids along the hillside
have ta'en their fearless way,
Till they come to where the rowan trees in lonely beauty grow
Beside the Fairy Hawthorn gray.*

*The Hawthorn stands between the ashes tall and slim,
Like matron with her twin grand-daughters at her knee;
The rowan berries cluster
o'er her low head gray and dim
In ruddy kisses sweet to see.*

*The merry maidens four have ranged them in a row,
Between each lovely couple a stately rowan stem,
And away in mazes wavy, like skimming birds they go,
Oh never caroll'd bird like them!*

*But solemn is the silence of the silvery haze
That drinks away their voices in echoless repose,
And dreamily the evening has still'd the haunted braes
And dreamier the gloaming grows.*

*Till out of night the earth has roll'd her dewy side,
With every haunted mountain and streamy vale below;
When, as the mist dissolves in the yellow morning tide,
The maidens' trance dissolveth so.*

—*The Fairy Thorn*
Sir Samuel Ferguson, 1830

And the Witch Queen shared her
prophecies and cures,
        visions and magic.

Lesson 10

Magickal Symbols

This hoop: what does it mean to us? What is the riddle of the hoop? How many men put it here? A small number? A multitude?[22]

In esoteric studies, the most enthralling information for the novice is magickal symbols, runes, and alphabets once used to encode the teachings of the Mysteries, for such items are indeed codes, not only used as a secret language to communicate information between adepts, but also to empower working tools and spellcraft, as well as for divination. In this chapter, we will look at the Irish ogham, the Gaelic alphabet, Celtic symbols, and numerology.

The Irish Oghams

Today, the most commonly acknowledged form of the Celtic oghams is called the Beth-Luis-Nion (Birch-Rowan-Ash) Alphabet, which takes its name from the series of sacred trees whose initials are the sequence of its letters. This ogham alphabet was described by the 17th century Irish bard, Roderick O'Flaherty, in his book *Ogygia*. According to O'Flaherty, his information came from the clan bard, Duald MacFirbis, of the O'Briens.

Scholars disagree on the origin of the ogham (dating the script as early as 2200 B.C.E.* and as late as the 2nd century C.E. †, and all agree, or at least speculate, that this tree-alphabet may have been created in a time when trees were worshiped as deities.

---

22 From the Irish epic *Tain Bo Cuailnge,* The Army Encounter Cu Chulainn, pg 70., translated by Thomas Kinsell, Oxford Unitersity Press, 1969/1990.

* This dating is based upon markings found on small chalk slabs by Alexander Keiller during excavations at Windmill Hill in southern England.

†This date is given by the ogham expert, Professor Brendan O'Hehir, of the University of Berkely, Calif.

The concept of the tree as a deity, containing the universe, deeply rooted in the earth, containing all the knowledge of the Underworld, with its branches spreading throughout the heavens, containing all that exists, can be traced through almost every major religion of the world.

Hebrew mysticism, as discussed in the Jewish holy book called the Qabbalah, focuses on the Tree of Life, a three-pillared, ten-branched universe. In the Muslim Koran, we read about the Tooba Tree, the paradise tree. The Scandinavian World Tree is known as Yggdrasil, while the World Tree in India is known as Asvattha, the fig. Buddha was known to sit under the Bo-Tree, which oversaw his enlightenment, and Christ carried the Palm leaves. In the southwestern United States, trees in desolate areas are said to have been the sites for the entrances used by the Anasazi Indians to journey to and from the third world and this one.

Whether the alphabet was developed out of reverence for deity, as a magickal system, or simply as a means of secret communications, it has been, and continues to be, a point of interest for many people who study ancient religions and systems of magick.

The ogham was used in Ireland some centuries before the introduction of the Roman alphabet, for there are several hundred known ancient ogham inscriptions on rock faces, stones, crosses, portable artifacts, and manuscripts. R. A. S. Macalister, a chief druid, published 385 known inscriptions from the British Isles in the early 1940s. Interestingly, 82 percent were found in Ireland, while the majority of the others were in Scotland and Wales, and the remaining in England and mainland Europe.

In Faery Wicca, we call the Irish ogham: Ogaim na nGadhel. In the Irish language today, the word *oghum* means ancient alphabet. Its invention is credited in *The Book of Ballymote* to Ogma* Sun-face, as shown below:

> From whence, what time, and what person, and from what cause did the ogham spring? The place is Hybernia's Isle, which we Scots inhabit; in the time of Breass, the son of Elathan, then king of all Ireland. The person was Ogma MacElathan, the son of Dealbadh, brother to Breass; for Breass, Ogma and Dealbadh were three sons of Elathan, who was the son of Dealbath.
>
> Ogma, being a man much skilled in dialects and in poetry, it was he who invented ogham, its object being for signs of secret speech known only to the learned, and designed to be kept from the vulgar and poor of the nation . . . It is called ogham, from the inventor, Ogma. The derivation is ogham, from "ghuaim", that is the "guaim" or wisdom through which the bards were enabled to compose; for by its branches the Irish Bards sounded their verses. "Soim" was the first thing written in ogham. On a Birch it was written, and given to Lugh, the son of Ethlem ...

---

* Ogma is one of the early gods who was pictured as a veteran Hercules with club and lion-skin, drawing crowds of prisoners along with golden chains connnected by their ears to the tip of his tongue. He was the Tuatha De Danann patron of literature.

The Standard Irish Oghams

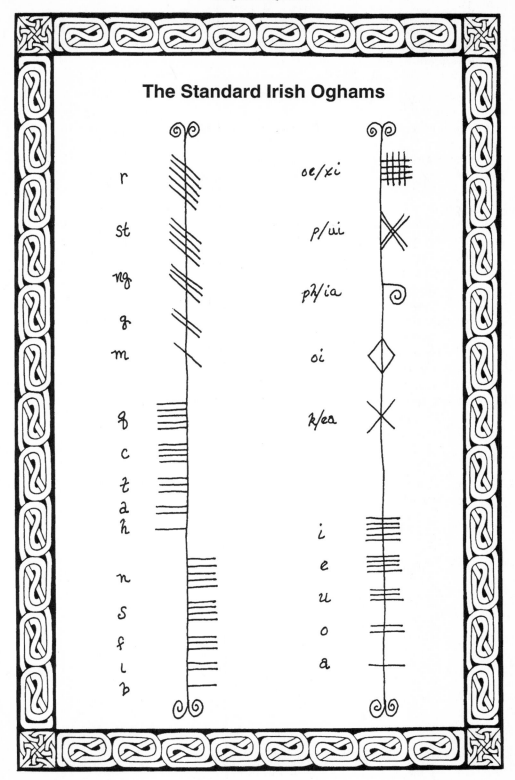

Figure 20

The symbols of the ogham are arranged along a line called the druim or principal ridge (Figure 20). All characters of the ogham are in contact with the druim, and are scribed either above, below, or through the druim.

Originally, the ogham was intended for inscriptions upon upright, or vertical, pillar/stones, or wood slats and posts, and were written from below to above. The markings equivalent for letters were notches cut across, or strokes made upon, one of the faces of the angle. The most common way of inscribing a message was, however, nicking the inscription on wooden billets.

When written horizontally, the upper side of the druim is counted as the left-hand side, and the lower side of the druim is counted as the right-hand side. Structurally, the ogham script is written from left to right just as the English language.

Originally, there were only twenty characters, but today the oghams number twenty-five (fifteen consonants, five vowels and five dipthongs), and are arranged in five basic divisions, each with five characters. According to *The Book of Ballymote*, the original divisions were: "B and her five; H and her five; M and her five; and A and her five"; the fifth division, bringing in the diphthongs, are explained further:

> *From whence come the figures and namesakes in the explanation of B, L and N ogham? From the branches and limbs of the Oak Tree: they formed ideas which they expressed in sounds, that is, as the stalk of the bush is its noblest part, from them they formed the seven chief figures as vowels, thus: A, O, U, E, I, EA, OI ... and they formed three others, which they added to these as helpers, formed on different sides of the line, thus: UI, IA, AE ... The branches of the wood give figures for the branches and veins of ogham, chief of all. The tribe of B from Birch, and the daughter, that is the Ash of the wood, is chief; and of them the first alphabet was formed; of L, from Luis, the Quicken Tree of the wood; F from Fearn, the Alder, good for shields; S from Sail, a Willow from the wood; N in ogham from Nin, the Ash for spears; H from Huath, Whitethorn, a crooked tree or bush, because of her thorns; D from Dur, the Oak of Fate from the wood; T from Tine, Cyrpess, or from the Elder Tree; C from Coll, the Hazel of the wood; Q from Quert, Apple, Aspen or Mountain Ash; M from Mediu, the Vine, branching finely; G from Gort, Ivy towering; NG from Ngetal or Gilcach, a Reed; ST or Z from Draighean, Blackthorn; R, Graif; A from Ailm, Fir; O from On, the Broom or Furze; U from Up, Heath; E from Edadh, trembling Aspen; OI, Oir, the Spindle Tree; UI, Uinlleann, Honeysuckle; IO, Ifin, the Gooseberry; AE, Amancholl, the Witch Hazel; Pine Ogham, that is the divine Pine from the wood, from whence are drawn the four 'Ifins', or Vineyard, thus #, per alios, the name of that branch.*

Before, we look at the Irish ogham, it is important to clarify the difference between the commonly accepted Beth-Luis-Nion alphabet being used today as the ogham, and the oghams used in Faery Wicca.

As mentioned above, the Beth-Luis-Nion* alphabet is ascribed to O'Flaherty. He listed the ogham characters with their names as: B, Boibel; L, Loth; F (V), Forann; N, Neiagadon; S, Salia; H, Uiria; D, Daibhaith; T, Teilmon; C, Caoi; CC, Cailep; M, Moiria; G, Gath; Ng, Ngoimar; Y, Idra; R, Riuben; A, Acab; O, Ose, U, Ura; E, Esu; I, Jaichim, which will not be the system under study here.

The Irish oghams consists of five vowels, each relating to a season or focusing on the solar energy. All the consonants of this alphabet form a calendar of seasonal tree-magick, of which all its trees figure prominently in European folklore. This seasonal tree-magick calendar is made up of thirteen true lunar months consisting of twenty-eight days, plus one extra day at the end of the calendar.

Both Irish and Welsh myths of the highest antiquity refer to this calendar in an old saying: A year and a day. The true lunar calendar of thirteen, twenty-eight day months is correct not only in the astronomical sense of the moon's revolutions in relation to the earth and sun, but also in the mystic sense that the moon, which is of a feminine nature, has a woman's normal menstrual cycle of twenty-eight days.†

Birch (Betula pendula)—**Beth** (beh)—Is the first tree letter of the Irish ogham alphabet. In modern Irish it is Beith, pronounced Be, and its phonetic equivalent is *B*. In Faery Wicca and Irish ogham tradition, a birch tree provided the first wood upon which an ogham word was inscribed. It is classified as the first peasant tree, with the sacred color of ban (white).

Beth is one of the thirteen moon oghams. The Birch month extends from December 24 to January 20, fixing its beginning just after the winter solstice, the midwinter day of purification and renewal. Birch is a healer of skin and joints, is ascribed the number five, and corresponds to the besan, the pheasant ('the best bird that flies') bird-ogham.

Birch is a pioneer tree, for it was the first tree to recolonize the treeless wastes left after the retreat of the glaciers at the end of the last Ice Age. Birch is the tree of inception and is indeed the earliest forest tree, with the exception of the elder, to put out new leaves. In some countries, its leafing marks the beginning of the agricultural year, because farmers used it as a directory for sowing their spring wheat.

The *Cad Goddeu,* or *The Battle of the Trees* (Appendix F) states that birch "armed himself but late," referring to the fact that birch twigs do not toughen until late in the year (which is also true of willow and rowan).

Birch rods were used in rustic rituals for driving out the spirit of the old year, and in ceremonies for expelling evil spirits. In Celtic symbolism, hats made of birch are associated with the dead.

---

* Several versions of this alphabet can be found in: Squire, *Mythology of The British Isles*; Macalister, *Secret Languages of Ireland*; Brynmore-Jones and Rhys, *History of the Welsh People*; Spence, *The Mysteries of Britain*; and even in the Oxford English Dictionary. All differ slightly between certain letters and their pronunciations and most are not the Irish ogham at all, but Bobileth and Beth-Luis-Nion.

† The magickal connection of the moon with menstruation is also of highest antiquity, and today is being remembered in the current revival of Goddess worship and the woman's movement. For an indepth study of the moon cycle and menstrual cycle, refer to my book *Sister Moon Lodge: The Power and Mystery of Menstruation.* Llewellyn Publications.

Rowan or Quickbeam tree (Sorbus acuparia)—**Luis** (loo-ish)— Is the second ogham character. In modern Irish it is called caorthann, and given the phonetic equivalent of *L*. Traditionally, this tree is a magickal plant, and is classified as the second peasant tree, and given two colors. In *The Book of Ballymote*, Luis is described as "Delight of the eye, that is Luisiu." This color is flame (the modern Irish luisne, a red glare) with the additional meaning of a sheen or luster. The other color correspondence is liath (grey).

The time of Luis extends from January 21 to February 17, and is the second moon month. The important Celtic feast of Oimlec falls in the middle of this month (February 2), which marks the quickening of the year, the coming of spring. In Ireland, February 2 is also the day of Brigid. The connection of rowan with the Oimlec fire-feast is shown by Morann Mac Main's ogham in *The Book of Ballymote*, when he gives the poetic name for rowan as "Delight of the Eye, that is Luisiu."

Rowan sustains and extends life, a quality attributed to the eating of its berries. The esoteric number of Luis is fourteen. In bird-ogham, Luis is lachu (duck), which swims on land in this season of floods. The duck is sometimes used as the sacred bird of river goddesses; for example, Sequana is depicted as riding in a duck-headed barge. The fairy godmother, Mother Goose, also rides on the back of a flying duck. The duck also appears in several ancient Irish manuscripts, as well as upon crosses and monuments, and at one time rowan-berry jelly was eaten with duck.

Rowan is also known as the mountain ash, quicken or quickbeam, and tree of life. Its round wattles, spread with newly-flayed bull's hides, were used by the druids as a last extremity for compelling demons to answer difficult questions, hence the Irish proverbial expression "to go on the wattles of knowledge," meaning to do one's utmost to get information.

The botanical name of rowan is Fraxinus, or Pyrus, Aucuparia, and later became known as the witch; the witch-wand of the cunning women, formerly used for metal divining, was made of rowan. Sacred groves of rowan existed at places of sanctity as magically protective and oracular trees.

In ancient Ireland, fires of rowan were kindled by the Bards and Ollamhs of opposing armies and incantations spoken over them summoning the Fenian Heroes, or the Morrigu to take part in the fight. The berries of the magickal rowan in the Irish romance of *Fraoth*, guarded by a dragon, had the sustaining virtue of nine meals; they also healed the wounded and added a year to a person's life. In the romance of Diarmuid and Grainne, the rowan berry, with the apple and the red nut, is described as the food of the gods.

In Danann Ireland, a rowan stake hammered through a corpse immobilized its siabra (ghost); and in the Cu Chulainn saga, three Hags spitted a dog, Cu Chulainn's sacred animal, on a rowan twig to procure his death.

Luis serves to protect its user against psychic attack and to develop the individual's powers of perception and prediction. In country tradition, rowan was planted outside the front door to ward off harmful spirits, energies, and on-lays.

Alder (Alnus glutinosa)—**Fearn** (fair-un)—The third letter is Fearn. In modern Irish, it is fearnog, and its phonetic rendering is *F*. Alder is classified as the second chieftain tree of Irish tradition. In the Irish Ossianic *Song of the Forest Trees*, alder is described as "the very battle-witch of all woods, tree that is hottest in the fight." Though it is a poor fuel tree (like the willow, poplar, and chestnut), it is prized by charcoal-burners as yielding the best charcoal. It has the corresponding color of flann, blood-red or crimson.

The alder was celebrated for yielding three fine dyes: red from its bark, green from its flowers, and brown from its twigs. Red for fire, green for water, and brown for earth. When the alder is felled, the wood at first appears white, but then seems to bleed crimson as though it were alive. The green and brown dyes were used extensively for cloth—such as the green dress of the Faery— while the red dye was often used as the crimson-stain on the battle-ready warrior's face.

Although Fearn is the third ogham, its moon month extends from March 18, when the alder first blooms (around the time of the vernal equinox) and is in full white blossom by the middle of the month, to April 14, which marks the drying-up of the winter floods by the spring sun, symbolic of the fire and its power to reduce water.

The healing of alder is a quality that deals with doubt. Its esoteric number is eight, which is the Celtic number of man, in a human rather than a gender sense. The bird-ogham is faelinn (seagull). The gull's calls were imitated by sea-witches in their magickal summoning of the wind.

The alder is also proof against the corruptive power of water; its slightly gummy leaves resist the winter rains longer than those of any other deciduous tree, and its timber resists decay indefinitely when used for water-conduits or piles. This fact is brought out in the *Romance of Branwen* when the swineherds (oracular priests) of King Matholwch of Ireland see a forest in the sea and cannot guess what it is. Branwen tells them that it is the fleet of Bran the Blessed come to avenge her. The ships are anchored offshore, and Bran wades through the shallows and brings his goods and people to land; afterward he bridges the River Linon, though it has been protected with a magick charm, by lying down across the river and having hurdles laid over him. It was said of Bran that no house could contain him. The riddle: What can no house ever contain? has a simple answer: The piles upon which it is built, which were alder.

Principally, the alder is the tree of fire, the power of fire to free the earth from water; and the alder branch in the *Cad Goddeu* is a token of resurrection; its buds are set in a spiral, representing the continuum of life.

Green alder-branches make good whistles and were used by the cunning women to conjure up destructive winds, especially from the north, in opposition to invaders. Musical pipes were also made from alder and called alder-pipes or Bran-pipes, and milk pails and other dairy vessels were also made from alder, as is poetically described in *The Book of Ballymote: Comet lachta or guarding of milk*.

Fearn is connected with the spirit known as Far Darrig (Red Man). According to legend, these beings are reputed to help human beings to escape from the Otherworld. But the Far Darrig is also a prankster, and in wintertime will ask permission to warm himself by the fire. Bad luck will dog anyone foolhardy enough to refuse.

White Willow (Salix alba) **or Sally tree—Saille** (sal-yeh)—The next tree-letter is Saille, phonetically *S*. In modern Irish, it is saileach. The willow is the third peasant tree, whose color is sodath (fine or bright). This tree, whose narrow crown is silvery-grey in color, is associated with the growth of lunar power, rooting in water. In Irish, its name is allied with the word *saill*, meaning fat, referring to its month which begins on April 15 and ends on May 12. This is known as the sacred moon month of the goddess, containing her wedding day to the god: La Baal Tinne (May 1st, May Day), one of the Four Sacred Festivals, now famous for its orgiastic revels and its magick dew.

The healing of willow is fevers and headaches. It is also the tree of enchantment and has the numerological equivalent of 16. Its bird-ogham character is seg, the hawk, mentioned in one of Amergin's poems referring to this month: "I am a hawk on a cliff."

Saille is an ogham of linking, a watery symbolism which brings itself into harmony with the flow of events, most notably the phases of the moon.

The wearing of the willow in the hat as a sign of the rejected lover seems to be originally a charm against the moon goddess's jealousy. The willow is sacred to her for many reasons: it is the tree that loves water most, and the moon-goddess is the giver of dew and moisture generally; its leaves and bark, the source of salicylic acid, are sovereign against rheumatic cramps at one time thought to be caused by enchantment. The willow, or osier, was sacred to all death aspects of the Triple Morrigu, and much worshiped by the cunning women. The words *witch* and *wicked* are believed to be derived from the same ancient word for willow, which also yields wicker. The willow also gives its name to Helicon, the abode of the Nine Muses.

The witch's besom (broom) was made of an ash stake, birch twigs, and willow binding—birch twigs because at the expulsion of evil spirits some remain entangled in the besom, of ash stake as a protection against drowning, willow for the moon owns it and its magick.

Druidical sacrifices were offered at the full of Moon in wicker baskets, and funerary flints were napped in willow leaf shape, although the ancient song: *The Song of the Forest Trees* indicates: Burn not the willow, a tree sacred to poets.

Gray and Black Ash (Fraxinus excelsior)—**Nuin or Nion** (knee-un)—The ash is the fifth letter of the oghams. It has the phonetic value of *N*, and in modern Irish it is fuinnseog. Ash is the first chieftain tree, whose color association is necht, clear.

Nion is the third moon month of the Celtic calendar, a tree of sea-power, or of the power resident in water, and governs the moon month which extends from February 18 through March 17, which traditionally was considered the month of floods. March is also the time when budding of trees and the fresh growth of herbs becomes apparent. In the first three months of the Celtic year, the nights are longer than the days, and the sun is regarded as still under the tutelage of night, or the moon.

The healing of ash is in its watery, moon nature, teaching one to learn of their inner-self, which will result in a stronger knowledge and much more effective expression of self. Its esoteric numerical equivalent is thirteen. In bird-ogham it is naescu, the snipe.

In Ireland, the Tree of Tortu, the Tree of Dathi and the Branching Tree of Usnech, three of the Five Magic Trees whose fall in the year 665 C.E. was said to have symbolized the triumph of Christianity over Paganism, were ash-trees. A descendant of the Sacred Tree of Creevna, also an ash, was still standing at Killura in the nineteenth century; its wood was a charm against drowning, and emigrants to America after the Potato Famine carried it away with them piecemeal.

The druid's wand with a spiral decoration, from the early first century, was ash, and in both Wales and Ireland all oars and coracle slats were made of ash, as were the rods used for urging on horses, except where the deadly yew was preferred. The bunches of fruits that resemble keys, signify the power to unlock the future. But just as the seeds in these keys germinate only in the second year after falling to the ground, unlocking of the future may take a considerable time.

Whitethorn or Hawthorn (Crataegus monogyna)—**Huath or Uath** (hoo-uh)—This is the sixth character of the ogham alphabet. In modern Irish, it is sceach gheal, and has the phonetic value of *H*. The hawthorn is classified as the fourth peasant tree whose color is huath (terrible), or purple, the forbidden color of the hag aspect of the goddess.

The hawthorn, or whitethorn, is the tree of enforced chastity and takes its name from the month of May. It is sometimes referred to as the May tree. The sixth moon month begins on May 13, which accounts for the mediaeval habit of riding out on May Morning to pluck flowering hawthorn boughs and dance around the maypole in anticipation of the sixth month when sexual interchange was looked down upon. The sixth moon month ends on June 9. Huath is the Goddess's tree of sexuality.

The healing of hawthorn relates to balancing the blood, nerves, and spirit. Esoterically, it has no numerical value, which could be a result of it being an ogham of the Underworld. The bird-ogham correspondence is hadaig, the night-crow.

In the Irish Brehon Laws, the hawthorn appeared as the scieth (harm), and was considered generally an unlucky tree. The ogham's name means terrible, referring to the hag, or destroying aspect, of the Threefold Badb.

The destruction of an ancient hawthorn tree in Ireland was attended with the greatest peril. Two nineteenth century instances are quoted in E. M. Hull's *Folklore of the British Isles*. The effect is the death of one's cattle and children, and loss of all one's money. In Vaughan Cornish's *Historic Thorn Trees in the British Isles*, he writes of the sacred hawthorns growing over wells in Goidelic provinces. He quotes the case of St. Patrick's Thorn at Tinahely in County Wicklow:

> *Devotees attended on the 4th of May, rounds were duly made about the well, and shreds torn off their garments and hung on the thorn. [He adds:] This is St. Monica's Day but I do not know of any association.*

However, St. Monica's Day, or the New Style, corresponds with May 15, the Old Style, a ceremony in honor of the hawthorn month, which had just begun. The rags were torn from the devotees' clothes as a sign of mourning and propitiation regarding the enforced abstinence of sexual intercourse because it was believed that children born from conception during this time frame would be evil, or demented.

In the book, *Magical Alphabets*, author, Nigel Pennick, provides a very recent example of bad luck encountered when cutting down a sacred thorn tree, and this was "the obliteration of such a tree to make way for the ill-fated DeLorean car factory in Northern Ireland. Local people ascribed the disastrous collapse of the business to the ill luck attending the removal of this holy tree."

Oak (Quercus robur)—**Duir** (der)—*Duir* is the seventh sacred tree of the oghams. In modern Irish, it is dair, and has the phonetic value of *D*. The oak is the most powerful of the trees, and classified as the third noble, or chieftain tree, whose color is dubh (black).

The seventh moon month begins on June 10 and ends on July 7, containing the high point of the year, summer solstice or midsummer, esoterically known as the door of the year; the day on which the oak king was sacrificially burned alive.

The healing of oak are qualities of cleansing and strengthening. The esoteric numerical correspondence is twelve, and the bird-ogham is droen, the wren, smallest of the birds indigenous to northern Europe, and one of the most sacred birds of the ancient Faery-Faith.

The oak is the Dagda, the chief of the elder Irish gods, as well as Zeus, Jupiter, Hercules, Thor, Jehovah, El, Allah and all the other Thunder-gods. The royalty of the oak tree needs no enlarging upon; for in this aspect, *Duir* is related to the Irish words *dur*, meaning hard, unyielding, durable, and *duranta*, meaning mysterious.

Midsummer is the flowering season of the oak, which is the tree of endurance and triumph, and like the ash is said to "court the lightning flash." Its roots are believed to extend as deep underground as its branches rise in the air, which makes it emblematic of a god whose law runs both in the Heavenly Realm and in the Under-world, such as the Dagda Mor's law.

The *Cad Goddeu* states that the "Stout Guardian of the door, His name in every tongue" is customarily made of oak. In other words, doors are made of the strongest and toughest wood. Appropriately, the name Duir is cognate with other words for door; in Irish door is doras. It is behind this great oak door that the old religion was shut when the oak-cult was swept away by Christianity.

The oak was the tree honored by the druids, who gave particular attention to its parasite, the mistletoe. At the winter season, the mistletoe could be found hanging throughout its branches. The oak symbolized life, endurance, and strength, and the mistletoe, though beautiful, is poisonous; thus, the combination was that of Life and Death.

Holly (Ilex aquifolium)—**Tinne** (tin-uh)—The holly is placed as the eighth ogham letter, although *The Book of Ballymote* gives alternative ascriptions. There, the Cypress (Cupressus sp.) or Rowan (Sorbus acuparia), are mentioned. But rowan is identified with Luis (caporthann), and most ogham users prefer to use holly. However, the modern Irish word for holly is *cuileann,* and conversely, the letter's magickal name is related to the Irish words tine, meaning fire, and teann, meaning strong or bold. Holly means holy. *Tinne* is also the Celtic word for any sacred tree. Its phonetic value is *T*. The *T* is the evergreen oak which rules the waning part of the year, the bloody, or scarlet oak, the holy oak; whereas the preceding letter of the alphabet, *D*, rules the waxing part of the year—the sacred druidic oak.

The holly of this alphabet was most likely the scarlet oak, or kerm oak, or holly oak, the evergreen twin of the ordinary oak. It has prickly leaves and nourishes the kerm, a scarlet insect not unlike the holly-berry, which was once thought to be a berry. It was from this that the ancients made their royal scarlet dye and an aphrodisiac elixir. The holly is classified as the fifth peasant tree, whose color is temen, meaning gray-green or dark gray.

Tinne rules the eighth moon month which extends from July 8 to August 4. Eight is also the number of increase and is well suited to the month of the barley harvest, although this is not the ogham's esoteric numerical correspondence. Within this moon month is found the Great Festival of Lughnasadh, August 1, which is celebrated in honor of Lugh, and is traditionally acknowledged as the time of the first harvest. The eighth moon is also known as the Spear month, or the Warrior's Moon, making the dark gray of iron, the warrior's metal, appropriate.

The holly approaches healing from the preventative and protective viewpoint. Its esoteric numerical correspondence is 11. The truith (starling) can be considered the bird-ogham symbol for this month, as the starling flies in armies, turning or moving as one with no apparent signal or communication. The message of the starling in this moon would be that battles are won by concerted, joint efforts, not by individual acts and broken unity.

The holly, which flowers in July, appears in the original Irish *Romance of Gawain and the Green Knight*. The Green Knight is an immortal giant whose club is a holly-bush. He and Sir Gawain, who appears in the Irish version as Cu Chulainn, make a compact to behead one another at alternate new years (midsummer and midwinter), but the Holly Knight spares the Oak Knight. However, the Holly Knight and the Oak Knight fought every first of May until Doomsday.

Since in mediaeval practice, St. John the Baptist, who lost his head on St. John's Day, took over the oak-king's titles and customs, it was natural to let Jesus, as John's merciful successor, take over the holly-king. The holly was thus glorified beyond the oak, as is demonstrated in both the *Holly-Tree Carol*: "Of all the trees that are in the wood, the Holly bears the crown"; and in the *Song of the Forest Trees*: "Of all trees whatsoever the critically best is holly."

Hazel (Corylus avellana)—**Coll** (cull)—The ninth tree letter is Coll, and its ancient name is the same in modern Irish. Its phonetic value is *K* or a hard *C*. The hazel is classified as the fourth chieftain tree, and its color is cron, nut-brown.

Hazel is a moon month, which extends from August 5 to September 1, and is the nutting season. The nut in Celtic legend is always an emblem of concentrated wisdom. The hazel is the tree of wisdom which contains something sweet, compact, and sustaining enclosed in a small hard shell. The saying, "this is the matter in a nutshell" is derived from the hazel tree.

The healing of hazel is the value of time and patience. The letter Coll was used as the Bardicu numeral nine, because nine is the magickal number of three times three, as well as the number sacred to the Muses. Also, the hazel fruits after nine years of growth. Its bird-ogham has the same name as its color correspondence: cron, which also means crane.

One of the ancient Irish topographical treatises, *The Dinnshenchas*, describes a beautiful fountain called Connla's Well near Tipperary, over which hung the nine hazels of poetic art which produced flowers and fruit of beauty and wisdom. As the nuts dropped into the well they fed the salmon in it, and whatever number of nuts any of them swallowed, as many bright spots appeared on their bodies. All the knowledge of the arts and sciences was bound to the eating of these nuts.

The hazel was the Bile Ratha (venerated tree of the rath)—the rath in which the poetic Sidhe lived. It gave its name also to a god named Mac Cool (son of the Hazel), who was one of the three earliest Milesian rulers of Ireland, along with his two brothers, Mac Ceacht (son of the Plough), and Mac Greine (son of the sun). They celebrated a triple marriage with the Triple Goddess of Ireland, Eire, Fodhla, and Banbha. This legend appears, at first, to be misleading as a record of the overthrow of the matriarchal system by patriarchal invaders; but since Grainne (the sun) was a goddess not a god, and since both agriculture and wisdom were presided over by the Triple Goddess, the invaders were probably goddess-worshippers themselves, and merely transferred their allegiance to the Triple Goddess of the new land.

According to the ancient Irish Fenian legend of *The Ancient Dripping Hazel,* the hazel appears as a tree of wisdom that can be put to destructive uses. It dripped a poisonous milk, had no leaves, and was the abode of vultures and ravens, birds of divination. It split in two when the head of Balor (the Fomorian king) was placed in its fork after his death, and when made into a shield by Finn mac Cumhaill, poisonous gases emanating from it slew his enemies. Finn's Shield is a poetic keening for magickal protection. It alludes to the optical illusion binding knots of Celtic interlace-patterns known as luaithrindi carried by Celtic warriors. Finn used its wood as a shield in battle, its noxious vapors killed thousands of enemy. Finn's hazel shield is also an emblem of the satiric poem that carries a curse on the subject of the satire.

In the *Cad Goddeau,* hazel was the druidic heralds' tree: "hazel was arbiter"; ancient Irish heralds carried white hazel wands as symbols of office, representing their ability to use words.

Crab Apple (Malus sylvestris)—**Quert** (kwert)—Quert is the tenth ogham and the final character of the second rubic. It is a magickal name, as the profane name of the apple is aball in modern Irish, and it has the phonetic value of *Qu.* Crab apple is the seventh peasant tree, whose color is given variously as apple-green and quiar (mouse-colored). Its bird-ogham is another version of brown, querc, the hen.

Quert was an added letter, and is coupled with the ninth moon of Coll. With the hazel and wild apple, the commonalty is immortality, attained through wisdom, or through inspiration.

Quert is placed after Coll, and its ogham of five lines drawn to the right, or above the dividing line, reflect the five-fold petals of the apple flower, the five receptacles for the seeds within the fruit itself. Unlike the cultivated species of apple, the crab apple bears thorns, making Quert a protective tree like the hawthorn and blackthorn.

In Celtic tradition, the apple symbolizes the tree of rebirth and eternal life. In Faery Wicca, the Silver Branch is made of apple wood. This is the branch, or tree, which is a passport into the Land of Faery.

Grape Vine (Vitis alba)—**Muin or Min** (muhn)—Muin is the eleventh tree of the oghams. In the Irish language, it is finium (vine). This plant is not indigenous to the British Isles, but it is believed that the Tuatha De Danann carried the tree itself northward with them, as well as the emblem, into Britain, which then became an important motif in British Bronze Age art. It may also have been introduced by the Celts from mainland Europe.

The Irish word *muine,* means a thicket of any thorny plant, so the correlation of this ogham with the vine may be a late connection. As a thorny thicket, it is nearer to a tree than a vine. Its phonetic value is of *M.* Muin is classified as the fifth noble or chieftain tree, whose color is mbracht, meaning variegated. Vine is the tree of joy, exhilaration and wrath. The tenth moon month extends from September 2 to September 29 and includes the autumnal equinox.

The vine, like the ivy, grows spirally. But unlike the ivy, the vine is a symbol of resurrection, because its strength can be preserved in wine. Thus, tonic healing is the effect of vine. Its numerical correspondence is six, and its bird-ogham is mintan, the titmouse, a bird of thickets.

The color of the berries and the shape of the leaf correspond to the bramble. However, it was the blackberry that was picked from the vine and made into a heady drink and enjoyed during the fruiting season. In all Celtic countries, there is a geasa (a taboo) against eating the blackberry—the reason being 'a cause des fe'es' (because of the fairies)—though it is a wholesome and nourishing fruit.

Ivy (Hedera helix)—**Gort** (gor-it)—The twelfth ogham character is the ivy in its flowering season. The modern Irish word for ivy is *eadhnean,* and the Irish word gort means a tilled field, not ivy. It is given the phonetic value of *G,* and its color is gorm (blue).

The ivy month extends from September 30 to October 27. Vine and ivy come next to each other at the turn of the year, and are jointly dedicated to resurrection, presumably because they are the only two trees in the Irish ogham that grow spirally. The ivy bush, however, is the sign of the wine tavern; hence the proverb: Good wine needs no bush. Ivy-ale is a highly intoxicating mediaeval drink and its leaves can also be chewed for their toxic effect. The ivy heals by calming and regulating the nerves. Its esoteric numerical equivalent is ten, and its bird is geis, the mute swan.

Ivy and holly became intertwined in mythology. Mediaeval carols between these two are not based on the tree of murder and the tree of resurrection, but rather a domestic war of the sexes. The last harvest sheaf to be carried was that bound around with ivy and called the Harvest May, or the May Bride, or the Ivy Girl: whichever farmer was latest with his harvesting was given the Ivy Girl as his penalty, an omen of ill luck until the following year. Thus, the ivy came to mean a carline, or shrewish wife, a simile confirmed by the strangling of trees by ivy. But ivy and holly were both connected to the winter solstice, and gave rise to a Yule custom in which holly boys and ivy girls contended in a game of forfeits for precedence, and sang songs of satirical natures against each other.

Symbolically, ivy is a tree of transformation, starting as a small, weak, herb-like plant, which finally, after centuries of growth, becomes an enormously thick, woody, serpentine tree in its own right.

Reed—**Ngetal**—Ngetal is the thirteenth ogham, and it is here that one will find a major difference between the Irish ogham and the Beth-Luis-Nion alphabet. The Irish word for reed is *giolcach,* and it has the phonetic equivalent of *Ng.*

According to bardic-tree classification, the reed is the first of the kiln or shrub trees. Ngetal's tree is not a tree, according to modern botanical definitions. However, it appears that the reed was classified as a tree because the scribes of ancient Ireland used the hard, resistant stems of the reed to make pens, and in ancient times, any plant with woody stems, such as a reed or ivy, was called a tree. The color classification of Ngetal is nglas, meaning glass-green—a clear, yellowish-green.

The thirteenth ogham's moon month extends from October 28 to November 24, making it the ogham of Samhain, the festival of the dead, marking the beginning of the new year in the Celtic calendar. The healing of the reed can be used for the ills caused by overindulgence. In bardic numerology, it signifies the number one. Its bird-ogham is ngeigh (goose), the bird that winters in the reedlands.

Traditionally, reed for thatching and other weaving is cut in November. To the Irish, it was believed that a house was not an established house until the thatched roof was on. The canna-reed, which grows from a thick root like a tree, was an ancient symbol of royalty, and was made into scepters. It is the tree from which arrows were cut and shot into every direction as a symbol of sovereignty, and in herbal remedies it was used to heal the wounds of an arrow. The reed was also the material from which a sort of paper, or papyrus, known as plagawd, was made.

The reed was a traditional rod of measure, used to delimit sacred enclosures. It is a symbol of music and is utilized and of great value in making woodwind instruments such as bagpipes and flutes. The greatest power of Ngetal is as a preserver. As a pen, the reed preserves memory and knowledge; as a rod, it preserves measure; and, as roofing, it preserves the house. Above all else, Ngetal is the ogham of written communication, thereby signifying conscious precision and the maintenance of order in chaos.

Blackthorn or Sloe Tree (prunus spinosa)—**Straif** (strauff)—The second character added, and the fourteenth ogham character, is *Straif*. The modern Irish name is *draion* or *draighnean*, and it is given the phonetic value of *St*. Blackthorn is one of the major trees of magickal power, a tree whose name has the connotations of punishment and strife. Its corresponding colors are sorcha (bright colored) and purple-black, the color of the blackthorn's fruit, the sloe. The ogham of Straif would be four diagonal lines crossing the dividing line, giving *Ruis* its five diagonal lines. Straif is coupled with the moon month of Ngetal.

In healing, blackthorn wards off evil spirits thought to cause illness. The once sacred alcoholic beverage made from the blackthorn's fruit, sloe gin, is a reviver and protector on another level. Straif does not have an esoteric numerical equivalent, perhaps because it is the greatest magickal power of the oghams. However, the bird-ogham correspondence is the smolach, the thrush, a bird reputed to impale snails on the thorns of the blackthorn bush.

Blackthorn is a shrub that produces suckers which can make a single plant the nucleus of an impenetrable thorny thicket. On a physical level, the thorns of the blackthorn proved a valuable defense in hedging; walking-sticks, shillelaghs, and cudgels were also made from this wood. Staves made from this wood were carried by witches and wizards. These were to have been renowned for their magickal power. It is no coincidence that the Irish word for a wizard is draoi, and that of a druid, drai, both relating to the mantic turning power of the sloe tree.

Elder or Bourtree (Sambucus nigra)—Ruis (roo-ish)—The fifteenth ogham character is *Ruis*, with the modern Irish *trom*, and the phonetic value of *R*. The elder tree is of great mantic power, for it is the second kiln, or shrub tree whose color is ascribed rocnat, one of the many forms of red which was described in tartan ogham as roebuck red.

The moon month of Ruis extends from November 25 to December 22, technically ending with the winter solstice. With the thirteenth moon month, the year ends, and with it the extra day, or the fourteenth month of one day which falls after the winter solstice. The number fourteen is a moon-number, the days of the lucky first half of the month, or the waxing phase of the lunar cycle. And thus, with the birth of the new sun, at the time of the Great Year, when the solar and lunar time were roughly synchronized, the sacred king's term of a year and a day came to an end.

Purification of both outer and inner body is the healing power of the elder. It is said to remedy influenza, and to keep away flies, and although the flowers and inner bark of the elder have always been famous for their therapeutic qualities, the scent of an elder plantation was formerly held to cause death and disease. Ruis is connected to the numbers fourteen, thirteen (as will be discussed in the next paragraph), and three, although no esoteric numerical equivalent is assigned it. Symbolically, Ruis signifies the three aspects of time present in the Triple Goddess (the Fates, Parcae, Norms, and Wyrrd Sisters). It represents the ever-present threefold aspect of existence: beginning, middle, and end. Its bird-ogham is the rook.

The white flowers, which are at their best at midsummer, were considered an aspect of the Great Goddess Dana. Associated to the number thirteen, the number of the Goddess, its most powerful time would be in its thirteenth month, thus marking the elder for a tree of doom in the sense that the Great Goddess also contained the ability to destroy that which she created.

In Ireland, elder sticks, rather than ash, were used by the cunning women as magick horses upon which they rode during certain magickal incantations. The elder was considered an unlucky tree and was believed to have been the Crucifixion tree. Elder-leaf shape funerary flints in megalithic long barrows suggest that its association with death is long-standing, and, since it rules the season of death and repose, one can comprise the understanding for this association.

Elm (Ulmus minor)—**Ailm** (all-em)—Station of the Winter Solstice; Season of Rebirth. The first vowel. In Old Irish, the word *ailm* stood for the palm, a tree not native to Ireland.

The palm, the birth-tree of Egypt, Babylonia, Arabia, and Phoenicia, gives its name phoenix, bloody, to Phoenicia, which formerly covered the whole Eastern Mediterranean, and to the Phoenix which is born and reborn in a palm. Its poetic connection with birth is that the sea is the Universal Mother and that palms thrive close to the sea in sandy soil heavily charged with salt; without salt at its roots a young palm remains stunted. The palm is the Tree of Life in the Babylonian Garden of Eden story.

In modern Irish, *ailm* has come to mean elm, under the influence of the Latin Classics, and its phonetic value is of *A*. The color assigned to ailm is blue. Elm has its station on the first day of the new solar year, the birthday of the Divine Child; the extra day of the winter solstice.

In healing, the elm is the tree of regeneration, for the elm regenerates from new shoots sent out from the roots. When an elm is cut down, and appears dead, new stems grow from the still-living roots. No esoteric numerical equivalent is assigned ailm. Its bird-ogham correspondence is the lapwing. Its qualities are boldness and fidelity, and it is considered a good-luck token when given to departing friends.

In the Beth-Luis-Nion alphabet, ailm is tied to the silver fir, the tallest European native tree. However, this fir tree is not indigenous to the British Isles, and the Irish word for a fir tree is giuis.

Gorse or Furze (Ulex europaeus)—**On or Ohn** (un)—Station of the Spring Equinox; Season of Spring. The second vowel. *On* is the seventeenth ogham. The modern Irish word for the gorse is *aiteann*, and it is given the phonetic value of O. The gorse or furze is classified as the seventh chieftain tree, and it is given the color of the pea-like gorse flowers: golden-yellow, saffron, dun, or sand.

Its golden flowers and prickles typify the young sun at the spring equinox—the time when furze fires are lighted on the hills. The effect of burning away the old prickles is to make tender new ones sprout on the stock, which sheep eat greedily; and to encourage the growth of grass— "The furze but ill-behaved, Until he is subdued."

The religious importance of furze, or gorse, is enhanced by its flowers being frequented by the first bees of the year, as the ivy's are by the last. The name On-niona, a goddess worshiped by the Gauls in ash-groves, is a compound of Onn and Nion, which supplies the date of her festival, namely the spring equinox at the close of the Ash-month. Its bird-ogham is the cormorant, a sea-bird.

The gorse grows only in open country, not in woodlands, and it is a plant that can be found in flower almost every month of the year. Because of this, On takes on the symbolical meaning of continuous fertility.

Heather (Erica sp)—**Ur** (or-uh)—Station of the Summer Solstice; Season of Summer. The third vowel. *Ur* is the eighteenth ogham, and its meaning presents a bit of a problem for Ur means fresh, new, or moist, with the associated meaning of the morning dew. In Irish the word for this plant is fraoch.

Ur is classified as the last of the eight peasant trees, whose color is purple, the color of its flowers, associated with the dark goddess. In tartan ogham, Ur is given the color of light-green. The heather is the midsummer tree, red and passionate, and is associated with mountains and bees. The goddess is herself a queen bee about whom male drones swarm in midsummer.

In the *Cad Goddeu,* the heather is referenced as "heather-ale," a restorative, when comforting the battered poplars, and in healing is used for its restorative properties. Like the other vowels, Ur, is not assigned an esoteric numerical equivalent, but its corresponding bird-ogham is the skylark.

This third vowel tree is sacred to Garbh Ogh, an ancient ageless giantess, whose car was drawn by elks, whose diet was venison milk and eagle's breasts and who hunted the mountain deer with a pack of seventy hounds with bird names. She gathered stones to heap herself a triple cairn and set up her chair in a womb of the hills at the season of heatherbloom, and then expired.

Aspen or White Poplar (Populus tremula)—**Eadha** (eh-thuha)—Station of the Autumnal Equinox; Season of Autumn. The fourth vowel. In modern Irish the name for this tree is *pobail ban*, and its phonetic value is E. Eadha is given the color silvery-white. The fourth vowel tree is the tree of the autumnal equinox and of old age. It is the shifting-leaved white poplar, or aspen, and is known as the shield-maker's tree.

In healing, the aspen, or white poplar, is used as a facilitator of the individual's curative powers, providing access to the real essence that underlies the sometimes misleading outer form, or symptom. Because of this, it is holistically viewed as the "Spirit that animates the flesh." It is not ascribed an esoteric number, but its bird-ogham is the whistling swan, which speaks to us of shape-shifting. In ancient legends, the Faery were known to often take the form of a swan when departing from this realm, or from a bad or negative situation.

The aspen is very hardy, living in a range of habitats from low-lying wetlands to exposed mountain ledges. It thus has the quality of hardy resistance to a variety of seemingly inhospitable conditions.

Yew (Taxus baccata)—**Ioho, Idho or Iubhar** (i-thho)—Station of the Last Day of the Year; Season of Death. The fifth vowel, and last character of the conventional rubric of the ogham script. In modern Irish the name of the yew tree is *eo*. Its phonetic value is *I*.

The yew is classified as the sixth kiln or shrub tree, and its color correspondence is dark greenish brown, the color of the tree's leaves, although the tartan ogham correspondence is given as royal scarlet and blood red, the color of the under-bark and resin.

The station of the yew is the last day of the year, the eve of the winter solstice. Ailm, the elm, and Idho, the yew of death, are sisters; they stand next to each other in the circle of the year. Together, the two are reminders that death is life, and life is death.

In healing, yew is used for releasing mentally and emotionally in preparation for rebirthing new ideas, attitudes, and visions. Again, like the other vowels, there is no esoteric numerical equivalent rendered yew. However, its bird-ogham is the eaglet, a very important symbol in Faery Wicca. The eagle is the symbol of valor.

The yew, or the death-tree, is sacred to the Crone, Badb. The yew contains the secret mysteries of the Great Goddess Dana, for yew groves emit an intoxicating breath which induces vision. The yew is the longest-lived tree, green throughout the year, and because of this continuity, it is a tree of eternal life, sacred to various divinities and saints of death and regeneration.

In Ireland the yew was the coffin of the vine; wine barrels were made of yew staves. In the Irish romance of *Naoise and Deirdre*, yew stakes were driven through the corpses of these lovers to keep them apart, but the stakes sprouted and became trees whose tops eventually embraced over Armagh Cathedral, revealing the secret mystery of the Great Goddess, that love conquers even death.

Yew makes the best bows, and the deadliness of the tree was thereby enhanced. The ancient Irish used a compound of yew-berry, hellebore, and devil's bit for poisoning their weapons. It is also one of the Five Magickal Trees of Ireland. This was the Tree of Ross, described as a firm straight deity (the Irish yew differed from the British in being cone-shaped, with branches growing straight up, not horizontally), the renown of Banbha (the death aspect of the Irish Triple Goddess), the Spell of Knowledge, and the King's Wheel; that is to say the death-letter that makes the wheel of existence come full circle; as a reminder of his destiny, every Irish king wore a brooch in the form of a wheel, which was entailed on his successor.

Fir is to yew as silver is to lead. The mediaeval alchemists, following ancient tradition, reckoned silver to the Moon as presiding over both metals from the same mixed ore: Fir, womb of silver pain, Yew, tomb of leaden grief.

In addition to the original twenty oghams, there are five diphthong characters now in modern usage, although they have less of an esoteric value than the preceding oghams.

Koad or Eoh—The equivalent of Koad is that of Eadha, the Aspen tree. *Ea*, the first of this unconventional rubric signifies earth. It has the bardic number of thirteen, the number of Death in the Tarot, and the yew-rune. Eoh is associated with death. Koad signifies the unity of all eight festivals of the traditional year. It can be described as the sacred grove, the location in which all things, hitherto separate, become connected together. At such a point, all things become clear. Its associated colors are the forty shades of green, or the "light green and speckled."

Oi or Oir— Oi is the gooseberry bush. The Irish word is *spionan*. Its color is usually white. Traditionally, this ogham is associated with childbirth, being used magickally to ease the passage of the baby from the womb into the world. Sometimes this ogham is called *Tharan*, with the phonetic value of *Th*, relating to Huath and Straif.

Uinllean—In *The Book of Ballymote,* this ogham is associated with the honeysuckle. However, modern ogham users connect it with the beech tree, a chieftain tree. The name of this tree in modern Irish is *fea*, and is a version of the name of the *F* ogham, Feoh. The magickal characteristics of this ogham are hardness and resistance, the solidity of knowledge, and tried-and-tested actions. It refers to the solidity of ancient wisdom, the cultural or physical foundation which must be in place before any constructions can be made, either physically or figuratively. Its color is tawny, the color of the leaves of the copper beech. Sometimes this ogham is rendered as *Phagos*, with the phonetic equivalent of *Ph* or *F.*

Pethbol—Pethbol is the twenty-fourth ogham character. It is associated with the guelder rose or snowball tree. It is the only additional character ascribed an esoteric number, which is given as three or five in the Irish bardic mysteries, and its color is pink, after the pale, transparent red fruits of the tree, which are ripe in September and October. *Peith* is not believed to have been the original letter, but rather a Brythonic substitute for the original letter *NG*, which was of no literary use to Brythons, but which was formed as part of the original series. Magickally, it is a character of mystery, about which is little known. Peith has been connected with the rune *Peorth*, with the meaning of a lively tune, meaning the dance of life.

Peine, Amancholl, Xi and Mor—The twenty-fifth ogham is given various names, and given the phonetic value of *Ae*. Peine is connected with the sacred grid of the four of the eight *ifins*. The tree of this ogham is the evergreen pine. In modern Irish, the name is *peine*. Its color is seen as blue-green, or sea-green. In esoteric lore, it is a tree which shows the way. It is a marker on the ancient trackways known as *leys*, where prominently visible clumps of pine mark the path ahead. Magickally, Peine is the bringer of illumination, both on an intellectual and spiritual level. This connection with the illuminating fire is apparent also in the ceremonial burning of the sacred buarcin (pine cone). When seen as *Xi*, this ogham represents Spirit, and when seen as *Mor*, it represents the sea.

The Gaelic Alphabet

The Gaelic alphabet is a forgotten alphabet not in modern use, but like the ogham, each letter corresponds with a tree, with the exception of two, which are fire and garden. There are seventeen full characters, with an eighteenth, the letter *H*, which is considered an accent and not a character in its own right. Each of the letters corresponds to an esoteric numerical equivalent, and the order in which the letters fall is the same as the Graeco-Roman system, unlike with the oghams (Figure 21).

In modern Wiccan and Pagan circles, the Futhark runes seem to be the alphabet system being put to use, but between the Irish oghams and the Gaelic alphabet, Faery Wicca has a wealth of its own secret alphabets just waiting to be used.*

It is the Gaelic alphabet that is used when writing in secret language that information reserved for the knowledge of the adepts.

A	Fhalm	Elm	One
B	Beath	Birch	Two
C	Calltuinn	Hazel	Three
D	Doir	Oak	Four
E	Eubh	Aspen	Five
F	Fearn	Alder	Six
G	Gart	Garden	Seven
I	Iubhar	Yew	Eight
L	Luis	Rowan	Nine
M	Muin	Vine	Ten
N	Nuin	Ash	Eleven
O	Oir	Furze	Twelve
P	Beith-bhog	Poplar	Thirteen
R	Ruis	Alder	Fourteen
S	Suil	Willow	Fifteen
T	Teine	Fire	Sixteen
U	Uhr	Yew	Seventeen

---

* For further study of magickal alphabets from around the world, refer to Nigel Pennick's book: *Magickal Alphabets.*

Figure 21: The Gaelic Alphabet. Line 1 is the variant letters of the Gaelic alphabet. Lines 2 and 3 are the Late-Celtic magickal alphabets. Lines 4 and 5 are the Medieval Irish alphabets.

Celtic Sacred Symbols

The art of understanding magickal and sacred symbolism has always fascinated humankind. Symbols represent an image which links us to higher levels of subjective intuitive experience, as well as to our immediate conscious awareness. Symbols are the midway point between what is outside ourselves, and what is deeply etched within.

Through symbolism we can see the soul awakening to the realization of true purpose, leading us to a higher level of spiritual evolution. The apprentice is often unaware that they are surrounded by symbols, the most obvious two being the sun and moon.

The sun represents the ancient symbol of light. On the physical realm, it is the bringer of life to this planet. On the spiritual realm, it represents the solar logos, or word of creation, as well as the masculine aspect of the creator: god.

The moon is the universal symbol of the Great Mystery. On the physical realm, it is the symbol of fertility. On the spiritual realm it represents the lunar logos, or intuition of creation, as well as the feminine aspect of the creator: goddess.

In symbolism, everything has some meaning and a purpose. When working with symbols it is important to be cognizant of what forces we are tuning into when contemplating a particular symbol, or when we use it as a base for meditation. The same stands true when we choose to engrave such symbols on magickal tools.

The study of symbols allows one to experience the symbol as the gateway to deeper thinking and living, we become aware that we have transcended the personality and touched deeply on our soul quality. When this happens, we then recognize that it is through the self that we make an inner contact with the Spiritual Benefactor on a level beyond reason or intellect. We become part of the whole, and recognize that the whole is also part of us.

Although symbols have no power of their own, they exert the influence for what they do represent. The powerful symbol is one that attracts beneficent energies for the growth and stimulation of the person working in it.

Turning to the magickal and sacred symbols of Faery Wicca, it must be noted that the ancient Celtic artist was forbidden to copy or portray the work of the creator, thus the artist's representation of natural creatures became highly stylized and abstracted; arms, legs, hair, and beard often intertwining in intricate patterns. The artist worked with stone, wood, metal, and paint in a style characterized by its abstract nature, balance of form, delicacy, brightness of color, and, most of all, by its spirals and interlacing designs.

There were seven created beings of the Celtic world featured in ancient artwork: plant, insect, fish, reptile, bird, mammal, and humans. Because the artwork of the Faery tradition was inspired by the supreme perfection of Dana's creation, it was made holy in their minds, and so, to show humility, an artist would deliberately leave parts unfinished so as to avoid the possibility of absolute perfection in their personal endeavor, and as an act not to insult the Ancient One. The following magickal symbols are the symbols considered most sacred to Faery Wicca.

Figure 22: Celtic Cross

The Celtic Cross—Although today the symbol we think of when we hear the word cross brings to mind the Christian cross, the Celtic cross is much older. The oldest examples of crosses are those engraved or painted on flat pebbles, dating from 10,000 B.C.E., found in a cave in the French Pyrenees. These ancestor stones were believed to contain the spirits of the dead.

The Celtic cross symbolizes the four roads of the four corners of the earth (forerunners of our parallels of latitude and longitude), and the meetings of these roads at a central point formed a cross, indicating the center of the world body. (Figure 22)

The center of the cross is also representative of the center place where all forces come together: the usual location of the Tree of Life, *axis mundi omphalos*, source of the four mystic rivers, summit of the world mountain, and other interpretations of the X that marks the spot.

The cross in the wheel has been used as a symbol for the sun and male gods who rule over all things—length, breadth, height, and depth.

Lozenge: The lozenge either has a dot in the center, or is divided into four equal parts with a dot in each compartment. This diamond shape has appeared with triangles on shrine walls, vases, seals, and, typically, on the pregnant belly or other parts of the Pregnant Goddess, starting in the seventh millennium B.C.E. (Figure 23)

The design is thought to be a symbol of fertility because of its vulva configuration. The lozenge with a dot in the four corners may denote planting in all four directions, whereas many dots within a diamond may signify multiplication of the seed, a general resurgence of life in the sown field.

Figure 23: Lozenge

The lozenge that is divided in equal parts suggests that all fat parts of the body were significant, considered to be growing, or pregnant. This sign, apparently, is representative of the Great Mother from whose womb we were given birth, and in whose womb still rest the countless unborn.

Knot Work Designs: The Celtic knot was considered the Thread of Life. To the Celts, the human soul was thought to be a fragment of the divine, which will ultimately return to its divine source. Through successive rebirths the soul rids itself of its accumulated, inherited impurities until it finally achieves the goal of perfection. (Figure 24)

The interlaced, or latticed, knotwork patterns, with their unbroken lines, symbolize the process of humankind's eternal spiritual evolution. When the cord is unravelled, it leads us on. A knot lattice can be used as an aid to concentration by occupying the conscious mind with a demanding repetitive task.

Figure 24: Knot Work Design

Spirals: Both single and double spirals were among the most sacred signs of Neolithic Europe. They appeared on megalithic monuments and temples all over the continent and the Celtic islands. Spiral oculi (double twists resembling eyes) appear prominently in places like the threshold stones at Newgrange in Ireland. (Figure 25)

The spiral is the cosmic symbol for the natural form of growth; a symbol of eternal life, reminding us of the flow and movement of the cosmos. The whorls are continuous creation and dissolution of the world; the passages between the spirals symbolized the divisions between life, death and rebirth.

The apprentice would pass a spiral barrier into an inner sanctuary on their journey of the sacred dance through the labyrinth to the sacred realms beyond the center. The labyrinth creates and protects the still center, allowing entry to knowledge only in the correct way—initiation. Before the knowledge can be imparted, old preconceptions must be discarded and the traveler must re-enter the preformal state of the earth-womb. At the center there is complete balance: the point where heaven and earth are joined.

The spiral dance that witches perform in sacred circles demonstrates the concept of As above, So below; mirroring the macrocosmic order of the heavens, the gyratory movement representing the whirling of the stars above the fixed earth. Winding in,

the spiral dance establishes the still center within, approaching the heart of the universe, or the womb which will give birth. Winding out, the spiral dance births the Spirit back to its divine source of existence.

Figure 25: Spiral oculi

Figure 26: Key Pattern

Labyrinths or Key Patterns: The Key lattice also represents the Sacred Dance with its step patterns, which are really spirals in straight lines. When connected, they become a processional path, leading through a complex maze to the sacred omphalos (the navel) at the center. (Figure 26)

Figure 27: Portcullis

Portcullis: The doors that lead to the inner, or Solar Sphere, were often adorned with a key pattern lattice archway. The combination of these two symbols was to prepare the apprentice for their journey into the Great Mysteries. (Figure 27)

The willingness to pass through the threshold was the first step every Initiate at one time took. This was a journey through progressive levels of experience, physical, mental, and spiritual, until the vortex at the center was reached, as conveyed by the key pattern labyrinth design of the lattice archway above the door.

Zoomorphic Ornaments: Animals and birds were considered sacred and were often used to represent the Ancient Ones. Shapeshifting was a common attribute of the Celtic goddesses and some of the gods. These semi-mythological characters, who adopted the form of an animal, were soon turned into art. (Figure 28)

Zoomorphic and anthropomorphic ornaments are symbols which show us that nothing is as it first appears. Often, such artwork looks like a beautiful mosaic of miscellaneous design and color until, upon closer examination, one identifies a head, or a tail, or a plant, all of which are interwoven with each other. These intricate patterns first appeared in the Bronze Age art of Ireland. The artisans fashioned them into a complicated contortion of bodies, but they kept the motif still logical and conforming with nature.

Because it was forbidden to duplicate Dana's creation in a perfect state, it is not unusual for animals to appear with human hands and feet, or even to see a calf's head on an eagle's body, or a human being with animal parts.

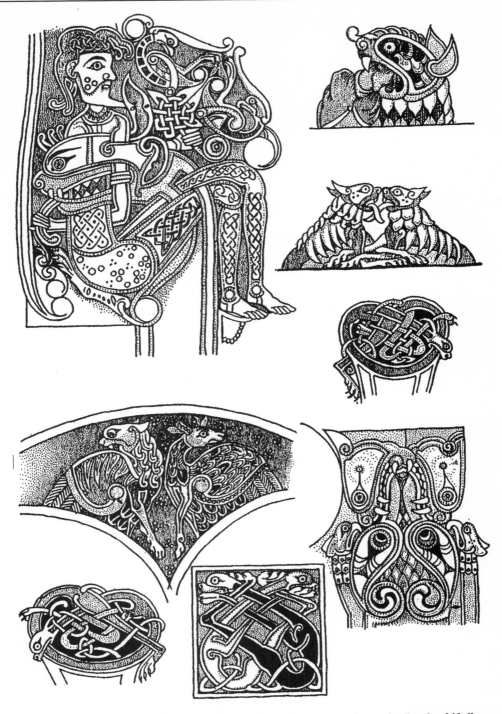

**Figure 28: Examples of Zoomorphic Ornaments found in the Historic *Book of Kells* —
Source: Dover Publications**

Celtic Numerology

The science of numerology is one based on harmonious vibration. Each letter of every alphabet carries a certain rate of vibration based on a number. Numbers have three aspects or degrees of comparison:

- The constructive.
- The negative.
- The destructive.

The belief is that if you understand the vibration of your name, for instance, then you have the power to choose to live a constructive life. The numbers show their negative side if we drift through life, they become destructive when we deliberately take action in the wrong direction, but by understanding these two aspects, you can attempt to change your life and express it through the constructive aspect which produces the most harmonious vibration.

This cosmic orchestra provides the roadmap to finding the fullest expression in living, while teaching us how to bring out the harmonies of the inner self. The clue to producing the personal harmony is found in the world around us, for, if we pause long enough to sense and feel it, we can realize the vibration.

The understanding of numerology is to find the inner harmony which will enable each of us to vibrate at an equal pace with the vibration of Mother Earth. The world travels at a rapid rate. Scientists have noted that the vibration of the earth increases at the rate of one hour a week, which means our inner vibrations will also continually shift. Numerology helps us to work with the vibrations rather than against them, taking our place in the orchestra and traveling at the rate that belongs to each one of us individually.

Although traditional numerology is based on the numbers one through nine, adding two master numbers of eleven and twenty-two, Celtic numerology places its main emphases on: four/five, eight/nine, twelve/thirteen, sixteen/seventeen, twenty-seven, and thirty-two/thirty-three. This system is based on multiples of even numbers, plus an odd number, except for twenty-seven, which is perfectly divided by nine three times, enacting the ancient magickal teaching: *by the powers of three times three.*

$$4 + 1 = 5$$
$$4 \times 2 \quad\quad 8 + 1 = 9$$
$$3 \times 4 \quad\quad 12 + 1 = 13$$
$$8 \times 2 \quad\quad 16 + 1 = 17$$
$$16 \times 2 \quad\quad 32 + 1 = 33$$

The implications that each of the odd numbers is completed by the addition of one is borne out by the fact that, both in old authorities and in modern Gaelic, the unit (even number) is transformed into an odd number when added to the center or leader, which is considered the unifying principle.

In ancient times, odd numbers were masculine, even numbers feminine. The Chinese express the fundamental duality of Yang (masculine) and Yin (feminine) in terms of odd and even numbers respectively. This concept of the additional unit as the unifying factor by no means expresses an inequity of even numbers, placing the odd or masculine numbers in a superior position but rather expresses a symbolism that to the principle of that which is material or set apart from the infinite is expressed through the even numbers, such as the number four: representing the earth and all material objects; while the number one, or the odd number, represents the outermost limits of the cosmos, is considered the source of all things, and thereby must be added to the physical in order to complete it. Therefore, whereas the center turns multiplicity into unity, the external factor sets it in the context of infinity, and between unity and infinity there is a strange identity with which our spirits merge.

In Ireland, one may still be confronted with the riddle: "Where is the middle of the world?" The correct answer is "Here" or "Where you are standing." The world, the universe, the directions, whatever the middle is referring to, is always oriented around wherever one *is*. This concept is why the traditional center of the Great Circle is the hearth-fire, for the fire represents the center, the Soul-Monad of each who stand within the Sacred Space.

Let us now take a brief look at the five numbers listed above as being a significant numerological part of Celtic lore.

Five—The figure five is the four of the cross-roads plus the swinging of the door which is the point itself of crossing, the moment of arrival and departure. The four is representative of the four elements, the four directions, while the fifth, the completing factor, represents the center where the four quarters meet and become whole. In Ireland, this whole is represented by every cairn (a mound of stones erected over a burial, or at some other point, with other-world associations) to be found.

In *The Champion of the Cairn*, given to Conchobar's son Cormac, it is noted that "some of the learned assert that every place wherein there are five stones, or any other five things, or the five provinces of Ireland, is properly called a cairn." This pattern of the whole is mirrored repeatedly throughout the myths of Ireland. Cormac as Nia in Chairn was "champion of the five provinces." A pillar stone at Keimaneigh is said to be a petrified woman, and in her are five cavities with five oval stones in them. Children playing fivestones unwittingly play with the symbols of the whole of Ireland and, finally, in the houses maintained by kindreds of the fuidir (tenant class), they do not incur liability unless they maintain five dwellings. The Irish baile biatach (ounce land), comprised of four quarterlands (the fifth element being the whole), was a tax unit. The faithche (similar to a ranch or farm), consisting of four fields, one on each side of a homestead was also considered a whole.

Although five is not the most prominent number in Celtic tradition, it appears in a large number of significant contexts. Ireland had five great roads, five celebrated hostels, five paths of law, five prohibitions for each of the four provincial kings (but seven for the king of Tara). Mythical personages wore fivefold cloaks, and Cu Chulainn had five wheels on his shield, representing the cosmos.

The Faery counted by fives. The secret fifth of the five families, or groups, of five signs each of which constitute the oghams, can also be found. The first three groups of five stand for the different consonants, while the fourth group stands for the vowels. The fifth set of five, however, called the supplementary family, denotes diphthongs and are represented not by hash marks as the other four groups, but by sacred symbols of the mystic center as we have already seen.

"Five words are adjudged to be a breath of the poet," or so it was noted in a medieval tract on language. In the Filidecht (philosophy, or the highest wisdom) learned at the royal palace Mur-Ollamh (The Wall of the Learned) in Tara, five kinds of language were taught:

- The language of the Feni, the precedents of the poets.
- The language of separation, the hidden (ogham).
- The language of the file (poet), in which they speak with one another.
- The language of iarmberla, such as cuich (five), that is a secret, and ballorb, a member which completes the poet.
- The fifth kind of language, learned by poets in their fifth year of training.

In war, chants were repeated five times upon spears, which would cause the spears to move from the chanter's hand and penetrate the enemies. In card games, the Irish trick is known as the cuig (five), unlike the modern card games in which are found four suits.

Five is the first number that was given only one form (the first four numerals were declined with feminine and masculine forms), thus combining, or unifying the polarities.

In the science of numerology, the vibration quality of the number five is one of expansion, awareness; the awareness of the five-senses, five fingers, five toes, in the form of two arms, two legs and the fifth part of torso, in the original five planets and five vowels. It is the five points on the pentagram, representing the four elements combined, which produce the fifth of Spirit, or which require the fifth of Spirit in order to become animated.

The constructive aspect of five is: freedom, progress, versatility, understanding, variety, adaptability, mental curiosity, life experience, cleverness, unattachment, sociability, change, discard, travel, adventure, companionability.

The negative aspect of five is: irresponsibility, procrastination, carelessness, self-indulgence, thoughtlessness, inconsistency, sensationalism, bad taste.

The destructive aspect of five is: libertinism, perversion, abuse of freedom, indulgence in drink, indulgence in drugs, perversion of sensuality.

Nine—This number figures so prominently in Celtic tradition that it can be described as the northern counterpart of the sacred seven of Eastern traditions. The most repeated reference made to nine is in the subject of houses. Houses of kingship comprised nine houses (or rooms) in one. Also a holding, consisting of a homestead and eight acres, was known as a kingdom.

There were nine hazels of wisdom, and a marvelous tree which grew from above downwards, with nine branches, of which the highest was the most beautiful, and in which pure white birds listened to the melodies to be heard there (the nine—in this case—representing the nine grades of heaven).

Nine, like five, symbolized the whole. Companies of nine abound in Irish literature. In many cases it is made clear that the nine consist of a leader and eight others. In the *Tain Bo Cuailnge*, Queen Medb rode with nine chariots: two before her, two behind, and two chariots at either side, her own chariot in the middle.

When King Loegaire set out to arrest St. Patrick, he ordered nine chariots to be joined together "according to the tradition of the gods." In the fiana, companies of nine, comprising a leader and eight others, were customary, these however, were grouped into larger units comprising three companies of nine plus a leader. In old authorities and modern Gaelic, eight persons are sometimes referred to as morochtar, "the great eight persons' signifies the 'nine'," the addition of the odd number being the center, or unifying principle.

Cu Chulainn had nine weapons, eight small and one large. Nine maidens are usually mentioned. At Beltain, nine sticks of wood, from nine trees, collected by nine men, are gathered for the hearth-fire, and sometimes the fire is kindled by nine-nines of first-begotten sons.

Nines, and particularly the ninth, is very important in divinations and folk cures. Even the waves of the sea broke in a series of nine, the ninth wave being larger and more fortunate than the rest.

The Irish terms *nomad* and *noinden* stand for units of nine time-spaces, and are believed, at one time, to have had significance in the Celtic calendar. The Celts may at one time have had a nine-day week, or rather a nine-night week. Three weeks of nine nights would give a twenty-seven night month.

In the science of numerology, nine is the vibration of universal love, and only through this principle can our power reach the whole world, becoming a servant to the Universe.

The constructive aspect of nine is: universal love, brotherhood/sisterhood, charity, compassion, the Higher Law, artistic genius, selfless service, philanthropy, humanitarianism, magnetism, sympathy, understanding, romance, generosity, breadth of viewpoint.

The negative aspect of nine is: emotionalism, amativeness, egocentricity, sentimentality, dissipation of forces, indiscretion, impracticality, fickleness, aimless dreaming.

The destructive aspect of nine is: dissipation, immorality, vulgarity, bitterness, moroseness.

Thirteen—The figure of twelve individuals around a king is ancient. In Ireland, the ancient king-idol, Crom Croich, was made of gold and around him twelve stone idols were placed. The twelve subsidiary idols were arranged in four rows of three, forming the familiar pattern of a center and three in each direction.

Thirteen is the number of times the average woman will menstruate during the year,* and the thirteen ancient stones described above easily demonstrates the twelve

---

* For an indepth study of menstruation, also called the blood mysteries, refer to my books, *An Act of Woman Power*, and *Sister Moon Lodge*.

constellations, with the thirteenth stone being that of the moon which lunates through each constellation in the course of one year.

Thirteen at one time was associated with the cunning women and the Women's Mysteries. It was the number of the moon-goddess, and in the more modern calendar, when the thirteenth of the month fell on a Friday (the day of Venus), it was considered a most auspicious day, and the attention of the people was focused on fertility, sexual union, and the eating of fish as an aphrodisiac. Through the institution of modern religions, Friday the thirteenth has become an unlucky day, and the number thirteen has been tainted as both an evil and unlucky number.

Interestingly, the numerological number of thirteen is four (1+3=4). Four is the representative of the four directions/quarters, the four elements, the four seasons. The four seasons are dually honored through the observance of the completion of the thirteen lunations of the moon: one year.

In the science of numerology, the vibration of the number thirteen, or four, is that of boundary. Four is the first manifestation in matter, as well as the formation of Spirit, Soul, Mind, and Body. The earth is considered the square of the four, or the boundary in which the physical, as we know it, manifests. The lessons of the four is to learn to cooperate within the four elements.

The constructive aspect of thirteen/four is: practicality, service, patience, exactitude, organization, application, devotion, patriotism, conservatism, pragmatism, divinity, economy, trust, worthiness, endurance, loyalty.

The negative aspect of thirteen/four is: plodding, narrowness, exaction, repression, minuteness, penuriousness, clumsiness, dogmatism crudeness, brusqueness, restriction, rigidity, sternness, dullness.

The destructive aspect of thirteen/four is: vulgarity, hatred, violence, jealousy, inhumanity, resistance, destruction, cruelty.

Seventeen—Partholan and Nemed between them cleared sixteen plains, which together with the Old Plain of Elta fashioned by Dana before any of the invaders arrived, make a total of seventeen. In *The Book of Rights,* seventeen kings accepted annual gifts from the king of Cashel, there were seventeen kingdoms in Meath, and seventeen townlands upon St. Ciaran. From the above, we can deduce that seventeen may have been a significant territorial unit.

Seventeen days, the seventeenth of the month, and seventeen years, occur in a number of interesting contexts. The Sons of Mil arrived in Ireland on the seventeenth of the moon, the Battle of Tailtiu began on the seventeenth of the moon, and there are several reigns of sixteen or seventeen years duration. Also, the Tuatha De Danann are listed in seventeen triads. Finn's womenfolk numbered seventeen, and seventeen chieftains in succession commanded the fiana.

Youths became men at seventeen in Ireland. Cu Chulainn had his first great exploit at seventeen. Fergus was exiled for seventeen years. Seventeen maidens lived on the Island of Women. The heavens are divided into sixteen regions, the cosmologies, or the center, denoting the seventeenth region. The year was also looked upon as seventeen: the thirteen months and the four seasons.

In Ireland, the seventeenth generation marked the limits to which kin could properly be reckoned, as noted in this saying: There is not an old seanchaidbe (storyteller) in Tirconaill that has not heard times without number of the seiseadh glun deag (the sixteenth generation), the seventeenth being the current one, and curses are invoked to the seventeenth generation.

The ancient kinship system incorporates all the uneven numbers which we have discussed thus far, classifying kindred into four categories according to their degree of remoteness.

- The geilfine extends to five persons.
- The deirbhfine extends to nine persons.
- The iarfine extends to thirteen persons.
- The innfine extends to seventeen persons.

The innermost circle of geilfine contains five persons, while each of the other three contains four additional ones, making a total of seventeen.

In the science of numerology, the vibration of seventeen is eight (1+7=8). Eight is the vibration of manifestation; the power to matter the forces of matter and the balanced judgement to use them for the good of humankind, and in the Irish sense, unto seventeen generations. In the lesson attached to this vibration, the key to success is in considering the effects one's decisions and actions will have on the kinship of the seventeenth generation (this concept is not unlike the Native American Indian seventh generation caretaking considerations). In Celtic numerology, eight also represents man and woman in myths.

The constructive aspect of seventeen/eight is: power, authority, success, material freedom, judgement, discrimination, executive ability, organization, leadership, management, practicality, thoroughness, dependability, self-reliance, control, the power to succeed.

The negative aspect of seventeen/eight is: strain, hardness, materialism, ambition for self and money, demand for recognition, intolerance, worry, scheming, love of power, carelessness, impatience, poor judgement, mis-spent energy.

The destructive aspect of seventeen/eight is: bullying, abuse, revenge, oppressiveness, injustice, cruelty, unscrupulousness.

Twenty-seven—This number is a derivative of nine, and so all the information listed under nine applies to twenty-seven, with the addition of the following: twenty-seven, in Celtic tradition, was frequently expressed as three nines. Three times nine plus a leader, making twenty-eight in all, seems to have been a numerical arrangement of considerable significance. Calatin with his twenty-seven sons insisted on their being regarded as a single warrior, claiming that all his offspring were constituent parts of his own body.

In the *Wooing of Emer*, Cu Chulainn was opposed by Emer's father, together with her three brothers, each of whom had eight men—a company of twenty-eight altogether. Companies of nine, comprising a leader and eight men were customary among the fiana.

In the evaluation of a nine-night week, three weeks of nine nights create a twenty-seven night month. The importance of the twenty-seven in Celtic mythology is related to the twenty-seven constellations of the lunar zodiac.

Thirty-three—Groups of men are primarily acknowledged as thirty-two, plus the leader: thirty-two leaders of the Tuatha De Danann, the thirty-third being Lugh; thirty-three men, of thirty-two years each, sit at tables in the Otherworld island-castle in Perlesvaus; Nemed reached Ireland with only one ship, thirty-two of his ships lost on the way; Cu Chulainn slays thirty-three of Labraid's opponents; and thirty-three Fomorian leaders are listed in *The Second Battle of Mag Tuired*.

In the science of numerology, the vibration of thirty-three is 6 [3+3=6]. Six is the vibration of union, harmonization, the completed form of polar opposites—as above, so below. The lesson to be learned through this vibration is one of extension: seeing one's own image in their children, their work, as being carried on through these extensions. The link between the image and the extension is thus reflected upon and the examination of the Soul initiated.

The constructive aspect of thirty-three/six is: love, harmony, home, responsibility, adjustment, musical talent, sympathy, understanding, domesticity, guardianship, stability, poise, protection, healing, firmness, balance, idealism, conscientiousness, justice, burden-bearing, service to humankind.

The negative aspect of thirty-three/six is: anxiety, worry, meddlesomeness, bustling activity, misplaced sympathy, mistaken ideals, interference, conventionality, pride, smugness, unwilling service, drudgery, despondency.

The destructive aspect of thirty-three/six is: cynicism, egoist , suspicion, jealousy, slavery, domestic tyranny.

Taking the above descriptions of the more important numbers referred to throughout Celtic mythology, one can see how the vibration is being used through the actions presented in the tales, and upon closer examination of where one may be in their own journey of apprenticeship.

From these examinations an understanding of the expression of the inner-soul is understood. You could ask yourself, "Am I vibrating in a constructive, negative, or destructive expression?" and, upon finding the answer, can choose to alter the harmony if it is a less than a constructive one.

Of course the study of the science of numerology is much more indepth then what has been provided here. The point to be made is that we are all affected by the vibrations that govern the Universe, for we are all a part of it. As a part of the whole, we are affected by every change in the Universal rate of vibration, but because we are individuals we also have a rate of our own. We choose the rate, or aspect, at which we vibrate. Therefore, when magickally working with numbers, it is wise to be aware of the number's vibration before scribing it on a magickal tool, or using it in ceremony.

o Rathlin's Isle I chanced to sail
When summer breezes softly blew,
And there I heard so sweet a tale,
that oft I wished it could be true.
They said, at eve, when rude winds sleep,
And hushed is ev'ry turbid swell,
A mermaid rises from the deep,
And sweetly tunes her magic shell.

And while she plays, rock dell and cave
In dying falls the sound retain,
As if some choral spirits gave
Their aid to swell her witching strain.
Then summoned by that dulcet note,
Uprising to th' admiring view,
A fairy island seems to float
With tints of many a gorgeous hue.

And glittering fanes, and lofty towers,
All on this fairy isle are seen;
And waving trees, and shady bowers
With more than mortal verdure green.
And as it moves, the western sky
Glows with a thousand varying rays;
And the calm sea, tinged with each dye,
Seems like a golden flood of blaze.

They also say, if earth or stone,
From verdant Erin's hallowed land,
Were on this magic island thrown,
For ever fixed, it then would stand,
But, when for this, some little boat
In silence ventures from the shore,
The mermaid sinks—hushed is the note,
The fairy isle is seen no more!

— The Enchanted Island
16th Century anonymous

Lesson 11

The Temple

Come to us, ye who do not know where ye are ...
Amazed ye look and do not comprehend, for your eyes
are set upon a star and your feet move in the blessed
kingdoms of the Sidhe!*

Getting set up is a relatively easy process; as mentioned earlier, Faery Wicca is closely connected to the land, and therefore all celebrations take place on the land, within the boundary of the Great Circle. I realize that in some locations working outside year round becomes an impossibility due to local weather patterns. Therefore, the need for a Temple might become vital.

Temples truly can be any type of dwelling that is consecrated as holy ground. For example, garages can be transformed into a Temple, the guest house, a spare bedroom, even the living room can be used.

Remember, when the Great Circle is cast, the space within the boundary of the circle becomes consecrated Sacred Space, albeit Temporary Sacred Space. Nevertheless, the Great Circle can also be looked upon as the Temple. Practicing Faery Wicca does not dictate a separate dwelling.

Creating a Permanent Temple

If you were to create a Permanent Temple, the space required must contain four quarter/province walls, each with its own altar, a main altar area, and, if a traditional Temple, a hearth pit in the center of the Temple (Figure 29).

In the North/Ulster Quarter/Province would ideally be the entrance into the Temple. On the wall would be hung the Warrior's Shield. The earth quarter altar would have a white or green altar cloth, a white or green votive candle, and the La Fal talisman.

In the East/Leinster Quarter/Province would be set living plants. On the wall would be hung the magickal athame. The air quarter altar would have a green or yellow altar cloth, a green or yellow votive candle, and the Sword of Nuada talisman.

In the South/Munster Quarter/Province would be set musical instruments. Upon the wall would be hung weavings, tapestries, or artwork. The fire quarter altar would have a red altar cloth, a red votive candle, and the Spear of Lugh talisman.

---

* James Stephens, *The Crock of Gold*, pg. 296-7, The Macmillan Company, New York, 1935

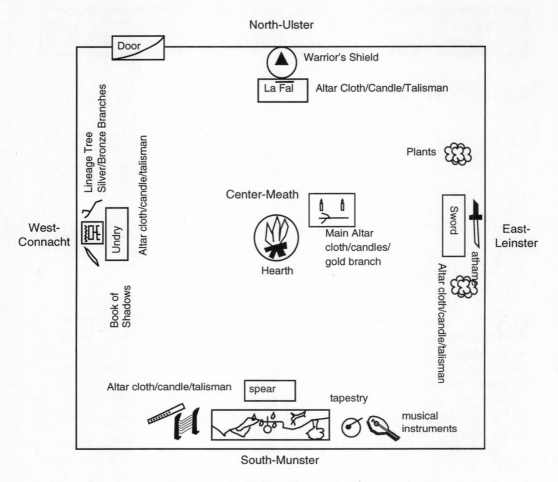

Figure 29: Example of the Temple Layout

In the West/Connacht Quarter/Province would be set the *Book of Shadows* on a podium. Upon the wall would be hung the Lineage Tree (Lesson Two), and the Silver and Bronze Branches. The water quarter altar would have a blue, gray, or black altar cloth, a blue votive candle, and the Undry talisman.

In the Center/Meath Province would be set the hearth (a circular barbecue can be used), and to the north or north-east of the hearth would immediately be the main altar. The main altar would have a green cloth, white and black altar candles, the Gold Branch, as well as the other items required for the particular altar face used.*

Once a Permanent Temple has been properly prepared, it is important to consecrate it, designating it as Sacred Space. The following ritual outline can be used to consecrate your Temple; it will require the quiet and undisturbed space of approximately 45 minutes to perform. Aside from the items required to properly prepare your Temple, have the following items ready:

---

* Altar faces are discussed in Section One, Lesson 6: Sacred Space

232

⤞ A silver hand-bell
⤞ Pure water
⤞ Holy oil such as heather or yarrow

Before you begin the ritual, ground and center yourself by using the three soft breaths followed by the three full-belly breaths for mind, body, and Spirit.

Consecrating the Temple Ritual
Take the pure water and walk around the perimeter of the room, espurging the water. You are doing this as an act of purifying the room.

With Faery wand or athame in hand, go to the North quarter and walk deosil around the Temple three times, tracing the circle boundary by sending the Blue-Energy* of sacredness through your tool. As the third round is completed, say:

The boundary of this Temple be
scribed thrice with Fire
under the protection of the Ancient Ones
until it is banished by the power
of the sacred and Holy water.†

When you return to the North, invoke the guardians and keepers of each quarter by raising your Faery wand, or athame, and pointing it toward the quarter and sending the blue flame. At each quarter, recite the following invocation, and finish each by ringing the silver hand-bell.

Mighty Guardians of the North [East, South, West]
Old Ones of the Way,
Keepers of the Power of earth [air, fire, water]
I invoke you this day,
Come empower this gateway
of the Temple _____ [name of Temple]
and make this place a Sacred abode
in which to honor the ancient Faery-Faith.

When you return to the North, anoint the North quarter votive candle and its talisman with the holy oil, and then light the candle. Perform this process for each quarter, each time saying:

With the holy oil I anoint thee,
and bring forth the power of earth [air, fire, water].
I smoor (light) the fire of the gateway
that leads to the sacred city of Falias [Gorias, Finias, Murias].
With the sacred talisman, may entrance be granted.
Thoet se (So must it be)!

---

* See Section Two: Magickal Faery Tools, Faery Wand Exercises.

† This sacred and holy water is the actual water from the Well of St. Bridged in Ireland.

Move to the hearth and main altar. Stand before the altar and anoint the candles, and light them, and say:

The Center is empowered!

The final act is lighting the heart-flame. When you feel ready, light the hearth fire and as the flames rise, call out:

Behold! I smoor the sacred flame,
just as the Tuatha De Danann smoored the sacred flame
in honor of Great Dana!
With the heart-flame now lit,
the Temple comes to life
and is dully consecrated.
Blessed by the power of Dana,
by the powers of earth and sea,
by the powers of moon and sun,
by the powers of starlight,
the Ancient Faith now lives once more!

Whether one has a Temple, or uses their living-room space to perform ceremony, the following journey provides an invaluable strengthening of the inner Temple within each one of us, while further demonstrating the meaning of Personal Sacred Space. To understand Personal Sacred Space, and actually have a real sense of what that means, brings about an energy balance that will only enhance your ability to cast the Great Circle, or work inside your actual Temple.

Personal Sacred Space

Once you have undergone this journey and created your Spirit Temple, your Personal Sacred Space will grow stronger and stronger. The importance of experiencing this type of Sacred Space becomes more apparent every time you meditate, go on a shamanic journey, create Temporary Sacred Space, or walk into a Temple.

Recalling Personal Sacred Space to the forefront of awareness, before undergoing any experience or situation involved with spirituality, builds a smoke-screen of protection. This shield, in time, will only allow those energies personally called forth to be experienced, while holding at bay any unwanted energies.

For example, if you experience a feeling of nausea when you visit a metaphysical bookstore, or when you take part in a public gathering ceremony, then you are in need of developing your Personal Sacred Space. This type of experience happens to many of us, and when it does we are being informed by our own bodies and our own awakened senses that we are what some call *sensitive*. This means, whether you want to or not, you attract and receive the energies (negative and positive alike) of everyone around you.

Shielding yourself becomes vitally important, because being a receptacle for unwanted energies is very exhausting. By creating Personal Sacred Space, you then reinforce your own etheric body in such a manner as to develop an astral stop light.

This stop light shuts out all energies (negative and positive alike) until you specifically invite them to come in.

In addition, as you begin to dwell in a state of perpetual sacredness, you provide a forum in which your five senses (sight, taste, touch, hearing, and smelling) align. Through this alignment the sixth sense (intuition) is generated and fine-tuned. Through Personal Sacred Space, intuition freely operates, providing you with daily direction for the welfare of Spirit.

This journey will require the quiet and undisturbed space of one hour. Sit before your Mirror altar and focus your attention on the altar face. Take a moment to peruse each item, checking to make sure you haven't forgotten anything, and taking time to really reflect on the symbols before you. When this mental exercise has ended and you feel your mind begin to quiet, perform the Preparation and Ground and Center formats.

Burn some incense to awaken the deeper memories of the Ancient Ones, light the hearth-fire for clarity and push the play button on your stereo to bring in the vibrational side of life which will begin your shapeshifting.

Relax, and let your eyes stop seeing by blinking a few times and relaxing the lids until they shut half-way and you are in soft-sight.

Focus on your breath, following it in and out. Follow the three soft-breaths in and out, moving deeper into your center, and then ground your awareness into your center by taking the three full belly breaths for mind, body and Spirit. Let your breathing resume its normal rhythm.

Spirit Temple Journey*

Every breath you take paves an inner road. This road leads you into a deep place within. As you breath in, a stretch of road is revealed. As you breath out, you move down the road. Follow this inner road of breath, and allow yourself to go deeper and deeper within.

> *Now I walk the beauty road,*
> *beauty is before me,*
> *beauty is behind me,*
> *above and below me,*
> *around and within me.†*

The inner road, is a road of beauty. Beauty is Spirit. As you walk this beauty road, you arrive at a very warm and comfortable place. Sit down in this place. Look around and sense the warmth and comfort around you. [pause]

As you sit in this place, open your Spirit eyes and see what this place looks like. Your vision will at first seem blurry, but slowly the darkness will recede, and the place will begin to materialize around you.

---

* Have someone act as mediator and read this to your group, or pre-record the journey on tape and play it as you enter your Personal Sacred Space.
† From an old Navajo prayer.

See the ground on which you sit. Are you sitting on dirt? Grass? Grass mats? Beautiful rugs? Allow the ground to completely materialize, and become aware of its every detail.

[pause]

See the structure begin to materialize. Are walls forming around you? Are you sitting within an open patio dwelling, its walls simply four corner poles? Or, are the walls made out of material, allowing you to see through and beyond them? Perhaps they are grass walls, or wood, or stone, or cement. Allow the wall structure to completely materialize, and be aware of every detail. [pause]

Above you the ceiling begins to materialize. Observe the shape it takes. Is it flat, arched, domed. Does it have skylights? Is part of it open? Perhaps it is lattice, or wood, or marble, or stone, or cement, or glass. Allow the ceiling to completely materialize, and be aware of every detail. [pause]

Around you a Spirit Temple has materialized. Stand and move into the center of the Temple. There you come to an altar. Look down at the altar face and see every detail on its surface. [pause]

On the altar face rests your Silver Branch. Pick it up and point it toward the east. Don't worry, you will automatically point your wand in the right direction. As you hold your Faery wand, close your eyes and feel the sacredness of your Temple. Breath-in the sacredness of your Temple, and as you breath out, the sacredness flows out your Faery wand in a blue stream of energy and touches the east corner of the Temple.

Continue breathing in sacredness and breathing out the blue stream of energy as you move the wand toward the south. When you arrive at the south quarter of the Temple, take another breath and shoot the blue energy to touch the south corner of the Temple.

Continue turning toward the west. Shoot the blue energy and touch the west corner. Continue turning toward the north. Shoot the blue energy and touch the north corner. Continue to turn toward the east, where you will once again shoot the blue energy to touch the east corner, sealing the boundary of the Great Circle.

Raise your Faery wand up to the heavens above you and shoot the blue energy to touch the Heavenly Realm, and then lower your Faery wand down to the ground below you and shoot the blue energy to touch the realm of the Underworld. You have completed connecting the six directions of the Great Circle, and are thus enclosed in Sacred Space.

Return the Faery wand to your altar, and once again, return your focus to the face of the altar. The time has come for you to ground the Sacred Space within your Spirit Temple. Relax and allow yourself to dance and sing. When you feel the full power of the energy raised by your body movements and vocal vibrations, fall to the floor and release all the energy, grounding it into the Spirit Temple.

[pause for a few minutes]

With the energy grounding now complete, become very, very still. Call to your Faery Fetch, and ask your companion to fetch your Spiritual Benefactor. When your Spiritual Benefactor arrives, relax and open to receive information from her/him.

[Meditation time permitted/approximately 15 to 30 minutes.]

Meditation with your Spiritual Benefactor comes to an end. Thank her/him for any messages she/he shared with you.

[pause]

Stand before the altar once more and look down upon its face. Take a full belly breath and exhale, committing any messages received from your Spiritual Benefactor to your conscious awareness.

[pause]

Take another full belly breath and exhale, imprinting the Great Circle of Sacred Space within your Spirit Temple.

[pause]

Finally, take another full belly breath and absorb the Spirit Temple entirely into your being.

[pause]

Allow your breathing to resume its normal rhythm. As you do so, the Spirit Temple slowly disappears. Before you forms the road of beauty. Breath in and expose a stretch of road. Exhale, and walk up the road. Continue breathing in and exhaling, moving farther up the road until you are completely back in your body, sitting before your physical altar.

Begin to blink your eyes open, and let them focus on the face of your physical altar. Begin to see the symbols that rest there. When your eyelids open back to a normal attention, focus on the hearth-flame. Take a deep breath and relax.

Within you now exists a Spirit Temple, dually consecrated and containing your Personal Sacred Space.

The Four Cities

The Tuatha De Danann came from another realm into this one, in which we now dwell. From the east, south, north, and west they came, from each of their great and sacred cities. Little is recorded regarding these four cities, and what little has been is obscure. What we do know is that each of the cities is a realm connected to one of the four directions, and each has a key or talisman.

In my experience with the four cities, I have come to understand that they are thresholds into a greater realm which we do not even identify or work with in any esoteric system. These four cities do not lead us into the Heavenly Realm, nor the Plains nor even the Underworld. Perhaps, they admit us into another Cycle of Existence, of which we cannot possibly conceive of nor understand, for no one who has passed through cares to come back and enlighten us.

Gaining deeper insight into the meaning of each city requires committed contemplation on each quarter, province, element, color, season, and talisman. All of these correspondences are the woof and warp of each city, and to weave the threads together through visualizations and meditation brings forth the truth or message connected to each.

Each city contains a guardian, a companion, a landscape, and a truth, or message. Before you can fully come to understand the sacred cities, you must be educated with the foundation of Faery Wicca. Further study of the four cities will eventually come, as it is a subject of great imagination and one that must be thoroughly experienced*.

Working with the Underworld

As already discussed in Lesson Five: The Land Of Faery, the Otherworld exist in this land, and access to it begins in our imagination.

When one consciously chooses to journey into the Land of Faery, they are subjecting themselves to a course of events beyond rational control, for one can never know what will be encountered. Not one of our natural laws is acknowledged in Faeryland, nor have they any effect. Linear time, for example, has no bearing. What may be a month in our time reference, is often but a day in the realm of the Fay. Because of this, one is likely to become disoriented upon attempting to journey into the Underworld.

The direction of such a journey is downward, in search of the light within the earth, the earth wisdom, and Ancient Ones. The most effective way in which to experience the Underworld is through the guidance of one who has already traveled there. Therefore, I share with you one of my first journeys into the Land of Faery:

I went on a journey to the Underworld. A spiral staircase took me down through an opening between this realm and that. At the bottom of the stairs, was an anteroom and at the end of it was a closed wooden door.

A light glowed over the archway of the door, and in the wood to the left of the archway were carved symbols: the first symbol was two *U's* stacked back-to-back; the second was the roman letter *i*.

Directly under the lamp was another symbol: a crescent-shaped boat. To the right of the arch were three symbols: the same stacked *U* symbol that was to the right; an *X*; the third symbol was more complex, it was an *X* with three vertical lines drawn through it and a dot centered over the first two lines.

The design of a serpent tail began near the bottom of the arch on the right, and continued on the floor before the door. It curved and wound up the left-side of the arch, forming into the head. The serpent's head, however, was molded out of a material and was actually three-dimensional, whereas, the entire body was painted on the arches and floor.

The serpent became real, disengaging itself from the wall, and slithered toward me. I became frightened.

"Why are you afraid?" the serpent hissed. My mind reeled as I watched horrified as the serpent grew larger and slithered between my feet, wrapping around my right ankle.

"Snakes are sly," I finally said. "They move without seeming reality." Then I thought: is the serpent a warning not to go forward?

No sooner had this thought crossed my mind, did the wooden door burst open.

"Ride me," the serpent instructed as it grew large, moving forward, propelling me through the archway on its back. Hills rose on either side, and I

---

* The four cities will be studied in depth in *Faery Wicca Book Two*; until then, I encourage you to begin your own contemplation of each of the four cities.

was aware that off in the distance, the horizon had a faint glow. For the most part, the initial light was grey, shadowy, muted.

As the serpent moved through the grass a mist rose around us, and the land soon became marshy. I soon felt the firmness of the ground give way as the serpent moved into water. I actually thought of the Loch Ness monster at this point.

The mist had turned into a heavy fog, and all I could hear was the sound of water, but the serpent's body compacted under me as it slid back on solid land. Instantly, the fog thinned into a light mist and before me formed a stone circle.

The serpent deposited me in the middle of the stone circle with the instructions to merge with the land by curling up in the center of the circle, inside a hollow-like navel.

No sooner did I curl up in the hollow did the land begin spinning like a spiral, and I lost all sense of direction. As the spinning slowed to a stop, four creatures stepped forward from each direction into the center where I lay.

I was told to choose a companion. I chose the Stone Creature. I stood and moved to it, throwing my arms around it. As I hugged it, warmth spread through my body, and I felt very comforted.

"Time to get back in touch with your bones," the creature groaned. "Solidness. Structure. Time to know the bones again."

Again, I felt another presence in the circle and turned toward it. There stood a beautiful woman, shining with a white light around her. She wore a shimmering silver gown and her tendril-like hair flowed out from her head and around her like a mermaid.

"Come with me," she said, holding out her hand. I took it, and she turned to lead me out of the stone circle, but a gust of wind rose up from nowhere and held me back. It was as if my body were weightless, for I dangled on her hand like a rag-doll.

"You can make it," she said, smiling. "Just come." And forward she moved, flying me like a kite. The landscape dissolved into blackness and huge doors suddenly spread before us. They were hundreds of feet high and as they opened, a magnificent hall came into view. The hall was lit, but it was by a light lighter than that of sunlight or moonlight, but not brightly lit like the sun when it blinds you.

She moved forward to cross the threshold and the wind grabbed at me, stronger than before. There we remained, her inside the threshold, me dangling outside the threshold. Turning to me, she smiled and grabbed both my hands.

"We shall dance in," she said and began moving round and round. We danced round and round through the doors and into the great hall. In the air we danced, for there really was no floor. We danced and I laughed and she let go of one of my hands and it was grabbed by another being and suddenly we were joined by hundreds of others, forming a gigantic ring of dancing bodies.

I felt free, and the wind was gone, or so it seemed, but suddenly the hands I held released mine and I went spinning to a halt before the throne of the King of Faery. He had a brownish-red beard and curly hair, green eyes and a ruddy complexion. He was dressed in brown breeches and a purple and green tunic; the colors of the tunic blending and merging together.

A second throne formed, and there sat the Queen of Faery. She had brown and red hair and green-grey eyes. Her long gown was colorful, yet colorless.

"Choose," she instructed. I started to turn to the King, for she intimidated me, but she came forward and placed her hand on my shoulder. The King's laughter spilled into the hall and soon laughter came from everywhere.

"There is much I must teach you," said the Queen. "I must prepare you, for we would like you to become the most powerful teacher of the Faery realm."

She held up a brilliantly clear crystal, at the same time she stuck her other hand into my heart and began scrapping out fatty tissue from the valve tunnels and heart itself.

"I must clear you first," she told me, and I asked what she was going to do with the tissue she was scrapping out. She lowered her hand and said, "I give it back to the water to be dissolved." And she lowered her hand, full of the glob, releasing it into the sound of water beneath our feet, but I saw the faint image of a horrible creature rise out of the water and open its jaws and feed.

"Feel the lightness?" she asked, bringing my focus back to her eyes. "Feel the clearness?"

An image of my heart breathing appeared before my eyes. She placed the crystal inside my heart. And I watched as it started to spin, first like the propeller of an airplane, and then around itself.

"Breath and feel the lightness," she said as the heart image disappeared, and I felt my own heart spinning with lightness.

"Time for you to return!"

I was instantly away from her, out of the hall and back at the spiral stairs. The wooden door was once again closed, and the serpent was attached to the wall, no visible life registering in its plaster head and ruby studded eyes.

I flew up the stairs, seeing the doorway through which I first entered the Underworld, which would take me back to my living room. I came back through the passage and stood facing my body as it sat on the floor. Slowly the room began to take shape around me and I sat down on my own image, feeling solidness form around me.

I blinked my eyes open, focused on my face in the mirror and then looked around. My journey to the Underworld had ended.

As an Ollamh of the tradition, I recognize the need to acquaint the readership with the traditional information of Faery Wicca as the first step in delving into the Otherworlds. Because of this, I leave the continued study and working with the Land of Faery to a following study on Faery Shamanism.

*ay-day! delightful day!*
Bright colours play the vale along.
Now wakes at morning's
slender ray
Wild and gay the blackbird's song.

Now comes the bird of dusty hue,
The loud cuckoo, the summer-lover;
Branchy trees are thick with leaves;
The bitter, evil time is over.

Swift horses gather night
Where half-dry the river goes;
Tufted heather clothes the height;
Weak and white the bogdown blows.

Corncakes sing from eve to morn,
Deep in corn a strenuous bard!
Sings the virgin waterfall,
White and tall her one sweet word.

Loaded bees with puny power
Goodly flower-harvest win:
Cattle roam with muddy flanks;
Busy ants go out and in.

Through the wild harp of the wood
Making music roars the gale -
Now it settles without motion,
On the ocean sleeps the sail.

Men grow mighty in the May,
Proud and gay the maidens grow;
Fair is every wooded height;
Fair and bright the plain below.

A bright shaft has smit the streams
With gold gleams the water-flag;
Leaps the fish and on the hills
Ardour thirlls the leaping stag.

Loudly carols the lark on high
Small and shy his tireless lay,
Singing in wildest, merriest mood,
Delicate-hued delightful May.

— May Day
Eileen O'Faolain, *Irish Sagas and Folk Tales,*
originally from *The Tain Bo Cuailgne*

Lesson 12

Ceremony and Ritual

*Beannachtai an tSeasuir agat. Slainte chuig na fir, agus go mairfidh na mna go deo. Go mbeire muid beo ar an am seo aris!**

The greatest joy comes through celebration. In Faery Wicca, music, song, dance, food, and drink are vital ingredients in all forms of circling, whether it be a weekly gathering, monthly esbat (new or full moon ritual), one of the Four Great Festivals, or any of the minor holidays or rites of passage found in the tradition. This chapter is dedicated to that joy, and the first area we must look at is casting a Faery Ring.

The Faery Ring
If one is celebrating on the land, then casting a Faery Ring is an important step to undertake before the festivities begin.

The Faery Ring is, technically, the boundary of the Great Circle, but it is specially measured out and marked before the actual casting of the circle takes place. The most invaluable tool required for casting a Faery Ring is a cord nine feet in length, preferably green, brown, or white (as these are the colors of earth. This cord is used only for the casting of the Faery Ring and once acquired needs to be consecrated as a magickal tool by using the Tool Consecration Ceremony provided at the end of the Magickal Faery Tools chapter.

There are six steps to actually casting a Faery Ring:

1. Find the designated location.
2. Determine where the center of the circle will be, and use a compass to determine where each of the four directions are located.
3. Make a loop in each end of the cord.
4. Slip the blade of your athame through the loop on one end of the cord and then stick the athame blade down into the earth in the spot where center has been determined.

---

* Traditional Irish saying: Blessings of the season to you. Health to the men, and may the women live forever. May we be alive at this time next year!

5. Slip your finger through the loop on the other end of the cord, gently stretch the cord away from the athame and the center, until the cord is at its fullest length. Begin walking deosil, dragging one of your feet—or have someone else walk behind you marking the circle—to create the boundary of the Great Circle.

6. When the circle boundary has been scribed into the earth, take fresh cut flowers and lay them end-to-end on the circle boundary, marking the Faery Ring.

Once the Faery Ring has been created, set up each of the quarter altars and dig the hearth-pit in the center of the Great Circle, or set up the circular barbecue. Place the main altar to the northeast of the hearth, far enough away so that it does not catch fire, adorn it, and then finish with any other decorations needed for the festivity.

Feast tables will usually be created inside the circle boundary, near the hearth, in which case the table is made of earth. This is performed by using the dirt dug out of the hearth-pit, or carrying dirt from outside the circle. The Feast table only needs to be an inch in height, so not much dirt is required. Cover the mound with an appropriate cloth.

Faery Music

Today not many people play an instrument, but if you have banshees (priestesses) and leprechauns (priests) in your circle who do play, then you are very fortunate. We are, however, provided with alternative ways of producing music. There are several forms of battery operated portable equipment that can be used (i.e. tape decks and CD players), and of course there is a wealth of recorded music nowadays.

Since Faery Wicca is connected to Ireland, recordings of Irish folk music can be purchased. Some popular recording artists are: Enya, The De Danann, The Chieftains, Kim Robertson, The Renaissance Singers, Kate and Anna McGarrigle, Ruth Barret and Cynthia Smith, and The Voice Squad, to name only a few.

Tiompans (lap harps), dulcimers, fiddles, bodhrams (traditional drums), flutes, harpsichords, Uilleann pipes (bagpipes), and tin whistles are the more traditional instruments, and so, any recording of such instruments can also be used. Figures 30, 31, and 32 contain traditional Irish music used for ceremony.

The Irish Jig and other Faery Dances

The Irish jig is an exhilarating dance and is difficult to learn from a book. To describe such movements on paper is futile, and so I encourage the reader to take an Irish folk dance class, or attend an Irish Festival.

The Irish jig consists of a lot of knee lifting and heel kicking, and, in some ways, is very similar to certain patterns found in our American square dance, as square dancing is an offspring of the Irish and Scottish folk dances. However, when the jig is used in our ceremonies it is an indication that each dancer is on their own and their movements can be anything.

Learning to do a basic grapevine step will help, as this step is used in circle dancing. The **grape-vine step** is very basic. The movement is always in a sideways motion, as the front of your body faces the front while the dancers move around in a circle.

For example: you step sideways with your left foot, then the next step is with your

Figure 30: Example of Fairy Music, written in 1888

Figure 31: Traditional Irish tune written for dulcimer

right foot, crossing in front of the left. The left foot steps to the left again, and this time the right foot steps behind the left foot. In other words the left foot moves you and the right foot weaves in front or behind the left foot each time you use it to step.

The Ronde is a moonwise or widdershin circle dance using the grapevine-step. **The Spiral Dance** moves sunwise or deosil in a circle, but the leader eventually breaks hold of the person to their left and begins to lead the dancers inward, forming a spiral of dancers. Once the leader reaches the center, they turn away from the center and begin winding the dancers out of the center. The effect is that of a labyrinth or a maze.

The Procession dance is performed at the beginning of each of the Four Great Festivals. The dancers move in a deosil pattern singularly, turning around themselves periodically to demonstrate the turning of the Wheel of the Year. Periodically the dancers couple-up, hooking their arms at the elbows and circling round.

The Snake dance needs lots of room, for the dancers undulate their lines in imitation of a snake's movement as they circle round the sacred site. The gyrations of the dancers are always westward in the track of the sun. The Snake dance can move into the Spiral dance if the leader so desires.

The Baila is a dance which forms two circles. The circling motions are that of the revolution of earth on her own axis, and the other is the movement of her ecliptic path around the sun. The oldest worship of the world was that of the sun and moon, of trees, wells, and the Great Mother, whose serpent gave wisdom.

The inner circle moving widdershin is comprised of either all women or all men, the determination based on the lesser number of each group. If less women, they comprise the inner circle, thus also representing the movement of the feminine energy

"That rake up near the rafters, why leave it there so long?
Its handle, of the best of ash, is smooth and straight and strong
And, mother, will you tell me, why did my father frown
When to make the hay, in summertime I climbed to take it down?"
She looked into her husband's eyes, while her own with light did fill,
"You'll shortly know the reason, boy!" said Rory of the Hill.

The midnight moon is lighting up the slopes of Sliav-na-man,—
Whose foot affrights the startled hares so long before the dawn?
He stopped just where the Anner's stream winds up the woods, anear,
Then whistled low and looked around to see the coast was clear.
The shieling door flew open—in he stepped with right goodwill—
"God save all here and bless your work!" said Rory of the Hill.

Right hearty was the welcome that greeted him, I ween,
For years gone by he fully proved how well he loved the Green;
And there was one amongst them who grasped him by the hand—
One who through all that weary time roamed on a foreign strand;
He brought them news from gallant friends that made their heart strings thrill
"My soul! I never doubted them!" said Rory of the Hill.

They sat around the humble board till dawning of the day,
And yet not song nor shout I heard, no revelers were they;
Some brows flushed red with gladness, while some were grimly pale;
But pale or red, from out those eyes flashed souls that never quail!
"And sing us now about the vow, they swore for to fulfil"—
"You'll read it yet in history," said Rory of the Hill.

Next day the ashen handle he took down from where it hung,
The tooth rake, full scornfully, into the fire he flung;
And in its stead a shining blade is gleaming once again—
(Oh! for a hundred thousand of such weapons and such men!)
Right soldierly he wielded it, and—going through his drill—
"Attention —charge—front point—advance!" cried Rory of the Hill.

She looked at him with woman's pride, with pride and woman's fears;
She flew to him she clung to him and dried away her tears;
He feels her pulse beat truly, while her arms around him twine—
"Now God be praised for your stout heart, brave little wife of mine."
He swung his first born in the air, while joy his heart did fill—
"You'll be a free man yet, my boy!' said Rory of the Hill.

Oh! knowledge is a wondrous power, and stronger than the wind;
And thrones shall fall, and despots bow, before the might of mind;
The poet and the orator the heart of man can sway,
And would to the kind heaves that Wolfe Tone were here today
Yet trust me, friends, dear Ireland's strength—truest strength is still
The rough and ready roving boys, like Rory of the Hill.

Fig. 32: Ancient Irish ballad written by Charles Kickham, Fenian leader and novelist who wrote *Knocknagow*, or *The Homes of Tipperary*

or the moon energy. The outer circle moving deosil becomes the circle representing the masculine energy or the sun energy. Either circle can be danced by both male and female, but each circle should be exclusive of one sex.

The Baila can also be danced with couples. When it is performed in this way, the movement is that of a traditional waltz; the turning of the dancers around themselves moving widdershin, while the direction of their dance takes them deosil.

Faery Dress

How to dress, according to tradition, can sometimes present problems, for if one were to dress according to the dress code of ancient Ireland, then one would be wearing a costume.

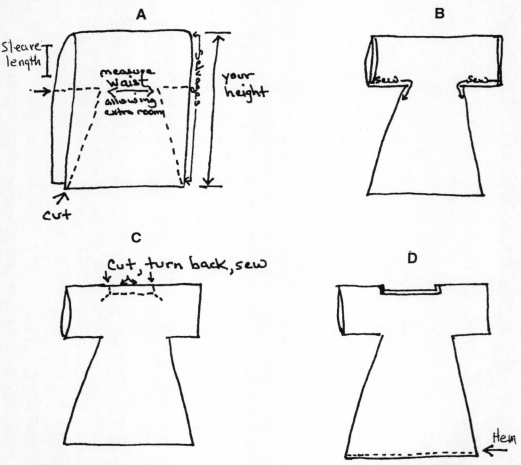

A: Fold 5 yards of fabric in half, selvages together; measure height, cut fabric off at measure; cut sleeves and skirt as indicated.

B: Sew bottom of sleeves together and sides of skirt; hem sleeves 1 inch.

C: Cut boat neck across fold and at diagonals front and back; turn under, using extra material as an intact facing and topstitch in place.

D: Turn under a 1-inch hem and sew.

E: Belt at waist and you're ready to go.

Figure 33: Traditional Faery Ceremonial Dress

Today, the traditional dress has become a simple gown (Figure 33) for women, the color depending on their rank, and either a gown, or breeches and flowing shirt, for men—again the colors depending on their rank.

Novices dress in white, representing the color of beginnings and their virginhood into the Craft. Their cloaks or capes can be either green or brown, which are the traditional colors of the Faery.

Initiates dress in white, red, or blue, representing the color of admittance into the Craft: white as a remembrance from where they came, red as a symbol of their new blood-line, blue as a symbol of their spiritual deepening. Their cloaks or capes can be either green, brown, or black.

Elders usually dress in the colors of power: black, purple, while occasionally using the white and red of the Novice and Initiates. Their cloaks or capes are usually black, but sometimes will be purple.

No unnecessary jewelry is worn into circle. Only those items that have been duly consecrated as a magickal piece are worn, such as the First Degree Initiate's pentacle necklace that was awarded them at the time of their initiation; the second degree Priests' and Priestesses' power ring that was awarded them at the time of their rite of passage; the Elder's crown that was awarded them at the time of their Becoming. Of course, wedding bands are worn after consecration, except at the time of the First Degree Initiation.

Faery Food and Faery Drink

In the ancient tales, warnings are always given against consuming any food or beverage offered the sojourner of the Land of Faery. For once eaten, the sojourner becomes trapped in the Land of Faery, and should they ever chose to return to the realm of mortals, they will turn to dust once their foot touches the soil.

However, in celebration we eat the Faery Food and drink the Faery Drink with joy and gladness, knowing that this is one way to partake of their energy without alienating ourselves from the world in which we belong.

Potatoes and corn are traditional foods, as are pot-pies, salmon, and other fish, nuts, fruits, berries, and bread. Ale, mead, elderberry wine, Sloe gin, water, and cream are the traditional drink.

Recipes for using potatoes and corn, making pot pies and fruit pies can be found in any cookbook, and therefore won't be provided in this book. However, I will provide two old recipes for Irish Soda Bread that can be used as the offering food to the Ancient Ones during the celebration of the Four Great Festivals.

All Faery Drinks can be purchased at most stores. Ale, mead, Sloe gin, and elderberry wine can be found at liquor warehouses, English import stores, and pubs. However, the following is a traditional recipe to make mead.

IRISH MEAD

1   tablespoon yeast   3½ pounds of raw honey
1   gallon pure water   2   dozen shelled hazelnuts

In a large pot combine water and honey. Bring to a boil, lower heat and cook for about 45 minutes, stirring occasionally. Put the hazelnuts into pot with the liquids, cover and let stand overnight. Remove the halzelnuts. Sprinkle the yeast on top of the liquid, cover, and let sit for two to five days. During this time the yeast will work into the liquid. Transfer the liquid into an air-tight bottle and let stand for three months. NOTE: Once mead is opened, the shelf-life is minimal. **Yield: 1 gallon**

IRISH SODA BREAD VARIATION ONE

2 cups unsifted flour
¾ teaspoon salt
1½ teaspoons baking powder
¼ teaspoon baking soda
1 cup buttermilk

Mix all the dry ingredients. Add the buttermilk. Stir until the ingredients are blended and dough is soft. Turn out on a lightly floured board and knead dough for about 1 minute. Shape into a round loaf and place in a round pan or on a cookie sheet. With a sharp knife, cut a Celtic cross (see Figure 22) into the top (about ¼ inch deep). Bake in a pre-heated oven at 350 degrees for about 40 minutes. When done, the loaf sounds hollow when tapped on the bottom. Cool the loaf on its side before cutting. This bread is wonderful when toasted. **Yield: 1 loaf.**

IRISH SODA BREAD VARIATION TWO

4 cups all-purpose flour   ¼ cup sugar
1 teaspoon salt   1 teaspoon baking power
1 teaspoon baking soda   ¼ cup butter or margarine
3 to 4 tablespoons caraway seed   2 cups raisins
1⅓ cups buttermilk   1 egg, beaten
Milk

In a mixing bowl, combine flour, sugar, salt, baking power and baking soda. Cut in butter until mixture resembles coarse meal. Stir in caraway seed and raisins. Combine buttermilk and egg; stir into dry ingredients just until moistened. Turn out onto a floured surface and knead lightly until smooth. Shape dough into a ball and place on a greased baking pan. Pat into a 7-inch round loaf. Cut a 4-inch cross about ¼ inch deep on top to allow for expansion. Brush top with milk. Bake at 375 degrees for 1 hour or until golden brown. **Yield: 1 loaf.**

The Four Great Festival Ceremonies

The following ritual outlines are provided for use in celebrating the four sacred holidays of Samhain, Imbolc, La Baal Tinne, and Lughnasadh. Although the ritual outlines provided are designed for group celebration, they can easily be adapted for private celebration.

When you begin celebrating the high holidays of the Faery Wiccan tradition, it is important to bear in mind that during the first year you are simply learning the meaning of each Sabbat, becoming acquainted with the energy of the ceremony. When you celebrate the Sabbats in year two, the rituals will take on new meaning and you will begin to feel the energy shifts taking place. By the third year of ritual celebration you will truly begin celebrating, and thus begin living the tradition.

Samhain—October 31

Temporary Sacred Space Preparations

Cast the Faery Ring. Set up the quarter altars, the main altar, the feast table and prepare the hearth-pit.

In the north province prepare a special Ancestor altar, upon which pictures, candles and food offerings can be placed by each participant. In each of the four quarters place large basins of cleaning water that will be used for washing hands and faces after the feast.

Decorate the site with items that represent the kingdom of death and the Spirit realm, i.e., ghosts, skeletons, hobgoblins, shimmering veils, lots of candles, tombstones, pomegranates, and carved pumpkins.

Ceremony Items to Construct

To perform a Ronde of the Dead (Dance of the Dead), have all or designated dancers create masks which they will wear during the dance. The masks can depict daemons, Spirits, creatures of the night, dead ancestors, elementals, or can be simply painted black to represent the Otherworld.

Ritual for Samhain

The Ollamh (Elder Priestess or Priest) walks widdershin (moonwise) around the outside of the Faery Ring three times, followed by all participants, who carry white candles, which are lit. While circling, each participant focuses on three things in succession:

1. Assisting the release of The Big Sun.
2. Surrendering to the Wheel of the Year which will very soon begin to turn anew.
3. Reflecting on The Little Sun, the moon, and her energy, which will begin to guide us into the first half of the year.

When the Ollamh arrives at the northern gateway, she/he leads everyone through it into the boundary of the circle. As each participant steps across and through the threshold, they speak:

For the Ancestors and all my relations,

in acknowledgement of all who have gone before, are currently living and who are yet to be born.

The Ollamh leads the circle deosil (sunwise) around the perimeter of circle, until all have crossed over and stand within, forming a circle.

Release the energy of the sun-god, Lugh, and the sun-goddess, Grainne, by using the following call/answer chant (or something of a similar nature):

Women call out:

Evoe Grainne

Men answer:

Ecco Lugh

Continue chanting back and forth until the energy begins to release, at which time the chant changes, becoming:

Women call out:

Grainne

Men answer:

Lugh

This continues until there is no longer a call/answer, but both *Grainne* and *Lugh* are being chanted together. Let the release of The Big Sun take place. (NOTE: this is not a cone of power chant, but quite the opposite. The chant gets quieter and quieter, and is eventually whispered until silence surrounds the site.)

All participants adorn the ancestor altar with pictures of deceased relatives and friends; each picture is occupied by a white candle which is lit. As this takes place, the participants speak the name of the one they are honoring, and share a fond memory. [NOTE: Each participant can go to the altar one at a time and share while the rest of the group listens, or participants can pair-up, or form small groups if there is a large number of people. Also try the chaos method of having everyone speak at the same time; this creates an incredible vibrational link of moving from the ending of the current or dying Wheel of the Year, to the birth or beginning of the new year cycle.]

The Ollamh casts the Great Circle by acknowledging the four provinces, beginning in the north, where everyone will naturally be after having adorned the ancestor altar.

North: *From the realm of Falias*
come forth earth strength
La Fail, La Fail,
solid, strong, foundation beneath!
Thoet se!

East: *From the realm of Gorias*
come forth clarity and truth
sunlight, starlight,
moonlight, shining bright!
Thoet se!

South: *From the realm of Finias*
come forth fire warmth
Heat of fire, fire of lighting
heat and energy, Spirit fire!
Thoet se!

West: *From the realm of Murias*
come forth fertility of plenty
Ocean circling the earth
sea flowing and ebbing!
Thoet se!

The Ollamh lights the sacred hearth-fire proclaiming:

The flame of life reaches up,
climbing and reaching
for the life that surrounds it,
within it's dancing,
it can destroy life,
but from the destruction,
from the ash covered death,
new life will sprout.
On this night we honor the dying year,
we honor the Ancestors,
we honor the Spirit realm,
Circle of Abred!

Ronde of the Dead

Designated dancers put on their masks, and form a circle around the hearth-fire. Those who are not dancing stand around the circle edge. The dancers revolve around themselves from east-to-west, three times, and then begin moving widdershin as a whole around the fire. They continue to dance until they feel the dance has been properly completed; sufficient energy raised. Those who are watching clap hands or play instruments, and chant or sing a song such as:

The circle is moving widdershin
the circle of life slowly resends
back to its place of origin
back to its place of beginning.

The circle is moving widdershin
the circle of life will begin again

into a new Circle of Existence
into a new cycle of life!

When the dance is completed and the dancers catch their breath, the Ollamh shares the ancient meaning of Sam-fuin, in honor of the Tuatha De Danann. She/he recites:

Let us honor Tuatha De Danann and remember the bloodthirsty Cromm Cruaich, The Bowed One of the Mound, the Fomorian God of darkness to whom the clans of Erin were forced to sacrifice their children until Tuatha De Danann rode out from Tir na nOg and conquered them. Let the cunning women—the banshees—chant in memory to those who died in this magnificent battle.

The cunning women—or banshee—chant:

There came Tigermas,
the prince of Tara yonder,
on Samhain eve with many hosts,
A cause of grief to them was the deed.
Dead were the men of Banba's host,
without happy strength,
Around Tigermas,
the destructive man in the north,
From the worship of Cromm Cruaich—twas no luck for them.
For we have learnt,
Except one-fourth of the keen Danann
Not a man or woman warrior alive—lasting the snare!
Escaped without death in their mouths.

The Feast of Sam-fuim
All participants gather round the earthen feast table. A special blessing is recited over the food. (I have found that this blessing should come from the heart and be birthed out of the energy of the ceremony, not written and memorized beforehand.)

The first plate that each participant makes is called the dumb-supper—the ancestral plate which is placed on the ancestral altar before the candle and picture of the relative or friend being honored. Once all the ancestors have been fed, the participants prepare their own plates and enjoy!

During the feast, share song and dance, explore divinations, and have a jolly time celebrating the turning of the Wheel of the Year into the new cycle.

When all have finished their feast, the participants break into four groups and move to the water basins in each of the four quarters. There, hands and faces are washed. At each of the quarters, a Leprechaun is chosen to enact the custom of throwing out the water. This individual will wash their hands and face last, then pick up the basin of water, move to the edge of the Faery Ring and face the dark of night.

In a loud voice, they cry out:

Hugga, Hugga, Salach! (Away, Away, Water!)

This warns the Spirits and the dead who were last buried and may still be wandering about, not to get their clothes wet!

As the water is tossed, all participants clap and shout:

Hugga, Hugga, Salach!

The time has come to acknowledge The Little Sun, and so all participants come to the center and form a circle around the hearth-fire by holding hands. A chant is shared:

Circling, circling,
Wheel of Life,
now comes the time
of The Little Sun.

The Ollamh acknowledges the goddess and god of The Little Sun.

Cailleach is reborn each Samhain,
Cailleach daughter of Grainne,
Oh Cailleach, we pay homage to you,
Oh, Winter Sun, Gentle Moon.

Cu Chulainn is the great warrior,
whose mighty spear conquers all evil,
Oh Cu Chulainn, we pay homage to you,
Oh, Winter Sun, Gentle Moon.

With the new year established, all participants move once, deosil, around the hearth before exiting through the northern gateway. They continue to move deosil, once, around the outside of the Faery Ring. When the Ollamh arrives back in the north, she/he proclaims:

The Wheel of the Year does move forward, and with it, let all those who
have passed and wish to re-enter the Circle of Gwynvyd, where the living
are stronger than the dead, let them prepare for rebirth during this season
of Ghemrath, in the cauldron of regeneration!"

All participants clap and hoot and holler. When all the excitement dies down, the Ollamh rings a crisp sounding bell four times in release of the quarter province energies. She/he then announces:

Tum Fostladh Dorus na Bliadhna uire chum sith, sonas is samchair! ("May the door of the coming year open for you to peace, happiness and quiet contentment.) This rite is over.

The Ollamh opens the Great Circle with a fifth ring of the bell, saying:

The Great Circle is open, but ever unbroken.
May the peace of the Ancestors dwell in our hearts.
Merry meet, and merry part, and merry meet again!
Thoet se!

Imbolc—February 1

Temporary Sacred Space Preparations
Cast the Faery Ring. Set up the quarter altars, the main altar, the feast table, and prepare the hearth-pit.

Ceremony Items to Construct
Processional torches to be used by all.

Ritual for Imbolc
A procession led by the Ollamh circles deosil, three times around the Faery Ring. All participants carry burning torches.

The Ollamh leads the procession through the north gateway and circles deosil, once around the inside of the Faery Ring. She/he leads everyone around the hearth-pit, wherein are laid brambles and other kindling woods. Upon a signal from the Ollamh, all converge on the pit and throw their torches into it, in an act of passing the power, and watch as the sun is birthed. All chant:

Bride is welcome,
Bride is come,
Bride is welcome,
Bride is come!

The chant is sung to welcome back the warmth of the sun-goddess to the earth. As the sacred fire grows in strength and brightness, all know the season is changing and all life will be warmed and rebirthed with the warmth of the Breo-saighit.

The Ollamh casts the Great Circle, invoking the quarter province energies.

North: *From the realm of Falias*
come forth earth strength
La Fal, La Fal,
solid, strong, foundation beneath!
Thoet se!

East: *From the realm of Gorias*
come forth clarity and truth
sunlight, starlight,
moonlight, shining bright!
Thoet se!

South: *From the realm of Finias*
come forth fire warmth
Heat of fire, fire of lighting
heat and energy, Spirit fire!
Thoet se!

West: *From the realm of Murias*
come forth fertility of plenty
Ocean circling the earth
sea flowing and ebbing!
Thoet se!

All sit around the fire pit. Celtic harp music is played to assist the Ollamh, who will guide all participants on an inner journey. Everyone closes their eyes and focuses on breath. The Ollamh guides the journey by reading:

The breath of Spirit moves in and out of your lungs, flowing and ebbing. The breath of Spirit moves throughout your bodies, filtering through all organs, tissue, bones. The breath of Spirit circulates around you, stilling you, quieting you, lifting and lowering your consciousness into the very center of nothingness, darkness. Rest in this nothingness, this darkness of Ghemrath.

The Wheel of the Year turns this night, edging away the darkness, bringing forth the Breo-saighit—Fiery Arrow—of inspiration in anticipation of the rebirth of your own inner light.

Within the nothingness where you now rest, a shining light appears above you, high, high above you. Shining brightly, growing bigger, it moves closer to you. It seems as if this shinning light is coming from the stars.

From the stars comes this shinning light. And from the center of this shining light, shoots a fiery arrow which sinks into the ground at your feet. The Breo-saighit has been sent to you from the Shining Ones, the Tuatha De Danann.

As you look down at its burning shaft, a face of energy begins to form. The goddess of fire has come to you. Breed, has come to share with you and inspire you through her gifts.

As you gaze down upon her face, you realize that one side of her face is ugly, yet the other side is very beautiful. A smile spreads across her lips, and she speaks to you. She says:

"It is I, the Breo-saighit, bringing you gifts. What will be your flame of growth this next wheel of learning? Will you develop your skills of physicalness; battle skills of the warrior, metal craft, jewelry maker, technical skills, musical training, dance, sculptor?

"Or will you develop your skills of mentalness; communications, writing, illustrating, poetry, song, drama? Or will you develop your skills of emotionalness; healing, herbcraft, counseling, parenting, relationships? Which area do you choose to develop?"

[pause]

As you look down upon the fiery arrow shaft, the face of Breed is once again the flame. Look into the flame and find which skill you will choose: physicalness, mentalness, emotionalness; and when you are ready, take hold of the shaft and pull it out of the ground and hold the fiery arrow to your heart.

[Meditation time is permitted, until all gathered hold their hands to their hearts.]

Breathe this fire of inspiration into your heart, into your mind, into your body. Own it. Become it.

[pause]

Very gently open your eyes.

When all gathered have opened their eyes, the Ollamh stands and points her/his Gold Branch at the flames of the hearth-fire and calls out:

Behold the flame of inspiration!
Let us acknowledge the Lady on Her day!
Every day and every night
That I say the genealogy of Brigid,
I shall not be killed,
I shall not be harmed,
I shall not be put into a cell,
I shall not be wounded.
No fire, no Sun,
No Moon shall burn me.
No lake, no water,
No sea shall drown me.
For I am the child of Poetry,
Poetry, child of Reflection,
Reflection, child of Meditation,
Meditation, child of Love,
Love, child of Research,

Research, child of Great Knowledge,
Great Knowledge, child of Intelligence,
Intelligence, child of Comprehension,
Comprehension, child of Wisdom,
Wisdom, child of Brigid!

Using holy (purified) water, preferably water from Tober Breda, each participant comes to the altar where they either anoint themselves or are anointed by the Ollamh. During this, those who are waiting to be anointed and/or have already been anointed, chant:

La Fheile Brid! (The Brigid's Day!)

A feast of milk and bread is shared, and many a tale is told as all gather round the sacred fire for warmth.

Ollamh thanks the Ancient One, whose energy graced the ceremony, dismisses each of the province quarters by ringing a crisp-sounding bell four times. She/he then announces:

The peace of Dana, the peace of women and men,
The peace of Brigid kindly,
Be upon each window, upon each door,
Upon each hole that lets in light,
Upon the four corners of each home,
Upon the four corners of each bed,
Upon each thing the eye takes in,
Upon each thing the mouth takes in,
Upon the body that is of earth
And upon the soul that came from on high,
Upon the body that is of earth
And upon the soul that came from on high. This rite is over.

The Ollamh opens the Great Circle with a fifth ring of the bell, saying:

The Great Circle is open, but ever unbroken.
May the peace of Brigid dwell in our hearts.
Merry meet, and merry part, and merry meet again!
Thoet se!

La Baal Tinne—May 1

On this day everyone is entitled to dress in green. The color green symbolizes eternal youth and rebirth, as in nature during the springtime when all vegetation after its death-sleep of winter springs into new life; just as the neophyte (apprentice), who during the ceremonies of Initiation into the Ancient Mysteries, leaves the physical body in a trance state, and in full consciousness, which is retained afterwards, enters the Otherworld and beholds all its wonders and inhabitants, and then coming out of that world is clothed in a robe of sacred green to symbolize their own spiritual resurrection and rebirth into spiritual life —for they have penetrated the Mystery of Death and are now an Initiate.

Herbs gathered on May Eve have a mystical and strong virtue for curing disease, and powerful potions are then made by the skillful cunning women, which no sickness can resist, chiefly of the yarrow, known to us as the herb of seven needs. Love is the central theme of all magick performed at La Baal Tinne.

Preparation of Temporary Sacred Space
When the ceremony of La Baal Tinne is enjoyed the participants prepare the Faery Ring lavishly—lots of flowers, ribbons, and lace. Although the Faery Ring is cast, the celebration area requires lots of room, as the main focus will be on performing the Baila dance, and the mystic Snake dance which winds westward in the track of the sun.

The quarter altars are set up with bunches of heather tied with colorful ribbons to each, and a heather bush is adorned and placed in the center of the circle next to the hearth-fire, but far enough from the pit to create a pathway between the two.

The main altar is adorned and a short distance outside the Faery Ring, the beautifully decorated May Pole is raised. The May Pole (the phallic) symbolizes the union of god penetrating goddess (the shaft of the pole planted into Mother Earth), which can be another aspect of the day's celebrations: that of fertility.

Ritual for La Baal Tinne
The Ollamh forms a circle around the outside of the Faery Ring, and begins moving widdershin, three times around. When the Ollamh arrives at the northern gateway, she/he leads everyone through into the boundary of the circle. The Ollamh leads the circle deosil around the perimeter of the Faery Ring until all have crossed over and stand within forming a circle.

The Ollamh casts the Great Circle by acknowledging the four provinces, beginning in the north.

> North: *From the realm of Falias*
> *come forth earth strength*
> *La Fal, La Fal,*
> *solid, strong, foundation beneath!*
> *Thoet se!*

East: *From the realm of Gorias*
        come forth clarity and truth
        sunlight, starlight,
        moonlight, shining bright!
        Thoet se!

South: *From the realm of Finias*
        come forth fire warmth
        Heat of fire, fire of lighting
        heat and energy, Spirit fire!
        Thoet se!

West: *From the realm of Murias*
        come forth fertility of plenty
        Ocean circling the earth
        sea flowing and ebbing!
        Thoet se!

All participants join hands and face the center of the circle. The Ollamh lights the great fire while the following is recited.

Tuatha De Danann,
Gun till do Cheum,
As gach cearn,
Fo Rionnac-iuil an dachaidh!
(Tribe of Dana,
may your steps return from all corners of the globe,
under the guidance of the star,
that points to home!)

The Ollamh begins the mystic Snake dance by guiding everyone around the Great Circle, deosil. Everyone continually chants:

We come from the stars,
we come from the stars,
shining, shining to the earth!

We come from the stars,
we come from the stars,
shining, shining to the earth!

Sun-light, life-light,
Moon-light, inner-light,
Star-light, shining bright,
shinny beings of light!

In this winding and undulating dance (that often times resembles the movement of a snake), the line of dancers move between the heather bush (May Bush) and the hearth-fire on their way out from the Great Circle. The Ollamh leads the dancers through the east gateway and circles three times around the outside of the Faery Ring before winding around the May Pole where the dance ends.

All remain holding hands and focus their attention on the May Pole. Again, the Ollamh speaks:

> *Tu mu slan dhan teine,*
> *Tu mu slan dhan chuideachd uile,*
> *Gun robh dion air ti-ionmhas!*
> *deach-bheus, slainte,*
> *saoibhreas, sonas!*
> *(Blessed be the fire,*
> *Blessed be the people all,*
> *may what you treasure be secure!*
> *Virtue, health,*
> *wealth, happiness!)*
>
> *Lugh, your mighty spear has joined the Mother!*
> *Grainne, your fertile womb has opened!*
> *Let your Sunlight heat and warm us All!*

Music begins playing; the sounds of bagpipes, harps, flutes, fiddles, dulcimers and the bodhrans resonate the entire area. Around the May Pole, the Baila is danced, either in couples or individually. (The Baila forms the two circling motions; that of the revolution of our planet on her own axis, and her orbit around the sun.)

Dancing and singing can go on for quite awhile, and end with feasting and love magick!

As the ceremony wanes, and before anyone departs, the Ollamh gathers all partici-pants into the Great Circle and has everyone form a circle around the hearth-fire by holding hands. Silence is allowed for a minute or two to quiet and ground the energy of the day. When the Ollamh senses the process has been completed, she/he gives thanks to the energy of the Ancient Ones who joined the ceremony, releases hold on the province energies by dismissing each quarter with the ring of the bell, and then closes the ceremony by reciting:

> *As we journey now, into the time of The Big Sun, and you begin your*
> *lessons of this seasons learning, and until we return once more to our time*
> *of togetherness, Gum biodh rath le do thurus! (May your quest be fruitful!)*
> *This rite has ended.*

The Ollamh opens the Great Circle with a fifth ring of the bell, saying:

> *The Great Circle is open, but ever unbroken.*
> *May the peace of Dana dwell in our hearts.*
> *Merry meet, and merry part, and merry meet again!*
> *Thoet se!*

Lughnasadh—August 1

Preparation of Temporary Sacred Space

The ceremony area will be bigger then the site chosen for the Faery Ring. Bushels of hay can be strategically placed designating the areas where the contests of skill will be performed.

Within the Faery Ring, an earthen mound is created for the Harvest Feast table, and bunches of wheat and fruits and vegetables are placed in baskets around the area. Natural abundance is the key decoration here. Each quarter altar is set-up, as is the main altar and the hearth-pit.

Ceremony Items to Make

A corn dolly, approximately twelve to eighteen inches long can be made and adorned to represent the Harvest Mother, Tailltiu. Lammas Towers made out of corn stalks can also be built and placed near the Faery Ring so dancers can circle around it while carrying the corn dolly to represent the continuation of life through the rebirthing of the corn.

Ritual for Lughnasadh

The Ollamh forms a circle around the outside of the Faery Ring, and begins moving widdershin, three times around. When the Ollamh arrives at the northern gateway, she/he leads everyone through into the boundary of the circle.

The Ollamh leads the circle deosil around the perimeter of the Faery Ring until all have crossed over and stand within forming a circle.

The Ollamh casts the Great Circle by acknowledging the four provinces, beginning in the north.

North: *From the realm of Falias*
come forth earth strength
La Fal, La Fal,
solid, strong, foundation beneath!
Thoet se!

East: *From the realm of Gorias*
come forth clarity and truth
sunlight, starlight,
moonlight, shining bright!
Thoet se!

South: *From the realm of Finias*
come forth fire warmth
Heat of fire, fire of lighting
heat and energy, Spirit fire!
Thoet se!

West: *From the realm of Murias*
come forth fertility of plenty
Ocean circling the earth
sea flowing and ebbing!
Thoet se!

The Ollamh has everyone sit in a circle around the hearth-pit. She/he then lights the sacred fire, speaking the following proclamation:

Behold, the fire of life!
Tha mi Smaladh an Teine,
Mar a smaladh Tuatha De Danann,
Tu mu Slan Dhan Teine,
Tu mu Slan Dhan chuideachd uile!
(I am Smooring the Fire,
as the Tribe of Dana would smoor,
Blest be the Fire,
Blest be the people all!)

The Ollamh will now take the participants on a shamanic journey to honor Tailltiu, the Harvest Mother, for providing us with yet another year of her abundance.

The following shamanic journey combines the use of a trance chant and the heartbeat as produced on a bodhran. The Ollamh instructs everyone to gaze upon the fire; the fire that will soon feed them in the form of the Harvest Feast of Tailltiu.

All participants are informed that as they gaze into the fire, they are to open and receive the whispering blessings of the Harvest Mother, who will give each a special message to apply to their lives. It may be a message guiding one deeper into their spirituality. It may be a message directing one to the final steps required in polishing a skill. It may be a message telling one how they might win a contest, or overcome an obstacle. But all must concentrate on the sacred flame, for "Thig sealdh a dichioll gadh beachd air an t-search dhiamhair cheilteach so!" (The power of concentration may bring success!)

The beating bodhran embraces the Great Circle, while all begin, and continue to, chant:

Tailltiu, tell us.

As the drumming and sacred flame lures everyone into their own state of trance, eventually the chant will end and eyelids will droop. The drumming should continue until everyone finally sits with eyes closed, or with soft-sight.

After the drumming has ended, within a very short time, all the participants will begin to open their eyes and naturally come out of trance.

Harvest Feast
A round of blessings are said over the Harvest Feast by everyone gathered. Then the Ollamh recites, before all enjoy in the feast:

Wisdom of serpent be thine,
Wisdom of raven be thine,
Wisdom of valiant eagle.

Voice of swan be thine,
Voice of honey be thine,
Voice of the son of the stars.

Bounty of sea be thine,
Bounty of land be thine,
Bounty of the Queen and King of Sidhe.

Invocation to Lugh

When the feast has ended, the Ollamh gathers everyone around the hearth-fire to honor Lugh by the recitation of his victory over the Fomorians. A male Ollamh or chosen Leprechaun recites the following:

A tathlum (concrete ball), heavy, fiery, firm,
Which the Tuatha De Danann had with them,
It was that broke the fierce Balor's eye,
Of old, in the battle of the great armies.

The blood of toads and furious bears,
And the blood of the noble lion,
The blood of vipers and of Osmuinn's trunks;-
It was of these the tathlum was composed.

The sand of the swift Armorian Sea,
And the sand of the teeming Red Sea;
All these, being first purified, were used
In the composition of the tathlum.

Bruin, the son of Bethar, no mean warrior,
Who on the ocean's eastern border reigned;-
It was he that fused, and smoothly formed,
It was he that fashioned the tathlum.

To the hero Lugh was given
This concrete ball, no soft missile;
In Mag Tuireadh of shrieking wails,
From his hand he threw the thathlum!
[Note: "The Second Battle of Motura" could also be read.]

After the story-telling has ended, all stand and hold hands. Three cunning women step forward and stand before the hearth-fire. They turn and look at the people, and together recite:

Peace mounts to the heavens,
The heavens descend to earth,
Earth lies under the heavens,
Everyone is strong, Hail Lugh!

Cheering and clapping and the stamping of feet breaks out. The men whoop and jump around and engage in mock wrestling matches with each other. The women cheer and throw kisses of encouragement to their champions. This is the scene that takes place for the remainder of the celebration.

Games of Skill:
Spear throwing for longest distance, tug-of-wars for strength, wrestling matches, horse-racing, volley ball or softball or foot races, games of tag, a chess tournament, contests of skill—any and all are engaged.

At the closing of the day, the Ollamh has all participants gather back around the hearth fire, forming a circle and holding hands. The energy from the celebration is grounded during a few minutes of silence. The Ollamh thanks the Ancient Ones, and follows by releasing each province with the bell. The Ollamh steps into the center of the circle next to the hearth-fire and recites:

> *Gun cuireadh do chupa thairis le slainte agus sonas,*
> *(May your cup overflow with health and happiness,)*
> *as this Lughnasadh comes to an end!*
> *This rite is over!*

The Ollamh opens the Great Circle with a fifth ring of the bell, saying:

> *The Great Circle is open, but ever unbroken.*
> *May the peace of Dana dwell in our hearts.*
> *Merry meet, and merry part, and merry meet again!*
> *Thoet se!*

Appendix A

Ancient Manuscripts and Books

Of the ancient Irish manuscripts, the earliest is in the possession of the Royal Irish Academy. It is one of the most important manuscripts, in spite of its dilapidated condition, because of the great source of ancient Gaelic mythology it contains. Unfortunately, it is reduced to a fragment of 138 pages, but this remnant preserves a large number of romances relating to the old gods and heroes of Ireland. Among other things, it contains a complete account of the epic saga called the *Tain Bo Cuailgne*, in which the hero, Cu Chulainn, performs his greatest feats.

This manuscript is called the *Book of the Dun Cow*, from the tradition that it was copied from an earlier book written upon the skin of a favorite animal belonging to Saint Ciaran, who lived in the seventh century. An entry upon one of its pages reveals the name of its scribe, Maelmuiri, who was killed by robbers in the church of Clonmacnois in the year 1106 C.E.

The Book of Leinster, compiled in the early part of the twelfth century by Finn mac Gorman, Bishop of Kildare, is far more voluminous than *The Book of the Dun Cow,* but a little less ancient. This book also contains an account of Cu Chulainn's mighty deeds which supplements the older version in *The Book of the Dun Cow*.

The Book of Ballymote and *The Yellow Book of Lecan*, belonging to the end of the fourteenth century, and *The Books of Lecan and of Lismore*, belonging to the fifteenth, are somewhat less important. However, they do contain ancient mythical lore such as the story of the Battle of Moytura fought between the gods of Ireland and their enemies the Fomorians.

Following is a complete list of the ancient manuscripts and books of Ireland.

Ancient Manuscripts and Books of Ireland

Agallam na Seanorach
Annals of Clonmacnois
Annals of Loch Ce
Annals of the Four Masters
Annals of Tighernach
Annals of Ulster
Arma Colm Cille
Battlebook of the O'Donnells
Book of Acaill
Book of Armagh
Book of Ballymote
Book of Durrow
Book of Kells
Book of Lismore
Book of Munster
Book of Rights
Book of St. Moling
Book of the Dun Cow
Book of the Ollams
Bruidean Da Dearga
Cain Fuirthime
Cain Padraic
Calendar of Aengus
Commemmoratio Laborum
Confession of Patrick,
    Magnum Opus
Cormac's Glossary
Cuilmen, The
Days of Lamentation, The

De Divisione Naturae
Dialogue of the Ancients, The
Dicuil's De Mensura
Dimna's BookSenchus Mor
Domnach Airgid
Epistle of Coroticus
Feilire of Aongus, The
Four Masters, The
Invocation of Amergin
Judgments of Creidne
Leabar Breac
Liber Hymnorum
Life of St. Malachy
Lives of the Saints
Martyrology of Donegal
Oisin, Lays of
Provinicarum Orbis Terrae
Psaltar of Tara
Saltair na Rann, The
St. Adamnan's Life of Colm
St. Molaise's Gospels
Stowe Missal, The
Tain Bo Cuailgne, The
Teagasc an Riogh
Voyage of Bran, The
Will of Cormac, The
Works of Columbanus
Yellow Book of Lecan

Appendix B

Euphemistic Names for the Faery

By the sixteenth century, and with the birth of the Diminutive Fairy, or literary fairy, a list of euphemistic names was birthed. The peasantry feared what they did not understand, and since the Roman Catholic Church had a strong hold on the people, superstitions regarding the ancient pagan ways began to develop. To protect oneself against the Fay, a pet name was used. In doing so, you were ensured one of two responses: the departure of a haunting fairy, or the power over such a creature.

The following list, though in no way complete, presents an excellent study of the many folk-names used for the fairy, and the meaning and origin of each name.

Folk Names for the Faery

Bendith y Mamau (ben-dith uh momay)—Mother's Blessing, which was the name of the fairies of the Carmarthenshire country in Wales; this saying became a prayer spoken to ward-off harm.

Brownie—His territory extends over the Lowlands of Scotland and up into the Highlands and Islands all over the north and east of England and into the Midlands. With a natural linguistic variation, he becomes the BWCA of Wales, the Highland *Bodach* and the Manx *Fenodoree*. In the West Country, Pixies or Pisgies occasionally perform the offices of a brownie and show some of the same characteristics, though they are essentially different. Border brownies are most characteristic. They are small men, about three feet in height, very raggedly dressed in brown clothes, with brown faces and shaggy heads, who come out at night and do the work that has been left undone by the servants. They make themselves responsible for the farm or house in which they live: reap, mow, thresh, herd the sheep, prevent the hens from laying away, run errands, and give good counsel at need. A brownie can become personally attached to one member of the family.

Bwca—The Welsh name for the Brownie.

Corrigan— Malignant nature spirits found in Brittany, often associated with phantoms of the dead.

Daoine Maithe—"The Good People"; Similar to the Gentry, they were said to be next to heaven at the Fall, but did not fall; Some think they are a people expecting salvation (Angels?).

Dwarfs—Germany/Isle of Rugen/Swiss mountains.

Ellyllon—The name given to the Welsh Elves. They are tiny, diaphanous fairires whose food is toadstools and fairy butter, a fungoid substance found in the roots of old trees and in limestone crevices. Their queen is Mab.

Elves—In Scandinavian mythology the fairy people were elves and were divided into two classes, the light elves and the dark elves, like the Seelie Court and Unseelie Court. In Scotland the fairy people of human size were often called elves and Faeryland was Elfame; in England it was the smaller Trooping Fay who were called elves, and the name was particularly applied to small fairy boys.

Fays—The earlier noun/archaic of the word "fairy"; also referred to as the Fatae (three fates).

Fair Family or Fair Folk—The euphemistic name used by the Welsh for the fairies. See Tylwyth Teg.

Farisees, or Pharisees—The Suffolk name for fairies. The Suffolk children used to be confused between the farisees and the biblical mentions of the Pharises.

Fary—The dialect name in Northumberland.

Feeorin—A small fairy that is indicated as being, green-coated, generally red-capped, and with the usual fairy traits of love of dancing and music.

Fees—The fairiers of Upper Brittany.

Feriers, or Ferishers—Another Suffolk name for the fairies.

Ferries—The usual name for the Shetland and Orcadian fairies.

Ferrishyn (Ferrishin)—A Manx name for the fairie tribe; the singular is "ferrish." They are the Trooping Fairires of Man, though there does not seem to be any distinction between them and the Sleih Beggey. They are less aristocratic than the fairies of Ireland and Wales, and they have no named fairy king or queen. They were small, generally described as three feet in height, though sometimes as one foot. They could hear whatever was said out of doors. Every wind stirring carried the sound to their ears, and this made people very careful to speak of them favorably.

Fetes— The Fates of Upper Brittany.

Foawr, (fooar)—Manx equivalent of Highland Fomorians/giants, stone-throwing.

Frairies—The Norfolk and Suffolk, local version of the word "fairy."

Gentry, the—The most noble tribe of all the fairies in Ireland. A big race who came from the planets and usually appear white. The Irish used to bless the Gentry for fear of harm otherwise.

Good Neighbors—One of the most common Scottish and Irish names for the fairires.

Good People—The Irish often referred to their Sidhe in this manner. See Daoine Maithe.

Green Children, the—The fairy are recorded in the medieval chronicles under such a name.

Greencoaties—The name for the fairies that dwell in Lincolnshire Fen country.

Greenies—The euphemistic name used for the fairies in Lancashire; associated with the Jacobean Fairies.

Grey Neighbours, the—One of the euphemistic names for the fairies given by the Shetlanders to the Trows, the small gray-clad goblins whom the Shetlandersd used to propitiate and fear, using against them many of the means used all over the islands as protection against fairires.

Guillyn Veggey—The Little Boys is a Manx term for the fairies who dwell on the Isle of Man.

Gwyllion (gwithleeon)—The evil mountain fairies of Wales. They are hideous female spirits who waylay and mislead travelers by night on the mountain roads. They were friends and patrons of the goats, and might indeed take goat form.

Henkies—One of the names given to the Trows of Orkney and Shetland.

Hobgoblin—Used by the Puritans and in later times for wicked goblin spirits, but its more correct use is for the friendly spirits of the Brownie type. In "A Midsummer Night's Dream" a fairy says to Shakespeare's Puck:

> *Those that Hobgoblin call you, and sweet Puck,*
> *You do their work, and they shall have good luck:*
> *Are you not he?*

Hobgoblin was considered an ill omened word. "Hob" and "Lob" are words meaning the same kind of creature as the Hobgoblin. They are on the whole good-humored and ready to be helpful, but fond of practical joking.

Host, The—See Unseelie Court.

Hyter-sprites—Lincolnshire and East Anglian fairies/small and sandy-colored, with green eyes.

Klippe—The Forfarshire name for a fairy.

Leprechaun—Generally described as a fairy shoemaker, this creature is a red-capped fellow who stays around pure springs and is known to haunt cellars. He spends his time drinking and smoking. One branch of the Leprechaun is known as the Fir Darrig, who is a practical joker; both are of the Solitary Fairies. Leprechauns have also been associated with the Earth-Elemental Gnome, and when so done, is described as being a merry little fellow dressed all in green, instead of wearing a red cap, a leather apron, drab clothes and buckled shoes, and the boy, who has fairy blood in him, succeeds in winning a wealth of treasure from an underground cave, keeps his gain secret, and is the founder of a prosperous family.

Li'l Fellas, the—Another Manx euphemistic name for The Good Neighbours.

Little Folk—See Sleight Beggey.

Little People of the Passamaquoddy Indians, the—There are two kinds of Little

People among the Passamaquoddy Indians, the Nagumwa-suck and Mekumwasuck. Both kinds are two and a half to three feet in height, and both are grotesquely ugly. The Passamaquoddy Indians, who lived close to the Canadian border, used to migrate to the ocean in the summer and move inland in the winter. When they moved, their fairies moved with them. The Little People can only be seen by the Indians. They live in the woods and are fantastically and individually dressed. Their faces are covered with hair, which strikes an alien note to the Indians. Oral tradition has it that they were made of stone.

Lunantishess—The tribes that guard the blackthorn trees or sloes in Ireland; they let you cut no stick on the eleventh of November (the original November Day), or on the eleventh of May (the original May Day).

Mooinjer Veggey (moo-in-jer vegar)—The Little People is a familiar Manxman term for the faeries who dwell on the Isle of Man; see Sleigh Beggey

Muryans—*Muryan* is the Cornish word for ant. The Cornish belief about the fairies was that they were the souls of ancient heathen people, too good for Hell and too bad for Heaven, who had gradually declined from their natural size, and were dwindling down until they became the size of ants, after which they vanished from this state and no one knew what became of them.

Old People, the—Another Cornish name for the fairies.

Pechs, or Pehts—The Scottish Lowland names for fairies and are confused in tradition with the Picts, the mysterious people of Scotland who built the Pictish brughs and possibly also the round stone towers. The Pechs were considered tremendous castle builders and were credited with the construction of many of the ancient castles. They could not bear the light of day and so only worked at night, when they took refuge in their brughs or "sitheans" at sunrise. It seems likely that some historic memory of an aboriginal race contributed one strand to the twisted cord of fairy tradition.

People of Peace— The Irish often refered to their Sidhe in this manner. The word *sidhe* means peace. See Daoine Sidhe, Lesson Two.

People of the Hills, the—Fairies who live under the green mounds, or tumuli, all over England.

Picts—The original peoples who dwelled in the northeastern coast of Ireland. They were called the "Cruithne" and migrated down from Gaul or Galia (France). As the conquering waves of invaders arrived in Ireland, eventually the Picts retreated to the woods and lived in caves and underground forts. They were a small, dark people and became known as the classic Faery-people. See Pechs.

Pigsies—See Pixies

Pixies, or Pigsies, or Piskies—These are the West Country fairies belonging to Somerset, Devon and Cornwall. There are varying traditions about the size, appearance and origin of the Pixies, but all accounts agree about their being dressed in green and about their habit of misleading travelers.

Plant Rhys Dwfen (plant hrees thoovn)—The family name of a tribe of fairy people who inhabited a small land which was invisible because of a certain herb that grew on it. They were handsome people, rather below the average in height, and it was their custom to attend the market in Cardigan and pay such high prices for the goods there that the ordinary buyer could not compete with them. They were honest and resolute in their dealings, and grateful to people who treated them kindly.

Pookas—Black-featured fellows mounted on good horses, they are horse dealers in Ireland. They visit race courses, but usually are invisible.

Portunes—Small agricultural fairies. It was their habit to labor on farms, and at night when the doors were shut they would blow up the fire, and, taking frogs from their bosoms, they would roast them on the coals and eat them. They were like very old men with wrinkled faces and wore patched coats.

Seelie Court—Blessed Court; Name of the kindly fairy host, or benevolent Faery of the positive polarity, and is generally used to describe the Scottish fairies. The malignant fairies were sometimes called the Unseelie Court.

Sidhe, Sith, or Si (shee)— The Gaelic name for fairies, both in Ireland and the Highlands of Scotland. Very tall beings that seem to either shine or appear opalescent. The shining beings belong to the earthly realm; while the opalescent beings belong to the heavenly world. As with any shamanic practice there are three great worlds which we can see while we are still in the body: the heavenly, the earthly, and underworldly realm.

Silent Moving Folk—The Scottish fairies who live in green knolls and in the mountain fastnesses of the Highlands. See Still-Folk.

Sleigh Beggey (sleigh beargar)—The Little Folk. A name given to fairies in the Manx tongue.

Sluagh (slooa)—The most formidable of the Highland fairy people; The Host of the Unforgiven Dead. By some scholars, they are regarded as the fallen angels, not the dead, but on the whole their accounts correspond closely to that given by Alexander Carmichael in *Carmina Gadelica* (vo. II, p. 357):

> *Sluagh, 'the host', the spirit-world. The 'hosts' are the spirits of mortals who have died. The people have many curious stories on this subject. According to one informant, the spirits fly about in great clouds, up and down the face of the world like the starlings, and come back to the scenes of their earthly transgressions. No sould of them is without the clouds of earth, dimming the brightness of the works of god, nor can any win heaven till satisfaction is made for the sins of earth. In bad nights, the hosts shelter themselves behind little russet docken stems and little yellow ragwort stalks. They fight battles in the air as men do on the earth. They may be heard and seen on clear frost nights, advancing and retreating, against one another. After a battle, as I was told in Barra, their crimson blood may be seen staining rocks and stones ('Fuil nan sluagh', the blood of the hosts, is the beautiful red 'crotal' of the rocks melted by the frost). These spirits used to kill cats and dogs, sheep and cattle, with their unerring venomous darts. They commanded men to follow them, and meno obeyed, having no alternative.*

It was these men of earth who slew and maimed at the bidding of their spirit-masters, who in return ill-treated them in a most pitiless manner. They would be rolling and dragging and trouncing them in mud and mire and pools.

Small People of Cornwall, the—Fairies were sometimes spoken of this way in Cornwall.

Solitary Fairies—The fairies who are chiefly malignant or ominous creatures, comprise this group, although there may be a few nature spirits or dwindled gods among them. An exception is the Brownie and its variants—though there are a few family groups among the Brownies—some think that they were unacceptable in Faeryland because of their ragged, unkempt appearance, and that they went off to the Seelie Court when they were properly dressed. However, this is only one school of thought on the subject. Other creatures, such as the Lepracaun, Pooka, and Bean Si, also comprise this group.

Sprites—A general name for fairies and other spirits such as Sylphs and nereids.

Still-Folk—The Scottish name for the Highland fairies. See Silent Moving Folk.

Themselves, They, or Them that's in it—The most common Manx names used in place of the word "fairy," which was generally considered an unlucky word to use. It is sometimes said that 'Themselves' are the souls of those drowned in Noah's flood.

Tiddy Ones, Tiddy Men, or Tiddy People—The Lincolnshire fenmen's nature spirits, which are also referred to as the Yarthkins or Strangers. Most of them were undifferentiated, a drifting mass of influences and powers rather than individuals. The one among them personally known and almost beloved was the Tiddy Mun, who was invoked in times of flood to withdraw the waters.

Trooping Fay or Faery—The Faery have been divided into two main classes: trooping and Solitary. It is a distinction that holds good throughout the British Isles, and is indeed valid wherever fairy beliefs are held. The trooping fay can be large or small, friendly or sinister. They tend to wear green jackets, while the Solitary Faery wear red jackets. They can range from the Heroic Faery to the dangerous and malevolent Sluagh, or those Diminutive Fairies who include the tiny nature spirits that make the fairy rings with their dancing and speed the growth of flowers.

Tylwyth Teg (terlooeth teig)—The Fair Family. The most usual name for Welsh fairies, though they are sometimes called Bendith Y Mammau, in an attempt to avert their kidnapping activities by invoking a euphemistic name. They are fair-haired, and love golden hair. They dance and make fairy rings. They are like the Daoine Sidhe, and dwell underground or underwater. The fairy maidens are easily won as wives and will live with human husbands for a time. The danger of visiting them in their own country lies in the miraculous passage of time in Faeryland. They give riches to their favourites, but these gifts vanish if they are spoken of.

Unseelie Court—Unblessed Court; They are never under any circumstances favorable to mankind. They comprise the Slaugh, or The Host, that is, the band of the unsanctified dead. The Unseelie Court are the malignant Faery of the negative polarity, made up of Solitary Faery.

Verry Volk—The name of the fairies in Gower of Wales; little people dressed in scarlet and green.

Wee Folk—One of the Scottish and Irish names for the fairies.

White Ladies, the—The use of White Ladies for both ghosts and fairies is an indication of the close connection between fairies and the dead. The White Ladies were direct descendants of the Tuatha De Danann.

Appendix C

The Etymology of the Word Fairy

You know that even forms of speech can change
Within a thousand years, and words we know
Were useful once, seem to us wondrous strange—
Foolish or forced—and yet men spoke them so.
                                    —Chaucer

According to a well-known law of our nature, effects suggest causes; and another law, perhaps equally general, impels us to ascribe to the actual and efficient cause the attribute of intelligence.

The mind of the deepest philosopher is thus acted upon equally with that of the unschooled; the only difference lies in the nature of the intelligent cause at which they respectively stop. The one pursues the chain of cause and effect, and traces out its various links till she or he arrives at the great intelligent cause of all, however she or he may designate it; the other, when unusual phenomena excite her or his attention, ascribes her or his production to the immediate agency of some of the inferior beings recognized by her or his legendary creed.

The action of this latter principle must forcibly strike the minds of those who disdain not to bestow a portion of their attention on the popular legends and traditions of different countries. Every extraordinary appearance is found to have its extraordinary cause assigned; a cause always connected with the history or religion, ancient or modern, of the country, and not infrequently varying with a change of faith.

This can best be demonstrated in the story of the lady and the vicar, viewing the moon through a telescope; they saw in it, as they thought, two figures inclined toward each other.

"Methinks," says the lady, "they are two fond lovers, meeting to pour forth their vows by earthlight."

"Not at all," says the vicar, taking his turn at the glass. "They are the steeples of two neighboring churches." Point, well-rested.

It is my intention to aspire to record some semblance of the origin of those beings who are our fellow-inhabitants of earth, and whose manners I aimed to describe in the text.

Like every other word in extensive use, whose derivation is not historically certain, the word *Faery* or *Fairy* has obtained various and opposite etymons.

Of a classic source, however unlikely, some derive fairy from a Homeric name of the Centaurs. In other words, centaurs is the root for deer. Other theories deduce the English fairy from the Persian Pheri.

The Paynim foe, whom the warriors of the Cross encountered in Palestine, spoke only Arabic; the alphabet of which language, it is well known, possesses no *P*, and therefore organically substitutes an *F* in such foreign words as contain the former letter; consequently Peri became, in the mouth of an Arab, Feri, whence the crusaders and pilgrims, who carried back to Europe the marvellous tales of Asia, introduced into the west the Arabo-Persian word fairy.

All that is wanting in this so very plausible theory is proof, and some slight agreement with the ordinary rules of etymology. Had Feerie, or fairy, originally signified the individual in the French and English, the only languages in which the word occurs, etymologists might feel disposed to acquiesce in it. But they do not.

The foregoing are all the conjectures of English scholars; for the English is the only language in which the name of the fairy has the canine letter to afford any foundation for them.

I will discuss the true origin of the words used in the Romantic languages to express the being which, it is believed, we name fairy. These are:

Faee or *Fee*, French
Fada, Provencal
Fata, Italian
The root evidently Latin: *Fatum*.

In the fourth century, this word was made plural, and even feminine, denoted by three female figures, with the legend *Fatis victricibus*, ascribing to it the attributes of the older Moerae, or Fates.

On the other hand, as celebrated in old romance, the definition of the word *Fee* expressly asserts that such a being was a woman skilled in magick; and such, on examination, I find to have been all the *Fee* of the romances of chivalry and of the popular tales; in effect, *Fee* is a participle, and therefore, the words *Dame* or *Femme* are to be understood.

In the middle ages, there was in use a Latin verb, *Fatare* (derived from *Fatum* or *Fata*), signifying to enchant. This verb was adopted by the Italian, Provencal and Spanish languages; in French it became, according to the analogy of that tongue, *Faer* or *Feer*. Of this verb the past participle is *Fae* or *Fe*.

From the verb *Faer* or *Feer* (to enchant, allude), the French made a substantive *Faerie* or *Feerie*; illusion, enchantment, the meaning of which was afterwards extended, particularly after it had been adopted into the English language.

In summary, the word *fairy* is late in origin, the earlier noun having been *Fee*, perhaps, a broken-down form of *Fatae*. Thus, I have endeavored to trace out the origin, and mark the progress of the word *fairy*, through its varying significations, and trust that the subject will now appear placed in a clear and intelligible light.

In this modern time, the term *fairy* covers a large area, the Anglo-Saxon and Scandinavian Elves, the Daoine Sidhe of the Highlands, the Tuatha De Danann of Ireland, the Tylwyth Teg of Wales, the Seelie Court and the Unseelie Court, the Wee Folk and Good Neighbors.

There are a score of euphemistic name-associations with the term *fairy* as shown in Appendix B: The Trooping Fay and the Solitary Fairies are included in it, the fairies of human or more than human size, the three-foot fairies and the tiny fairies, the domestic fairies and those that are wild and alien to man, the subterranean fairies and the water fairies that haunt lochs, streams, or the sea.

These euphemistic species run into and are so confounded one with the other; the actions and attributes of one kind are so frequently ascribed to the nature of another. It is important to remember that all these beings once formed parts of ancient and exploded systems of religion, and that it is chiefly in the traditions of the peasantry, or in the deepest wisdom of the Occult traditions, that their memorial has of late been preserved.

It cannot be expected that our clarifications should vie in accuracy and determinateness with those of natural science. The human imagination, of which these beings could very easily be the off spring, works not (at least that I can discover) like nature, by fixed and invariable laws; and it would be hard to exact from the fairy historian the rigid distinction of classes and orders which I expect from the botanist or biochemist. What matters most is not that there is an origin to the English word *Faery* or *Fairy*, but an origin to the beings of whom such words are attached.

Appendix D

Irish Gods and Goddesses

The following are complete lists of Celtic gods and goddesses provided here for a continued study of the Irish Pantheon.

Celtic Gods

All-Father—A title (in various languages) given to many gods.

Ambisagrus—Continental Celtic, equated by the Romans with Jupiter.

Amergin—The bard and spokesman of the Milesian invaders of Ireland in the Mythological Cycle, and one of their leaders against the De Danann. Traditional author of the poem *I Am a Stag of Seven Tines*.

> *I am a stag of seven tines*
> *I am a wild flood on a plain,*
> *I am a wind on the deep waters,*
> *I am a shining tear of the Sun,*
> *I am a hawk on a cliff,*
> *I am fair among flowers,*
> *I am a god who sets the head afire with smoke,*
> *I am a battle-waging spear,*
> *I am a salmon in the pool,*
> *I am a hill ofr poetry,*
> *I am a ruthless boar,*
> *I am a threatening noise of the sea,*
> *I am a wave of the sea,*
> *Who but I knows the secret of the unhewn domen?*

It was he who granted the wish of the three De Danann queens, Eire, Fodhla, and Banbha, daughters of the Dagda, that Ireland be named after them. He is said to be buried under Millmount hill in Drogheda.

Balor—The old god who appears in legend as king of the Fomors. Husband of Dana or Ceithlenn, father of Eithne and thus grandfather of Lugh, the bright young god who supplanted him. He had a poisoned eye which could slay with its glance; it took four men to raise his eyelid in battle. At the "Second Battle of Magh Tuireadh," Lugh killed him by hurling a slingstone into his great eye. The Welsh equivalent is Beli.

Bith—In Irish legend, he is son of Noah and father of Cesara, the first occupier of Ireland. His wife was Birren.

Bormanus—An early Continental Celtic god.

Borvo *[to boil]*—Continental Celtic god of hot springs, in which role he replaced Sirona, said to be his mother. Equated by Romans with Apollo. May be the same as Borve in the Welsh legend of Llyr.

Bres—Son of a Fomorian father and a Tuatha De Danann mother, he was married to Brighid, daughter of the Dagda, in a dynastic alliance. He became king of the De Danann but lacked the necessary qualities of generosity and lost his title when he was satirized by the bard Cairbre and boils appeared on his face. This led to renewed war between the Fomorians and the De Danann and to the latter's victory at the Second Battle of Magh Tuireadh.

Bussumarus [large-lipped]—Continental Celtic god, identified by the Romans with Jupiter.

Camulos—A king of the Tuatha De Danann, fused with some earlier god; he may have been Cumhal, warrior king father of Finn, and the origin of King Cole of the nursery rhyme.

Cernunnos—The only known name of the Celtic Horned God. The name appears only on the altar of Nautes, now in the Cluny Museum in Paris. He is portrayed in many Celtic artefacts, from a rock carving at Val Camonica in northern Italy (fourth century) to the famous Gundestrup Cauldron which was found in a peat bog in Denmark. He is portrayed on the medieval market cross in the center of Kells, Col. Meatha, and a few miles farther off, on a stone in the churchyard on Tara Hill.

He is usually portrayed with horns and accompanied by animals. He usually either wears or has looped on his horns the torc (circular necklet) of Celtic nobility. Often, as on the Gundestrup Cauldron, he holds a serpent with a ram's head or horns.

The Irish saints Kieran and Ciaran (5th- and 6th-century) had characteristics of this pagan deity. Both had animal legends attached to them. St. Kieran of Clonmacnoise had a tame fox who used to carry his writings for him. Just before his death, he asked for his bones to be left on a hilltop "like a stag," and for his spirit to be preserved rather than his relics. St. Kieran of Saighir built his hermit's cell with the help of a wild boar, his first disciple, to which he soon added a fox, a badger, a wolf, and a stag, which obeyed his every command.

Cian—Son of Dianchecht, and father by Eithne of Lugh. may be equated with Mac Kinely.

Credne—Bronze-worker hero of the De Danann who, together with the smith Goibniu and the woodworker Luchtain, made the weapons with which the De Danann defeated the Fomors.

Crom Cruaich [The Bowed One of the Mound]—Also known as Cenn Cruaich, the Lord of the Mound, and Crom Dubh, the Black Bowed One. An ancient sacrificial god particularly associated with the festival of Lughnasadh. The last Sunday in July is still called Domhnach Chrom Dubh [Crom Dubh's Sunday], even though it has been Christianized as the day of the spectacular pilgrimage up St. Patrick's mountain, the 2,410-foot Croagh Patrick in County Mayo.

Delbaeth—Son of Oghma Grainaineach. Father of the triple goddess Badb [Neman, Macha, and the Morrigan]. According to one account, also father of Boann, goddess of the River Boyne.

Diancecht—Healer god of the De Danann. His son Miach and daughter Airmid made the silver hand which replaced the one lost by Nuada at the First Battle of Maigh Tuireadh.

Donn—Irish lord of the dead.

Essus, or Esus—Early Continental Celtic agriculture god, worshipped by the Essuvi. His consort may have been the bear-goddess Artio.

Fergus—Name of several legendary characters, but this particular one's virility was such that, when his wife, the woodland goddess and ruler of beasts, Flidais, was away, he needed seven ordinary women to satisfy him sexually.

Fergus Mac Roi—King of Ulster who loved Nessa, mother of Conchobar; he suffered exile for her sake, and Conchobar inherited his throne. Later became tutor to Cu Chulainn, Conchobar's nephew; but he took Queen Maeve's side in her war with Ulster.

Fintaan—Husband of Noah's granddaughter Cesara, first occupier of Ireland in the Mythological Cycle. They left for the western edge of the world forty days before the Flood, with Cesara in charge of the expedition. Cesara appears to have been a pre-Celtic matriarchal goddess, with Fintaan as her less-important consort.

Fionn Mac Cumhal [Finn Mac Cool]—Son of Cumhal, king of the De Danann. As a child, he burned his finger on the Salmon of Knowledge, sucked it and thus acquired all knowledge. Became leader of the Fiana, a famous mobile group of warriors and hunters. Said to have lived 200 years.

Gadel—Said to have been an ancestor of the Milesian, and to have divided the Gaelic language into five dialects—for soldiers, poets, historians, physicians, and the common people. Perhaps originally an Achaean deity of the River Gadylum on the southern shore of the Black Sea.

Gavida—A smith god, brother of Mac Kinely. Equivalent of Gobniu, and the Welsh Govannon.

Gebann—Druid of the De Danann. Father of the South Munster goddess Cliona of the Fair Hair, renowned for her great beauty and connected with the O'Keefe family.

Goibniu—Smith of the De Danann, who with Credne and Luchtain made the weapons with which the Tuatha defeated the Fomors. Uncle of Lugh. Equivalent to Gavida and the Welsh Govannon.

Grannos—Early Continental Celtic god of mineral springs. An inscription to him was also found at Musselburgh, near Edinburgh.

Holly King—Celtic god of the waning year. The cycle of fertility has been expressed in many god-forms. One of these, or rather one pair, which has persisted from pagan times to contemporary folklore is that of the Oak King and the Holly King, gods respectively of the waxing year and the waning year.

The Oak King rules from midwinter to midsummer, the period of expansion and growth; the Holly King from midsummer to midwinter, the period of withdrawl and rest. They are the light and dark twins, each being the other's alternate self. They are not good and evil; each represents a necessary phase in the natural rhythm, so in this sense, both are good.

At the two change-over points, they meet in combat. The incoming twin slays the outgoing one. But the defeated twin is not truly dead; he has merely withdrawn, during the six months of his brother's rule, into the Castle of the ever-turning Silver Wheel.

The custom of the Holly King can be seen in the survival of the folk-custom—Hunting the Wren at the winter solstice. The wren is the Holly King's bird. In scattered places in Ireland, adult Wren Boys, wearing conical straw hats completely covering their heads and faces, still dance and sing around their villages on St. Stephen's Day, December 26. More universally on the same day, in the West of Ireland, children, usually in fancy dress and with their faces made up, go from door to door carrying bunches of holly and reciting:

The wren, the wren, the king of the birds,
On Stephen's Day was caught in the furze;
Up with the kettle and down with the pan,
And give us some money to bury the wren.

Although the Holly King's reign is one of withdrawal, culminating in apparent lifelessness, his symbology reminds us all the time that he is his brother's other self and holds life in trust while it rests. The holly's leaves are evergreen, and its bright berries glow red when all else is bare of fruit.

The Holly King is the true origin of Santa Claus, rather than the 4th-century bishop of Myra who is his official prototype and whose factual history is virtually non-existent, in contrast to his body of kindly legend.

Iuchar—Iuchar, Iucharba, and Brian were three sons of the goddess, Anu and grandsons of Balor. Said to have married Eire, Fodhal and Banbha, the three goddesses after whom Ireland was named. [See also Mac Cecht, Mac Cuill and Mac Greine.] One account makes them the joint fathers of Lugh by Clothru, a ring of red circles on his neck and belly showing which part each had fathered. Another version makes them murderers of Lugh's father Cian, for which crime they had to gather the Treasures of the Tuatha De Danann.

Leucetios—A Continental Celtic god of thunder.

Litavis—An early Celtic god, possibly Breton in origin; Llydaw is the Welsh name for Brittany.

Lir—The Shakespearian King Lear is modeled after this god. He is both a Welsh and Irish god. In Irish mythology, he is the father of Manannan Mac Lir. He was also a king of the De Danann; his first wife was Aebh, by whom he had a daughter, Fionuala, and three sons, Hugh, Fiacha, and Conn; Aeb then died. His second wife was Aoife, who turned the four children into swans out of jealousy. The Children of Lir flew around Ireland as swans for 900 years, until the hermit Mochavog baptized them and they changed to aged human shape and died.

Mac Cecht—Son of the Plough, or Whose God was the Plough. Husband of Fodhla, the mother aspect of the triple goddess symbolizing Ireland. He represented the earth element.

Mac Cuill—Son of the Hazel, or 'whose god was the hazel' or Whose God was the Sea. He was husband of Banbha, the crone aspect of the triple goddess symbolizing Ireland. He represented the primordial water element.

Mac Greine—Son of the Sun, or 'whose god was the sun'. He was husband of Eire, the maid aspect of the triple goddess symbolizing Ireland. He represented the fire element.

Mackinely—Son of Balor and Ceithlenn, and father by Eithne of Lugh. He may be equated with Cian.

Miach—Son of Diancecht, the father of medicine, and himself a physician. With his siter Airmid, made King Nuada's silver hand, for which Diancecht killed him. Healing grasses grew on his grave.

Moccos, or Moccus—A Continental Celtic pig god, or god of a pig totem clan. He is identified under Roman influence with Mercury.

Mullo—A Continental Celtic god known as the patron of muleteers. Sometimes he is identified with Mars. His probable totem was the ass.

Nemed—He was the leader of one of the early peoples to occupy Ireland in the Mythological Cycle. Husband of Macha, the (probably pre-Celtic) Ulster goddess.

Oak King—Celtic god of the waxing year. [See Holly King entry above.] The Oak King rules from midwinter to midsummer, the period of expansion and growth. His bird is the robin; its red breast symbolizing the reborn sun.

Oberon—The fairy king invented by Shakespeae. He has magickal powers and rules a kingdom called Mommur. He is a dwarf, though with an angelic face, and son of Julius Caesar and the Lady of the Hidden Isle.

Oisin, or Ossian [fawn]—Son of Fionn Mac Cumhal and the deer goddess Sadhbh. She was lured away from Fionn's house by magic before Oisin was born, and turned into a deer; Fionn never found her, but the boy Oision came to him and grew up to be an inspired poet. The only man on record to stand up to St. Patrick in argument. He went with Niamh of the Golden Hiar to Tir na nOg, where she bore him two sons (Fionn, after Oisin's father, and Osgar, He Who Loves the Deer), and one daughter (Plur na mBan [Flower of Women]).

Segomo—A Continental Celtic god of war; also known as Cocidius.

Shoney—This god is both Irish and Scottish. A sea god to whom libations of ale were offered till late into the nineteenth century by fishermen in Ireland and the Isle of Lewis.

Tethra—A chief of the Fomorians who was also king of Lochlann, their mythical undersea haome.

Celtic Goddesses

Achall—The Hill of Achall near Tara was memorialized after her when she died of sorrow upon the death of her brother in battle.

Achtan—She mothered Cormac mac Art, who at birth was separated from her, found and suckled by a wolf. Although the child grew up wild, he was healthy. The hunter, Luinge Fer Tri happened up the child and returned him to Achtan. Together the mother and child climbed the wild Irish mountains and reached the seat of Irish sovereignty, the Hill of Tara, where Cormac took his father's place as king. Achtan settled down with Luinge.

Adsullata—A Continental Celtic goddess of spring; may be equated with Sul, the sun goddess of another pantheon.

Aeife [eye-fy]—Literally means Reflection. She was recorded among the Goddesses as one of the governmental and/or martial leaders, and soldiers. She was also among the instructors of Cu Chulainn, whom he married for a year and who bore him a son.

Aeife was one of three foster-daughters of Bodb the Red; Aebh, Aeife, and Aibhe, the children of Ailioll of Arran. The great Sea-God, Lir came to visit Bodb the Red after is first wife died, and Bodb the Red offered him one of his three foster-duaghters. Lir chose Aebh for his wife claiming, "She is the eldest, so she must be the noblest of them." They were married, Aebh bore four children to Lir, the eldest was a daughter called Finola, a son Aed, and two twin boys called Fiachra and Conn, but in giving birth to the twins Aebh died.

Again Bodb the Red offered Lir another of his foster-daughters. Ler chose the second, Aeife. Aeife, was associated with swans and as legend goes, changed Aebh's four children into swans for 300 years, and they dwelled at Lake Darvra. It was not long after this incident that gods and mortals ceased to associate. As Aeife's punishment she was asked to tell her father Bodh "what shape of all others, on the earth, or above the earth, or beneath the earth, she most abhorred, and into which she most dreaded to be transformed."

Aeife was obliged to answer that she most feared to become a demon of the air. So Bodb the Red struck her with his wand, and she fled from them, a shrieking demon.

Aeval—A Faery queen of southwestern Munster. In her district a debate was launched on whether the men were satisfying the women's sexual needs. In a midnight court, Aeval heard both sides and then decreed the men wrong and sentenced them to overcome their prudishness and accede to the women's needs.

Aibheaog—In the County of Donegal, she was worshiped at Tober Breda. The well's waters were held to be an effective remedy against toothache, so long as the petitioner left a little white stone beside the well as a substitute for the sore tooth. It is believed that she was also an ancient fire-goddess.

Aige—In Irish legend she was turned into a fawn and wandered across the island until she died by plunging into a bay, which today bears her name.

Ain—A twin sister of Iaine. She was the mythical reason for women's high status in ancient Ireland. When the two sisters married their two brothers, the men invented war so that each could claim as large a share of the island as possible. As a result of the conflict the rights of women, single or married, were spelled out carefully in the Brehon Laws. The laws were singularly comprehensive in assuring women's property rights and freedom.

Aine [aw-ne]—This is the Bright Faery goddess to whom the mountain Knock Aine on the shores of Lough Gur is dedicated, and she is one of the great goddesses of ancient Ireland who has survived in modern times as the queen of the fairies of south Munster. The reference made to her brightness may indicate that she was originally a sun-goddess.

She is the daughter of Tuatha king, Egogabal, and a shapeshifter, her alternate forms that of a swan and Lair Derg (Red Mare).

Aine is recognized as a moon-goddess, and patroness of crops and cattle. She is attributed to giving the meadowsweet its scent. Her name derives from the same root as Adeh, "fire," and therefore she could be identified with Bridget.

The Midsummer festivals were once celebrated in honor of her before they were transferred to St. John's Day. On this night, farmers carried torches of straw in procession around Knock Aine and waved them over the cattle and the fields for protection and fruitfulness.

Her energy is most effective during the "Time of the Big Sun," which is from Beltain to Samhain.

Knock Aine and Knock Fennine on the shores of Lough Gur were dedicated Aine and her sister Fenne. Aine is known to take the form of a swan, as illustrated in the tale below.

One day, as Aine was sitting on the shore of Lough Gur combing her long golden hair, Gerold, the Earl of Desmond, saw her and fell in love with her.

He gained control over her by seizing her cloak, and made her his bride. Their child was Earl Fitzgerald, and the geasa imposed upon his father was that he must never express any surprise at anything his son might do.

One night, however, showing off his skill to some maidens, he jumped into a bottle and out again, and his father could not restrain a cry of surprise.

Fitzgerald at once left the castle and was seen swimming across the lough in the form of a wild goose towards Garrod Island, under which his enchanted castle was said to lie. At the same time, Aine disappeared into Knock Aine as a swan.

Airmed [er-ma]—A Tuatha De Danann who had great magickal powers, particularly in the cunning arts of herblore. She knew the uses of every plant, the knowledge gained after the death of her brother Miach, from whose grave sprang innumerable plants. These were all the herbs of the world, and as Airmed tended her brother's grave, the plants instructed her in their use. Thus we have a Tuatha who works with the Devas and is the birther of the art of herbcraft.

Almha, or Almu [al-va]—Although nothing remains of her myth, she is connected to the Tuatha De Danaan. A hill in southern Ireland was named after her.

Andarta, or Andrasta—The goddess of Victory invoked by the Celtic Queen Boadicea.

Anu, or Anann—One of the Deae Matronae [the Mothers] of Ireland, and a goddess of Fertility, Prosperity and Abundance. Two neighboring hills in Kerry are called the

Paps of Anu. She is perhaps a local goddess and may be connected with Black Annis of the Dane Hills in Leicestershire, and it is possible that Dana and Anu are the same. Anann is worshipped in Munster as a goddess of Plenty. There are hints that she was also a Fate goddess.

Aoibhinn—Queen of the Faery of North Munster.

Aynia—A Faery Queen of Ulster.

Ban-Chuideachaidh Moire—The midwife to the Virgin Mary, and a title given to St. Bridget.

Banfathi [bahn-fy]—The goddess who often accompanied troops into battle, and was relied upon for advice and strategy. She based her advice upon listening to the sounds of the streams, and studying the eddies and currents of the waters.

Ban Naomha, or Banna Naomha—A fish goddess of Kil-na-Greina, the Well of the Sun, in County Cork. The well was a place of prophecy and wisdom and only those with the second-sight could see Ban Naomha after performing a magickal ritual which consisted of taking three drinks from the well three times, crawling around the well three times between drinks and laying a stone the size of a dove's egg on the altar with each circle.

Becuna Cneisgel—A goddess of fertility.

Biddy Mannion—A midwife chosen by the Faery's of Inishshar, a tiny island off the Irish coast. She was reputed for healing and brought many Faery babies back to life when they died at birth.

Birren—Wife of Bith, Noah's son, and mother of Cesara.

Black Annis—A cannibal Hag with a blue face and iron claws supposed to live in a cave in the Dane Hills in Leicestershire. There was a great oak at the mouth of the cave in which she was said to hide to leap out, catch and devour stray children and lambs. The cave, which was called Black Annis Bower Close, was supposed to have been dug out of the rock with her own nails.

Originally on May Day, and later on Easter Monday, it was the custom to hold a drag hunt from Annis' Bower to the Mayor of Leicester's house. The bait dragged was a dead cat drenched in aniseed. Black Annis was associated with a monstrous cat. This custom died out at the end of the 18th century.

Black Annis and Gentle Annie are supposed to derive from Anu, or Dana [see Lesson Three]. However, the Leicester Chronicle of 1842 mentions a tomb in Swithland Church to Agnes Scott, an anchoress, and suggests that she was the original of Black Annis, and yet up until the December of 1941, Black Annis was reportedly still alive and lived in the Danehills.

Black Virgin, The—The Goddess worshipped by the Dryadesses of Sena on the Isle D'e Sein. One of their major religious sites later became the Chartres Cathedral.

Blathnat [blah-na]—Daughter of Midir, King of the Gaelic Underworld. She helped Cu Chulainn steal her father's magick cauldron.

Boadicea, or Boudiga [bow-di-cea, or buh-oo-di-gah]—Queen of the Iceni tribe, who personally led a rebellion against the Romans in 61 A.D. Boudiga occurs as a name of a goddess meaning Victory.

Boand [bo-unn]—The Divine Ancestress of the Celtic Boii tribe. Her name literally means "white cow," and she was linked with the River Boyne in Ireland as the Boyne's source, which was said to be a pool where the Salmon of Knowledge fed on nuts dropping from the nine Hazel trees surrounding it.

Her son was Aengus Mac'Og (Mac'Og means Son of the Virgin—in the old sense of one who is an independent goddess in her own right, and not a mere consort). Her mating with Dagda was on November 1.

Bo Find—The white cow of Erin who gave birth to magickal twin claves, one male and one female, from them descended all the cattle of Ireland. Some legends say that Bo Find was originally a woman, who could not regain her human form unless she slept for centures on the summits of Erin's three highest mountains and was awoken by an Irish high king. It is most probable that Bo Find is also an ancient fertility goddess.

Bri—A beautiful fairy queen of Ireland.

Bronach [bro-naw]—A Hag of western Ireland, especially in the rocky northern Burren near the Cliffs of Mother. One of the highest of these cliffs is Hag's Head, or Ceann Cailighe. Another of her titles, Caileach Cinn Boirne, means "the Hag of Black Head," another of the Mother Cliffs.

Buana [boo-awna]—Which means Good Mother. The Irish goddess as a cow, similar to the Egyptian Hathor or Cow-Eyed Hera of the Greek pantheon. She is a milk-giving Mother who represents wealth or plenty. Her name may stem from Ana.

Buannan [boo-awn-in]—Means The Lasting One. A warrior goddess, who was one of the Amazon instructors of Cu Chulainn.

Caer—She was a swan-maiden who every year, when summer was over, went with her companions to a lake called Dragon-Mouth, and there all of them became swans. She was also the Dream-Maiden that appeared every night, for a year, in the dreams of Angus, son of Dagda. When Angus found her, he proclaimed his passion and his name to her, and she promised to be his bride, if he too would become a swan. He agreed, and with a word she changed him into swan-shape, and thus they flew side-by-side to Angus's Sidh, where they retook the human form, and lived as changeable immortals.

Caileach Cinn Boirne—The literal meaning is the Hag of Black Head, which is one of the Mother Cliffs in the rocky northern Burren located in western Ireland. This is also another title worn by Bronach.

Cally Berry—The Ulster goddess, who has been reduced from a nature spirit, the personification of winter and the guardian of the wild deer, to a malignant supernatural Hag. Her name may derive from the East Indian goddess, Kali-Ma, the goddess of birth and destruction.

Canola—The music created by the wind blowing through the rotted sinews clinging to the skeleton of a whale inspired Canola to recreate the magical and beautiful sound, and so she created the first harp. She was a goddess of music.

Caolainn—The ruler of a healing well in County Roscommon devoted to Brigid. Another form of the Cailleach.

Carman—A Wexford goddess, whence Gaelic name of Wexford, Loch Garman (Loch gCarman). May have a Phoenician or Greek connection; one source says three men from Athens, with their mother, came to Wexford Bay to settle, and that Greek merchants traded at the Fair of Carman Festival—August 1.

Carravogue—Another name for the Hag of winter. One legend has it that this woman, after eating berries on the way to church, became a monstrous snake. St. Patrick was called upon to throw holy water at her, and she dissolved into lakes from which she will someday rise again. The legend clearly shows the Christianization of Ireland over the banishment of the Faery-Faith. Other names associated with this same myth are—Gabhog and Gheareagain; all three, however, are connected to the Cailleach Bera.

Cebhfhionn [y-von]—A goddess of inspiration who stood next to the Well of Knowledge constantly filling a vessel with its water and pouring it out without letting wisdom-seeking humans taste it.

Ceithlenn—The Crooked Tooth; Wife of Balor, the old god who appears in legend as the King of the Fomorians.

Cesara, or Cessair—In The Mythological Cycle, Cesara was considered the first true occupier of Ireland. I provide her in this list because she is acknowledged as being one of the "mothers of the various nations of the world," and because of this she may bridge the gap between Pagan Ireland, Celtic Ireland, and Christian Ireland. She is considered to be daughter of Bith, who is the son of Noah. Cesara and her husband, Fintaan, were sent with Bith and his wife, Birren, by Noah "to the western edge of the world" forty days before the Flood, to escape it. Cesara was in charge of the expedition. One account says she rejected Noah's god and took her own with them. Accompanying them were fifty (or 150) women who were originally the "mothers of the various nations of the world." Cesara appears to be a Goddess of pre-Celtic days of another pantheon.

Cetnenn—A great warrior in Irish legend; however, little is written about her.

Cliodna of the Fair Hair—The tributary Queen of Munster, who rules from a sidh near Mallow in County Cork; goddess of great beauty.

Coventina—Mother of Covens; the goddess who was patron of healing wells and springs.

Cred, or Creide—The Faery queen of the Paps of Anu. Her palace, heavily guarded, kept mankind from entering. Cred swore to never sleep with a man until she found one who could create the most magnificent poem for her. A bard named Coll came to her and sang his poem, which contained one line that convinced her to marry him. The line was:

Wounded men spouting heavy blood
would sleep to the music of fairy birds
singing above the bright leaves of her bower.

Crobh Dearg—Which means red claw, was an ancient goddess who was said to be the sister of Latiaran.

Delbchaen—Daughter of Morgan, who lived on an island somewhere in the sea. Art, the son of Conn, was bound by a geasa to procure marriage with her.

Derbforgaille [der-va-la]—A Swan maiden, who fell in love with Cu Chulainn, and was wounded by him.

Dil—A cattle-goddess of ancient Ireland.

Domnu—Goddess of the Fir Domnann; the goddess brought in with the wave of the Firbolg invasion.

Dornoll [doorr-nuhl]—Literally means Bigfist. A warrior goddess who was among the Amazon instructors of Cu Chulainn, and whose sexual advances he refused.

Druantia—A fir-tree goddess.

Dubh Lacha—A sea-goddess.

Eadon—A goddess of poetry and inspiration.

Ebhlinne, or Ebhlenn [ev-lynn]—The goddess worshipped in the sountern County of Tipperary. Her home was in the Twelve Mountains of Ebhlenn, the highest of which was called Mathair-Shliabh, the "Mother Mountain." In the Dindshenchas (the geographical poetry of Ireland), Ebhlinne was said to be the daughter of Guaire from the Brugh na Boine, and was married to a king of Cashel. She ran away with his handsom son. The traditional celebration in her honor was at midsummer in her mountains.

Ebliu—The mother of Libane.

Echtghe Aughty—Daughter of the god Nuada. Her lover gave her a range of mountains in the west of Ireland known as Sliabh na Echtghe (Slieve Aughty). The area surrounding the hills, Feakle Parish, was the haunt in the early part of the century of Biddy Early, the White Witch of Clare, whose magical blue bottle rests beneath a lake somewhere in the hills, its power waiting to be reclaimed. She may be an ancient form of Anu.

Eithne—Daughter of Danu and Balor; wife of Mackinely or Cian, and mother of Lugh. May be equated with the Welsh Arianrhod.

Ele, or Eile [el-lie]—The sister of Queen Maeve.

Emer—In the legend, *The Wooing of Emer*, Cu Chulainn was her suitor. She was endowed with everything a woman could possess—wisdom, talent, and wit. She was lovely to look upon and well-mannered. In her conversations with Cu Chulainne, Emer proudly acknowledged her own excellence—"I am a Tara among women, the whitest of maidens, one who is gazed at but gazes not back; I am the untrooden way" before demanding heroic exploits of him before she would sleep with him, reasoning that her superior endowments warranted them.

Eorann—Goddess of the woods, married to Suibhne, the hero who went mad after being cursed by Saint Ronan for desecrating the church. Thereafter he led the life of a vagabond in the woods. Eorann was forced to remarry for political and economic reasons, but she did not forget Suibhne, whom she still loved, and when she met him in the forest she sang to him:

> Welcome to you, dear, dear, splendid fool:
> Although sleep may be its lot,
> My body has been ravaged since the day
> When I learned you were no more,
> Although the king's son leads me
> Into the joyful falls of feasting,
> I would prefer to sleep in a tree's small hollow,

With you, my mate, if only I could...
If the choice had been left to me
By the men of Ireland and Britain,
I would prefer to live on cress and water,
With you, without sin...
I am sad, O mad one, to see you blind and in distress,
It grieves me that your skin has changed colour,
That briars and thorns tear you...
I wish that we be together
And feathers grow on our bodies,
In light and in darkness,
I would wish to wander with you, each night and day.

Eri—The mother of the beautiful god Bres. She had beautiful golden hair and was of the Tuatha Da Danaan.

Ernmas [airr-in-mosh]—Which means murder. She is the mother of the Morrigu.

Ess Euchen—A war goddess killed by Cu Chulainn when avenging the death of her three sons, whom he had killed.

Estiu—A warrior and bird-goddess.

Etain, or Edain—Was also known as Etain Echraidhe, or horse-riding. Etain was also a symbol of reincarnation. She was the wife of Midir, but was stolen away from him by Angus. Then King Eochaid heard of her beauty; she is described as being so beautiful that "all who might before have been thought beautiful are as nothing beside Etain ... all blondes cannot match her."

So, he himself went to see her, and chose her to be his queen and gave her a splendid dowry. Midir heard of these and came to retrieve her. It took Mider two years to get Etain back; the final act was when he spoke to her the following verses.

O fair lady! will you come with me
To a wonderful country which is mine,
Where the people's hair is of golden hue,
And their bodies the colour of virgin snow?
There no grief or care is known;
White are their teeth, black their eyelashes:
Delight of the eye is the rank of our hosts,
with the hue of the fox-glove on every cheek.
Crimson are the flowers of every mead,
Gracefully speckled as the blackbird's egg;
Though beautiful to see be the plains of Inisfail,
They are but commons compared to our great plains.
Though intoxicating to you be the ale-drink of Inisfail,
More intoxicating the ales of the great country;
The only land to praise is the land of which I speak,
Where no one ever dies of decrepit age.
Soft sweet streams traverse the land;
The choicest of mead and of wine;

Beautiful people without any blemish;
Love without sin, without wickedness.
We can see the people upon all sides,
But by no one can we be seen;
The cloud of Adam's transgression it is
That prevents them from seeing us.
O lady, should you come to my brave land,
It is golden hair that will be on your head;
Fresh pork, beer, new milk and ale,
You there with me shall have, O fair lady!

Ethniu—Was the daughter of the Fomorian god, Balor. She was married to Cian of the Tuatha De Danann at an attempt of alliance. She was also the mother of the Celtic god of light, Lugh, who became one of the Tuatha De Danann and reigned after Nuada and the Dagda.

Etrange—Mother of the goddess Macha.

Fachea—A goddess of poetry and inspiration.

Fand [fahnn]—Goddess of healing and pleasure, lover of Cu Chulainn, and wife of the sea-god, Manannan mac Lir, who deserted her. Her name is analogous with the Latin Venus and the Norse Vanir.

Fand, after being deserted by her husband, sent her sister Liban to Cu Chulainn as an ambassador of love. At first he refused to visit her, but ordered his charioteer, to go with Liban to the Happy Plain to spy out the land.

Laeg returned enraptured. "If all Ireland were mine," he assured his master, "with supreme rule over its fair inhabitants, I would give it up without regret to go and live in the place that I have seen."

So Cu Chulainn himself went and stayed a month in the Celtic Paradise with Fand, the fairest woman of the Sidhe. However, Cu Chulainn was already betrothed to Emer and his grief touched her so that he swore to her that she was pleasing to him and would be as long as he lived. Because of Cu Chulainn's pledge to Emer, the goddess Fand gave Cu Chulainn's love back to Emer.

It was then that Lir heard of Fand's trouble, and was sorry he had forsaken her. So he came, invisible to all but her alone. He asked her pardon and she herself could not forget that she had once been happy with the "horseman of the crested waves." and still might be happy with him again.

The god asked her to make her choice between them, and when she went to him, she shook his mantle between her and Cu Chulainn. It was one of the magic properties of Lir's mantle that those between whom it was shaken could never meet again. Then Fand returned with her divine husband to the country of the immortals.

Fea—The war goddess wife of Nuada, king of Tara and the Tuatha De Danann.

Feithline—A seer who lived in the Cruachen (Gateway to Hell), hill in western Ireland and appeared to Queen Maeve (see Lesson Three), attired in a golden crown with seven burnt-gold braids hanging down her shoulders, to foretell the queen's death.

Fenne, or Finnen—Which literally means "White," is the fairy goddess to whom, with her sister Aine, Knock Fennine and Knock Aine on the shores of Lough Gur are dedicated.

Finchoem—The mother of Conall, an Irish hero.

Findabair [finnavar]—Daughter of Queen Medb, who died of shame when Medb offered her as the reward for any champion who would go against Cu Chulainn and slay him. All perished, and Findabair, when she finds out how she is being promised to a fresh suitor every days, dies of shame.

Finncaev—Which means fair love, was a powerful Faery queen.

Finola—The eldest daughter of Ler, who was turned into a swan by Aeife, for 300 years.

Fiongalla—The fair-cheeked one, who lived in southwestern Ireland and was held in enchantment by the powerful Druid Amerach of Ulster. She made Fiongalla vow never to sleep with a man until one brought magical yew berries, holly boughs, and marigolds from the earthly seat of power. Feargal performed the task, freeing Fiongalla from Amerach's power.

Fithir—The younger daughter of an Irish king. The king of Leinster, in southwestern Ireland, wanted to marry her but her older sister Darine was still unmarried and their father refused to let the younger daughter wed before the elder. The king of Leinster then kidnapped Darine and locked her away, with nine handmaidens, in a tower in the woods. He returned to the palace at Tara, claiming Darine was dead. Fithir was then, although in mourning for her sister, free to wed. One day while wandering in the woods, Fithir happened upon her beloved sister. The shock killed Fithir; Darine, seeing her sister dead, killed herself with mourning.

Flaithius—Which means royalty, was a Kundry (a female divinity), who originally appears as a repulsive Hag, and then once kindness has been given her, turns into a beautiful woman.

Flidhais—Woodland goddess, ruler of beasts; the Cattle of Flidais were named after her. She rode in a chariot pulled by deer. Her husband was Adammair, or Fergus, whose virility was such that when Flidhais was away he needed seven ordinary women to satisfy him sexually. She nurtured many heroes and led them on mystic adventures. When they died she took them to Tir na nOg, where some grew horns and became stag-gods.

Fodhla, or Fotla [fot-lah]—One of the three queens of the Tuatha De Danann, and one of the three daughters of Dagda, who asked the Milesians to name Ireland after them. The name derives from the compound fo, under, and tla, earth.

Garbh Ogh [garv-ogh]—An ancient ageless giantess, whose car was drawn by elks, whose diet was venison milk and eagles' breasts and who hunted the mountain deer with a pack of seventy hounds with bird names. She gathered stones to heap herself a triple cairn and "set up her chair in a womb of the hills at the season of heather-bloom'; and then expired."

Gentle Annis, or Annie—The weather spirit responsible for the southwesterly gales on the Firth of Cromarty. The firth is well protected from the north and east, but a gap in the hills allows the entry of spasmodic squally gales. These give Gentle Annis a bad reputation for treachery. A day will start fine, luring the fisherman out, then, in a moment, the storm sweeps round and his boat is imperilled. Annis may come from Anu, which has been suggested as the origins of Black Annis of the Dane Hills.

It may be, however, that these half-jocular personifications have no connection with mythology.

Gillagriene—Daughter of the Sun in Irish legend.

Grian—Literally means sun. A Faery Queen with a court on Pallas Green Hill, County Tipperary.

Gwyddynod of Gloucester, The nine [gwuh-thynn-oth]—Warrior goddesses who are rarely mentioned in literature, and who are possibly connected to the smith-god, Gwydion.

Gyre-Carling—A Fairy Queen of the Fife who is a spinner. Superstitious females in Fife are anxious to spin off all the flax that is on their rocks, on the last night of the year; being persuaded that if they left any unspun, the Gyre-Carling, or—as they pronounce the word—the Gy-carli, would carry it off before morning.

Hag—The Cunning Woman (witch woman) of Erin. The term *Hag* is the last shadow of the primitive nature Goddess, the Cailleach Bear, Black Annis, or Gentle Annie.

Inghean Bhuidhe—Which means The Yellow-Haired Girl, who was the sister of Latiaran. She was honored in Pagan Ireland on May 6 with rituals around a sacred well.

Iseult, Isolde, Esyllt, or Essyllt Vyngwen—Which means of the Fine Hair. She is a goddess connected with healing. In the tale of Tristan, she represents the sun personified; the feminine power.

Lavercam—Was the nurse to Deirdre, in the famous tale of *Deirdre of the Sorrows*. Although her role was primarily that of nursemaid, she was also a poet who foresaw the death of Deirdre and her lover Naoise.

Latiaran—A Harvest goddess. She had two sisters—Lasair, which means flame, and the middle sister, Inghean Bhuidhe, which means yellow-haired girl. They survived into the Christian era disguised as saints. Lasair ruled spring; Inghean Bhuidhe ruled the summer, and; Latiaran ruled the harvest-time. The story that survives of Latiaran is that each morning she carried a seed of fire from her nun's cell to a nearby forge. One morning the smith complemented her on her beautiful feet, and she, vainly, looked down. As she did, her apron caught fire, but though her clothes burned she remained unharmed. Then she sank into the ground under a heart-shaped stone and was never seen again.

Leanan-Sidhe [lyaan-nawn shee]—Which means The Faery Mistress, or Mistress of Peace; the spirit of life. She is one of many of the beautiful goddess of inspiration to the poet and singer, as the Bean Si is the spirit of death, the foreteller of doom. In exchange for her spirit, she burns them up; living off their life spirit so that their earthly life is brief.

Liban—Irish goddess of healing and pleasure. With Fand, she appeared to Cu Chulainn in a dream in which they beat him with horse-whips— but only to teach him a lesson which ended in happiness.

She was the daughter of Etain and Eochaid. She was considered the "sanctified mermaid," who may possibly account for the presence of some of the mermaids who so often occur in church carvings.

Her story is as such:

In the year 90 a sacred spring which had been sacrilegiously neglected overflowed its bounds and formed the great water of Lough Neagh. Eochaid and all his family were overwhelmed and drowned, except his two sons, Conang and Curman, and his daughter Liban.

Liban was indeed swept away by the waters, but she and her pet dog were supernaturally preserved and carried into a subaqueous cave where she spent a year in her bower with no company except her little dog.

She grew weary of this after a time, and prayed to Dana [see Lesson Three] that she might be turned into a salmon and swim around with the shoals of fish that passed her bower. Dana granted the prayer and gave her the tail of a salmon, but from the navel upwards she retained the shape of a beautiful woman. Her dog was turned into an otter, and the two swam around together for 300 years or more.

In this time Ireland had become Christian and St Comgall had become Bishop of Bangor. One day Comgall dispatched one of his clergy, Beoc, to Rome to consult Pope Gregory about some matters of order and rule. As they sailed they were accompanied by a very sweet voice singing from under the water. It was so sweet that Beoc thought this it must be an angel's voice. At that Liban spoke from under the water and said—'It is I who am singing. I am no angel, but Liban, and for 300 years I have been swimming the seas, and I implore you to meet me, with the holy men of Bangor, at Inver Ollarba. I pray you tell St Comgall what I have said, and let them all come with nets and boats to draw me out of the sea.

Beoc promised to do as she asked, pressed on his errand, and before the year was over had returned from Rome, in time to tell St. Comgall of Liban's prayer. On the appointed day a fleet of boats was there and Liban was drawn out of the water by Beoan, son of Inli. They half-filled the boat in which she was caught with water, and crowds of people came to see her swimming around.

A dispute arose as to who had the right to her. St. Comgall thought she was his as she was caught in his diocese; Beoc claimed her because she had made her appeal to him; and even the man who had drawn her out of the sea staked his claim.

To avoid dissension all the saints of Bangor embarked on a night of fasting and prayer. An angel spoke to them and said that on the next morning a yoke of two oxen would come to them. They were to put Liban into a chariot and harness the oxen to it; wherever they stopped, that was the territory. It was a method employed in many saints' legends to settle the place where a church should be erected, and the expedient did not fail this time.

The oxen drew their chariot undoubtingly to Beoc's church, Teo-da-Beoc. There she was given her choice whether to die immediately and ascend at once to heaven or to stay on the Earth as long as she had lived in the sea, and to ascend to heaven after 300 years.

She chose immediate death. St. Comgall baptized her by the name of Murgen, or sea-born, and she made her entry into heaven. She was accounted one of the Holy Virgins, and signs and wonders were done through her means in Teo-da-Beoc.

Libanie—Which means Beauty of Women, was a mermaid goddess associated with Lough Neagh.

Logia—The goddess worshipped at the Lagan River in Ireland.

Luaths Lurgann—Which means Speedy Foot. She was the aunt of the hero Finn, who raised the boy, teaching him all the physical arts. She received her name when carrying Finn, outrunning his enemies who were fearful of his eventual power. However, Finn accidently killed his aunt. An enemy was pursuing them and Finn picked up his aging athlete aunt and ran as fast as he could; so fast that the wind he created tore her body apart, leaving only her thighbones. Finn planted these in the earth, where they formed Ireland's Loch Lurgann.

Mab—Fairy Queen, whose name meant mead, a red drink representing sovereignty which she gave to each of her many consorts. The claret in the lap of the Fairy Queen, appears to be a concoction of the queen's own menstrual blood as the feminine wine of wisdom. She is linked to the Celtic Faery goddess Maeve (see Lesson Three) of Ireland, who was a warrior goddess.

Mal—The goddess of Hag's Head, the most famous of the Cliffs of Mother. The village of Miltown Malbay was named after her.

Moingfhion, or Mongfhinn—Literally means The White-Haired One. She is associated with Samhain; and is therefore a crone, or goddess of winter.

Morgan le Fay—It is important to mention Morgan le Fay of the Arthurian Legends, because she is a derivative of an earlier goddess of Fate—Fata Morgana. Though Morgan le Fay was considered a Celtic fairy and Priestess of Avalon, she is not connected to the Celtic Faery of Ireland. Reference is often made to the Morgans of Wales and Brittany which were originally mermaids of the same breed as the Breton Morgens, which are also mermaids. It is possible that Morgan le Fay is also connected to the legends of the mermaids, since she is also known as the Lady of the Lake.

Moruadh, or Moruach—A sea maiden who had a magic cohuleen druith (cap) that allowed her to breathe beneath the sea.

Muime Chriosda—Which means Foster Mother of Christ, was a title given to Saint Bridget (see Lesson Three), emphasizing her maternal qualities.

Muireartach—Which means Eastern Sea, was the goddess of the stormy ocean. She was a one-eyed crone who lived beneath the waves.

Munanna—A bird-goddess, whose cranelike figure flew around the cliffs of Inishkea, crying "revenge, revenge," on the Scandinavian sea pirates.

Nair, or Nar—A fertility, earth goddess. Any king who slept with her apparently died.

Nessa—Which means Ungentle, was originally called Assa, or gentle one. She was a warrior goddess of Ulster who defeated king after king and kept a strong hand on the reins of government. She was captured while bathing by the Druid Cathbad, who kept her hostage. However, Nessa outwitted Cathbad by swallowing little worms with the water from his magickal well and conceived and gave birth to the famous king Conchobar.

Niamh [nee-av]—A goddess of great beauty who appeared to the Fenians when they were hunting near Lake Killarney. She told them she was the daughter of the Son of the Sea. The following eighteenth century poem, reweaves the ancient story of her beauty.

> *A royal crown was on her head;*
> *And a brown mantle of precious silk,*
> *Spangled with stars of red gold,*
> *Covering her shoes down to the grass.*
> *A gold ring was hanging down*
> *From each yellow curl of her golden hair;*
> *Her eyes, blue, clear, and cloudless,*
> *Like a dew-drop on the top of the grass.*
> *Redder were her cheeks than the rose,*
> *Fairer was her visage than the swan upon the wave,*
> *And more sweet was the taste of her balsam lips*
> *Than honey mingled thro' red wine.*
> *A garment, wide, long, and smooth*
> *Covered the white steed,*
> *There was a comely saddle of red gold,*
> *And her right hand held a bridle with a golden bit.*
> *Four shoes well-shaped were under him,*
> *Of the yellow gold of the purest quality;*
> *A silver wreath was on the back of his head,*
> *And there was not in the world a steed better.*

Such was Niamh of the Golden Hair, Lir's daughter; and it is small wonder that when she chose Ossian from among the sons of men to be her lover, all Finn's supplications could not keep him. He mounted behind her on her faery-horse, and they rode across the land to the seashore, and then over the tops of the waves. As they went, she described the country of the gods to him in just the same terms as Ler himself had pictured it to Bran, son of Febal, as Mider had painted it to Etain, and as everyone that went there limned it to those that stayed at home on earth.

> *It is the most delightful country to be found*
> *Of greatest repute under the sun;*
> *Trees drooping with fruit and blossom,*
> *And foliage growing on the tops of boughs.*
> *Abundant, there, are honey and wine,*
> *And everything that eye has beheld,*
> *There will not come decline on thee with lapse of time.*
> *Death or decay thou wilt not see.*

Notre Dame Sous Terre—Which means Our Lady Beneath the Earth. The goddess worshipped by the Dryadesses on whose sacred grounds were built the church of Mont Saint Michel.

Onaugh [oo-na]—The most beautiful of the Faery queens, who had golden hair so long it swept the ground. She flew through the earth robed in gossamer silver bejeweled with dew. Onaugh lived with king Finnvara, who was constantly unfaithful to her with mortal women. However, regardless of his infidelity, she retained an even, benevolent temperament.

Sadhbh, or Sadb [sav]—Literally means deer, or hind. She was the daughter of Bodb the Red, the wife of Fionn, and the mother of Ossian, whom the *Ossianic Ballads* are atrributed. A rival goddess lured Sadb away from Fionn's house by magick when she was pregnant with Ossian and changed her into a deer. Sadv, the hind goddess, or goddess of hinds, is related to the ancient image of Artemis-Diana, the sun goddess of those peoples who came to Western Europe before the Indo-European.

Scathach [scae-thoch]—A war goddess and prophetess from Alba [Scotland], who taught the martial arts to Cu Chulainn, and whose name means the woman who strikes fear.

Scota—Was the wife of the Milesian leader, and mother of the bard Amergin. She was also the daughter of the Pharaoh of Egypt, Necbetanus, who died in the invasion of Ireland and was buried near the dolmens on Sliabh Mis in County Kerry.

Sequana—The Divine Ancestress of the Sequani tribe of France, who was also linked with the River Seine of France. A healing shrine dedicated to Sequana stood at the headwaters of the Seine near the modern-day city of Dijon. There has been some hypothesis that the Sequani were also linked to the River Sankarya of Anatolia, the river that was known as the Sangarius to the Greeks, and cited by Homer as an area in which Amazons had lived. Sequana's name was later linked with the River Shannon (see Sinnan below) of Ireland. There is a remote possibility that this goddess was also known as a warrior Goddess.

Sheila-Na-Gig—The accepted name for the bas-reliefs found outside many old churches, priories and convents, and sometimes on castles, of a naked female figure squatting and displaying exaggerated genitals with a yawning vulva. The Great Mother in her crudest, Female Generative Principle aspect.

Sin—Which means sigh, was the name of a goddess Dryadess who married Muirchertach, the King of all Ireland. She later caused his death by her magick spells. She was the victim of a conflict of duty and love, and when she was asked why she acted in this way, she said:

> *I myself will die of grief for him*
> *The noble king of the western world,*
> *For the burden of all misfortunes*
> *I have heaped on the ruler of Ireland.*
> *I, alas, made the poison*
> *That vanquished the king of noble troops.*

Sinnan [shannon]—A granddaugher of the sea-god Lir. She was a nymph of a river which became known as the Shannon. According to legend, the Shannon river burst, like the Boyne, from an inviolable well.

Tea—Goddess of Tara, its co-founder with Tephi, both described as Milesian princesses. Second wife of Erimon. She chose the mound Drum Chain (Beautiful Hill) as her marriage price, and it was named Temair (Tara), which means The Wall of Tea, after her.

Tephi—Goddess of Tara, its co-founder with Tea.

Turrean—The wolfhound-goddess who helped Finn MacCool, a Finian Hero.

Uairebhuidhe—A bird goddess.

Uathach [oo-ah-thoch]—Which literally means The Very Terrible. She was the daughter of Scathach, and became Cu Chulainn's lover.

Appendix E

Principles of Wiccan Belief

The following set of thirteen principles was adopted by the Council of American Witches, in April, 1974.

1. We practice rites to attune ourselves with the natural rhythm of life forces marked by the phases of the Moon and the seasonal Quarters and Cross Quarters.

2. We recognize that our intelligence gives us a unique responsibility toward our environment. We seek to live in harmony with Nature, in ecological balance offering fulfillment to life and consciousness within an evolutionary concept.

3. We acknowledge a depth of power far greater than that apparent to the average person. Because it is far greater than ordinary it is sometimes called supernatural, but we see it as lying within that which is naturally potential to all.

4. We conceive of the Creative Power in the universe as manifesting through polarity—as masculine and feminine—and that this same Creative Power lies in all people, and functions through the interaction of the masculine and feminine. We value neither above the other, knowing each to be supportive to the other. We value sex as pleasure, as the symbol and embodiment of life, and as one of the sources of energies used in magickal practice and religious worship.

5. We recognize both outer worlds and inner, or psychological, worlds sometimes known as the Spiritual World, the Collective Unconscious, Inner Planes, etc.—and we see in the interaction of these two dimensions the basis for paranormal phenomena and magickal exercises. We neglect neither dimension for the other, seeing both as necessary for our fulfillment.

6. We do not recognize any authoritarian hierarchy, but do honor those who teach, respect those who share their greater knowledge and wisdom, and acknowledge those who have courageously given of themselves in leadership.

7. We see religion, magick, and wisdom in living as being united in the way one views the world and lives within it—a world view and philosophy of life which we identify as Witchcraft—the Wiccan Way.

8. Calling oneself "Witch" does not make a Witch—but neither does heredity itself, nor the collecting of titles, degrees, and initiations. A Witch seeks to control the forces within her/himself that make life possible in order to live wisely and well without harm to others and in harmony with Nature.

9. We believe in the affirmation and fulfillment of life in a continuation of evolution and development of consciousness giving meaning to the Universe we know and our personal role within it.

10. Our only animosity towards Christianity, or towards any other religion or philosophy of life, is to the extent that its institutions have claimed to be "the only way," and have sought to deny freedom to others and to suppress other ways of religious practice and belief.

11. As American Witches, we are not threatened by debates on the history of the Craft, the origins of various terms, the legitimacy of various aspects of different traditions. We are concerned with our present and our future.

12. We do not accept the concept of absolute evil, nor do we worship any entity known as Satan or the Devil, as defined by the Christian tradition. We do not seek power through the sufferings of others, nor accept that personal benefit can be derived only by denial to another.

13. We believe that we should seek within Nature that which is contributory to our health and well-being.

Appendix F

Cad Goddeu

Although the *Cad Goddeu* —The Battle of the Trees—is of Welsh origin, it does have a position in Faery Wicca because it contains the esoteric teachings, as pertaining to the Faery tradition regarding the tree-lore found in the Irish oghams.

The Cad Goddeu is based on a Welsh myth that tells the battle between Arawn King of Anwm (The Bottomless Place), and the two sons of Don, Gwydion and Amathaon. The original is written in short rhyming lines, the same rhyme often being sustained for ten or fifteen lines. The following, however, is a mid-Victorian translation of the original.

I have been in many shapes, Before I attained a congenial form. I have been a narrow blade of a sword. I have been a drop in the air. I have been a shining star. I have been a word in a book. I have been a book originally. I have been a light in a lantern. A year and a half. I have been a bridge for passing over Three-score rivers. I have journeyed as an eagle. I have been a boat on the sea. I have been a director in battle. I have been the string of a child's swaddling clout. I have been a sword in the hand. I have been a shield in the fight. I have been the string of a harp. Enchanted for a year. In the foam of water. I have been a poker in the fire. I have been a tree in a covert. There is nothing in which I have not been. I have fought, though small, In the Battle of Goddeu Brig, Before the Ruler of Britain, Abounding in fleets. Indifferent bards pretend, They pretend a monstrous beast, With a hundred heads, And a grievous combat At the root of the tongue. And another fight there is At the back of the head. A toad having on his thighs A hundred claws, A spotted crested snake, For punishing in their flesh. A hundred souls on account of their sins. I was in Caer Fefynedd, Thither were hastening grasses and trees. Wayfarers perceive them, Warriors are astonished At a renewal of the conflicts Such as Gwydion made. There is calling on Heaven, And on Christ that he would effect Their deliverance, The all-powerful God. If the God had answered, Through charms and magic skill, Assume the forms of the principal trees, With you in array Restrain the people Inexperienced in battle. When the trees were enchanted There was hope for the trees, That they should frustrate the intention Of the surrounding fires.... Better are three in unison, And enjoying themselves in a circle, And one of them relating The story of the del-

301

uge..., The alder trees in the first line, They made the commencement. Willow and quicken tree, They were slow in their array. The plum is a tree Not beloved of men; The medlar of a like nature, Overcoming severe toil The bean bearing in its shade An army of phantoms. The raspberry makes Not the best of food. In shelter live, The privet and the woodbine, And the ivy in its season. Great is the gorse in battle. The cherry-tree had been reproached. The birch, though very magnanimous, Was late in arraying himself; It was not through cowardice, But on account of his great size. The appearance of the... Is that of a foreigner and a savage. The pine-tree in the court, Strong in battle, By me greatly exalted In the presence of kings, The elm-trees are his subjects. He turns not aside the measure of a foot, But strikes right in the middle, And at the farthest end. The hazel is the judge, His berries are thy dowry. The privet is blessed. Strong chiefs in war Are the mulberry. Prosperous the beech-tree. The holly dark green, Was very courageous: Defended with spikes on every side, Wounding the hands. The long-enduring poplars, Very much broken in fight. The plundered fern; The brooms with their offspring: The furze was not well behaved Until it be tamed. The heath was giving consolation, Comforting the people. The black cherry-tree was pursuing. The oak-tree swiftly moving, Before him tremble heaven and earth, Stout doorkeeper against the foe Is his name in all lands. The corn-cockle bound together, Was given to be burnt. Others were rejected On account of the holes made By great violence In the field of battle. Very wrathful the Cruel and gloomy ash. Bashful the chestnut-tree, Retreating from happiness. There shall be a black darkness, There shall be a shaking of the mountains, There shall be a purifying furnace, There shall first be a great wave, And when the shout shall be heard-Putting forth new leaves are the tops of the beech, Changing form and being renewed from a withered state; Entangled are the tops of the oak. From the Gorchan of Maelderw. Smiling at the side of the rock the pear-tree not of an ardent nature. Neither of mother or father, When I was made, Was my blood or body; Of nine kinds of faculties, Of fruit of fruits, Of fruit Goddess made me, Of the blossom of the mountain primrose, Of the buds of trees and shrubs, Of Earth of earthly kind. When I was made Of the blossoms of the nettle, Of the water of the ninth wave, I was spell-bound by Math Before I became immortal. I was spell-bound by Gwydion, Great enchanter of the Britons, Of Eurys, of Eurwn, Of Euron, of Medron, In myriads of secrets, I am as learned as Math. I know about the Emperor When he was half burnt. I know the star-knowledge Of stars before the Earth, Whence I was born, How many worlds there are. It is the custom of accomplished bards To recite the praise of their country. I have played in Lloughor, I have slept in purple. Was I not in the enclosure With Dylan Ail More, On a couch in the centre Between the two knees of the prince Upon two Blunt spears? When from heaven came The torrents into the deep, Rushing with violent impulse. Four-score songs, For administering to their pleasure. There is neither old nor young, Except me as to their poems, And other singer who knows the whole of the nine hundred Which are known to me, Concerning the blood-spotted sword. Honour is my guide. Profitable learning is from God. Of the slaying of the board, Its appearing, its disappearing, Its knowledge of languages. The light whose name is Splendour, And the number of the ruling lights That scatter rays of fire High above the deep. I have been a spotted snake upon a hill; I have been a viper in a lake; I have been an evil star formerly. I have been a weight in a mill. My cassock is red all over. I prophesy no evil. Four-score puffs of smoke To every one who will carry them away: And a million of angels, On the point of my knife. Handsome is the yellow horse, But a hundred times better Is my cream-coloured one, Swift as the sea-mew, Which cannot pass me Between the sea and the shore. Am I not pre-eminent in the field of blood? I have a hundred shares of the spoil. My wreath is of red jewels, Of gold is the border of my shield. There has not been born one so good as I, Or even known, Except Goronwy, From the dales of Edrywy. Long and white are my fingers, It is long since I was a herdsman. I travelled over the Earth Before I became a learned person. I have travelled, I have made a circuit, I have slept in a hundred islands; I have dwelt in a hundred cities. Learned Druids, Prophesy ye of Arthur? Or is it me they celebrate, And one relating The history of the Deluge? With a golden jewel set in gold I am enriched; And I am indulging in pleasure out of the oppressive toil of the goldsmith.

Table of Irish Pronunciation

Irish has many sounds not found in American English, it depends on inflections to show the relationships between words in a sentence. In other words, whereas in an English sentence the order or sequence of words determines the meaning, in an Irish sentence the meaning is primarily determined by changes in spelling and pronunciation within the individual words.

The Irish alphabet consists of eighteen letters, containing all but eight of the English alphabet (j, k, q, v, w, x, y, and z). However, Irish has two very important diacritical marks not found in English (which are not used in this volume). They are important because they affect both pronunciation and meaning in essential ways. They are: a dot called a seimhiu (SHAY-voo) above certain consonants (represented in Roman script by a following *h*) which aspirates or softens them; and an accent mark called a fada (fodah), which can occur above all vowels, that lengthens them. It is necessary to understand from the beginning that there is no simple relationship between the pronunciation of Irish words and their appearance in modernized Roman script. The following guide to pronunciation is very rough, and subject to exceptions, but may be some help.

Consonants—At the beginning of a word consonants have the same value as in English (c always = k). Elsewhere:

b = v
c = g or k
ch = guttural, as in German
d = dh (as in *then*)
g = gh, a soft guttural
m = v
t = d
s followed or preceded by e or i = sh
th = th, as in *thin*.

Vowels—Short vowels have the same value as in Latin. Long vowels (marked with an accent) are pronounced awe, ay, ee, owe, oo (accents are not shown on capitals).

ai = a in the first syllable and i elsewhere
a final e is sounded
iu = u but with the i slightly sounded
ei = e

A conversation course in Irish (Gaeilge) can be purchased through: Educational Services Corp., 1725 K Street, N.W., Suite 408, Washington, D.C. 20006

Bibliography

Adler, Margot. *Drawing Down the Moon: Witches, Druids, Goddess-worshippers and Other Pagans in America Today*. Beacon Press, 1979.

Bain, George. *Celtic Art: The Methods of Construction*. Dover Publications, Inc., 1973

Barker, Cicely Mary. *Flower Fairies of the Countryside*. Peter Bedrick Books, 1923/1989.

Bradley, Marion Zimmer. *The Mists of Avalon*. Del Rey, Ballantine Books, 1982.

Briggs, Katharine. *An Encyclopedia of Fairies, Hobgoblins, Brownies, Bogies and other Supernatural Creatures*. Pantheon Books, 1976.

— *The Vanishing People: Fairy Lore and Legends*, Pantheon Books, 1978.

Buckland, Raymond. *Buckland's Complete Book of Witchcraft*. Llewellyn Publications, 1986.

Caldecott, Moyra. *Women in Celtic Myth: Tales of Extraordinary Women From the Ancient Celtic Tradition*. Destiny Books, 1988/1992.

Campbell, Joseph. *The Hero with a Thousand Faces*. Bolligen Series XVII, Princeton University Press, 1973.

— *The Power of Myth*. Doubleday, 1988.

Carter, Angela, ed. *The Old Wives' Fairy Tale Book*. Pantheon Books, 1990.

Claiborne, Robert. *The Roots of English: A Reader's Handbook of Word Origins*. Times Books/Random House, Inc., 1989.

Coghlan, Ronan, Ida Grehan and P. W. Joyce. *Book of Irish Names: First, Family and Place Names*. Sterling Publishing Co., Inc., 1989.

Cyr, Donald L. ed. *Celtic Secrets*. Stonehenge Viewpoint, 1980.

Davis, Courtney. *The Celtic Art Sourcebook*. Blanford Press, 1991.

de Groat, Florence. *A Fairy's Workday*. self-published, date unknown.

de Waal, Esther, ed. *The Celtic Vision: Prayers and Blessings from the Outer Hebrides*. St. Bede's Publications, 1988.

di Givry, Grillot. *Witchcraft, Magic and Alchemy*. Dover Publications, Inc., 1931.

Eisler, Riane. *The Chalice and the Blace: Our History, Our Future*. Harper and Row Publisher, Inc., 1988.

Farrar, Janet and Stewart. *A Witches' Bible: Volume I: The Sabbats*. Robert Hale, Ltd., 1984.

— *A Witches' Bible, Volume II: The Rituals*. Robert Hale, Ltd., 1984.

—*The Witches' Goddess,* Phoenix Publishing, Inc., 1987.

—*The Witches' God.* Phoenix Publishing, Inc., 1989.

Fife, Graeme. *Arthur the King: The Themes Behind the Legends.* Sterling Publishing Co., Inc., 1991.

Foyle, Kathleen. *The Little Good People: Folk Tales of Ireland.* Frederick Warne and Co., Ltd., London and New York, date unknown.

Gardner, Edward L. *Fairies: The Cottingley Photographs.* A Quest Book, Theosophical Publishing House, 1982.

Gimbutas, Maria. *The Language of the Goddess.* Foreward by Joseph Campbell, HarperCollins, 1991.

—*The Civilization of the Goddess: The World of Old Europe.* HarperSan Francisco, 1991.

Graves, Robert. *The White Goddess.* Amended and Enlarged Edition, Farrar, Straus and Giroux, 1966.

Green, Miranda J. *Dictionary of Celtic Myth and Legend.* Thames and Hudson, 1992.

Hansen, Chadwick. *Witchcraft at Salem.* George Braziller, Inc., 1969.

Hodson, Geoffrey. *Fairies at Work and Play.* A Quest Book, The Theosophical Publishing House, 1925.

Hull, Eleanor. *Cuchullin Saga, The, in Irish Literature.* David Nutt in the Strand, 1898.

—*Pagan Ireland.* M.H. Gill and Son., Ltd. 1904.

Joseph, Frank. *Sacred Sites: A Guidebook to Sacred Centers and Mysterious Places in the Unites States.* Llewellyn Publications, 1992.

Katlyn. *To Summon the Faery: Traditions and Origins of the Ancient Faery Faith.* Mermade Magickal Arts, self published, 1989.

Keightley, Thomas. *The Fairy Mythology.* Bohn Library, London 1850.

Kramer, Heinrich and James Sprenger. *The Malleus Maleficarum.* translated with an introduction, bibliography and notes by the Reverend Montague Summers, Dover Publications, Inc., 1971.

Laing, Lloyd and Jennifer. *Art of the Celts.* Thames and Hudson, 1992.

Mabinogion, The. Translated by Lady Charlotte Guest, J.M. Dent and Sons, Ltd., 1906.

MacCrossan, Tadhg. *The Sacred Cauldron: Secrets of the Druids.* Llewellyn Publications, Inc., 1991.

MacManus, Seumas. *The Story of the Irish Race: A Popular History of Ireland.* The Devin-Adair Company, 1921.

Markale, Jean. *Women of the Celts.* Inner Traditions International, Ltd., 1986.

Matthews, Caitlin, ed. *Voices of the Goddess: A Chorus of Sibyls.* The Aquarian Press, 1990.

—*The Celtic Book of the Dead.* St. Martin's Press, 1992.

McAnally, Jr., D.R. *Irish Wonders: The Ghosts, Giants, Pookas, Demons, Leprechawns, Banshees, Fairies, Witches, Widdows, Old Maids, And Other Marvels of The Emerald Isle, Popular Tales as told by the People.* Weathervane Books, New York, 1938.

McKillip, Rebecca. *Celtic Designs.* Stemmer House Publishers, Inc., 1981.

Mitchell, John. *The Earth Spirit: Its Ways, Shrines, and Mysteries.* Avon Publishers, 1975.

Monaghan, Patricia. *The Book of Goddesses and Heroines.* Llewellyn, 1990.

Moray, Ann. *A Fairstream of Silver: Love Tales From Celtic Lore.* William Morrow and Co., 1965.

Nichols, Ross. *The Book of Druidry: History, Sites and Wisdom.* The Aquarian Press, 1990.

O'Faolain, Sean. *The Story of the Irish People.* Avenel Books, New York, 1949.

Packer, Alison, Stella Beddoe and Lianne Jarrett, *Fairies in Legends and the Arts.* Cameron and Tayleur, 1980.

Pennick, Nigel. *Magical Alphabets: The Secrets and Significance of Ancient Scripts— Including Runes, Greek, Ogham, Hebrew and Alchemical Alphabets.* Samuel Weiser, 1992.

Pickston, Margaret. *The Language of Flowers.* Penguin Group, 1968.

Rees, Alwyn and Brinley Rees. *Celtic Heritage, Ancient Tradition in Ireland and Wales.* Thames and Hudson, 1990.

Roderic (Llandovery), D. J. *Barddas of Iolo Morganwg.* Longman and Co., 1862.

Ronan, Margaret. *Hunt the Witch Down: Twelve Real Life Stories of Witches and Witchcraft.* Scholastic Book Services, 1976.

Ryall, Rhiannon. *West Country Wicca: A Journal of the Old Religion.* Phoenix Publishing, Inc., 1989.

Scott, Reginald. *The Discoveries of Witchcraft.* Southern Illinois University Press, 1885.

Sechrist, Elizabeth Hough. *Heigh Ho for Halloween,* Macrae Smith and Company, 1948.

Seymour, St. John D. *Irish Witchcraft and Demonology.* Causeway Books, New York, 1973.

Spenser, Edmund. *The Faerie Queen.* Penguin Classics, 1590/1987.

Spock, Marjorie. *Fairy Worlds and Workers.* St. George Publications, 1980.

Squire, Charles. *Celtic Myth and Legend.* Newcastle Publishing Co., Inc., 1975.

Stepanich, Kisma K. *An Act of Woman Power.* Whitford Press, 1989.

—*The Gaia Tradition: Celebrating the Earth in Her Seasons.* Llewellyn Publications, Inc., 1991.

—*Sister Moon Lodge The Power and Mystery of Menstruation.* Llewellyn Publications, Inc., 1992.

Stephens, James. *The Crock of Gold.* The Macmillan Company, New York, 1935.

Stewart, R. J. *The Underworld Initiation: A Journey Towards Psychic Transformation.* The Aquarian Press, 1985.

—*The Prophetic Vision of Merlin.* Routledge and Kegan Paul Inc., 1986.

—*The Mystic Life of Merlin.* Routledge and Kegan Paul, Ltd., 1986.

— *Living Magick Arts: Imagination and Magic for the 21st Century*. Blandford, 1987.

—*Advanced Magick Arts*. Element Books, 1988.

—*Cu Chulainn: Heroes and Warriors, Hound of Ulster*. Illustrated by James field, Firebird Books Ltd., 1988.

—*Earth Light, The Ancient Path to Transformation Rediscovering the Wisdom of Celtic and Faery Lore*. Elements Books Limited, 1992.

—*Power Within the Land: The Roots of Celtic and UnderWorld Traditions Awakening the Sleepers and Regenerating the Earth*. Elements Books Limited, 1992.

The Tain. From the Irish epic *Tain Bo Cuailgne*, translated by Thomas Kinsella, Oxford University Press, 1969/1990.

Thorsson, Edred. *Futhark: A Handbook of Rune Magic*. Samuel Weiser, Inc., 1984.

Van Gelder, Dora. *The Real World of Fairies*. A Quest Book, The Theosophical Publishing House, 1977.

Wentz, W.Y. Evans. *The Fairy-Faith in Celtic Countries*. University Books, Inc., 1911, Library of the Mystic Arts, 1990.

Wilde, Lady. *Ancient Legends, Mystic Charms and Superstitions of Ireland*. Lemma Publishing Corporation, 1887.

— *Irish Cures, Mystic Charms and Superstitions*. Sterling Publishing, Co., Inc., 1991.

Yeats, W. B. *Celtic Twilight, The*. A.H. Bullen, London, 1893/1902.

—*Irish Folk and Folk Tales*. Walter Scott, London, 1893.

Youngs, Susan, ed. *The Work of Angels: Masterpieces of Celtic Metalwork, 6th–9th centuries A.D*. British Museum Publications, 1989.

Stay in Touch

On the following pages you will find listed, with their current prices, some of the books now available on related subjects. Your book dealer stocks most of these and will stock new titles in the Llewellyn series as they become available. We urge your patronage.

To Get a Free Catalog

You are invited to write for our catalog, *Llewellyn's New Worlds of Mind and Spirit*. A sample copy is free, or you may subscribe for just $10 in the United States and Canada ($20 overseas, first class mail). Many bookstores also have New Worlds available to their customers. Ask for it.

In *New Worlds* you will find news and features about new books, tapes and services; announcements of meetings and seminars; helpful articles; author interviews and much more. Write to:

Llewellyn's New Worlds of Mind and Spirit
P.O. Box 64383, Dept. K694-7
St. Paul, MN 55164-0383, U.S.A.

To Order Books and Tapes

If your book store does not carry the titles described on the following pages, you may order them directly from Llewellyn by sending the full price in U.S. funds, plus postage and handling (see below).

Credit Card Orders: VISA, MasterCard, American Express are accepted. Call toll-free in the USA and Canada at 1-800-THE-MOON.

Special Group Discount: Because there is a great deal of interest in group discussion and study of the subject matter of this book, we offer a 20% quantity discount to group leaders or agents. Our Special Quantity Price for a minimum order of five copies of *Faery Wicca, Book I* is $79.80 cash-with-order. Include postage and handling charges noted below.

Postage and Handling: Include $4 postage and handling for orders $15 and under; $5 for orders over $15. There are no postage and handling charges for orders over $100. Postage and handling rates are subject to change. We ship UPS whenever possible within the continental United States; delivery is guaranteed. Please provide your street address as UPS does not deliver to P.O. boxes. Orders shipped to Alaska, Hawaii, Canada, Mexico and Puerto Rico will be sent via first class mail. Allow 4-6 weeks for delivery. International orders: Airmail – add retail price of each book and $5 for each non-book item (audiotapes, etc.); Surface mail – add $1 per item. Minnesota residents please add 7% sales tax. Mail orders to:

Llewellyn Worldwide
P.O. Box 64383, Dept. K694-7, St. Paul
MN 55164-0383, U.S.A.

For customer service, call 1-800-THE-MOON
In Minnesota, call 291-1970.

Prices subject to change without notice

The Book of Ogham
The Celtic Tree Oracle
Edred Thorsson

Drink deeply from the very source of the Druids' traditional lore. The oghamic Celtic tradition represents an important breakthrough in the practical study of Celtic religion and magick. Within the pages of *The Book of Ogham* you will find the complete and authentic system of divination based on the letters of the Celtic ogham alphabet (commonly designated by tree names), and a whole world of experiential Celtic spirituality.

Come to understand the Celtic Way to new depths, discover methodological secrets shared by the Druids and Drightens of old, receive complete instructions for the practice of ogham divination, and find objective inner truths concealed deep within yourself.

The true and inner learning of oghams is a pathway to awakening the deeply rooted structural patterns of the Celtic psyche or soul. Read, study and work with the ogham oracle . . . open up the mysterious and hidden world within . . . and become part of the eternal stream of tradition that transcends the individual self. Come, and drink directly from the true cauldron of inspiration: the secret lore and practices of the ancient Celtic Druids.

0-87542-783-9, 224 pp., 6 x 9, illus., glossary, softcover $12.95

Witchcraft Today, Book One
The Modern Craft Movement
edited by Chas S. Clifton

For those already in the Craft, and for those who stand outside the ritual circle wondering if it is the place for them, *Witchcraft Today, Book One* brings together the writings of nine well-known Neopagans who give a cross-section of the beliefs and practices of this diverse and fascinating religion.

The contributors live in cities, small towns and rural areas, from California to Ireland, and they have all claimed a magical birthright—that lies open to any committed person—of healing, divination, counseling and working with the world's cycles.

Written specifically for this volume, the articles include:
- "A Quick History of Witchcraft's Revival" by Chas S. Clifton
- "An Insider's Look at Pagan Festivals" by Oz
- "Witchcraft and Healing" by Morwyn
- "Sex Magic" by Valerie Voigt
- "Witchcraft and the Law" by Pete Pathfinder Davis
- "Witchcraft and Shamanism" by Grey Cat
- "Being a Pagan in a 9-to-5 World" by Valerie Voigt

0-87542-377-9, 208 pp., 5¼ x 8, softcover $9.95

Witchcraft Today, Book Two
Rites of Passage
edited by Chas S. Clifton

This book is about the ritual glue that binds Pagan culture. In contrast, much writing on modern Paganism, whether it be Witchcraft or some other form, seems to assume that the reader is a young, single adult—a "seeker." At most, the reader is seen as a member of a coven or other group made up of adults. This collection of writings, however, takes a wider view with the long-term goal of presenting a living Pagan culture. If modern Pagan traditions are to persist and have any effect on the world community in an overt way, they must encompass people of all ages, not just young adults. *Witchcraft Today, Book Two: Rites of Passage*, therefore, is organized according to some of life's significant markers: birth, puberty, adulthood, partnership, parenthood, Wicca conversion, maturity or eldership, and finally death. None of these occur in a social vacuum, but always in relation to other people.

0-87542-378-7, 288 pp., 5¼ x 8, softcover $9.95

Witchcraft Today, Book Three
Witchcraft & Shamanism
edited by Chas S. Clifton

This book is a compelling and honest examination of shamanic techniques (both classical and neo-) as they are being practiced in Neopagan Witchcraft in the 1990s. Shamanism is a natural adjunct to the ritualistic and magical practice of many covens and solitary Pagans. In this ground-breaking volume, you will discover how others have integrated techniques such as trance journeys, soul retrieval, and altered states of consciousness.

Discover how shamanic ideas influenced Greek philosophers, Platonists, Pythagoreans and Gnostics ... learn how evidence from the old witch trials suggests that at least some Europeans may have practiced shamanic journeying in the past ... incorporate caves for ritual and inner journeys, both literally and in visualization ... find out who is out there retrieving souls and curing elfshot ... compare the guided visualizations common to modern magickal practice with the neo-shamanic journey ... learn how spirit contacts are made, how guides are perceived and what "worlds" they reside in ... and much more.

1-56718-150-3, 288 pp., 5¼ x 8, photos, softcover $9.95

The Faerie Way
A Healing Journey to Other Worlds
Hugh Mynne

Now is the time for an ecology of the invisible. We must interface with our sisters and brothers of other planes so that Earth Mother's wounds may be healed. *The Faerie Way* extends an invitation to you to become part of this process.

Faeries are energy beings who take on any form to speak to the pure-hearted through the symbolic language of the right brain. *The Faerie Way* offers a vision of the universe as dizzying and dazzling as the wildest speculations of quantum physicists. In the same way that the American Indians rely on power animals, so does the Faerie Way rely on helpers and allies. Practical techniques for working with the Faerie, or Sidhe, world, include meditation to establish a private mental space, relaxation, purification and energization. Get back in touch with the natural world by contacting your own animal helper and faery allies. Journey to the Faerie Realm to experience rebirth, love, peace and death, and to gain the power of these energy beings. Bring your inner world back into harmony, and then return to the outer world with your gifts of vision and harmony. This is how we can rebuild our shattered world. This is *The Faerie Way.*

1-56718-483-9, 6 x 9, 168 pp., illus. $12.95